Hispano Nation

Hispano Nation

The Rise and Decline of Spanish Identity in New Mexico

Phillip B. Gonzales

University of New Mexico Press
Albuquerque

Printed in the United States of America

Library of Congress Cataloging-in-Publication Data

Names: Gonzales, Felipe, 1946– author
Title: Hispano nation : the rise and decline of Spanish identity in New Mexico / Phillip B. Gonzales.
Description: Albuquerque : University of New Mexico Press, 2026. | Includes bibliographical references and index.
Identifiers: LCCN 2025054256 | ISBN 9780826369727 hardcover | ISBN 9780826369734 paperback | ISBN 9780826369741 epub
Subjects: LCSH: Spanish Americans—New Mexico—Ethnic identity | Spanish Americans—New Mexico—Attitudes | Spanish Americans—New Mexico—Intellectual life | Spanish Americans—New Mexico—Social life and customs | Spanish Americans—New Mexico—History | Spanish Americans—Land tenure—New Mexico | BISAC: HISTORY / United States / State & Local / Southwest (AZ, NM, OK, TX) | SOCIAL SCIENCE / Ethnic Studies / American / Hispanic American Studies
Classification: LCC F805.S75 G665 2026 | DDC 978.900468—dc23/eng/20251229
LC record available at https://lccn.loc.gov/2025054256

Founded in 1889, the University of New Mexico sits on the traditional homelands of the Pueblo of Sandia. The original peoples of New Mexico—Pueblo, Navajo, and Apache—since time immemorial have deep connections to the land and have made significant contributions to the broader community statewide. We honor the land itself and those who remain stewards of this land throughout the generations and also acknowledge our committed relationship to Indigenous peoples. We gratefully recognize our history.

Cover illustration: Adapted from photograph by Jim Thompson.
Designed by Isaac Morris
Composed in Marion and Stern Pro

To the memory of my parents,
Angelita Sánchez Cabrera
Benerito Domingo Gonzales

Contents

Illustrations

Preface

Like John Nieto-Phillips, who authored *The Language of Blood*, a substantive book on New Mexico's Spanish identity, my earliest fix on the peculiarity of Spanish identity occurred when I was young. I vividly recall my preteen bewilderment when a neighbor, a construction foreman from a northern New Mexico village, reacted to someone calling us "Mexicans." "We are Spanish," he corrected with redoubtable conviction.

My father's genealogy is steeped in the culture of northern New Mexico. The family's ancestry hunters have traced our descendance from Juan Bautista Gonzales, born in Questa in 1750, and his bride, Antonia Baca, whom he married in 1777. These ancestors may well have come from a direct line of Spaniards for all we know. Yet I cannot remember that my father ever impressed in the minds of his children the idea that we were Spanish as Nieto-Phillips's mother did to him.

On the other side, that my mother was born to a family fleeing the chaos of the Mexican Revolution, circa 1915, is proof of a Mexican pedigree. The ties to kin in Parral and Sombrerete were frayed between my mother and her siblings and snapped for their children. Yet our maternal grandmother, whom we knew as a lone parent in Belen, New Mexico, was most assuredly a Mexican matron who, from what I can recall, never spoke a word of English. Moreover, the accounts of our uncle Pedro Ornelas, husband of our oldest *tía*, who rode with Pancho Villa, vouched for a Mexican ancestry.

While a graduate student in the 1970s, I was surprised to encounter "Hijos de los Conquistadores," "Children of the Conquerors," a chapter in Marc Simmons's *People of the Sun: Some Out of Fashion Southwesterners*—surprised because while in the Chicano Chicana Movement, I naively believed that we had erased Spanish identity from our people's collective awareness. Instead, Simmons argued for a "single fact" needing to be grasped, that the Southwest "is the home of not one, but two different cultures whose roots lead back to Spain. The older is the Spanish or Hispano culture of northern New Mexico and southern Colorado. The second, and more recent, is the Mexican American, or Border culture, concentrated along the international boundary from Brownsville to Tijuana."[1]

As one can imagine, my lived experience hardly resonated with the Simmons's cultural duality. Yet I found myself piqued into wanting to understand the staying power of Spanish identity. A foray into the work and life of Aurelio Espinosa, the pioneer *Nuevomexicano* folklorist known in academic circles as a premier Spanish promoter, seemed a good way to start. In 1933, Espinosa headed the Department of Romance Languages at Stanford University and served on the editorial board of the *New Mexico Historical Review.* During a search for biographical information on Espinosa in the journal's archive, I discovered three letters between him and its editor, Lansing Bloom, that started to open doors.[2]

Espinosa asked Bloom if he would be "good enough" to let him know whether "that questionnaire about which there was recently so much discussion in New Mexico and drawn up by Professor Page from the University has been sent out? If so, what results were obtained?" In his response, Bloom got some things wrong but confirmed that the "questionnaire" was sent to some high schools and was suddenly halted. Its "scientific value" was compromised by "the deplorable form of publicity which was given to it" and because of the governor's meddling in the project. An investigation committee had finished its hearings and its findings were expected soon, Bloom explained. Bloom expressed hope that "some constructive good" would come out of "the mess—for example, some Spanish Americans on our board of regents—if the governor will make his appointments above the plane of petty politics." Sounding less than sanguine, Espinosa objected to what was an attitude scale, saying he was not surprised that it "stirred up so much trouble."

Sleuthing about, I came upon the Richard M. Page papers and from them I discovered what I came to call the Racial Attitude Confrontation: a statewide protest alleging that the University of New Mexico discriminated against "Spanish Americans." The insulting characterizations of the Spanish-speaking people of the Southwest that Page included in his survey fueled the fear that he was spreading race prejudice against the Spanish American people.

What proved particularly intriguing was the force with which people identifying themselves as "Spanish" challenged the university because it was commonly maintained at the time that Spanish identity reflected a nonconfrontational politics and a reluctance to admit of racism existing in New Mexico. Simmons himself had written that Spanish Americans disdained militant activism; other writers had said the same. And yet here I beheld aggrieved Spanish Americans unleashing their wrath on Page, an acting assistant professor in the Psychology Department, on the charge that in his research he sought to promote prejudice against their people—and that the fault for this transgression lay with the university itself. Clearly something was amiss in the usual way Spanish identity was looked upon by critics and believers alike.[3]

The Racial Attitude Confrontation became the topic of my PhD dissertation (so long ago). Material from that study formed the basis of my first peer-reviewed article. Throughout my long academic career, I returned to the subject of Spanish identity with some regularity. I always found things that I considered new and enlightening about it. That part of my research career has trailed its way into this volume in which I strive to sum up my long-running interrogation of Spanish identity and more. In addition to new material, I bring in previous work at certain points but sometimes to reinterpret or even correct some things I've said about the topic in the past. I hasten to add that much of my description of Nuevomexicano identity formation in the nineteenth century can be seen as a kind of ideological adjunct to my structural study of Nuevomexicanos contributing to the political development of territorial New Mexico presented in *Política: Nuevomexicanos and American Political Incorporation, 1821–1910.*

Acknowledgments

Over the years, I gained a great deal from the responses of audience members to whom I have reported portions of this endeavor at meetings of the American Sociological Association, the Western History Association, the National Association of Chicana and Chicano studies, the National Hispanic Cultural Center, and the Sociology Departments of the University of California Los Angeles and of the University of New Mexico.

John Nieto-Phillips gave inestimable advice, counsel, critiques, and recommendations on the content and organization of the manuscript. Maria E. Montoya and Rosina Lozano provided cogent assessments and pertinent recommendations. I have profited greatly from discussions and conversations with Durwood Ball, Casandra Salgado, Sarah B. Horton, Ramón Gutiérrez, Deena González, Raúl Coronado, Tomas Almaguer, Paul Espinosa, A. Gabriel Meléndez, Genaro Padilla, Edward Gonzales, José María Carlos Higinio, and Esteven Rael-Gálvez. As they were for my previous book on nineteenth-century Nuevomexicano politics, Arely Guerrero, Erika Derkas, Bryan Turo, and Melina Vizcaino again proved themselves super research assistants.

The usual suspects at the Center for Southwest Research at the University of New Mexico Libraries—Christopher Geherin, Samuel Sisneros, and Nancy Brown Martínez, among others—proved invaluable assets across a wide range of requests I presented to them. I am grateful to Caitlyn Carl, Hannah Abelbeck, and Heather McClure for their guidance and patience regarding materials at the Fray Angélico Chávez Library, New Mexico History Museum. On matters digital, Robert O. Valdez, Shoshana Handel, Mark R. Montoya, Mason Parrish, and Molly Montgomery came through. Jane E. Egan, Special Assistant in the Office of the Cabinet Secretary, New Mexico Department of Cultural Affairs, graciously took time from her busy schedule to help me resolve a logistical matter. At the University of New Mexico Press, my oversight editor, Michael Millman, kept my confidence bristling in what often seemed like an interminable "bookmaking" process, James Cruise proved a copy-edit partner, and Isaac Morris designed the deeply textured dust jacket. Finally, in relation to material costs associated with producing the book, I am grateful for the support of the University of New Mexico's Center for Southwest Research, Sociology Department, and Center for Regional Studies.

Introduction

ETHNIC COLLECTIVE IDENTITY has been a staple of public life throughout the history of modern society. At times, adherents have styled their identity complex so strikingly that it gains special fame and reputation. Thus, among those in the know and those who claim to be in the know concerning things Mexican American, nothing bespeaks "New Mexico" more instantaneously than the group labels "Spanish," "Spanish American," and the related "Hispano." The reason is clear. So many Nuevomexicanos and Nuevomexicanas (who trace their ancestry to New Mexico's Spanish colonial era) have over many generations declared themselves ethnically "Spanish." The surveys that poll Nuevomexicano/a samples for their ethnic identity testify to the durability of Spanish identity in the state's cultural field.[1]

Historically, Nuevomexicanas/os have not only declared themselves Spanish; they have laid claim to a Spanish heritage with a pride that is pronounced and even outsized. It was in grand evidence, for instance, when New Mexico celebrated the four hundredth anniversary of its Western founding by the Spanish imperial official Juan de Oñate. In addition, the activation of Spanish identity has been responsible for many a community commemoration of its origins, for the public monuments to New Mexico's historical Castilian figures, and the Spanish naming of streets, schools, and other structures.

Nuevomexicano Spanish identity has been a staple within New Mexico's greater adoption of the Spanish heritage for its regional identity. At the same time, considerable antagonism has condemned Spanish identity. As we shall see, Spanish identity has divided persons of Mexican American extraction. Countless Chicanos and Chicanas have contested what they deem the pretentiousness of claiming to be Spanish. In addition, for decades now Native critics, particularly New Mexico's Pueblo communities, as well as their indigenous allies, have bedeviled the oppressive symbolism that accompanies the portraying and heralding of the Spanish conquest of their homelands. In return, Spanish Americans have passionately defended the history of New Mexico's Spanish presence in all its manifestations and the emblems that have represented their cherished heritage. The feud that developed in this contention has been one for the books.

We shall in due course immerse ourselves in the controversy, not least for the changes it has wrought in New Mexico's public sphere. But first, a detour. As John Nieto-Phillips has recently commented, Spanish identity has remained an enigma. Considerable ambiguity pervades the general understanding of what has driven Spanish identity to prominence despite the substantial attention we have given its raison d'être and teleology—an attention, I would emphasize, that is without comparison among other ethnic identities in the plural Southwest. Academics have contributed a great deal to the community's understanding of the origins of Spanish identity, of its self-serving justifications for existing, and its functioning in the social worlds of Nuevomexicanos/as. Accordingly, before I move on to a head-on interrogation of the history and meaning of Spanish identity, it will help greatly to familiarize ourselves with the literature.

The first thing to realize is how a type of canon, or established consensus, has coalesced among authors. As for the beginnings of Spanish identity, this canon maintains that it came to fruition between the last two decades of the nineteenth century and the first two of the twentieth century, that is, during New Mexico's initial industrial economy. At that, it is accepted that Spanish identity sprouted as an unorthodox or anomalous phenomenon.

In one explanatory thread within the canon, Nuevomexicanos took to expressing Spanish identity as a reaction to the anti-Mexican attitudes Euro-American newcomers brought into the territory. As the folklorist Arthur Campa has argued, the trouble with "all the terminology developed in New Mexico" is that "anomalies" that have attempted to "justify prejudices and defense mechanisms." People, he urges, use reflexive reasoning in dealing with social categories, and those "who think in terms of the past century insist that the New Mexican is a Mexican." However, the "New Mexican resents this, not on the basis of nationality but on the assumption that he belongs to a different race. He makes the mistake of thinking that Mexican is a racial term." But Nuevomexicanos took to race-thinking only after Anglo Americans introduced it. Since the New Mexican was no different in appearance from the inhabitants below the Rio Grande, "Americans classify him [*sic*] in the same category despite his American citizenship."[2]

Class and immigration were mixed in. The art patron and ethnographer Mary Austin noted that Nuevomexicanos (not her word) were "affiliated by inheritance and economic influence" with incoming Mexicans, yet middle- and upper-class persons took to fancying themselves "Spanish" to deflect the race prejudice engendered by Anglos from Texas and Oklahoma and as the numbers of lower-class Mexican nationals began to swell in the Southwest.[3]

In a variation on a theme, so-called Anglos are said to have triggered Spanish identity. Chris Wilson, for example, notes that the Santa Fe *Daily New Mexican* of the 1890s "rarely used the term 'Spanish-American,' and then only to describe the upper level of the local society." Only when Spanish-surnamed people voted for an Anglo business initiative did the daily congratulate young "Spanish Americans for coming down on the side of progress." Moreover, the staff of the Museum of New Mexico were Anglo arrivals who "realized that tourists were more interested in romantic tales of the Spanish conquistadors than in the still foreign and threatening presence of the Mexican working class." Wilson also claims that the "rhetoric of tri-culturalism, with its shift from the term *Mexicano* to Spanish-American was helped by the effects of the Mexican Revolution of 1910 on the U.S. side of the border."[4]

Charles Montgomery's influential *The Spanish Redemption* relied on Carolyn Zeleny's observation of tension in the social relations between upper-class Anglos and elite Nuevomexicanos.[5] The Spanish heritage made for a lens to focus objective facts "and the constructed meanings of everyday life." In public arenas, "Spanish culture," "Spanish history," and "Spanish-Americans" papered over a simmering conflict and by doing that "mask[ed]," "cloak[ed]," and "divert[ed] attention" from problems affecting *paisanos* and more privileged Hispanics. A glorified Spanish heritage sustained Anglo social dominance. Higher class Spanish Americans who lost land and historic community power assuaged themselves by posing as proud "Spaniards."[6]

Laura Gómez's treatment of the rise of Spanish identity in New Mexico sees the progressive politician LeBaron Bradford Prince strategizing to promote Spanish identity with a myth of three cultures—Anglo, Spanish, Native—living in harmony. Prince used Spanish heritage to defend the civil rights of the Mexican citizens of New Mexico. In the process, Nuevomexicano elites got "a collective psychological boost by being allowed to claim whiteness within the American context of white supremacy." The claim to Spanish "proved an ideal tool" for co-opting those Mexican Americans who traded on their mestizo heritage to divide themselves from Pueblo neighbors.[7]

Juan Gómez-Quiñones makes the case more explicitly that "Spanish" labels signaled a "social and political ploy introduced by prejudiced Anglos and adopted by mixed-blood mestizos to curry favor," which frequently led to anti-Mexican and anti-Native attitudes.[8] In dissociating from *lo mexicano*, Nuevomexicanos denied their membership in a shared culture, mixed bloodline, and historical association "with the independence of the Republic of Mexico."[9] The "euphemistic identity of 'Spanish'" enabled "their dealings with 'Anglos' as in the phrase, '*la raza española*'" (the Spanish race). A claim to Spanish descent facilitated the goals of those who sought social mobility in Anglo society, the price for "strenuous efforts to assimilate."[10]

John Nieto-Phillips has emphasized the link between the rise of Spanish identity and the process in which New Mexico became a state. He sees Nuevomexicano reaction to Euro-American impositions while recognizing a significant Nuevomexicano collaboration with Anglo-sponsored nostalgia projects. In his key finding, the value placed on blood purity, established in medieval Spain and streamed into the caste system of colonial America, remained in Nuevomexicano culture, but not surfacing prominently until the turn of the twentieth century. The ideologues of Manifest Destiny demanded "whiteness" for those who strove for inclusion in the American body politic while targeting the "mongrel" Mexicans for exclusion. The old connotation of Spanish blood purity demonstrated to Nuevomexicanos their equality with white Anglo-Saxons, which, they believed, qualified them for full American citizenship and convinced them that Congress needed to make New Mexico a state.[11]

In *Border Dilemmas*, Anthony Mora placed Spanish identity squarely in the field of the canon, "members of the Euroamerican territorial elite deploy[ing] a tricultural New Mexican identity after 1880" with prominent Mexican Americans joining in this "regional discourse with equal enthusiasm."[12]

As far as they go, these and similar works shed bright lights on Spanish identity, especially in the era they focus on; this study draws on much from that body of work. Yet, as I rejoin the conversation in this volume, I take advantage of research that has gone back further than fin-de-siècle New Mexico and that jets to the virtual present. In a key reckoning, I flesh out Nieto-Phillips's notation of the ideational roots of modern Spanish identity lying in Spanish colonial and Mexican epochs by demonstrating that the link was not as subterranean as he has suggested, but more open and direct. Also coming under scrutiny are the canon's psychologically reactive, compensatory, and sycophantic models. It is true: Euro-American racism greatly charged Nuevomexicano identity greatly, but Nuevomexicanos were too savvy to confuse the difference between nationality and race as Campos maintained. In addition, while Euro-Americans did indeed play important roles in sustaining the Spanish heritage, the notion of Nuevomexicanos being herded powerlessly over something as primal as collective identity denies their agency and belies the toughened personas that will populate the pages to follow.

The rise of Spanish identity in nineteenth-century New Mexico involved, as this book emphasizes, hard-boiled politics. What I argue is that many of the mysteries of Spanish identity are clarified if we understand that in the nineteenth century Nuevomexicano identity reflected *ethnic nationalism.* It was in some ways a prototypical instance of the regional nationalisms that commonly appeared in Western states in the twentieth century. My effort here is not the first time that Spanish identity has been tied to ethnic nationalism. I have previously alluded to the connection, and anthropologist Sarah Horton used the concept of ethnic nationalism to organize her study of the modern-day Fiesta de Santa Fe.[13] As such, *Hispano Nation* provides a conceptual backbone for the thesis of Spanish identity as ethnic nationalism. That is not to say that "Spanish" was and is a "true" identity, whatever that might mean, nor does it signify agreement with the idea that Spanish identity has been an irrational construction. It is, rather, a tool for understanding what Nuevomexicanos were doing as they configured their ethnic identity, and for peeling off the layers of significance that have lain inside and about Spanish identity, some of which the canon avoided, such as the formation's acute historical relations to Indigenous nations.

How then will ethnic nationalism play out? In classic parlance, a "nation" simply meant "a people." The Roman *natio* referred to distant tribes, but it has since evolved to mean "all 'peoples'" with distinctive traits.[14] As an ideal, it referred to a bounded community held together by cultural, social, and material ties, linked by custom, self-made institutions, and a conception of the object people's "place of birth."[15] Such a coherence was readily perceived in hinterlands, while in reference to Western society, whether "nations" existed in these terms has been debated. So-called primordialists have argued that they did and do because of surviving cultural and genetic features.[16] With his concept of *ethnie*, Anthony Smith set out to demonstrate the premodern cultural roots of modern ethnic groups.[17]

"Constructivist" critics, however, have cautioned against taking subjects' accounts at face value. For Walker Connor, a nation refers not to "what is," but to "what people believe is." Nation "connotes a group of people who believe they are ancestrally related," or "a group of people characterized by a myth of common descent."[18] A nation exists "when a significant number of people in a setting consider themselves to form a nation or behave as if they formed one."[19] Benedict Anderson's influential "imagined community" signifies the investments people make in "cultural artifacts," which may change yet "command . . . profound emotional legitimacy."[20] "Imagined" is not to be confused with "imaginary," not a question of fact in all cases but of claims made about a "people's" history, language, territory, customs, religion, race, etc., often filled with heartfelt, spiritual meaning.[21]

Relatedly, nationalism means "loyalty to the ethnic group." Ethnonationalism is a "psychological, emotional, or generally subjective bond" based on a notion of shared blood and culture, pivoting on an abiding affection and love for "the ancestral land, land of our fathers, this sacred soil, land where our fathers died, the native land, the cradle of the nation, most commonly, the *home*—the *home*land of our particular people."[22] Commonly codified as territorial *primacy*, it signals the value placed on "a people's" rootedness in their patria.[23]

Also to consider are the "attitudes and ideologies which characterize the behavior of nationalities engaged in the struggle to achieve, maintain, or enhance their position in the world."[24] Frederik Barth has countered the old anthropological notion of cultural differences politicizing ethnicity by contending instead that social boundaries formed in social contact and interaction, regardless of cultural distinctions, are what count.[25] Claims to difference stem from pressures that suggest "widespread evidence of ethnic divisions, precipitating or intensifying nationalist urgings."[26] Political nationalism means often that ethnicity will be public in nature, meaning that ethnicity is "incessantly negotiated through discourse." Conceptions of ethnic nation depend on the "narrative accounts and arguments [brought] to bear in 'controversial discourse.'" "Strategies of remembrance" around "transgressions, or resistance" reflect "critical history," the "othering of opponents, oppressors, or competitors." Significant as well is "historical forgetfulness," as it conveniently, covertly, or inadvertently leaves out important, even countervailing events that critics may well point out.[27]

The use of a name to identify, designate, or signify one's group is far from simple. More than a mere tag, a name can "convey powerful imagery." Proposing, imposing, and accepting names "can be a political exercise."[28] Discursive naming "is not a neutral practice. To give a place [or a group] a name is to situate it within a knowable universe and to assert a form of possession."[29] Examining the debate among the "Coloureds" in South Africa, Immanuel Wallerstein concludes that "pastness" in the sense of history was represented by a particular name. It is "a mode by which persons are persuaded to act in the present in ways they might not otherwise act." Moreover, "pastness is a tool persons use against each other."[30]

A committed intelligentsia is key for constructing and naming "a people." An educated elite strives to "gain and/or maintain its political ascendancy in the community and to control the conduct of its public affairs."[31] According to Siniša Malešević, "identitarian intellectuals" emerge organically from a community, "intensifying ethno-nationalist mobilization."[32] Defined generally, not specifically,[33] identitarians are heritage visionaries, social-action thinkers who are connected by "feelings of mutual concern and loyalty" and who "make their demands by means of the depth and intensity of the special concern for others that they inspire."[34] Books, essays, and other publications, including nationalist tracts, generate sentiments, attitudes, and values to serve the fortunes and fates of a nation against the threats or competitions of collective rivals.[35]

Ethnic nationalism is often at the core of the nation-state.[36] Andreas Wimmer proposes "ethno-national dominance" to "embrace dominant ethnicity and dominant nationhood."[37] In the United States, for example, dominant ethnic identity is often (but not always) cast in terms of "white nationalism."[38]

On a variant scale, ethnic nationalism can also reflect regionalism, for example, as a consequence of a state expanding and acquiring land belonging to a neighboring state. Ethnic annexation thus transpires when a state enlarges its borders "by incorporation of adjoining areas inhabited by people of different culture and/or historical origin."[39]

In what I call "forced annexation," a state acquires foreign territory illegally, largely through military occupation. A special case involves a state expanding its existing international borderline "empire fashion,"[40] forcibly taking control of contiguous lands. What follows this type of expansionist annexation is critical. "Internal colonialism" is a trusty way to signal the social positioning of an ethnic group living on land taken by a neighboring state. In one variation, the imperial power exploits the colony for its natural resources. In Michael Hechter's cultural division of labor, for example, conquered elements are channeled into a particular labor force, held there by racism and the denial of civil rights.[41] Richard Schermerhorn's concept of "annexation sequences" is more flexible. In an initial phase, ethnocentrism, racism, cultural tensions, and forced assimilation arise.[42] In that model, native identitarians react "passionately" to violations of their "people's" homeland birthrights.[43] Invoking historical, pseudo-historical, or fabricated accounts, a discursive intelligentsia frames issues on a value of autochthony, that is, taking "great pride" in being native to their occupied territory.[44] Aggrieved subnationalists clamor for justice based on their people's longstanding belonging to their pre-annexed land.[45]

Should problems persist, an ideological movement surges among the colonized "for the attainment and maintenance of autonomy, unity, and identity" for an "actual or potential nation."[46] The aspiration for "self-determination" is consonant for a political community "whose boundaries were established [or reinforced] by the colonizer."[47] In this manner, ethnic identity affords "a new set of avenues to power and privilege for members of strata hitherto excluded from a share in both."[48] Nationalism's own doctrine holds that culture is the "basic social bond," and the size and power of the culture group should match the scale of a sovereign governance that ethnic nationalism defines for itself.[49] Three essential pathways to self-determination have come out of forced annexation: secession (including irredentism), ethnic autonomy, and subnational constitutionalism.

Secession—a movement to pull the homeland away to form an independent state—means the annexed have refused to legitimize the conquering state. Invoking the "language of discrimination" and drawing attention to "unacceptable levels of ethnic or racial inequality," annexed subjects reject the validity of the imperial power.[50] An example would be the secession movement in Catalunya, Spain, where a culture region bewailing discrimination mounts a secessionist movement.

Irredentism is a form of secession aimed at returning the regional homeland to its original country, as illustrated by the aim of Northern Ireland's Irish Republican Army in the twentieth century.[51] Native secessionists can demand irredentism, going along with the demand of the original sovereign to have its former land returned.[52] Inherently revolutionary, separatism and irredentism would rupture the dominant state.[53]

Regional autonomy arises to deflect the possibility of violent secession. In response to the call of regional subnationalists for self-determination, the central government agrees to devolve political, economic, and cultural control of the annexed territory to its native residents while that territory remains in the state. In "consociational democracy," a "grand coalition" of ethnic leaders and federal representatives[54] establish "ethnic federalism," a system of minority group representation in the federal government,[55] as in the case of the Quebecois in Canada.

Subnational constitutionalism evolved as a solution to problems of internal colonialism based on the legitimation that the conquered group grants to the imperial state. While ethnic partisans bang the drum of nationhood, demanding the fulfillment of homeland rights for their people, self-determination emerges within the federal unit that encloses the regional homeland. It is a "tool to ensure the continued existence of diversity and uniquely different cultures" in the federal entity.[56] It works in polities where departments, cantons, or internal states inscribe their own charters.[57] Subnational constitutionalism has generally involved participation rights, which constitute "a guaranteed and institutionalized special influence on the decision-making process [through] the democratic integration of these [colonized] groups" under the federal unit's constitution as a power-sharing arrangement.[58] In self-rule, the annexed group monopolizes the electoral procedures of the federal unit and in that manner ensures its "self-determination."[59]

The Nuevomexicano Case

That the United States forcibly annexed New Mexico is commonly recognized. In 1846, President James K. Polk, a Democrat who favored US westward expansion, misled the country by calling a minor skirmish between Mexican and American troops on the disputed international border an attack on the United States. Polk and the Congress used it to declare war on Mexico. Military forces launched a multi-flank invasion of its neighbor to the south. In one thrust, Colonel Stephen W. Kearny marched his Army of the West into New Mexico where he occupied Santa Fe without Mexican resistance. The United States never relinquished control of the territory.

Kearny's occupation manifested internal colonialism. In a complication, it was organized on the precepts of "liberal imperialism," as I have argued elsewhere.[60] Scholars associate liberal imperialism with Western polities and define it as an ideology to justify imperial control, as when the British argued that its dominion over India benefitted colonial subjects by bringing superior liberal values and ideas to areas historically ruled by despots.[61] The same discourse came with the annexation of New Mexico as Kearny promised America's enlightened values and republican politics to loosen Nuevomexicanos from the grip of Mexico's misrule.[62]

Nuevomexicanos legitimized the American conquest of their homeland due in no small measure to liberal imperialism. It happened in a convoluted manner. Nuevomexicano leaders were originally split on Kearny. One faction known as the "American party" was disgruntled over Mexico City's neglect of New Mexico. Admiring the United States for its robust democracy and wealth, members who regarded the US takeover as a good thing went on to collaborate with Kearny in his occupation.[63]

It looked like a peaceful conquest. However, the so-called "Mexican party" resisted the occupation, and in January 1847 Nuevomexicanos and Taos Puebloans assassinated Kearny's appointed governor, Charles Bent, along with members of his entourage, including two Nuevomexicano collaborators.[64] In the Taos Revolt, resistance spread across northern New Mexico.[65] Casualties were taken on both sides. In the end, the occupying military and a Euro-American militia defeated the resistance. The pro-American Donaciano Vigil was appointed New Mexico's governor. Conquerors charged captured rebels with treason, conducted an (internationally illegal) trial, found several of the accused guilty, and executed them by hanging.[66]

With its superior military, the United States prevailed with dispatch over Mexico. The Treaty of Guadalupe Hidalgo, which formally ended hostilities in February 1848, made provisions for the United States to purchase Mexico's entire northern half. Former defenders of Mexican sovereignty resigned themselves to the conquest, making Nuevomexicano legitimation to US nationality complete. A late nineteenth-century Nuevomexicano remembered that "After the first impulses of resistance, the Mexicans of the territory submitted in good faith" and accordingly accepted the new laws and institutions as theirs to work with.[67]

The provision in the Treaty of Guadalupe Hidalgo that granted US citizenship to Nuevomexicanos factored into Nuevomexicano legitimation. Commentators, though, have criticized this measure for having failed to prevent the racial othering of Nuevomexicanos and for denying them equal citizenship.[68] While largely true, in the immediate context of annexation, citizenship permitted the inclusion of the annexed elements into the American political system.

Kearny's occupation anticipated the Treaty of Guadalupe Hidalgo by giving the mass of male Nuevomexicanos the right to vote, a right that did not exist in the Mexican era except for the political elite. As both Texas and California became states in the mid-nineteenth century, Mexicans in both were not permitted the advantage of exercising control over Euro-American settlers.[69] Matters differed in the New Mexico colony. With American settlers forming a small portion of the population, popular elections assured that Nuevomexicanos would control the territorial position of delegate to Congress until the late 1880s, as well as the territorial legislature until the first decade of the twentieth century, and finally local and county governments in the northern, central, and far southern districts along the Rio Grande.[70] Elected politicians came from prominent families and thereby formed what Michael Alarid calls the "Hispano bastion."[71] Government was conducted mostly in Spanish, making the political participation of the recently annexed Mexicans both striking and significant.[72]

While under internal colonialism, conquered elements tended to be excluded from mainstream parties and their patronage, Nuevomexicanos virtually built their territory's two-party system.[73] And while nineteenth-century American parties fell short of fulfilling genuine democracy,[74] Nuevomexicanos put enormous energy into running seasonal elections, activating local parties for territorial and county conventions, serving as worker-ant organizers for nominating conventions, and acting as convention officers.[75] As such, a party made for a "political community,"[76] valued by those elected to office not least for the status payoffs it afforded. In 1864, for example, the *Nuevo Mexicano* weekly newspaper congratulated Tomás Gutiérrez for his chance "to be of great utility for the advancement of his *paisanos* of New Mexico."[77]

Nuevomexicanos expressed strong patriotism toward the country that conquered them. Colonial states often imposed a different kind of patriotism, dominant so as to subversively undermine primary patriotism to the ethnic group.[78] Nuevomexicanos, however, came under the influence of the hegemonic national loyalty that still coursed through American society in the extended wake of independence from Great Britain. In addition, their political involvement confirmed the concept of a democratic "civilian will" and the "superior nature of the republican government."[79] The 1872 commemoration in Albuquerque of its founding and patron saint, San Felipe de Neri illustrates. "Both in front and rear of the procession," a Euro-American correspondent wrote,

> were a number of men and boys on horseback, wearing red or blue scarves and hat bands, carrying different kinds of flags. All the flag scarves used during these ceremonies were surmounted by a cross with the exception of the splendid American flag borne by Mariano, son of Don Ambrosio Armijo, which was surmounted by a spread eagle.[80]

Ambrosio Armijo, chair of the county Democratic Party, served as marshal and commander of the mounted escort.

Finally, US military service solidified "allegiance citizenship."[81] Nuevomexicano leaders served as officers in New Mexico's war with the Confederacy and took on the responsibility of organizing militia companies, divisions, regiments, and brigades.[82] Militiamen confronted Texas rebels at the Battle of Valverde.[83] Officers and infantrymen, including former opponents of Kearny, distinguished themselves in battle at Glorieta Pass.[84] After the war, public relations festooned veterans with the notion of "no more loyal people than the Nuevomexicanos."[85]

Despite the channels of inclusion, problems of a colony persisted. Administratively, the organization of federal territories proved problematic. In context of what Ned Blackhawk calls the "settler colonial state,"[86] Congress exercised a laissez-faire policy toward its territories. Congressional delegates appeared before a committee hat in hand pleading for needed resources or specific regulations. Patronage determined who the president appointed as territorial governors, secretaries, and supreme court justices. This defect was especially detrimental to Nuevomexicano inclusion.[87] In general, as Ian Lee has noted, "Congress and other federal officials in Washington, D.C. accorded very little significance to New Mexico, giving greater importance to the growing sectional disputes and other matters to the east. They gave very little heed to concerns emanating from a territory thought to be so inconsequential to the overall value of the United States."[88]

Annexation meant more than the absorption of individuals. A whole regional social formation was swallowed up by a voracious state. Externally driven forces disrupted accustomed ways of life, not least a long-standing Catholic tradition and a communal system of landholding.

Racial distinctions were infamously ingrained in Manifest Destiny.[89] Americans since the 1820s, David Weber has noted, disparaged mixed-blood Mexicans, charging them with having "inherited the worst qualities of Spaniards and Indians, [the result of which was] a 'race' still more despicable than that of either parent group."[90] Coming from national and territorial sources, this tendency to stigmatize affected Nuevomexicanos/as up to the twentieth century. As Nieto-Phillips and others have shown, it was a major reason why American nationalists kept New Mexico from becoming a state for over thirty years.

As Laura Gómez points out, a key question in nineteenth-century New Mexico concerned the fit of Nuevomexicanos in the territory's racial order.[91] American colonizers ranked on top. Some of them forged alliances with Nuevomexicanos for purposes benevolent and ill. Many married Nuevomexicanas, often for financial gain, while others kept *la gente* (the people) at arm's length.[92] The national entitlement of "white American" counted for a great deal even as "whiteness" was a social construct.[93]

Euro-American culture brokers factored in as significant colonizers. They spawned earlier than what the canon claims. Serving as agents of the ideology of liberal imperialism, they followed (not preceded, it is important to note) Nuevomexicano identity formation. In their multifaceted project, they could grease the rails of Nuevomexicano integration, but their culture work also served their own material interests when Spanish colonial history and heritage suited their civic goals, economic plans, and personal ambitions.

Nuevomexicanos were driven to construct a primacy identity. To engage liberal imperialism, Nuevomexicano identitarians stressed their belonging to plural America, for their people were clearly not members of the American "white" nation. At the same time, hindrances to full inclusion required a "common rhetoric" and "cultural framing" to turn grievances into agendas.[94] How the rhetorics of ethnic naming and the constructions of cultural heritage intersected with these imperatives form the crux of the historical excursions I undertake in the chapters to follow.

The order of the chapters charts the career arc of Nuevomexicano ethnic identity in American New Mexico. On the frontier in the first thirty-five years, identity was encoded by Spanish, Mexican, and colloquial labels. Spanish identity grew prominent when the railroad revamped territorial society. The successful struggle to gain statehood and decolonize the Nuevomexicano people advantaged Spanish identity by encouraging the notion of a distinct people. In the early statehood period, the popularity of Spanish identity expanded. It's decline began slowly in the 1930s and accelerated in the coming decades, declining precipitously once it came under the opposition of Mexican American, Chicano/a, and Indigenous activism.

The narrative for the early period maps the discursive milestones that sustained public expressions of Nuevomexicano identity. An educated elite fulfilled the role of an identitarian intelligentsia. The first generation came to the United States from Mexico in 1848, and many in the second generation were its progeny. Significantly, the intelligentsia was steeped in the history of New Mexico,[95] composing in this sense a "community of memory."[96] Sometimes it was an actively networked community. At other moments, individuals stepped up to advocate for the interests of their territorial people.

In the essential thread, homeland identity was founded on two interrelated themes: in one, the claim of a cohesive "nation" having been fulfilled (even if it meant some important hedging), and, in the other, the power of this people's primacy on the New Mexican land, predicated on its long-standing settlement and the grittiness of their belonging to it. Any of several ethnic identifiers helped signal primacy including that of "Spanish." To highlight peoplehood, identitarians romanticized key events, heroic figures, and a beloved *poblador* (settler, community). Ancestor worship, a glorified Euro-Hispanic civilization, the people's exploits of settling in, and claims of blood purity instilled nationness. As it happens in cases of minority ethnic nationalism,[97] the rhetoric of a people's dignity and nobility elevated the value of Nuevomexicano heritage above that of Americans and indigenous Natives in equal measure.

Nuevomexicanos tried consolidating a sophisticated social movement organization to spearhead a fight against Euro-American hierarchy, but it imploded, as we shall see. In general, then, the oft-dispersed intelligentsia transmitted identity in the territory's developing channels of public discourse in both Spanish and English.[98] In an era in which American nationalism tended to denigrate their heritage, Nuevomexicanos showcased their historic culture and life-experiences in a rhetorical device I call the "heritage script."[99]

Heritage scripts came in three sizes. Most commonly, the curt, bite-sized signifying trope stood for and broke down the epistemic complexity of a master historical narrative, say, or of a great event, a cultural feature, or some politics rendered as familiar as clichés to ensure easy transmission and repetition across space and time. The intermediate "heritage account" was a more detailed or informed script. Sometimes incorporating signifying tropes, heritage accounts contextualized a given issue in the scope of, for example, a policy statement. Finally, the "monographic discourse" was a substantial account with a beginning, a middle, and an end.

In identifying heritage scripts across time, we sense the working construction of ethnic nationalism. Identity dropped in scenarios writ large and small; it was inscribed in government documents, election circulars, charters of volunteer organizations, speeches published in newspapers, the resolutions of spontaneous protest meetings, Spanish-language folk dialogues, and theatrical performances. Just as Benedict Anderson underscores the vernacular press of historically territorialized nations, so were the three kinds of identity scripts carried in the columns of Spanish-language newspapers, whose number increased in the late nineteenth century. Much identity scripting occurred in the Spanish language, yet the process was not isolated from mainstream English language discourse. We see it, for instance, in how Euro-Americans adopted scripts and accounts that originated in Spanish for their contributions to the debates and politics over Nuevomexicano/a standing in the territory and the United States. Accordingly, readers can expect a parade of healthy heritage scripts dug from the territory's discourse channels, intended as a methodological presentation of data on Nuevomexicano/a, Euro-American, and Indigenous identity and to savor a shifting historical prose.

In framing Nuevomexicano identity as ethnic nationalism, Spanish identity gets a fairer shake to account for itself than ever before. However, ethnic nationalisms harbor chauvinisms of their own making. As Nuevomexicano identity-makers dealt in the violence of engaged Plains Natives on what they deemed *their* homeland, they took in the air of superiority over the "savage." That "othering" ironically became a source for reinforcing the Nuevomexicano sense of primacy on New Mexico soil. They bent the posture toward the sedentary Puebloans as well in a significant performative heralding of their conquistador ancestors in the sixteenth and seventeenth centuries described in chapter 2.

The Spanish heritage greatly influenced the formation of New Mexico's modern civil society. As chapter 3 discloses, a range of informal and officious activities made for a "Realm of Spanish Memory" in the territory, one that provided for convivial relations between Euro-American and Nuevomexicano agents. Yet, a critical ethnic nationalism operated within it as well. In the most telling expression, identitarians set out to compose their people's own history to contravene what they judged to be the distorted portrayals of their people by "foreign" Euro-American writers.

In the 1890s, a new ethnic name for denoting Nuevomexicanos/ as sprung. Under "Hispano," Nuevomexicano journalists catalyzed what could have functioned as an anticolonial initiative. Reflecting a tendency to think in terms of ethnic nationalism, it held great potential for building a central movement organization. However, it stumbled into a trap borne of legitimation Nuevomexicanos gave to US imperialism, the partisanship of American electoral politics.

Euro-Americans often believed that Nuevomexicanos wanted to return to Mexico.[100] They hardly needed to worry. As for outright secession, small ethnic nations find the asymmetric power relation with a conquering state daunting and the material costs of launching a separatist movement overwhelming. Moreover, any secessionist movement requires an extensive solidarity to mobilize "large numbers willing to confront state repression."[101] Such unity went sorely lacking among Nuevomexicanos. Intense division often followed the "pervasively partisan" politics existing in the United States.[102] Parties competed fiercely for Nuevomexicano loyalty, each advertising that it was the one to truly represent the people.[103] As one journalist editorialized on the absence of Nuevomexicano solidarity, "No se une en política, porque la política es un necesario antagonismo" (there is no unity among us because politics is a necessary antagonism).[104] But it was not just party loyalty that aggravated Nuevomexicano solidarity; party competition broke down the colonizer-colonized boundary. To ensure election success, the party maintained cross-ethnic ties so that rank-and-file members could support standard-bearers regardless of ethnicity.[105]

Ethnic federalism was also out of the question. The United States lacked the capacity for consociated negotiations between territorial leaders and federal authorities. Empowering the states, Congress relied on per se citizenship and civic principles.[106]As Nathan Glazer argues, this appeared at Independence before any issues of regional fragmentation might encourage a nonwhite ethnic option for control of a territory. The politics of states' rights was pushed in the nineteenth century by "politically dominant English-origin elements" in the states. While great diversity in a state's legislation prevailed, the climate did not favor the rise of territorially concentrated ethnic groups struggling to control a state. Glazer sensed the possibility of an ethnic-federal tie for populations having "national characteristics," but, as he claims, in no instance did an ethnic community develop a subnational consciousness.[107] He shortsighted Nuevomexicano, native Hawaiian, Alaskan Native, and Native identity. Yet the structural blockages to ethnic autonomy were clear.

Self-determination for Nuevomexicanos thus lay in the possibility of subnational constitutionalism, embodied in the movement to gain statehood for New Mexico. The size and culture of the Nuevomexicano populace well-suited the scale of sovereignty that the Articles of Confederation defined for member states. Delegations represented the interests of their states in Washington on a plane with the other states. States' rights guaranteed "self-determination" in the inscriptions of idiosyncratic state constitutions.[108]

As Porter Stratton has glimpsed, Nuevomexicanos favored statehood while they still had a majority of New Mexico's population "and would be able to ensure that their rights would be protected in the constitution of the new state."[109] Howard Lamar passingly notes that Nuevomexicanos looked forward to seeing themselves at the center of self-rule under statehood.[110] New Mexican denizens appealed to Congress to pass statehood bills for congressional policy expected continental territories to become states, and the Treaty of Guadalupe Hidalgo stipulated that New Mexico would become one "at the appropriate time." Nuevomexicanos either led or collaborated in organizing statehood campaigns seven times between 1849 and 1876 and were determined fighters for statehood from 1887 to 1910.[111]

Nevertheless, as chapters 5 and 6 address, white citizens, congressmen, and even presidents used xenophobic degradations of the Nuevomexicano people to forestall New Mexico statehood. Even when statehood appeared propitious, statehood bills were tied into congressional knots. Nuevomexicanos responded with invigorated primacy sentiment. Indignant, often angry heritage scripts sailed under different ethnic names. In the burst of expressive energy, Spanish identity flashed noticeably.

In the Constitutional Convention of 1910, which Congress approved in preparation for final statehood, Nuevomexicano delegates, working in a frame of subnational constitutionalism, negotiated to have certain participation rights for their people inscribed in the Constitution. The discourse of that project, presented in chapter 7, involved a discursive wrestling match with congressional restrictions on certain Nuevomexicano political participation rights. The whole controversy lent itself to the privileging of Spanish identity.

When statehood finally arrived, Spanish identity came into its own among Nuevomexicanos despite the disappointments in effectively realizing the participation rights encoded in the state constitution. As chapter 8 tells, Nuevomexicanos basked in the institutionalization of their Spanish heritage after decades of pushing their primacy inheritance.

Any established identity complex is likely to fall from grace. Time takes its toll; social change alters the structural supports of imaginary growth; alternative interpretations of heritage emerge among younger ethnics. Of considerable significance, external forces provoke enmity.[112] As chapter 9 relates, heritage scripts that in former times defined a Nuevomexicano people became stale. Mexican Americans and Chicano/Chicana activists invigorated Mexican identity. The First Nations movement packed a powerful, conceivably mortal discursive punch to Spanish identity scripts as popular historical memory condemned the human effects of classic European imperialism. In the late twentieth and early twenty-first centuries, Pueblo heritage memory made a formidable bid to bring the oppressions of Spanish conquest to heel symbolically, which winnowed down the power of public Spanish identity.

The conclusion takes the fair measure of historical Spanish identity. Was it a wayward definition of New Mexico's regional *paisanaje* (homelanders), or did sufficient truth lie in its folds to have made the effort to construct and advance it worthwhile politically or otherwise?

PART I

Posting Primacy, 1830–1900

CHAPTER 1

"Scattered Broadcast"

Scripting the Frontier

Creole Identities in the Mexican Period

BEFORE NEW MEXICO became a part of the United States, Nuevomexicano/a society was markedly hierarchical.[1] The top tier of literate *hacendados* and government administrators included an important Creole element. In New Spain, *criollos* were the offspring and direct descendants of Iberian rulers. As ethnic Spaniards born and raised in the Indies, criollos belonged to the upper crust of colonial society.[2]

Criollos arrived in New Mexico after 1692 when Diego de Vargas established what would become permanent settlements of the Spanish empire.[3] In the eighteenth century, the "fifteen or so tightly interwoven leading families" who "ran the colony," John Kessell writes, were of Iberian extraction. If they had Pueblo mates, their children carried the criollo line in "Spanish" homes.[4] Creoles formed what France Scholes calls a "fairly well defined" aristocracy based on family service to the Crown. "Sons followed fathers in the profession of arms and as holders of local political and military office," and it was they who constituted the "small caste of professional soldier-citizens."[5] In 1789, Governor Fernando de la Concha referenced in an official report the provincial military officers who prided themselves in coming "from the first families of the country or were descended from the original conquistadors of New Mexico."[6] Most of the Franciscan friars in parishes and missions were criollo, born and trained as Catholic clerics in New Spain.[7] In the countryside of independent Mexico, Creole haciendas dominated.[8] Similar holdings of Creoles in New Mexico who identified as *españoles*, some of them wealthy, others not so much,[9] were set among the field of *vecinos*, the vernacular "neighbors" who formed the core farmers of the territory.[10] In 1812, the men who had submitted reports so that Don Pedro Baptista Pino, New Mexico's deputy to the territory, could compose his exposition to the Spanish Cortes on the economic conditions of the New Mexico province, were most certainly Creole descendants.[11]

In New Spain, Creoles owned land, mines, and mercantile stores or worked as middle administrators. They were, however, deprived of the top offices of the viceroyalty. Executive appointments in government and the church went solely to Iberians as rewards for service to the Crown. *Gachupínes* (Spanish settlers in America), moreover, scorned the less educated Creoles for lacking sophistication, treating them as their social and cultural inferiors.[12]

Criollos developed strong attachments to the colonial homeland they knew; in addition, they resented their exclusion from controlling colonial posts and the social prejudices they incurred. Becoming a great aggrieved class, they generated an ideological insurgency that eventuated in the campaign starting in 1810 to free New Spain from the royal empire. Mexico won its independence in 1821, and the Constitution of 1824 decreed that people born in Mexico would be regarded and should see themselves as *mexicanos* and *mexicanas*. The "Mexicano" label came into widespread use, especially as a referent for persons of mixed ancestry, including those from the Borderlands region.[13]

At independence, Creole politicians organized Mexico's political structure. Conservative Spanish royalists succeeded in producing Mexico's first independent government. The constitutional monarchy of General Agustín Cosme Damián de Iturbide aimed to make a hereditary emperor and a "Catholic republic" permanent.[14] Iturbide was overthrown in 1823 and royalists faded politically. Power went to the so-called radical liberals whose immediate roots stemmed from the promulgation of the liberal Constitución política de la monarquía española (Political Constitution of the Spanish Monarchy) in Cádiz in 1812 by young leaders who were influenced by the Enlightenment and the doctrines of the French Revolution.[15] In Mexico City, radical liberals led in the bringing down of Iturbide. They went on to determine who would serve as government officials and maintained a strong belief in upholding national sovereignty, the general will, and democracy, in the process rescinding the Church's *fueros* (privileges), including large land assets.[16]

Modern radical liberals considered their kind as the core nation of Mexico while judging Native culture a hindrance to progress and tribalism a contradiction of state citizenship. Aiming to assimilate Native Americans, liberals dismantled the colonial laws that had protected their properties. The Native was "more than a depressed peasant or proletarian in the European sense," a historian notes. "He was ethnically as well as socially different from the Creole elite." Liberals accordingly saw the infusion of European blood infusions (intermarriage) as the way to eliminate "the indigenous problem."[17]

As the historian Marc Simmons emphasizes, the decrees and directives that came out of the 1812 Spanish constitution "reached Santa Fe and were duly digested by the [New Mexican] authorities."[18] That the identity of a political liberal also gestated in New Mexico is illustrated by the clutch of governors in the Mexican period who traced their ancestries to the conquest of New Mexico, conquistadors in general, or acclaimed Spanish administrators of New Spain.[19] Among the citizenry, Donaciano Vigil was the most renowned of the region's liberals. As an American at the time described, he was "an outspoken and effective friend of liberty."[20] As Vigil himself recalled, when Mexico attained its "glorious independence we in New Mexico seconded it with such enthusiasm. We were swept up by patriotic discourses that circulated among us. We expected to enter a new era of happiness, and this word and the word 'liberty' were those that were most used and most repeated."[21] Vigil's family tree matched typical Creole generations, men trained for public service and the military. Donaciano in his career served as a militia officer and government official. In a society of low literacy, the Vigils owned books and retained the identity of "old Spaniards." Creole families typically taught their children at home, and this was true for Vigil. Indeed, he, his brother, and cousin "gained a reputation as 'the best educated men in public life.'"[22]

Quite likely, the youthful Vigil and his father were familiar with Mexican books of liberalism that they acquired in travels to the trade fairs in Chihuahua and Durango, as well as in their visits with Mexican officials such as Antonio Barreiro who was commissioned by the central government in the 1830s to author a report on the social and economic conditions in New Mexico.[23] Moreover, deputies to the Mexican Congress would have been important sources, such as Francisco Pérez Serrano y Aguirre, New Mexico's first delegate to Congress.[24]

From the standpoint of radical liberalism, Vigil's parents opposed New Mexico's official support of the church, calling it "a fanatical religiosity, by which the government sustained religion with no toleration of any other." Additionally, a discomfort with Native Americans and mixed blood *castas* (castes), a bias going back to Spanish colonial New Mexico,[25] played a part in Donaciano's cultivated radical liberalism. A criterion was *limpieza de sangre*, the devotion to blood purity dating to Spain's conflict with Muslims after the Reconquest of the Moors.[26] The bodies of indigenous groups in Mexico contravened limpieza de sangre,[27] which was "intended to affirm prestige and honor among propertied aristocrats and learned ecclesiastics," and which partly defined New Mexico's stratification order.[28]

While the evidence is sparse, it is probable that New Mexico criollos, like the Canary Islanders in San Antonio, Texas, "took great pride in preventing any marriage with mixed races" and indigenous people.[29] Vigil and his Creole colleagues were reinforced in such beliefs by their own fairer complexions that their future generations would inherit.

In 1846, Vigil asked the assembly to petition the central government for arms and munitions so that *la rasa* [*sic*] *Española* (the Spanish race) could protect itself from "barbarous" Native raids. By the Spanish race, Vigil stated that he meant the "descendants of the ancient discoverers and conquerors of this immense continent," who, as *españoles*, had "not degenerated in New Mexico," that is, by intermixing with *indios*.[30]

Another Creole faction never forgot that Mexico's independence movement was lit by Father Miguel Hidalgo y Costilla, whose *Grito de Dolores* in Guanajuato called the people to arms. Hidalgo led his largely mestizo insurgents toward Mexico City before Royalist troops captured and executed him by firing squad. Another priest, Father José María Morelos, succeeded Hidalgo in leading the war and occupying southern and central territories before he was captured, defrocked in an Inquisition trial, and also executed in 1815.[31]

These clerics fought under the banner of *la Virgen de Guadalupe*, the Marian figure who in Native legend appeared before the peasant Juan Diego, speaking to him in his Nahuatl tongue and instructing him to spread the word of her coming as protector of the poor. Creole philosophers Fray Servando Teresa de Mier and Francisco Javier

Clavijero Echegaray advanced the Jansenist messianism of Hidalgo Guadalupismo.[32] Inspired by the Jesuit historian Clavijero, the influential lawyer, journalist, and historian Carlos María de Bustamante took to "welding together a nationalist ideology which bound the cause of independence to the events of the sixteenth century" to advocate for the civic and cultural rights of Natives. The historical *indigenismo* of independence "survived to become an integral part of the national mythology." In the remembrance of Hidalgo as the martyred embodiment of Mexicanness, Bustamante persuaded Congress to adopt the anniversary of El Grito as the national commemoration of independence.[33] As the Catholic hierarchy virtually collapsed after independence,[34] Clavijero rallied a "priest's consciousness." Drawing inspiration from that notion, Bustamante supported in speeches and writings a weaponized Catholicism through a "Creole priesthood."[35]

Hidalgo Guadalupismo had a home in New Mexico. Fatefully, five young Nuevomexicanos from well-to-do families—Antonio José Martínez; the Ortiz brothers Rafael and Fernando and their cousin, Juan Felipe; and Ramón Ortiz—enrolled at the Tridentine Seminary in Durango, Mexico, in 1816 just as the desired outcome of the war for Mexican independence was being realized. Signifying his Creole stock, Martínez called his parents "noble by class."[36] Trained in "the nursery of a new generation of seminarians" and excelling academically, he fixed on the rising spirit of "Catholic Enlightenment and National Liberalism,"[37] adopting Mexican patriotism "when the country came into being."[38]

Martínez did the most to land Hidalgo Guadalupismo in New Mexico. It was not an exaggeration when his biographer said that everything he "proposed or tried to carry out as a self-designated priest-politician in his own homeland" was inspired by Hidalgo.[39] As opposed to Donaciano Vigil's elite formal liberalism, Martínez's brand of liberalism reflected a populist ideal. His obituary thus praised the priest for his "unbounded admiration" for Hidalgo.[40] It signaled New Mexico's version of a "priest's consciousness" that he and another young priest proposed (though unsuccessfully) that New Mexico be made a federal state with the name of Hidalgo.[41] (Similarly, the parish priest at Santa Cruz de la Cañada, Manuel de Jesús Rada, proposed that a school be established in Santa Fe and named for the father of Mexican Independence, Miguel Hidalgo.[42])

At an 1832 commemoration of Mexico's independence, Martínez delivered a sermon on Spanish colonialism, comparing Hidalgo and companions "to the Maccabees of Scripture who steadfastly resolved to sustain the rights of their nation," just as Jesus Christ, "the liberator of the world," had done, adding the Virgin of Guadalupe, "patroness of the struggle for freedom."[43]

With Hidalgo as his example, Martínez became "champion of the people," who provided alms to lower-class mestizos.[44] Treating the common folk as the true Mexican nation, he assisted those who were "deprived of their rights for the lack of the necessary means, suffering insults and injuries without . . . the protection of the law,"[45] and who also chafed under the taxes and restrictions of the central government, for which Martínez said he suffered "persecution."[46] From his family farm, he aided humble vecinos who struggled against the mercantile monetization of wealthy Nuevomexicanos and speculating American merchants.[47] He also tended to the welfare of indigenous people, advising Mexico City to defend the non-Christian Navajos, Utes, and Apaches against authorities who would exterminate them and against predatory Americans who plied them with munitions and alcohol.[48] Like Hidalgo and Morelos, Martínez and his clerical colleagues were political creatures.[49] Martínez served in the departmental assembly from 1830–1831, 1836–1837, and 1845–1846.[50] He also gave warning about foreigner ambitions, as in Americans who connived to illegally acquire large tracts of Nuevomexicano land.[51]

In Mexico City, liberals condemned Guadalupe Hidalgos, those who, they said, interpreted Hidalgo's revolt as the principal source of Mexican nationalism.[52] Vigil likewise criticized what he called the "imperious [parish] exactions and oppressions of the priests."[53] Liberal *españolismo* and Hidalgo Guadalupismo went toe-to-toe in government. As a French visitor observed in the 1840s, those "who are of the Spanish race boast of the purity of their blood, and those of mixed race all claim to be descended from Montezuma." Those of the "Spanish race" had "the upper hand," holding "all the [political] places, even that of governor, distinct from those who called themselves "sons of Montezuma."[54] Donaciano Vigil's camp and Martínez's clergy quarreled over such issues as the propriety of priests in political office, alliances with American entrepreneurs, and the treatment of *los indios bárbaros.*[55]

Transforming the Creole Configuration

Annexing Spanish and Guadalupe Identities

As the United States took control of New Mexico, the exponents of both liberal factions played political roles in Col. Stephen W. Kearny's provisional government. First, Kearny appointed Donaciano Vigil territorial secretary and made his radical compatriot, Antonio José Otero, one of the transformed territory's three territorial judges.

After the assassination of Governor Charles Bent and members of his staff, Col. Sterling Price made Vigil interim governor. Vigil carried out policies against the priests, seeking the removal of Juan Felipe Ortiz as New Mexico's vicar forane, likely for his political activities.[56] He also disparaged mestizos.[57] The liberal Constitution of 1824 provided New Mexico with organized local government. The *ayuntamiento* was centered on an *alcalde mayor* (quasi mayor) and a prefect. Governors preferred literate and administratively experienced elites for these positions, but often they had little choice but to appoint lower-class mestizos.[58] To Otero, Vigil complained of the impropriety of a prefect in the Bernalillo County election who failed to uphold the oath of neutrality in counting votes. It was an all-too-common problem in the "fawning and flattery" of public officials, Vigil remonstrated, "maldita condición de los hijos de Montezuma y de la mescla con sangre Española" (a damned condition of the sons of Montezuma and of the mixing of Spanish blood). Vigil called such faults the result of an inveterate *raza embolicida* (a lying race).[59]

From the priesthood, Padre Martínez was elected president of the first American territorial legislature in 1847. In 1849, after the United States–Mexico conflict ended, Martínez headed a nineteen-member delegation organized to petition the US Congress to replace New Mexico's military rule with a territorial form of government. When Congresses enacted the policy in the Compromise Act of 1850, Martínez was one of five on the Territorial Council, which included Vicar Ortiz, Father José Francisco Leyva, and Padre José Manuel Gallegos. Martínez served in the assembly until 1853, pushing legislation to serve vecinos.[60]

In 1850, American Catholic bishops established a vicariate apostolic in New Mexico, a preliminary step in forming a diocese.[61] A bishop came with the office. The Vatican named the French clergyman Jean Baptiste Lamy New Mexico's first-ever bishop. Nuevomexicano priests welcomed Lamy and his assistant, Father Joseph Projectus Machebeuf, with a procession. Relations soon soured. Lamy and New Mexico's priests entangled themselves in a momentously unfortunate, perhaps needless, dispute.[62]

At bottom of the conflict were Mexican priests who came from a liberal Latin American religious tradition while Lamy and Machebeuf were trained in a conservative European reaction to the anti-Catholic Enlightenment and the French Revolution. Because of their adherence to puritanical strictures of piety, an ordered liturgy at mass, and a distancing from community conventions, Lamy and Machebeuf criticized the predominantly secular priests who charged parishioners for sacramental rites, said Mass with little sermonizing, practiced celibacy quite loosely, enjoyed popular entertainments, and played politics.[63] Lamy could have enacted a reform program for what he deemed a debauched bunch. Instead, he reacted to reports of sinning priests by suspending them one by one.[64] Stepping up as legal counsel for his nativo colleagues, Martínez accused Lamy of denying them due process, a breach of Canon Law as he called it. Martínez aided discontented parishioners who accused Machebeuf of breaking the secrecy of confession. One scholar calls Martínez's defiance a "resistance against foreign domination."[65]

Assailing a homegrown institution while a strong anti-Catholicism coursed through the United States,[66] Lamy effectively undercut Hidalgo Guadalupe identity. A booming American nationalism, pumped by a resounding victory over Mexico, would not have tolerated such a strong Mexican identity. The priests were left to declare a regional attachment. It was tellingly revealed in the clash of identities that occurred in the halls of the US Congress between the defrocked Padre José Manuel Gallegos[67] and Miguel Antonio Otero I, a quick-witted member of Donaciano Vigil's liberal circle.

Gallegos—who was prepped for seminary studies by Padre Martínez—pastored Albuquerque's San Felipe de Neri Parish. Lamy approved Vicar General Machebeuf's recommendation that Gallegos be suspended on charges of scandalous merrymaking at fandangos, prioritizing a mercantile business over ecclesiastical duties, and having intimate relations with a woman. Layman Tomás Cabeza de Baca rallied parishioners and forwarded letters to Lamy defending Gallegos against charges of sacerdotal malfeasance and accusing Machebeuf of wanting Gallegos's parish for himself. Meanwhile, Gallegos, who was a member of New Mexico's legislature, ran for election as the territory's first delegate to an American Congress.[68]

Gallegos handily won the Democratic Party's nomination for delegate to Congress as most delegates were his friends, including one who had protested against Lamy. The opposition nominated William Carr Lane, who had the support of liberal Creoles, including Donaciano Vigil, and that of Bishop Lamy. Democratic Party Euro-Americans supported Gallegos as a son of the soil who had been unfairly suspended by a foreign bishop. Gallegos won the election narrowly. While in office he took on the (now) Archbishop Lamy by sending to the Vatican the territorial legislature's formal charges of Lamy's abuse of priests and Machebeuf's betrayal of the confessional seal. Machebeuf journeyed to Rome to respond to the charges where he successfully argued Lamy's case against recalcitrant priests.[69]

When Gallegos ran for reelection, friends of Lamy put up Miguel Antonio Otero I, the younger brother of the Donaciano Vigil ally, Antonio José Otero, whom Kearny appointed to the territorial judiciary.[70] Gallegos won the election by ninety-nine votes, but Otero contested the results on the grounds that Gallegos's partisans had engaged in voting irregularities and that Gallegos himself was unqualified to serve in Congress because he could not speak English.[71]

The contestants presented their cases before a House committee. In his translated statement read by the clerk of the House, Gallegos validated his right to represent his constituency and accused Lamy of importing priests to defeat him.[72] In a national climate in which Americans commonly regarded Mexicans as a "mongrel" species,[73] Gallegos refrained from calling his people "Mexicans." Rather, he anchored them in New Mexico with the key appellation "native." Among things American, Gallegos emphasized, the English language was still foreign in New Mexico, and he had always defended the "native [Nuevomexicano] folk" in their "very soil." He claimed that same identity for himself: "I am and have ever been one of that very people." They had chosen him as a representative of "their true type," and he bore no shame in what was common to them and himself. In a glint of Hidalgo modeling, he called himself "to the manor born" so that the insults he faced about his native language he wore like a badge of honor. One other thing as well: English fluency was not, Gallegos declared, a requirement for serving in Congress.[74]

Educated in the United States, Otero boasted that he was the "first native citizen" to go before the Congress "of our adopted fatherland and address it in the language of its laws and its Constitution." Otero in turn denied that Washingtonians had ridiculed Nuevomexicanos. Scoffing at his opponent's appeal for House magnanimity, he implied Gallegos's Creole betrayal, and implored the House Speaker thus: "When, sir, in the history of the race [of] which [Gallegos] claims to be a *type*, did Castilian blood ever congeal in the presence of power, and so far degrade itself as to seek to crawl into favor?" (his emphasis). Matching Gallegos's claim of a people's advantage, Otero said he, too, was a "native of New Mexico," though a native "of unmixed Spanish descent." Yet he was "proud to know that my own people at home do not consider me the less qualified to represent them in this body, whatever may be the opinion of the sitting Delegate."[75]

Otero prevailed in his contest. As Fray Angélico Chávez figured, the "honorable House of Representatives must have been naturally elated by Otero's oratory, coming as it did from a genuine 'Spaniard' of New Mexico who corroborated what they themselves had heard or read about those horrible Mexican priests."[76] In the implicit competition of identities, then, Otero's Spanish identification infiltrated the public discourses of the American territory quite definitely. Five years later, Otero rebuked the editor of the *New York Tribune* who editorialized against statehood for New Mexico because its people were unfit for such inclusion due to their hybrid Spanish-Native mixture, exclaiming that "ever since the conquest and colonization of the valley of the Rio del Norte, under the prowess of Don Juan de Oñate in the latter part of the seventeenth century, the Spaniards and the aborigines, or Indians, have been separated and distinct from each other, and have so remained up to this day."[77]

As historian William S. Kiser notes, Otero's "illusory claims marginalized the multiethnic population derived from well-entrenched systems of involuntary servitude and fictive kinship." Nevertheless, Otero inaugurated the script of Spanish Blood Purity, which would go on to regular usage among the Nuevomexicano intelligentsia in territorial New Mexico. Otero's long letter of protest was published in the *New York Tribune* and other national news outlets abroad and in the *Santa Fe Gazette.* As such, his "denials of truth" regarding the mestizo majority in New Mexico "began at the local level with territorial officials, legislators, and newspaper editors, and spread to a national audience among congressional representatives and sectional ideologues."[78] Regionally, Spanish identity would until the early twentieth century find its sustenance among the descendants of the legacy Creoles who passed into the United States after 1848.

Of course, many of them would not forget that they were Mexicans as we shall see. Yet, the evisceration of Hidalgo Guadalupe identity, important as it was for Mexican independence, was effectively done for in US territorial New Mexico, symbolized by Lamy's directive to excommunicate Padre Antonio José Martínez for his insurgency, which effectively silenced his historic voice.[79]

Early Euro-American Settlers and the Spanish Heritage

In continental annexation, the power of the "higher authority" rests "firmly in the hands of the victors," as David Montejano points out.[80] Yet, it is imperative that the conquered accept the terms of the social, as well as the formal governance structures being established over them, if peaceful accommodation is to prevail. In 1852, New Mexico's second American appointed governor, the self-same William Carr Lane who had run against José Manuel Gallegos for delegate to Congress, categorized Nuevomexicanos as Spanish to keep the peace in the territory. Fearing that they might turn their backs on America and rebel against membership in the United States because of the ill-treatment that their people suffered at the hands of US soldiers, Euro-American administrators, and appointed judges,[81] he advised members of the territorial assembly not to reject the "Anglo-Saxon wave now rolling from East to West across the continent." According to the commonly understood epistemic, it would be anomalous, for had they not "voluntarily" attached themselves to the United States?[82] To realize "a common destiny," Lane called for "harmonious co-operation between the natives of the country and strangers in all matters affecting the public welfare," for "good or evil awaits all alike—whether the parent stock be Castilian or Anglo-Saxon." New Mexicans must learn English and adopt the American customs "that are suitable and proper for this country." Yet they should not change their "beneficial or praise-worthy customs, nor," he added, "do I advise them to forget their parent stock, and the proud recollections that cluster around Castilian history." Still, Lane felt obligated to judge the territorial legislature as "a unique construction," the "defective laws" of which left communities in a "deplorable state."[83]

Lane sat squarely in the box of liberal imperialism. In his policy of "harmonious cooperation," he reflected what political scientist Karuna Mantena observes about how the British faced Indian resistance to assimilation by adopting a syncretic policy of reconciling with native customs.[84] It was true up to a point, for, as Lane hinted, tradition had a stranglehold on politics. In John Stuart Mill's liberal imperialism, "enlightened agency" was needed to realize the highest level of modern civilization.[85] Lane implied that such progressive agency would need to lift New Mexico's "defective" legislature to American standards. Playing the part of colonizer-monitor in what started to become an important discursive platform, W. G. Kephart, editor of the Santa Fe *Weekly Gazette*, complimented Lane for affording a "fair opportunity of testing the capabilities of the descendants of the Spanish race under free [i.e., not Spanish dictatorial] institutions, the maintenance of which depends upon the morality and intelligence of the people."[86] Nevertheless, in spite of the interactive accommodation, tension between ruling Euro-American colonizers and subordinate Nuevomexicanos would characterize nineteenth- and early twentieth-century social relations.

Seven years later and a decade after annexation, leading Euro-Americans saw the need for New Mexico to start catching up with the norms that steered the civic development of states and territories. As Chief Justice Kirby Benedict of the territorial New Mexico Supreme Court noted, New Mexico was "the only important peopled territory added to our matchless Union during its unparalleled march whose story had not as yet been thoroughly told by historians."[87] In 1743, the American Philosophical Society in Philadelphia, showcasing Pennsylvania's social, cultural, and historical legacies, initiated the practice of having individual states craft an identity for themselves. The bourgeois historical society as innovated by the Massachusetts Historical Society in 1791 became the key instrument. By the time of

Benedict's comment on New Mexico's lack of a history, one hundred sixty historical societies existed throughout the country.[88]

In December 1859, a handful of "gentlemen" gathered to sketch a constitution for the Historical Society of New Mexico. Two of the five were Nuevomexicanos: Facundo Pino (reputed to have plotted against Kearny in 1847), a veteran territorial legislator, twice elected president of the council; José Guadalupe Gallegos, a former Bernalillo County legislator and council president. Of the first twenty-four members of the Society, Jesús María Sena y Baca, a clerk of both assembly chambers, was the lone Nuevomexicano.[89] Other Nuevomexicanos would join, yet the proportion of their representation reflected what would become a territorial characteristic, their subaltern positionality in public structures.[90] While it was a subordinacy, it nevertheless reflected a significant presence as it represented the upper core of the majority population and with extensive local power.

In delivering the keynote address at the Historical Society's first anniversary observance, Justice Benedict had his opportunity for bringing some of America's civic values to this remote corner of the country while socializing Nuevomexicanos to America's institutional framework. Fortuitously, American and Mexican cultures shared certain pieces of a Latinate legacy. In constructing its own historical identity after the triumph of independence from Great Britain, the United States could hardly fall back on the nation it had broken from so bitterly. "The colonists needed a legitimate heritage that did not include Britain, and a name that stood beside Britannia in equality, without the mother/child relationship," historian Claudia Bushman writes. "These they found in Columbus and Columbia."[91]

From the 1760s on, a rolling campaign in US cultural and institutional fields romanticized Christopher Columbus as the "discoverer of America," epitomizing him as both the founder of the United States and the personification of its moral character.[92] The movement's high point came in 1828 with the publication of Washington Irving's reverential biography, *The Life and Voyages of Christopher Columbus.* As Bushman notes, Irving's "adulation" of Columbus, "prepared the way for a major work of scholarship for grownups, the most important in installing historical Columbus as a mythic and celebrated figure on the American scene. The importance of Irving's biography in establishing the Mariner as an

American hero cannot be overestimated." For his Columbus biography, Irving earned immediate favor throughout the country.[93]

After discoursing in his anniversary speech on history's value for revealing "Man's Existence and Destiny" (liberalism's imperial universalism[94]), Benedict, who had been in the territory seven years, drew upon "our Irving" and other like-minded historians[95] to stoke what would become for New Mexico the useful script of Columbus the Great, enshrining the original "discoverer" of the New World as "one of the grandest adventurers in history." With his "fiery heart and an iron will," the great discoverer valiantly ordered "the Cross taken to heathen lands."[96]

Benedict expanded his vision to the popular genre of *Hispanismo*, which historian Bailey Diffie calls "a liberal movement based on the principles of the Enlightenment."[97] In tandem with the worshipping of Columbus's voyage, Hispanismo spotlighted Spain's golden era of nation-building. Benedict obliged by tapping into an early version of "imperial nostalgia," exemplifying what N. Fisher-Onar calls "post-national pluralism," invoking an "imperial cosmopolitanism" as a means for "managing diversity." Postimperial nostalgia typically acclaimed Spanish glory hyperbolically while glossing over the shortcomings of imperialism.[98] In a genderized nostalgia, Isabella's Spain became to Benedict "a nation of enthusiastic adventurers and warriors, bred to danger, and familiarized with victory and conquest, in the Old and New Worlds."[99]

Benedict initiated the project of designing a popular history for New Mexico, having the romances of Spanish exploration at the ready. At that time the figure of Alvar Nuñez Cabeza de Baca garnered considerable attention. In 1528, Cabeza de Baca and two companions wandered to the West on foot after surviving the wreckage of Pánfilo Narvaez's ship off the Florida coast. The three reached the El Paso area before heading south along the Sea of Cortez to Culiacán.[100] Notwithstanding, the Cabeza de Baca Legacy script had him "discovering" New Mexico. Benedict (mis)credited him, Alonzo del Castillo Maldonado, and Andres Dorantes for being the first Europeans to "trod the soil of New Mexico," passing, as he said they did, "from Pueblo to Pueblo in the year 1534."[101] The propitious scenario suited the purpose of ceremoniously recognizing elite Nuevomexicanos while they appeared as a resource for developing a history of New Mexico. Before the "descendants" of Spanish stalwarts who sat up front, Benedict related how the determined Spaniard "excited Spain and interested his relatives in behalf of this region, which never died out in the family. Later, one after another left their homes, and journeyed until New Mexico was reached, and from such sources have descended the large, intelligent, and highly influential family of CABEZA DE BACA in this territory."[102]

Benedict, it bears emphasizing, acquired the idea of descendance of Spanish discoverers from Nuevomexicanos; in that way he "inhabited" the discourse of the colonized.[103] As liberal imperialism, the rhetorical device served two interrelated purposes—carve a civilizational memory and promote an etiquette for relations with a subject clientele. As Benedict gushed, all informed readers knew "how daring and adventurous, chivalric and gallant at that day was the Son of Spain." Spain's nobility of intrepidness included "no common, ordinary spirits" but "men and women of the stoutest heroic qualities" who settled "the most wild, picturesque and variegated countries in all North America." For both national optics and local consumption, a proper racialism was called for. The future historian of New Mexico would, in Benedict's contrivance, "stand at the base of the height of more than three hundred years of the white man's life," at the "introduction of the Spanish or white race into New Mexico," at the importation of the laws and civilization with which Spaniards were "instructed and reared in the lands of their birth."[104]

Much as a shared whiteness glowed in the hall, Benedict took note of the Spanish empire's key shortsightedness: "One of the great evils which existed here under the Spanish form of provincial government" being the "almost total want of responsibility of official authorities to the people where they bore rule." While the people remained poor,

> the man of official power must grow rich in his position. By honest and just official patronage, he could not well become so. His desire and aim were to amass a fortune and then retire to live in pomp and luxury upon some more favored portion of the globe. To accomplish his objective, he shrunk not from the

> commission of sore and cruel oppressions and despotic exactions. No effort was made to develop the intellect of the masses and give it discipline and direction by systems of education.

Thus were commoners raised in "mental ignorance and darkness.[105]

The prominence of this view in America of Spaniards as "grasping adventurers who came to the New World, not to seek liberty or better homes for their families as did the English, but to search for treasure and to live in idleness on the sweat of enslaved aborigines,"[106] did not contradict the enrapturing of Columbus who was "distanced from other wicked Spanish conquerors."[107] More pointedly, it snugly fit into Creole identity. Recall Donaciano Vigil hailing the "*descendants* of the ancient discoverers and conquerors" (emphasis added). Benedict thus toasted the "purely Spanish blood" that "preserved its caste, education and refinement, and to this day is as clear to the discriminating observer as it was one hundred and fifty years ago."[108]

In this contact situation, Benedict's memory rite of concordance massaged social boundaries and smoothed out cultural differences. The *Santa Fe New Mexican* extracted parts of the speech referencing Spanish blood[109] and a Euro-American translated the judge's remarks into Spanish.[110] When Benedict's commission as a territorial justice was set to expire, the mostly Nuevomexicano legislative assembly unanimously petitioned President Abraham Lincoln to reappoint him, not least for his having become familiar with the Spanish language and "well acquainted" with not only the laws of New Mexico but also the customs of the people.[111]

Ten years later, Territorial Collector of Revenue G. A. Smith replicated Benedict's socializing ritual. Americans used public events to forge a sense of national identity and ease divisions "created by unavoidable regional, class, or political differences," Anthony Mora writes. "Community celebrations, parades, and various other cultural events became a means for individuals to imagine themselves as defining and partaking in American nationalism during the early years of the republic."[112] In his Fourth of July speech, Smith gendered Spain's heroics to further sew Nuevomexicano belonging to the American flag. Retreading the Generous Spanish Queen script,

Smith avowed, "I cannot forget on this occasion to recall to your memory our indebtedness to Spain . . . for the discovery of America, and, my fair countrywomen,

> it is to one of your sex we are specially indebted. You all remember the hopes, the trials, and the sacrifices of Queen Isabella—how she even disposed of her Jewels to enable Columbus to prosecute his work. I congratulate you, her descendants, and rejoice to see you participating in the blessings and fruition of her work.[113]

Smith fulfilled a speaker's obligation, speaking directly to his Santa Fe audience, predominantly Nuevomexicana families, and, as a bonus, served to keep them close to America's bosom.

Soon, there was nothing about the conjoining of American and Spanish imperial legacies that a Nuevomexicano could not perform. Indeed, the lawyer and former co-owner of *La Revista de Albuquerque,*[114] Tránsito Mata, braided the two memory schemes in his 2,100-word, Spanish-language Fourth of July speech delivered in Albuquerque in the year the United States celebrated the centennial of the Second Continental Congress's signing of the Declaration of Independence. The national celebration was being staged in Philadelphia, where, Mata explained, the American banner was unfolded and raised "to the atmospheric regions in whose flight with its modulated symphonies incited a veneration among all of its hearers." Mata reinforced Nuevomexicano readiness to do what America asked: accept what she proposed; dissolve what she deemed in need of dissolution; unite what she said should be bound, including themselves mutually; and welcome immigrants.[115]

For the founding of the United States, Mata linked the scripts of Columbus the Great and Royal Spain's magnanimity. The "Divine Providence flowering in Italy" led the "eminently erudite" Columbus to realize from his astronomical tools that the earth was an orb. The King and Queen of Spain provided the ships for him to navigate the seas. Hearing of Columbus's good fortune in colonizing the isles of the Bahamas, Cuba, Santo Domingo, the "western Indias," and all

South America, other Europeans dispatched their armadas of families at great cost and risk. That is how America grew, Mata explained, "and we owe it to the generosity of the sovereigns of Castile."[116]

Alternating Spanish and Mexican

Nuevomexicanos broke down the proposition of a Spanish heritage residing only in a Creole minority on urgencies that called for mass regional unity and national belonging. At the outbreak of the Civil War, the joint resolution of the Nuevomexicano-run territorial assembly warned citizens to prepare for the impending invasion of Texas Confederates. In Brian Delay's adage, violence on the frontier "constituted community, and community constituted violence."[117] The legislators' long, penetrating statement thus imagined a territorial Nuevomexicano community not only to support the Union but also to protect its legacy homeland.

The self-styled "manifesto" thus teemed with collective primacy. The threat from abroad called for defense of the land "of our brave ancestors." Left to brave contemporaries then was to ensure the "peace, security and integrity of [their] soil and homes" from an enemy able to subsist only by "plundering our people." "Now is the day to feel the tinglings of the ancient and unconquerable Castilian blood that our ancestors brought to this land." At this point, though, no conceivable reason existed to be exclusive about invoking a Spanish-style heritage. "Let every Mexican in the territory rally to the brave in the field," the cresting paragraph heralded, "your fathers, sons, and brothers." It is notable that the proclamation was signed by Territorial Council President Facundo Pino, a Creole member of the Historical Society of New Mexico, and José Manuel Gallegos, the former priest who had lost his congressional seat to the Creole liberal Miguel Antonio Otero in 1855.[118]

The logic of the legislative assemblyman's call brought common-folk vecinos, mestizo laborers, and even Genízaro elements into the communion of worthy Castilian descendants. But Spanish identity also emanated after the war from the local level. In 1867, the nonelite Fraternidad Piadosa de Jesús Nazareno in Taos registered in the weekly *El Nuevo-Mejicano* a protest of the "false and malicious" accusations being charged against them by members of the legislative assembly.[119] No assemblymen were named as offenders; they may have been Nuevomexicanos as then only two Euro-American legislators were seated,[120] although quite relevantly, the Francophone Church at the time criticized the brotherhood on charges of practicing "degenerate" rites and the Protestants, both Anglos and Nuevomexicanos, called them medieval relics.[121] What proves telling is the script of Conquest Honor that the brothers of the Fraternidad brought forth, that is, the virtues of piety, humility, and brotherly care that "derived from" and "were brought and transmitted to us by the Spanish conquistadors of this country, our ancestors."[122]

The origins of the penitential organization in New Mexico are both vague[123] and contested,[124] yet evidence suggests that flagellant practitioners came with Oñate's founding of New Mexico.[125] In this sense, the Taos settler community had historical warrant to rationalize their objections to prejudice in the name of a privileged Spanish colonial legacy.

Hidalgo Guadalupismo may have left the premises, but the moniker mexicano/mexicana/Mexican roamed the countryside. Queried in an 1876 legal proceeding about whether he was "Mexican by birth," one Manuel Rodriguez responded, "I am."[126] To sidestep the complication of those from Mexico, "Mexican" often coupled up with "citizen," a Spanish weekly, for example, providing a *lista de ciudadanos mejicanos* (list of Mexican citizens) registered to vote.[127] In a twist, *americano* often meant Euro-American even as Nuevomexicanos were technically Americans. A probate judge thus reported to the territorial attorney general that "two Mexicans and an American" escaped from the Bernalillo County jail.[128]

Many a Euro-American vented racially against "the Mexicans,"[129] prompting Nuevomexicanos to challenge discursively. In one instance, the Nuevomexicano-led territorial assembly filed a protest to President Andrew Johnson on the false accusations Major General James Carleton, commander of the New Mexico Ninth Military Department, issued that "the Mexican people of this country" committed crimes, which Nuevomexicanos took to be "vilely calumniating our [Mexican] people."[130]

In 1872, Socorro County rancher Antonio Gonzales rallied the electorate in a Spanish-language weekly to back Congressional Delegate José Francisco Chaves's bill proposing statehood for New

Mexico. Gonzales directed his self-described "manifesto" *á los Mejicanos*, in this sense appealing to the grassroots as his statement would be conveyed to the masses by a literate reader. Straightaway he stressed the importance of self-rule, emphasizing how the "Right legislators" and "loyal guardians" would keep watch on "the interests of our land" and stand vigilant for "our general well-being." Statehood would raise the "social edifice of our people to form the fundamental codes for reposing our rights, principles of liberty and sovereignty" as Gonzales called for. In subnational parlance, Nuevomexicanos were said to be ready for *la emancipación de nuestro patria* (the emancipation of our homeland) so as to win the "great victory . . . in the American Union" for "our beloved territory." Adumbrating what would become the commonly expressed script of Derelict Mexico and Washington, the people's "pure, unblemished patria" was orphaned by both Mexico and the United States, left on a "twisted, retrograde road" bereft of progress in a "reprehensible oblivion." As such, self-government under statehood would provide *el país* with "security in life and property, [the] development of industry . . . and . . . public education for our youth." In a state, Nuevomexicanos/as more than any other segment in the territory would meet their "sacred duty to leave a fundamental legacy to your patria and our posterity."[131]

Gonzales further introduced the Nuevomexicano International Membership script, which would find future repetition, placing his folks among "the peoples" of the world and in the community of nations that "sought to realize an epoch of fortune and progress," in this latter sense reflecting what John Stuart Mill called the driving force of "developmental liberalism."[132] In the script of Imminent Advancement, Gonzales assured that statehood would deliver economic and educational resources to the Nuevomexicano nation.[133]

With only a third of the expected turnout voting, the statehood proposal went down to defeat, leading its proponents to feel certain that they had failed to sufficiently agitate on its behalf.[134] Nevertheless, for Nuevomexicano identity, Gonzales's manifesto reveals an intelligentsia imaginary treating a Nuevomexicano people according to what Helen Ting calls the legitimacy of claims "on the normative ideals linked to the concept of nation, a social classification linked to the attribution of rights and entitlements," a "dual quality" of "'already there, but not quite yet.'"[135]

"Spanish" and "Mexican" referents were bundled in a remarkable contention over public education. Michael Keating points out that two types of regionalism arose in the late nineteenth century. The conservative one, "supported by traditional social classes and religious groups[,] opposed social change imposed by modernity."[136] Here, insular (isolated) communities defined culture preservation as a "historical right" against the disruptions of modernization.[137] The other, "progressive and modernizing," responded favorably to the consolidation of the nation-state and its policy of promoting a homogeneous citizenry.[138] In a striking contradiction, some Nuevomexicanos believed that decolonization depended on a defense of traditional values and ways while others, influenced by liberal imperialism, maintained that progress paved the road to self-determination and enlightenment for the Nuevomexicano nation. This split strikingly inhabited the controversy over public education in the 1870s.

Mainstream America touted public education to promote social integration, a common culture, and opportunity.[139] A public-school movement that generally targeted immigrant families saw Nuevomexicano youth in serious need of education. While upper-class Nuevomexicano children received instruction at home or by hired tutors, the majority were taught irregularly or not at all—thus, for example, an 1879 census identified an 85 percent illiteracy rate.[140] As a result, Euro-Americans embarked on that mighty goal of liberal imperialism, the "civilizing mission."[141] In 1847, the *Santa Fe Republican* prioritized schooling for renationalizing Mexicans, a task "of first and major importance." Schools would give "the best benefits that they can confer to the children" and provide the knowledge "so essential to a free government, so necessary to constitute a great people." Women needed the "rudimentary of education," the paper noted, "and we await that soon we shall see schools for girls."[142] Another emphasized in Spanish that the "*mexicano* people" needed the "intellectual mind," else those children would "not be considered nor treated as equal by the coming strangers," making them "a minority in their own land."[143]

Progressive Nuevomexicanos agreed. An 1853 memorial to Congress from the territorial assembly noted that in no part of the United States "are the means of education so deficient as in New Mexico."[144] However, Congress denied a request for schools in 1857 even as public lands were offered as collateral.[145] In Archbishop Lamy's parochial schools, select Nuevomexicano youth and Euro-American children were taught according to Vatican pedagogies and instruction was conducted in Spanish and English.[146] But of course the Church could not educate the bulk of the territory's children.

Euro-American newcomers looked aghast at the significant presence of Jesuits, with their "Catholic" orientation, in territorial schools.[147] One called it "extraordinary," "un-American," and pedagogically ineffective. "The Romish priests have had the education of the people of New Mexico entirely in their own hands for nearly a century and a half," the comment held, "and what is the result? Not one in three of those who have passed the age of twelve years can read, and I doubt whether one in ten can read and write."[148]

In a message to the 1871–1872 assembly, Governor Marsh Giddings and Territorial Secretary William Ritch called on lawmakers to rectify the people's being, "educationally speaking, in a darker condition than when first brought into our nation."[149] Legislators reserved part of an ad valorem tax for schools; imposed a fee of one dollar on every male citizen over twenty-one for building them; had precincts elect a school supervisor to hire teachers and establish a four-member schoolboard whose members must have resided in the territory not less than five years, be heads of families, owners of real estate, and US citizens.[150]

These were clearly designed to keep priests, most of them immigrants, from teaching and serving on schoolboards. The bill passed but proved ineffective. According to a Protestant minister, the clergy made sure they had a priest on each board, one practitioner "of priestcraft" claiming the "whole Catholic Church" as his family and on this interpretation took the oath of office on a board.[151] Senator Jacinto Armijo of Las Cruces introduced Ritch's next bill that denied funds to schools controlled by religious personnel; prohibited the influence of "any sect, religious society, [or] denomination whatever"; banned the Bible and other religious texts for instruction; and, aiming at the Church's gender segregation, required boys and girls to learn in the same classroom. The Council passed the measure 9–4.[152]

A traditionalist going by the initials C. R. condemned Jacinto Armijo's cultural treachery. In the Traitorous Nuevomexicano script as it would become, Armijo was said to have sponsored a law meant to bury the "religious-moral-innocence of our families." How could it be, C. R. bemoaned in the terms of a Nuevomexicano Founding Ancestral Church script, that Armijo *no conoce la religión que nuestros antecesores sembraron y la que reina?* (does not know the religion our ancestors planted here and that reigns today).[153]

Traditionalists condemned secular schooling for not including morality in its teaching. US founders believed that mass education should be built on a religious foundation but with many Protestant denominations vying, the fear of a sect controlling education was serious. In what historian Timothy Smith calls the "Protestant consensus," public schools would be "nonsectarian but essentially religious." As public schools spread westward, the Protestant consensus led to teaching on a nonsectarian basis but with a strict promotion of an educational awakening for poor families. It was considered "vital to the highest interests" of communities "that universal education . . . be taken up as a great Christian enterprise." An "evangelical consensus of faith and ethics had come to dominate the national culture" and most Protestants were "willing to entrust the state with the task of educating children, confident that education would be 'religious' still."[154]

Catholics, however, saw no spiritual element in the schools. C. R. thus faulted the law for excluding "our Sacrosanct Apostolic Roman Religion from our schools," leaving the people "at the mercy of the winds of corruption that the great *Obscurantísimo* inculcated by means of teachers." More so, the traitor Armijo handed the children to the *cueras de ladrones* (straps of thieves). Schools without religion were but *máscaras de los infiernos*, masks of the underworld. It mattered little that the "foreigners" in New Mexico were Jews or Protestants; they sought to "destroy the harmonious peace concentrated for centuries in Spanish Catholicism." C. R. challenged Armijo: "Why have you, *ficticio Español* [false Spaniard] put yourself in the service of casting out religious instruction from the schools?" It was a sacrilegious betrayal of Nuevomexicano primacy. If any individual wanted to "do harm and cause ruin *á su país* [to their homeland]," it was he. Armijo was forewarned: "We want our historic religion and systems of teaching. As for the rest, we shall decide" (in elections).[155]

The Jesuits headquartered in Las Vegas (New Mexico) took up the traditionalist cause as clearly its own. Reverend Donato M. Gasparri, head of the New Mexico Society of Jesus, called out Protestant effrontery.[156] Priests lobbied at the capital for defeat of the Armijo bill. Father Agustín Truchard, pastor in the midsouth community of Socorro, hailed the colleagues who had downed the previous bill of "enlightened Mexicans" who were hostile to their own Church.[157] Truchard denied opposing progress and knew the sad state of education, yet he urgently defended the Nuevomexicano nation. As he swore,

> we will never consent to the establishment of a school system in New Mexico where not even the name of God is to be pronounced, because such schools in a country entirely Catholic [New Mexico] would lead to the ruin of faith and morals, for it is true, that schools without religion are seminaries of impiety and immorality.[158]

Truchard pleaded with authorities to "respect the belief and customs of Catholics, as we respect the belief and customs of others; that they attempt not to usurp the rights and privileges of the Catholic Church, guaranteed to them by the . . . Constitution."[159]

The proxy Nuevomexicano ethnonationalist journal *La Revista Católica* counselled Nuevomexicanos to unite in building a party of their own. Lawmakers had locked horns "over the altar of the land" with the "choleric fear" of "prepotent politicians" imposing their will. Bad laws were to be feared. Honorable legislators protected the "citadel of union," sacrificing personal interest and affecting patriotism, but "the day of hate among one another" would come "under the aspect of party difference," for the spirit of party was "a most fierce enemy." In New Mexico, it brought subordination to a foreign influence. To have unity, the "universal and continuous harms of party" must be reined in.[160]

If C. R. invoked a "Spanish" Church, the clergyman militantly pushed a Mexican ethnonationalism, not surprisingly given the expelling of the Society of Jesus from the Spanish empire. "Banish, then, the ancient quarrels," Truchard demanded. "What Democrats and what Republicans? Be Mexicans." As he piled on:

> In saying "Be Mexicans," it is not our intent to set one of two races living in this territory against the other. Better, we would like to always see narrower and

> stronger ties that unite the noble sons of Moctezuma and Pelayo [a mestizo allusion] with the generous and tireless descendants of the Edmunds and Edwards. If the first are here the ancient owners, they received but the seconds of the Constitution that guarantees to them peace and interior prosperity, friendship, and respect among the nations of the universe. We say, however, be Mexicans; that is to say, let unity be our politics in all that is necessary for the conservation and development of the inherent interests of the land.[161]

Unified, Mexicans could control; divided, they would be controlled, not by the "whole American portion, but by a few adventurers that over you and over the Americans will extend their usurping arm. But of those who will suffer most, without doubt, will be yourselves." This Settler Colonial script would appear in discourses to come. The messenger of religious primacy called on the people to let the past be "a useful and memorable lesson for the future."[162]

Pierced by the rhetorical extremism, the *Santa Fe New Mexican* argued that the "Italian *refugees* [who] sought and obtained shelter under our flag to create disturbances between the citizens of the United States resident in New Mexico on account of nationality . . . deserve a severe reprimand." As the weekly prosecuted:

> We call ourselves, for want of a better term, Americans; the citizens of Mexico call themselves Mexicans. Under which flag, cunning priests do you desire to live? Not Mexico, for they would not permit you to live there an hour; they have had too bitter a taste of your mischievous teachings [the chasing of Jesuits from New Spain]. Then if you intend to become a citizen of the United States by adoption, why do you teach these young men to sink all party ties and bind themselves together as Mexicans against Americans? Whose flag floats over the building in which they sit? Whose money pays for their valuable services? Whose Army guards protected your seditious heads from violence [in the Taos Revolt], and New Mexico

> from border raids and Indian massacres? Mexico? Bah! Treacherous Jesuit, this is America, the United States—Uncle Sam's country—Yankeeland. If you don't like it you can leave it.[163]

As the colonizer concluded, "We came to stay, to introduce for our use and benefit our common schools, our railroads, and our laws and language."[164]

The public school debate subsided. The miniscule property taxes and the difficulty of reaching widely scattered children limited school construction.[165] Yet the controversy yields identity sentiments that swirled around a technically colonial institution. The secular education issue would come home to roost in the later politics of statehood. Traditionalists would have their moment of resistance before the handwriting on the wall appeared: If New Mexico were to become a state, it must adopt the means of modern education.

Colloquial Self-Designations

The informal title *hijo del país* (literally, child of the homeland) fostered territorial primacy in its very semantics.[166] In running as a delegate to Congress and calling for self-rule under statehood, José Francisco Chaves was, as Euro-Americans had labeled him, an "American hater," intent on disenfranchising them. Chaves said he only opposed the racially biased governor, territorial secretary, and chief justice. He told his partisan foe Diego Archuleta in a letter that Euro-American corruption "ought to inspire us to unity of action for the purpose of combatting the suicidal policy of these adventurers." Archuleta needed to be on guard, Chaves informed his colleague, "against [his party] friends, in whom [you have] so much confidence. We ought, as *hijos de Nuevo México* and descendants of a noble race" make common cause against the policy "of our common enemy." Instead, Archuleta fed Chaves's letter to the *Santa Fe Weekly Gazette*, which condemned the delegate's un-American thinking and advised the people to "conduct themselves as citizens of the United States and not 'Sons of New Mexico and descendants of a noble race' in the sense that Mr. Chaves and his supporters would have them understand it."[167]

Nativo and "native" carried considerable discursive weight as well. When an anonymous European going by *Viagero* (traveler) praised Archbishop Lamy for ousting Nuevomexicano priests, Un Observador sarcastically called him a "glorious apparition in our continent" with his "blood-thirsty phrases." Those were not random derelicts Lamy took out, Un Observador sneered, but esteemed *eclesiásticos nativos.* The bishop offended the people when he swept away *los ministros hijos del país.*[168] Nuevomexicanos called themselves "native" to claim more authority over Euro-Americans "because they had a stronger connection to New Mexico as descendants of the 'first' colonizers."[169] But while Euro-Americans commonly called Native Americans "natives,"[170] Nuevomexicanos to my eye hardly, if ever, used nativo when referring to indigenous people.[171] Rather, they followed Spanish practice dating to the sixteenth century of calling them *naturales,* as Hernán Cortez did in his *cartas de relación* (letters to the Spanish court),[172] and when an official document referred to *un Yndio de nación tagno, Natural de las Salinas* (an Indian from the Tano nation, a natural [not born within the Church] of Salinas).[173] *Indígena, las huestes indígenas* (indigenous hosts), and *nación indio* were commonly used as well.[174]

Most intriguingly, nativo for Nuevomexicanos had what Leonard Doob calls a "We were here first" significance, what Chaim Gans calls a "first occupancy conception."[175] How could this be when the presence of indigenous nations predated Spanish exploration of the area by far?[176] Basically, as Rosina Lozano puts it, Nuevomexicanos "pushed to be described as 'natives' to emphasize their place on the land (and to rewrite the space for themselves rather than American Indians)."[177] What logic did they use for this? In charmed conceit or through coercion, the title "nativo" belonged to what Gans calls sovereignty in the "formative territories conception,[178] or what Ting calls a "figured world of nationhood," the origins of which traced to a "world system of nation states."[179]

In staking their belongingness on the New Mexico terrain, Nuevomexicanos were backed subconsciously and formally by a land transfigured by Western decree, basically an institutionally framed homeland. The Doctrine of Discovery promulgated by Pope Nicholas V in 1492 proclaimed the right of Christians to take possession of lands held by "barbarians" to save their souls and bring them within the bastionate (stronghold) of Western Civilization.[180] "Native of the Kingdom and Provinces of New Mexico" signified a jurisdiction managed by provincial authority,[181] inscribed potently on parchment with imperialist writing and record-keeping.[182]

Nativo thus signified citizen, as in the transition of vecinos in the eighteenth century from "settler" to "citizen" of the Spanish kingdom. "By its very nature," Ross Frank notes, the taking of a colonial census defined vecinos as against Native Americans "and those deemed not a part of the province."[183] Don Pedro Bautisa Pino, New Mexico's first deputy to the Spanish Cortes, defined the terms under which the Cortes would admit people as citizens. "All Spaniards who, on both sides of the family, derive their origin from the Spanish dominions of either hemisphere, and who are settled in any town in the said dominions" were automatic citizens.[184]

It was a spatiality for a privileged community. As the editor of *La Revista de Taos* recalled in 1918, New Mexico was "an entity well formulated and distinctly delineated since the epoch in which it was colonized by the Europeans from Spain with the firm proposition of presenting and establishing it on its own soil."[185] From the perspective of their bounded community, citizens perceived much of humanity as an "aggregate of more or less un-friendly foreigners."[186] Between 1700 and 1880, "an estimated five thousand *indios de rescate* [Native captives redeemed through purchase] and genízaros entered New Mexico," in many cases, spending their lives "as objectified outsiders and servile bondspeople in their communities."[187] Not even the sedentary, so-called "civilized" Puebloans qualified for inclusion if they were not Christians. People of the Plains, "untamed, gentile Indians," were antithetical to the "civilized *gente de razón*" (people with reason). "Barbarity" and "savagery," were quasi-official titles.[188] They signified not just a propensity to irrational violence; "barbarous nations" referred to ways of life, heathenism, superstition, and crass modes of dress. As Estevan Rael-Gálvez puts it, indigenous peoples were "savaged" to establish and maintain colonial rule.[189] In this sense they were not, or so it appears, equal in common discourse to "nativos."

Warfare and No-Name Primacy

After Diego de Vargas reestablished New Mexico for Spain in the eighteenth century, peaceful trade and social relations obtained between vecino settlements and Plains tribes only to see a rise in military campaigns and raiding especially by Comanches, Apaches, Kiowa, Utes, and Navajos.[190] After another time of peace, Nuevomexicano-Indigenous conflict spiked in the Mexican period, fueled by an irresolute Mexican policy that turned Navajos and Apaches into rock-solid enemies.[191]

Both the Treaty of Guadalupe Hidalgo (which in Article XI cited the "savage" threat) and Kearny the Occupier guaranteed pacification to the Mexicans, yet Nuevomexicanos grieved at what became a sustained pattern of Native fighting.[192] The record of experienced raids from the 1850s to the 1880s was for the ages. In southern New Mexico violence involving Mexican settlers and Comanche and Lipan Apaches "escalated to a 250-year high in the immediate aftermath of the U.S.-Mexican War."[193] In 1857, troops from Fort Craig tracking Mogollon Apaches south of Socorro "discovered several 'Mexicans killed and scalped.'"[194] An 1862 report said of Mescaleros that they killed forty-six ranchers with scores of children kidnapped and dozens of cattle, horses, sheep, and mules driven off.[195] In an 1863 memorial to President Lincoln, the territorial assembly requested authority to raise two regiments of volunteers to assist US troops, based on the toll in the northern counties of sixty-two dead, thirty-four wounded, seven captured, and thirty-five thousand livestock animals lost.[196] In 1864, San Miguel, Anton Chico, La Cuesta, and El Pueblo along the Pecos River retaliated for slain sheepherders, kidnapped children, and stolen livestock.[197]

For "the want of proper protection against the various barbarous tribes of Indians," citizens appealed to New Mexico's delegate to Congress for statehood.[198] In 1865, Governor William Connelly assured territorial legislators that statehood would lead to the curbing of the Native "menace," the expenses of a state a small price to pay for the "'entire subjugation and colonization of the Native tribes which have so long desolated and retarded the progress of our people.'"[199] As the *Santa Fe New Mexican* reported on September 1, 1868, it had "almost daily published instances of robbery, murder, and outrages of all descriptions in different parts of the territory."[200] Twenty-three incidents occurred in ten months with an estimated $40,000 in damages.[201] One J. J. filed notice of increased raiding throughout southern New Mexico.[202] A member of the 1869 assembly made an impassioned appeal for military protection against "the savages in Socorro county."[203] The *Santa Fe New Mexican* denied that the problem was the "inefficiency" of military authorities, but rather "the foolishly wicked policy pursued by our general government" of working treaties "with brutal savages."[204]

In January 1872, rancher Luis Baca said of Kiowa riflemen that they wounded a shepherd in El Arroyo de los Yutas; raided the ranches of his brothers; killed two shepherds; stole clothes, dishes, food, $1400 in animals including mules; and killed cattle worth $1200. Baca feared a campaign on the Sierra Grande to slay Mexicans and steal horses. Three days later, Cimarron Utes killed seventy cattle and many sheep, as well as threatened the Bacas with death if they did not leave their ranch.[205] Participants in a mass meeting in Abiquiu on the San Juan River petitioned authorities for protection since the "frontier county of Rio Arriba had continuously suffered the depredations, robberies, and outrages of Indians of different bands and tribes, and when our petitions were directed to authorities rarely were they attended to."[206] A Territorial Republican Convention that year earnestly appealed to the administration for military posts "for the protection of the lives and property of our people against the murderous savages who infest our territory and annually murder large numbers of our citizens."[207]

Not reported was the extent to which vecinos instigated aggression. Brian DeLay lays main responsibility for all the pain and destruction on the sustained captivity raids of Mexicans. For Native Americans, the narrative rang "of alienation and belonging, . . . about loved ones alienated from those to whom they belonged." The taking, keeping, and enslaving of family members conjured "collective grief," DeLay states, a Navajo describing the crying and mourning of Chiefs for two hundred of their children who were taken from their homes by the Mexicans.[208] The Diné (Navajo) experienced Mexican and American expeditions as invasions of *their* homeland. As the great Manuelito—who fought for the freedom of his people from the clutches of General Carleton's Long Walk of Diné to the concentration camp at Bosque Redondo—explained to his wife Juanita, whose suffering from battles hindered her ability to maintain the family: "I will shed my blood on my land and my people will have the land even if I die." Historian Kate Nelson describes Manuelito's perspective: "The Great Spirit had given Diné Bikéyah to the Navajos, the valleys and the high mesas and the four sacred mountains. The people were supposed to be there, and they would not leave."[209] Utes cherished the area around the San Luis Valley as their spirit domain and center of life. They repeatedly drove off Nuevomexicano families who settled in their winter hunting ground. As the official Indian agent John Greiner reported, the place contained "the bones of their Fathers, and they will not give it up quietly. If they needed to, they would fight to the death."[210]

What comes into play, however, is James Brooks' supplementary narrative of *la gran ladronería* (the great theft), "simultaneously a place and a process organized around systematic thievery." Brooks links the forty years of mutual banditry in the New Mexico territory, "unsavory and often illicit," to a "constellation of wealth and market circuits necessary for successful capitalist development," involving "exogenous laws of property and propriety and functioning within an alternative spatial culture of ladronería." Animal thieves, pillagers, and slave raiders—"Comanches, Kiowas, Apaches, New Mexican comancheros, transborder Tejanos, Mexican peones, and Anglo-Texan filibusteros—found niches for themselves that for a time worked very much in their favor. Both the interests of capitalist expansion and the interests of those ultimately swept aside by its momentum were, ironically, served well."[211]

Brooks points to the "reciprocal retribution in captive raiding [feeding] the pervasive insecurity and anger in the borderlands,"[212] yet what proportion of events constituted raid and retribution is hazy. In the oral histories of D`iné, rogue thieves on their own attacked and raided settlements for power and material wealth.[213] As Frank McNitt notes, "constant warfare was contrary to Navajo nature and totally disruptive of normal Navajo life," yet there were the "relatively few Navajo ladrones and *pobres* whose raids upon the river settlements continued unremittingly through the winter of 1860–61."[214]

It was on the incidences of "unremitting" raiding that Nuevomexicanos and Euro-Americans fixed on for public reporting over a much longer time. The importance of raiding is suggested by the constant campaigns of troops in military installations, such as Fort Craig, "responding to recent 'murders and robberies,'" seeking to capture raiders, pursuing stolen stock, attempting to interdict raiding that wore heavily.[215] The raiding, even if episodic, offered grist for the milling of identity, again confirming DeLay's aphorism of violence constituting community and community constituting violence.[216] The equation of aggressive mobile tribesmen and settled Nuevomexicanos encouraged a one-sided ethnic partisanship. Inevitably, fateful tragedies tilted ethnic identity toward a narrative of Native hostility, greed, and ultimate culpability even as the Indigenous claim would stress the original Western invasion of native lands. In the assembly's memorial to Congress, "candor and justice require us to say that the protection of our people against Indian hostilities has not been improved by the transfer of our Territory [to the United States]."[217]

While Manuelito communicated to his people via D`iné clan networks, Nuevomexicanos utilized public venues, archived testimonies, printed statements, and official appeals. Politicized scripts of Native plunder and savagery justified claims of a Nuevomexicano right to a peaceful life on "their" homeland. Setting off indigene others with bold social boundaries and portrayals of raiding, pillaging, and predation, they brought together vecino diversity—mestizo sheepherders and their strongmen *patrones*;[218] modest farm families, some identifying as Spanish; captive servants;[219] light-skinned wealthy sheep-ranchers; legacy Genízaros who were rapidly mixing into Nuevomexicano households;[220] Hermanos and laity; the diminishing Creole distinction[221]—into a singularity of interest forged by hard experience on the land.

In proposing a militia of a thousand men to deal with Navajo "depredations," a citizen junta in Santa Fe organized a correspondence chain across counties to strategize defenses and report on raids.[222] A Spanish-language broadside called the people to action against raiders while condemning government inaction. "For months, the bells of your sacred buildings have run incessantly in honor of your citizens who have been struck down. For months, their mangled bodies have been crowding your cemeteries."[223]

Assemblymen disseminated an emerging Indian Scourge script, warning vecinos to steel themselves with the awareness that "a savage tribe of Indians should be your enemies," that "plunder and murder" were "not a thing new or unexpected," and it must be remembered because assaults have been Native "habits since our brave ancestors first possessed the Valley of the Rio Grande."[224]

In accepting his party's nomination for delegate to Congress in 1880, Tranquilino Luna—born in 1847 as the scion of a Valencia County sheep barony[225]—bracketed his personal qualifications with scripts of Indian Scourge and Intrepid Poblador Ancestors. As he affirmed,

> I am native born to this soil; my father, grandfather, and in fact, all my ancestry, as far as the memory of man runneth, were the same. They have fertilized it with their blood, both in wrestling it from the savage Indian and subsequently in making the country fit for civilized men to settle and live upon. The bones of my ancestors are scattered broadcast over elevated mountains and beautiful plains—monuments of their patriotism, loyalty, and bravery.[226]

Luna's family was every Nuevomexicano family that had experienced the pangs of blood-stained competition with Natives even as the illegal civilian assaults and robbing of Native ranks went unrecorded. Luna's declaration gave voice to ethnonational motifs: "Our getting here has been an achievement involving risk and sacrifice on our part,"[227] and "crucial events and personages in the history of the ethnic community . . . invested with sacred significance."[228] Deeper still, Luna harmonized Nuevomexicano primacy with a kind of political indigeneity, "nativeness" representing a Christian civilization, not unlike Native identity in the twentieth-century understanding their First Nation rights, particularly in a context of a liberal democracy.[229] Well after the bloody period ended, Nuevomexicanos would remember the scripts Luna and his ethnic compatriots constructed on the frontier.[230]

And so, the concluding thought of this chapter: Nuevomexicanos, aided by Euro-American agents on the unstable frontier, made their belonging to New Mexico and the United States the substance of their public identity. A Spanish calling and other designations worked for exhibiting a distinct territorialized people now harbored in the American nation. In the next chapter, I look at the further parsing of territorial primacy by Nuevomexicanos, this time on the backs of the Pueblo nations, thereby adding a Spanish conquistador legacy to their identity quiver.

CHAPTER 2

Performative Primacy

"Spanish" and "Mexican" in the Tertio-Millennial Exposition

TRAINS REVAMPED LIFE in America to such a degree that Michael Lind refers to that altered life as the "railroad society."[1] After a decade of breathless anticipation, the Atchison, Topeka & Santa Fe Railroad reached Raton Pass in 1879,[2] raising the curtain on New Mexico's part in that modern drama of locomotion.

Portending good times, the railroad's arrival made for exciting news. Yet some Nuevomexicanos worried. In a legendary encounter, Diego Archuleta, the president of the territorial council, is said to have faced down the vice president of the Santa Fe Railroad, exclaiming, "We don't want you damned Yankees in the country. We can't compete with you; you will drive us out, and we shall have no home left us. We won't have you here."[3]

While the episode may be apocryphal, a Euro-American editor definitely crowed over "a few *ricos* who have, so to speak, been able to 'run' the Territory, and who feel that railroads, factories, and schools will destroy their power and remove the potence of [their] prejudice."[4] Another commentator claimed to have spotted a hatred of Americans, of "their language and institutions." The malcontents would do better to accept "the signs of the times," the observer said, for soon the territory would find itself "traversed by railroads north and south and east and west and Americans will have a controlling influence, numerically and otherwise." Repugnant though it seemed to the opinionator, "time will verify it."[5]

The prophecy of a Euro-American wave dominating New Mexico's railroad society at the expense of Nuevomexicanos would be realized indeed. In the political field, for example, Carlos Ramírez documented the decline of the "hereditary members of the native ruling class," beginning in the 1880s until in the first decade of the twentieth century they counted but four in the territorial Council and six in the

House of Representatives.[6] Some of the higher-class Nuevomexicanos accommodated the new ethnic overlay, others found ways to take advantage of it, and some resisted when necessary. Experiencing the modernisms of New Mexico's railroad society assured the permanence of their primacy identity.

The Business of Culture

On a frosty February morning in 1880, an agglomeration of Santa Feans crowded the platform of a new depot to welcome the train for the first time. The "immense" gathering featured Governor Lew Wallace, Chief Justice L. B. Prince, the commanding general of the New Mexico military Edward Hatch and his staff, all of the territorial legislature, the county commission, teachers and pupils from St. Michael's College, the parading Ninth Cavalry band, and citizens borne on carriages and covered wagons.[7]

Signifying biculturalism, two sovereign banners furled at the head of the procession, the American flag and the colors of Spain. However, the lineup of special guests failed to realize the implied equality because, in a subaltern moment, of the five men who nailed the final spikes on the track, only County Commissioner Antonio Ortiz y Salazar represented the Nuevomexicano folk.[8]

At least Santa Fe County Sheriff José D. Sena gave one of two speeches. Born in 1836, Sena was a legacy Creole, former officer in the Civil War, a former candidate for delegate to Congress, and a legal apprentice who gained admission to the Territorial Bar.[9] His remarks in Spanish went unpublished. According to a press report, he rejoiced at the prospect of the end of the disadvantageous "old days of Santa Fe." The railroad, that "promoter of civilization," he reportedly noted, would bring immigration and wealth. Spiting Diego Archuleta's alleged skepticism of domineering strangers flooding in, Sena had his hometown ready to "step into the ranks of the richest mineral and agricultural states of the Union."[10]

The other speaker, LeBaron Bradford Prince, was the new chief justice of the territorial Supreme Court. Prince spoke elegantly of the railroad's binding New Mexico to the "great throbbing central heart" of the country, to its talent, wealth, resources, and the "power and the glory of the great American people." The newcomers, capital, and enterprise would, in Prince's dream, "cause our hills to give up that hidden treasure of gold and silver, which will make every stream resound with the busy hum of mills which cover over prairies with flocks and herds, and make New Mexico the orchard, the vineyard, and the garden of the great west, which in short will develop every natural resource and stimulate every industrial enterprise."[11]

New Mexico's railroad society would spawn a forceful, domineering sector of Euro-American culture brokers with Prince as its incarnation. Already, on July 2, 1879, five months after Prince arrived in Santa Fe, the *New Mexico Herald* reproduced an interview he gave to the *New York Mail* regarding New Mexico's little-known people, "their traits, characteristics, etc."[12] In that article, Prince introduced his theme of "three cultures," raving that in New Mexico "we find three distinct civilizations, side by side, yet each making a contrast with the other and with our own condition of things in the east."[13] Later at the train station, Prince spoke of a "union" among two of the three civilizations:

> Here is the historic race of old Spain, full of spirited chivalry, of hospitality, and generosity, preserved through more than two centuries, free from the selfishness and greed which have often been the accompaniments of the intense activity of modern Euroamerican and Eastern life. And coming now is all the enterprise and energy, the determination and perseverance, the aspiration and ambition of the American character, fraught with the characterization of many foreign lands.[14]

This Cultural Accommodation script worked to break down Euro-American and Nuevomexicano boundaries. More than ever, the modern culture broker sought to shade New Mexico toward the American nation.

Prince embroidered the theme: "If in the mingling of these elements, the best of each be preserved, may we not look for a population in New Mexico such as the world has never seen equaled before?" It would mean a "unity of our whole people as we have not seen in the past. Shall we not today determine forever to drop use of the terms 'American' and 'Mexican' as heretofore too much employed as words of division among those who are equally American citizens!" Present to confirm the point were the "bright eyed boys" present, Nuevomexicanitos he meant, born under American government, marching "under the national flag."[15]

Many US nationalists seriously considered Prince's amalgamation impossible. It showed when Congressional Delegate Tranquilino Luna submitted a bill to make New Mexico a state. An anonymous writer from Trinidad, Colorado, forwarded a screed to the *New York Times* with the title "Greasers as Citizens" to argue why statehood for New Mexico was "simply detestable." It is important to convey the litany of disparagement the writer unloaded to illustrate the lengths that the dominant nationalism of the United States would go to preserve the homogeneity of its core people, all the while aiming to do harm to a foreign-bred element. Thus, "the character, manners, sentiments, wishes, and general condition" reflected "the mongrel breed known as Mexicans, a mixture of the blood of Apache, negro, Navajo, white horse-thief, Pueblo Indian and old-time frontiersman with the original Mexican stock." With such a mix, "You may sift and rake this Mexican population, and you will scarcely find man, woman or child who does not hate with a passionate hatred everything that is known to him or her as American" that they would "cover [over] with obsequiousness." Any "American" knowing Spanish quickly learned that "back of the Mexican's deference, behind his servility, there is lurking a spirit of abhorrence that only waits an opportunity to burst out."[16]

The script of Nuevomexicano Deficiency would be so repeatedly invoked by nineteenth-century nationalists that "New Mexicanism" is in order as a shorthand for its prominence. As an ideological codeword, New Mexicanism parallels Edward Said's "orientalism," the master codeword for the West diminishing or othering the East, upholding Western values, principles, and customs—the products of imperialism—as superior to their lesser, unrefined, or not fully civilized counterparts in the East, which altogether underscores the presumptiveness of imperial powers.[17] New Mexicanism had a boilerplate in *El Gringo; or, New Mexico and Her People.* Former Territorial Secretary W. W. H. Davis's 1857 tract catalogued the racial, cultural, and psychological faults of the Nuevomexicano element, as in their having the "cunning and deceit of the Indian, the politeness and spirit of revenge of the Spaniard, and the imaginative temperament and free impulses of the Moor." All classes believed in the superstitions of the Catholic Church; immoral priests dealt in politics, not saving souls; ignorant Mexicans refused education; women were sexually loose; the corrupt *patrón*, boss, kept the peons downtrodden; "Castilians" affected blueblood "grandees."[18]

Twenty-five years later, the Colorado discursive sniper's Davis mimetic spewed about uneducated Mexicans, their ignorance of American civic history and political parties, their "animal nature" restricting them to "small affairs of their neighborhood," priests having "a thick finger in the political pie." A parody of oversexualized Mexican women played to prurient interest: "in no other part of Christendom are the women of an entire community so generally without a sense of the beauties of virtue and so led to prove their insensibility for a money consideration." These "civilized people" did not know who their fathers were. A Mexican woman "living first with this man and then with another as his de facto wife is not considered by her female neighbors to be committing a serious impropriety, at least not such a heinous offense as should debar her from the countenance and society of others of her sex assumed to be leading a regular life."[19]

Like Alfred James Balfour's lecturing the British House of Commons on Egyptian civilization with "no attitude of superiority" (British statesmen knowing it better than anyone[20]), the Coloradan denied any intent to present "a stern censor of morality."[21] Yet as Said argues, the point behind orientalism was to colonize and exert control over the other. As the Nuevomexicano critic badgered, "a community run on the free-love principles and practice of the Mexicans of New Mexico is eminently undesirable as an addition to the number of States." For should the Mexicans fail to use statehood to secede from the Union, misrule would prevail based on "unlettered" Mexican voters, "perhaps not unwilling tools of sharpers of their own race," willing to be "controlled by or 'stand in with' white rascals bent on prey," while "American stock-raisers, miners, merchants . . . would be tied, hand and foot, gagged, and turned over to the mercy of insatiable leeches." Mexicans would fill the legislatures, courts, juries, and executive offices with their own kind, forcing the "'Americans' to submit to wrongs."[22]

It was to Prince's astonishment that a proposal for statehood could motivate such a "mass of slanders and misrepresentations." The chief justice called out the "tirade of abuse" which represented "that strange enjoyment which some persons seem to feel in irresponsible newspaper writing, which they consider spicy and smart in proportion as it is untrue and libelous."[23] He disabused the horror by borrowing from his Three Civilizations theme, as well as Miguel Antonio Otero's claim back in 1857: Pueblo villages lying "quite near Spanish towns" yet "no marriage or similar connections tak[ing] place between the races," their being "as separate in such respects as if a Chinese wall ran between them." The mixing with Navajo and Apache was also unknown as the latter resided on government reservations. Totally ignoring a valid mestizo legacy, Prince misleadingly pointed to the "fact" that "there is not now and has not been for a long time any such mixture, with very rare exceptions; fully as rare as in other sections of the country where the Caucasian race meets the Indian."[24]

Prince imparted an extensive contravention on behalf of Nuevomexicano worthiness. No more generous or "hospitable people" could be found "on earth than those of New Mexico," he declared. Worthy Americans "with the culture and manners which bespeak the gentleman or lady" would find a welcome "both swift and hearty" from them. To the accusation of their hating the Americans, Prince spoke of "rude Americans, adventurers, impostors and swindlers," imposing on the generosity and hospitality "of their hosts." Strangely, he held that "these noble qualities have not been utterly chilled." Instead, that "sad experience" made "the New Mexican, who originally was too confiding and unsuspicious, become circumspect as to the character of his new acquaintances," yet it had "not lessened the warmth of welcome to those who deserve it. New Mexicans exercised a "patriotic response" to the Southern rebellion, Prince emphasized, with "over 6,000 volunteers, larger in proportion to the population than could be claimed by many "of the most loyal states." After centuries of isolation, they were rapidly remedying illiteracy with the use of territorial funding of schools and the rise in Spanish and English newspapers. That their press "fitly" mourned the death of President Garfield was "surely . . . not evidence of dense ignorance."[25]

In attacking the offender's misogyny, Prince paid great homage to Nuevomexicanas. That "any man born of woman, and perchance with sisters and daughters whom he respects, should make such a wholesale denunciation [of them] is beyond comprehension," he declared. The presence of the American military is what caused any evident prostitution, no different than elsewhere. "No more high-bred, noble, and pure-minded women are to be seen on earth than among the Spaniards of New Mexico," their being brought up "with a care similar to that seen in Europe, and which seems almost too strict to us who are accustomed to the freedom of girl life in general in the United States." "Good daughters, faithful wives, and noble matrons" came out of cultural modesty and modest self-assertion. The virtue of "our countrywomen" was "too sacred a thing to be flippantly slandered wholesale by any writer," Prince pressed on, "least of all by one who is nameless." Finally, New Mexico was in no haste to become a state. The territory had progressed, "and in a short time would be 'a great and important one.'"[26]

It was an honorable defense of Nuevomexicanos/as that Prince presented, reflecting his experience as a Lincoln Republican in New York.[27] His rally in some ways fell in with progressive reformers who during Reconstruction acted as friends and protectors of African Americans.[28] At the same time, a sense of interest convergence—that is, a white person being liberal toward a minority insofar as it coincides with their interests[29]—was suggested in 1882 when Prince ran for New Mexico's delegate to Congress. "Like any Anglo Republican," a scholar notes, Prince relied on the support of Spanish-speaking voters,[30] yet, as an opposition editorial charged, he "with the cunning of a fox, is making love to the native population."[31] Prince lost the nomination to the incumbent Tranquilino Luna, a better-known and perhaps more trusted cultural standard-bearer.

Nevertheless, for Prince it was a way-stop. His journey to carve a public culture for New Mexico's railroad society had just begun. To that end, he became the vice president of the resuscitated New Mexico Historical Society.[32] Other Euro-Americans served as officers.[33] At the Society's first-anniversary celebration, its president, Territorial Secretary William G. Ritch, promoted Prince's Three Peoples vision. Two sections of his speech were devoted to the Native legacy. Under "Spanish Explorations," he recited the erroneous belief in Cabeza de Vaca's discovery of New Mexico and added a paragraph each to Coronado, the Espejo Expeditions (in search of mines, 1582), Oñate's settling the New Mexico province, and the Pueblo 1680 Insurrection. The main Hispanic epochs were: "Following the [Spanish] Restoration of 1691" (Diego de Vargas's reconquest after the twelve-year exile of Spanish colonists in the Pueblo Revolt), "The First Merchandise," and "The Mexican Republic." Like Justice Benedict patronizing ethnic contemporaries, Ritch saluted the "long line of names prominent in the history of the territory," specifically hailing the Chaves, Otero, Baca, Romero, Martínez, Abreu, Luna, Armijo, Sánchez, Valdez, and Ortiz families, following up with a parallel list of names from "The American Occupation."[34]

Ritch branched out to new duties and varied responsibilities brought by the "mighty change that has been wrought in this ancient and once isolated frontier during the last few months." In the script of New Mexico's Hidden Resources, Rich harked the "latent possibilities of our rich valleys and pastoral ranges and richer mountains and placers of wealth" just lying in wait for a "magical" transformation under the "indomitable energy of the individual American." In the vision, "silence and repose which for ages has reigned unbroken in so many places over the remains of an ancient population will be lifted."[35]

A stubborn obstacle obtained, however: New Mexico lacked the finances to roll out a powerful economy. Outside capitalists would have to be coaxed to build manufactures, mines, and industrial agriculture.[36] Inspired by the Denver Exposition of 1882 and Albuquerque's inaugural territorial fair,[37] Santa Fe's business lights concocted the Santa Fe Tertio-Millennial Anniversary Exposition (Tertio-Millennial) as a means of attracting outside capital.[38] As Tertio-Millennial president W. W. Griffin envisioned, the exposition would reveal "one of the principal wealth producing commonwealths of this wonderful republic."[39] "Tertio-Millennial" signaled the anniversary of Santa Fe's founding 333 years earlier. It missed the actual date by fifty-nine years; nevertheless, the notion of a Tertio-Millennial seemed best for seizing on New Mexico's market potential.

Many men served as officers of the incorporated Santa Fe Tertio-Millennial Anniversary Association. Of sixteen executives (president, three vice presidents, a secretary, a board of directors, and an executive committee), two were Nuevomexicanos.[40] The subalternity carried over to the New Mexico Bureau of Immigration, another organization for promoting development.[41] Nuevomexicano representation exemplified Susan Olzak's "niche overlap," elements of a largely segregated ethnic group present in dominant circles of power.[42]

COLLOSSUS OF ROADS.

FIGURE 1. The New Colossus of the Roads. New Mexico's Territorial Secretary William G. Ritch used this image in his book on the territory's resources and needs (*Illustrated New Mexico,* 23) to symbolize the ambitions of Santa Fe's business class for revolutionizing New Mexico's economy. It was a reproduction of a poster produced by the Atchison, Topeka and Santa Fe Railroad, which describes "A grenadier striding across the country personifies the route" of the railroad from Kansas to California and Mexico. Source: *Kansas Memory.* https://www.kansasmemory.gov/item/212835.

While Griffin stood prominently as Tertio-Millennial president, General Manager Charles W. Greene operated as its "prime mover."[43] Greene was editor/manager of the *New Mexican Review* (*NM Review*), the Santa Fe weekly recently purchased by the Santa Fe Railroad.[44] The *NM Review*'s coverage of the Tertio-Millennial often lapsed into exaggerated promotion, yet to a significant degree it respected modern journalism's aim of presenting factual coverage of important events, making its accounts useful for unpacking the details of the Tertio-Millennial Exposition.

A litany of columns described artifacts, thematic tableau, and Chautauqua. Paramount displays featured products from horticulture, agriculture, livestock raising, fruit orchards, wineries, Southwestern jewelry, forestry and fledgling manufactures. In a prepared space off the Plaza, crowds were treated to fun horse and burro races, Native dances, "sham" Native wars, lectures on antiquities, gold-panning demonstrations, competitive fireman drills, high-wire acts, and sports. The *matachín* dances of San Juan Pueblo Natives were said to have originated "many centuries back, in the misty rites and traditions of the Aztec race."[45]

In the master plan, New Mexico's culture groups were to serve as crown jewels not simply to enhance the tourists' gaze but to offset the "much maligned" territory in the states.[46] As advertised, the "general host of people, representing every nationality and from every nook and corner in the United States" were in for a treat, a "novel intermingling and blending of bloods, of nationalities and of civilizations, which are to be found in New Mexico."[47] Prince organized much of what a local (self-interested) historian called the "wonderful" exposition.[48] He wanted to have his new book of New Mexico sketches ready to provide historic information for visitors,[49] but it didn't arrive in time and so the exposition would present history visually to tell the story "more plainly than [written] words."[50]

The Tertio-Millennial's culture format blazed with the romance of Spanish imperial nostalgia. In formally opening the program, New Mexico Governor Lionel A. Sheldon stressed "founding" and "antiquity." In a petty but useful boast, he called Santa Fe "a youth of fifteen summers when a European foot was first set upon Florida's most [hoary] spot," a fact "which has been put beyond dispute that [Santa Fe] is the oldest Caucasian settlement within our domain."[51]

Sheldon spiced this founding heuristic with the Daring Explorer script that Kirby Benedict inaugurated. The Spanish of old were "more adventurous and enterprising than any other people," Sheldon affirmed. Spain was appreciated as the "greatest maritime power," possessing "the most nautical skill." Driven by the search for precious metals, Castilian explorers manifested the energy, perseverance, and courage to eclipse "all competitors in efforts to possess and dominate over the new world"[52] (eliding Queen Elizabeth I's defeat of El Rey Felipe II's Spanish Armada).

The specter of Francisco Vasquez de Coronado haunted the Exposition. Even the organizing committee called itself the Knights of Coronado. Coronado, Sheldon extolled, carried on in the "spirit of adventure which so thoroughly engrossed men of mind and courage with the expectation of finding an El Dorado."[53] It was an isomorph of Sheldon's business contemporaries scouting in search of fabulous riches.[54] The *NM Review* joined the Coronado reverence. If, according to legend, Montezuma traversed from a far north point in New Mexico to Tenochtitlan (Mexico City), Coronado's aim was "a matter of profound interest to discover the hive from which [the Aztecs] swarmed so far southward." As fortune and the exposition imaginary equated, the spot of this hive and that of the Tertio-Millennial were the same. In the countryside, dotted with "peaceful villages and industry," the people, though "crude and clumsy," supplied Coronado's men with "a coarse and simple plenty." Ever so loosely it alluded that Coronado "undoubtedly" established Santa Fe as the "capital in a league of free pueblos."[55]

Sheldon drew on the script of the Brave and Intrepid Pobladores pioneered by the territorial assembly in its proclamation at the start of the Civil War, intersecting it with that of Nuevomexicano Historical Isolation and the Indian Scourge. Notwithstanding their isolation, destitution, and exposure to attacks from numerous tribes of hostile, "warlike and savage Indians," the governor dramatized, they remained by the "shining wealth encased within the ribs of the rocky ranges" amid the resources that had sustained a "large unskilled population." In touch with what Leo Marx calls "sentimental pastoral," Sheldon painted Nuevomexicanos/as with "health, vigor, a bright and constant sunlight, and a place surrounded by beauty and grandeur,"[56] a brighter gild than that of Nuevomexicano identitarians in which ancestral settlers struggled in a constant battle with the elements, natural and human.

Prince seems to have ghostwritten much of Sheldon's speech. In the trope of Contacting European Civilizations, for example, the "Northmen" embarked on their migration later than the Spaniards and across a broader span of the continent, yet "Today, the whole continent is inhabited and controlled by Caucasians." New Mexico was until recently an "internal community, inaccessible except by a long, weary and dangerous march, and to the mass of the nation was practically terra incognita." The two forces coming from different directions had "but recently met within her borders. The American people are wont to watch closely the course of events and to speculate and philosophize upon results. This union has undoubtedly excited the attention of thoughtful men all over the country," the governor intoned, "and they are all solicitous as to the effect thus far, and as to what the finale will be."[57]

Sheldon presented amalgamation in a more assimilation spirit than Prince's pluralistic suggestion. Unless there was "a common religion, language, memories and dangers," he claimed, there could not be "real harmony and national sentiment among people under any form of government." New Mexico presented the "best possible test" for it had "no common religion or language, nor are memories the same among all our population." New Mexico showed the facility and rapidity with which "incongruous elements could fuse under the influence of popular institutions, and with the application of the good sense and justice of the general American mind."[58]

Such an allusion did not quite fit the tendency of Nuevomexicanos to privilege their traditional culture. However, Sheldon needed to reassure investors of the region's conducive possibilities. Going out with the liberal gentleman's judicious hark for this colonial outpost, he proclaimed, "this celebration indicates to the world a resolution on the part of the people of Santa Fe, that it shall not be truthfully said 'age thou art ashamed,' or 'thou hast lost the breed of noble bloods.' It has been determined that not age alone, but all that elevates and ennobles man shall entitle this city in this mountain region of the southwest to her rightful place at the head of the column."[59] Nuevomexicanos would have some things to say about the importance of age and its legacies for Santa Fe and New Mexico.

Publicizing the Memory of Conquest: Taking Possession

The Fourth of July in 1883 went into the Tertio-Millennial tent. A "huge" crowd, reportedly, heard the peripatetic Prince adopting Latin America as the children of American liberty, whose birthright the Declaration of Independence had inscribed. On the abiding question of New Mexico's national integration, he returned to Contacting European Civilizations, "two great streams of history, Spanish from the south and Anglo from the east in this Rocky Mountain area."[60] In his paean to America's cultural diversity, Ralph Waldo Emerson spoke of the United States as the "asylum of all nations, the energy of Irish, Germans, Swedes, Poles and Cossacks, and all the European tribes, of the Africans and Polynesians, [who] will construct a new race as vigorous as the new Europe which came out of the smelting pot of the Dark Ages."[61] Hopping on, Prince had New Mexico welcoming Germans, "prominent in all mercantile matters"; the French "largely in the priesthood"; the "versatile Irishman" found "in all walks of life"; the Italian "raising lasting monuments to his skill, and others all harmoniously working together under the protection of the same government and same flat building as one homogeneous American people."[62]

The Mora Valley rancher Rafael Romero followed Prince. Born and raised on his father's prosperous ranch on the Mora Land Grant forty miles northeast of Santa Fe,[63] Romero graduated from Notre Dame and Georgetown Universities.[64] Like his intelligentsia *colegas*, he had what Doris Meyer called a "sophisticated understanding of the Neomexicano historical situation," a perception of the "dialogic dimensions of a society in transition, in which two cultures interact and shape one another in a struggle for power."[65]

According to historians, Coronado failed miserably in his four-thousand-mile search for coveted gems and grand civilizations while exacting ruthless punishment on Puebloans if they did not deliver on demand the necessities for survival, all to the bitter memory of those on whom he visited atrocities.[66] None of it counted in the Tertio-Millennial, which hyped the legend of Coronado exploits. In Romero's Coronado the Originator script, Coronado went from the "stormy, tumultuous" conquest of Mexico to the "discovery" of this "bright land to the northward whereupon we now celebrate." The adventurer wintered in Arizona in 1542, pressed eastward to Quivira, and hoofed it to the Rio Grande Valley where the virtual founding of Santa Fe took place. Finessing the script to the occasion, Romero relayed the legend of Coronado followers "so taken with the beauties of the upper Rio Grande, the climate and the precious minerals that they refused to return with him, and thus by accident, it may be said, occurred Santa Fe's first European colonization in 1543, for even then this was known to be the chief city of all this region."[67] For the priest and Franciscan friars the allusion would have rung hollow because, in opposing the explorer's brutality, they left Coronado for Pecos Pueblo, where they remained.[68] Romero omitted this detail.

Quite importantly, Romero ignored Prince's three-cultures tribute and his amalgamation theme. Had he done so, the *NM Review* would have surely reported it. Instead, he prioritized Nuevomexicano belonging in the ethnonational discourse of the "power of precedence on the land."[69] Plucking the chord of Nuevomexicano autochthony—"the idea that certain individuals or groups are the original inhabitants of a particular territory"[70]—on *terra firma*, Romero placed his people's legendary background "on par with the ancients"[71] so that his ancestors would continue to "perform important roles in the present."[72]

New Mexico history occupied center stage two weeks later in the Tertio-Millennial's design of presenting the characteristics of the three civilizations "since the first occupation of the territory by the Spaniards in 1550."[73] In three days, a crowd said to be ten to twelve thousand in size witnessed the "Spanish pageant," an event the *NM Review* lauded as "one of the most unique and resplendent parades that was ever witnessed by an American assembly, royalty and barbaric magnificence the like of which can never be duplicated outside of New Mexico."[74]

In the opening act, glittering actors moved "in crimson, black and gold, with high boots, helmet and sword, and mounted on a spirited charger." Euro-Americans played honorary conquerors. W. T. Thornton, a superior court justice and president of the Knights of Coronado, was "arrayed in green satin," representing a gallant Spanish knight "to perfection."[75] Otherwise, the act clearly belonged to the Nuevomexicanos. José D. Sena, who helped greet the train at its Santa Fe debut, led the procession as its chief marshal. Sena traced his ancestry to rico families involved in the Spanish founding of New

Mexico.[76] He was a veteran of Catholic processions, yearly preparing one of the elaborate altars where celebrants of Corpus Christi paused in prayer. In addition, there had been a "Coronado procession" in the Fiesta de Santa Fe,[77] although, as figure 4 suggests, only a single Nuevomexicano stood among the six Coronado guard members, which included Prince and Griffin.

As eyewitness Ralph Twitchell noted, Native Americans had the year before engaged in deadly combat with the US Army, yet in the parade, Apache chiefs, warriors, and hunters walked behind the Thirteenth US Infantry Band, "their gleaming spears and buckskin robes adorned with beads of many hues." Their participation stemmed from their wardship in the Bureau of Indian Affairs.[78] Apache warriors walked alongside the "Oriental, and innocent-looking Zunis of the sixteenth century. The mild[-]mannered [Picurís] with their Christ-like wreaths of native willow, made up the first section of the novel pageant and aroused the admiration of the highest pitch by the characteristic wildness of their make-up." The "sun-dried and good herd" San Juan Native Americans walked with bows and arrows.[79]

It is important to emphasize that the main procession featured Nuevomexicano actors. Felipe Delgado—former Superintendent of New Mexico's Indian Agencies (appointed by President Lincoln), veteran member of the territorial legislature, former probate judge, a county commissioner, and on the Santa Fe School Board—played Coronado for the *Entrada* on horseback.[80] Court officers and a guard of twenty richly robed knights rode under the captaincy of don Vicente Mares. Espejo, played by Frank Chaves, filed through with his command. A "brilliant" *escuadrón* trailed don Gabriel Martínez. Captain Carlos Conklin, of a Euro-American father and a Nuevomexicana mother, led a "host of handsome lieutenants and a band of fifty Spanish warriors covered with gold and silver, varnished with helmets, spears and shields."[81] Former "Indian fighter" Román Baca played don Diego de Vargas, the famed 1692 re-conqueror of New Mexico.[82] A half dozen black-robed, barefoot Franciscan friars hoisted banners "in memory of the good fathers of the Holy Faith, who centuries ago braved the trials of this vast wilderness and first planted here the cross of the Christian religion."[83] The sheer volume of participation suggests both the spread and depth of Nuevomexicano identification with their Spanish conquest heritage at this moment in time.

FIGURE 2. (*above*) Corpus Christi procession on the Plaza, Santa Fe, New Mexico, n.d. The religious procession gave José D. Sena the capacity to organize the Nuevomexicano participation in the Tertio-Millennial Exposition, 1884–1892. D. B. Chase, photographer. Courtesy of the Palace of the Governors Photo Archives, negative number 056988.

FIGURE 3. Men on horseback in Spanish costume. Left to right: L. Bradford Prince; unidentified man; Arthur Boyle; possibly William W. Griffin; Roman Liberato Baca; William Taylor Thornton; and unidentified man. For Tertio-Millennial Exposition, Santa Fe, New Mexico, 1883. Unknown photographer. Courtesy of the Palace of the Governors Photo Archives, negative number 011001.

FIGURE 4. (*above*) Coronado procession, Fiesta de Santa Fe, New Mexico, 1880–1882. Henry Brown, Bennett and Brown, photographer. Courtesy of the Palace of the Governors Photo Archives, negative number 015258.

FIGURE 5. Apache headquarters at Tertio-Millennial. Santa Fe, New Mexico, 1883. Ben Wittick, photographer. Courtesy of the Palace of the Governors Photo Archives, negative number 015922.

As the procession passed by a Spanish–Pueblo battle awaited. The wars with Plains tribes had recently passed into history, but the Spanish conquest of the Puebloans—whose two-score farming communities lined the Rio Bravo and Chama Rivers and mountain basins, extending to the western desert—bestirred older memory. The battle as played out in the Tertio-Millennial modeled the encounter between the re-conqueror of New Mexico, don Diego de Vargas, and the Tewa Native Americans of Santa Fe in 1692.[84]

Here it is critical to pause over that legacy not only for its background to the present scene but also because both Pueblo and Spanish American collective memory would call it up formidably from each's perspective in the late twentieth and early twenty-first centuries. In keeping a "marvelous" heritage afloat, Spanish scripts would not, could not admit to what José de la Cruz Pacheco Rojas and José Rabasa call out: that Spanish conquerors of New Mexico failed to obey *Las Ordenanzas de descubrimiento*, the laws that Bishop Bartolomé de las Casas had forged quite prominently amid strenuous debate and conferencing, forbidding Catholic evangelism from forcing indigenous communities to political obedience and economic servitude.[85] Studies thus unfold the imperial yoke that New Mexico's governors strived to lay on the Pueblos. Governmental and religious oversight proved highly repressive. In the words of one Native American historian, the regime involved "crippling tribute demands, religious oppression, and enslavement, all enforced with the peculiar 'legal and rational' forms of social violence negotiated between the Spanish Crown and the popes in the administration of Indians."[86]

On entering the territory that the Spanish empire had named *Nuevo México*, Oñate kneeled and recited the important vestige of the original *Requerimiento* (Requirement), a long, detailed manifest that *adelantados*[87] were ordered to pronounce so as to legalize the taking of frontier lands, converting them into kingdoms and provinces of the empire while bringing Indigenous groups under legal jurisdiction.[88] Originally a formal rationale for "just wars" (which were abolished in 1552 because Spanish officials too often abused Native Americans),[89] the Requerimiento came to be called "acts of obedience and vassalage," which, when dictated to indios, compelled them to accept Spanish rule, adopt Catholicism, pay tribute to the colonial economy, or face punishment and war.[90]

From his encampment, Oñate visited seven Pueblo homesites, in each performing *la toma de posesión*, the act of taking possession of them and their lands.[91] In the standard ritual, a large cross was planted in the center of the Indigenous site. A friar led in the singing of the "Te Deum Laudamus" (Thee God we Praise). Children were baptized and rosaries handed out as a sign of absolution for apostasy. The chief conquistador himself announced the official taking of the land in the name of the Crown and the Pope, followed by the *cuadrilla* shouting three hails to the king and church. The proceedings of la toma de posesión were supposed to be translated, even though Puebloans likely understood little if any of what was being told to them.[92] Nevertheless, historians have accepted the account of Gaspar Pérez de Villagrá—who was with Oñate and penned an epic poem to describe his taking of New Mexico—on how the Puebloans beheld and kissed the wooden cross in the religious commissary's right hand, obeying General Oñate's command to make Philip their king, and submitting their children to be baptized.[93] As Rabasa notes, when Native Americans "surrendered" in this typical scene, they likely anticipated the injuries that would result from war if they disobeyed; or accounts like Villagra's could have been the "Spanish interpretation of Indian traditions and practices of hospitality—or even forms of entrapment."[94]

Spanish colonial law gave conquering Spaniards the right to exact tribute from local Natives. Yet, in an environment of scarce resources, the demand for tribute in foodstuffs, clothing, and wood often proved debilitating for subject Pueblos. The consequence of the policy calls to mind the iconic episode at Acoma Pueblo, sixty-five miles west of the Río Grande River, eight months after Oñate secured the region.[95]

Passing by Acoma with his squad of horsemen, Oñate's nephew, Captain Juan de Zaldívar, tried confiscating more cornmeal, fuel, and water for his soldiers than what Acomas could afford. Acomans killed him, two captains, eight soldiers, and two servants, the remainder jumping off the bluffs of the sixty-four square acre high rock mesa. Oñate ordered Zaldívar's brother, Sargeant Major Vicente, to offer Acomans the opportunity to surrender peacefully—and the force they should expect if they did not. As Acomans refused to surrender, Zaldívar's men scaled the mesa, firing cannons and torching buildings. Eight hundred Acomas were killed, five hundred captured, while no Spanish died. Prisoners were marched to Oñate's headquarters where they were tried and convicted as rebels and murderers. All Acoma males over the age of twenty-five were to have one foot cut off and made servants of Spanish officers or soldiers for twenty-five years. Women, elderly men, and children aged twelve to twenty-five were sentenced to twenty-five years servitude.

Forced tribute under drought conditions, the crass undermining of Pueblo religion, and the Franciscan's taking of Pueblo land continued. Some Puebloans adopted Christianity, but most kept to their spiritual traditions, often clandestinely to avoid clerical sanctions. In general, Puebloans "passed an uneasy and sometimes resentful existence," a Native scholar describes, adding, "the unrest becoming more pronounced until they attained sufficient strength and union to warrant successful revolt."[96] The first attempts by Pueblo leaders to carry out a unified rebellion came in the 1640s. Governor Fernando de Arguello suppressed one uprising and ordered the hanging of twenty-nine Jemez Puebloans and others imprisoned for allying with Apache warriors and killing a settler-farmer. Rebels from Isleta, Alameda, San Felipe, Cochití, and Jemez were hanged. Citing treachery and sorcery, General Fernando de Villanueva also had Piro Natives hanged while torching Senecú Pueblo.

Spanish dominance intensified in the 1660s and 1670s. European diseases decreased the Pueblo population significantly. Military and church officials offered no protection from Apache raids. To head off resistance plots, laws prohibited Native gatherings in sacred kivas. Underground ceremonial chambers were destroyed. Governor Juan Francisco Treviño conducted public whippings of suspects, imprisoned forty-seven Puebloans, and hanged four medicine men. Seventy Pueblo warriors muscled their way into the governor's quarters, forcing Treviño to release prisoners.

The Pueblo Revolt exploded as Governor Antonio de Otermín and War Secretary Francisco Xavier attempted to demolish traditional beliefs. The unremitting persecution of medicine men included the San Juan leader Po'pay.[97] Po'pay proved an effective organizer. War chiefs and mestizos who had learned Spanish ways in the missions designed a secret plan, selecting the day to strike. Otermín was informed of the plot. Tesuque rebels killed a Spanish settler and targeted the local friar.

Otermín alerted alcaldes to defend churches and settler families to gather in Santa Fe for safety. Picurís rebels engaged enemies, Santa Clara warriors attacked a Spanish escort, and Jemez men looted estancias. Puebloans from Tesuque to San Juan blocked passages to Santa Clara, killing two friars, and, in Pojoaque, carried off the wife and children of a Spanish captain, slaying another captain and the families of two settlers. With the Spanish settlements around the Santa Fe capital and the Río Abajo region under siege, Otermín heard that five hundred nearby warriors from Pecos, San Cristóbal, San Lázaro, Galisteo, and La Cienega waited for reinforcements from Taos, Picurís, and allied Apaches.

After peace talks failed, twenty-five hundred rebels bore down on San Miguel Church in Santa Fe. Otermín ordered a hundred men with firearms to dislodge enemies from the villa. A wounded Otermín executed forty-seven prisoners. With the determined opposition of practically all the Puebloans and bereft of provisions and horses, the governor's council received permission to leave the Spanish jurisdiction. After a difficult journey with enemy threats, the bedraggled colony of 1,946—most of them mestizos, Native servants, and Piro Pueblos who sided with Otermín—reached La Salineta outside El Paso. An estimated 380 men, women, and child settler, as well as 21 Franciscan friars, perished in the revolt.[98]

Spain never relinquished its claim of New Mexico. "The apostasy of formerly Christian inhabitants [would] inevitably continue to be a reproach to the spiritual conscience and pious zeal of their erstwhile masters," one historian notes. Moreover, reports of silver and quicksilver in the region continued to be believed.[99] Inevitably, Puebloans needed to be punished and made an example to deter tribal disrespect of Spanish authority.[100]

Refusing to commit resources for a return to New Mexico, the Spanish government announced a pledge to award a governorship to an individuals wealthy enough to underwrite a settler expedition. The adelantado contract for designing a plan for regaining New Mexico went to Diego de Vargas Zapata y Luján Ponce de León in 1890. General de Vargas came, predictably enough, from a titled noble family with twenty years of government service in northern Mexico, including campaigns against the Apache.[101] He would take the region by force, if necessary, then return to Mexico to gather the personnel and resources to reinstall the Spanish province.[102]

The de Vargas troupe of forty soldiers, ten civilian settlers, fifty Native allies, and ten Franciscan friars crossed the Río Grande with a company of soldiers joining later. He then set out to capture one village at a time. At his approach, some Puebloans fled, others greeted him with hostility, but they presented no direct challenge to his party, mostly because of dissensions arising among the multilingual Pueblos.[103]

As he approached the Pueblo at Santa Fe, de Vargas invoked the traditional "Praise be the holy sacrament." Inside the walled community Pueblos looked well on the toma de posesión since certain Catholic rites coincided with Pueblo traditions.[104] Other Pueblo leaders pledged allegiance to the King of Spain and Jesus Christ. The Picurís governor brought animal skins as gifts and for trade. The jaunt to Pecos produced successful stops at Tesuque, Cuyamungué, Nambé, Pojoaque, Jacona, San Ildefonso, Santa Clara, and San Juan. Captain General de Vargas was well received at San Cristóbal, San Lázaro, Taos, and Picurís. Playing peacemaker between the archenemies of Taos, the Tewas, and Tanos, de Vargas took possession of their plazas, baptizing ninety-six children. Similar contact with variations occurred at Pecos, Santa Ana, Cochití, San Marcos, San Felipe, Zia, and Cerro Colorado.[105]

Three hundred resistance warriors greeted de Vargas at Jemez, but leaders wearing crosses fell on their knees, instructing rebels to lay down weapons. After the posesión ritual, de Vargas and his men were invited to sup. The routine occurred at the western Pueblo of Acoma, site of the infamous Oñate battle of 1599–1600, and at Zuñi and Moqui [Hopi]. Having peacefully restored twenty-three pueblos and ten tribal communities to King Charles II, de Vargas returned to Mexico to prepare for the reset of missions, a presidio, government, and estancias. He returned to New Mexico with 234 persons: seventy settler families (twenty-seven "full-blooded Spaniards") returning to their former haciendas; a mix of mestizos and blacks; eighteen friars, and sixty-two other families who joined on the way.

En route to Santa Fe de Vargas found some Pueblos, especially those allied with Navajo and Apache, hostile and armed. Significantly, Santa Fe turned defiant. Governor de Vargas had to plan his

FIGURE 6. Tlaxcalan acceptance of Catholicism. This is Plate 05 of El Lienzo de Tlaxcala, ca. 1515, showing the reception of Christianity by Tlascalans before Hernán Cortez, the Spanish conqueror of Mexico, without violent opposition. Courtesy Homenaje á Cristóbal Colón: Antigüedades mexicanas. México: Oficina tipográfica de la Secretaría de fomento, 1892. Fray Angelico Chavez History Library/New Mexico History Museum, Bourne 972 MEXH.

announcement of occupation. As a Spanish squadron approached to surveil the villa, warriors lined the top of the walls, shouted war whoops, yelled anti-Christian blasphemies and pelted the squadron with stones and arrows. As de Vargas rode up singing the Blessed Sacrament, he commanded the people to surrender. Chiefs said they would respond to his entreaty that evening. Pecos allies in tow, de Vargas marched to the city. Pueblos shouted they would kill all enemies except missionaries whom they would enslave. The Siege of Santa Fe was on.

One hundred ninety years later, this scene was played out in the Tertio-Millennial Exposition. A building on the promenade where a crowd gathered represented a Pueblo fortress. The de Vargas court and "Indian slave attendants" advanced to enforce the order that the tribe submit to Spanish authority, only to be welcomed by war whoops, cat calls, and arrows. Role-playing Spanish soldiers enacted the attack.[106] As Twitchell recalled in bonny remembrance, "a beautiful and realistic combat waged [on] in the presence of the assembled thousands."[107]

The actual battle in 1692 raged all night. By morning, de Vargas had vanquished. The conqueror had the royal Spanish banner fixed on a wall, a sign of victory. When the Pueblos were bid come for a pardon, only women and children complied; warriors hid. As de Vargas's boldness won over, a five-foot cross went up in the patio. The imperial leader kissed the cross on one knee and the people climbed down from rooftops. With the royal standard raised in one hand, de Vargas addressed those assembled through an interpreter. Asking for peace and gratitude, he offered pardons and requested that they return to the king's vassalage and God's church. As his soldiers stood in line with swords unsheathed, de Vargas took formal possession of the *Villa de Santa Fe.* The royal standard was raised three times, each time de Vargas crying out, "Long live our king, Carlos the Second! May God spare him! King of Spain and all this New World, and of the realm and provinces of New Mexico, and of these subjects newly won and conquered." At each recital, de Vargas's men answered, "May he live many years and rule happily!" They tossed their hats into the air and missionaries fell to their knees, thanking God. A priest intoned the Te Deum Laudamus and blessed the people with holy water to clear their heresy, followed by the "praise be to god" chorus, which many of the women and children repeated. The people were implored to "pray every morning and evening before the holy cross in the patio as the Spaniards were accustomed to doing." Most Pueblo people wore crosses and nodded in ascent to the friars' admonitions.[108]

For the Nuevomexicano intelligentsia of 1883, the account of the religious taking of Santa Fe lived in the institutional memory of the church. Moreover, the wording survived in Spanish sources, such as that of Secretary Francisco Xavier's report of Governor Otermín's recital in Isleta[109] and Carlos de Sigüenza y Góngora's history of de Vargas's first incursion into Pueblo country. Based on de Vargas's journals, Sigüenza y Góngora's account was published in *El Mercurio Volante* (The Flying Mercury), a precursor to newspapers that imperial authorities had disseminated as a "newssheet" or gazette for journalistic purposes in New and old Spain.[110] We know that in 1839 there existed a partial draft of the history of the conquest of New Mexico in the governmental office of the province, which likely drew from these sources, after the governor at the time, Juan Bautista Vigil requested that Carlos Maria Bustamante undertake to write the history of Mexico as well.[111]

The memory of de Vargas's Santa Fe toma de posesión in the Tertio-Millennial played true to legend. Before a crowd of tourists and locals,

> the Indians, all kneeling and with right hands raised, took the oath of allegiance to the Spanish government, and swore to remain ever faithful subjects of the king, while at the same time the banner of the sacred cross was thrice waved about the heads of the assembly and planted by Major Sena. Vargas and his escort having dismounted and handed their steeds over to the care of servants, they advanced and, ever the true gentlemen, shook hands with the Indians, their all falling [*sic*] into mutual embraces.[112]

Impaling the ground with the Holy Cross, the de Vargas player blessed it as "our guide in this virgin soil in the name of the king of Spain for all time." Reflecting the moment's Castilian primacy, he asked all to "implore the divine Providence, that with it we may also plant the first seed of civilization and Christianity among this unfortunate people." True to script, de Vargas calls for "three cheers [*vivas*] for his majesty the King of Spain."[113]

Even though the actual Pueblo rebellion went on another four years before de Vargas finally won out,[114] the 1883 toma de posesión performance breathed an air of finality, the "refounding" of Santa Fe and the Nuevomexicano claim to the city. Euro-American sponsors had an economic rationale for organizing the Tertio-Millennial Exposition,[115] but in objectifying "conquest" and "founding,"[116] the practiced Nuevomexicano identity implied a statement about the priority of their presence in New Mexico.

The performativity of the Tertio-Millenial's Spanish procession and conquest represented a kind of cultural claims-making as it plopped the representation of Spanish history onto Santa Fe's civic field. It is confirmed by the ethnonationalist elocutions Nuevomexicanos voiced afterward. As Chief Marshal Sena proclaimed in his remarks to the audience, "It is now 333 years since our ancestors, the conquerors of this country, came here. They came here as you see them represented by their descendants here assembled." In this "transference," as Slavoj Žižek would call it, Sena set the illusion that the meaning of the Spanish conquest was from the "very beginning its immanent essence," which the Nuevomexicano people made present.[117] In his critical nostalgia, Sena emphasized how "our race has been the most daring race and has accomplished, decidedly, the most remarkable victories and discoveries that are yet known." In that sacralized moment, the audience heard "Great and glorious was the day for our dear mother country, Spain, when her banner and the standard of her religion (the holy cross) was planted upon this unknown world, but greater still for us, the happy sons of these Christian heroes. Spain naturally deserves the esteem and respect of every civilized nation of the world."[118]

In representing his ancestral conquest, Sena cued up Creole nationalism. "In the year 1810," he extolled in the script of "Oppressive Iberia,"

> our brothers, the citizens of Mexico, tired of suffering the cruelty of the Spanish rulers, proclaimed the war of Mexican independence. On this occasion the [Creole] Spaniards of Mexico, our brothers, inspired by the courage imbued in them as an inheritance, came

> forward, and as men of resolution headed by such heroes as Morelos, Cura Hidalgo and a number of other patriots, made themselves an independent nation.[119]

It was clearly in the interest of Sena's movement to hold the boundaries with Euro-American colonialism firm. He thus denied what "prejudiced persons" claimed, that his people were conquered: "Any man that has read the Treaty of Guadalupe Hidalgo will understand that it is a false assertion." The strengthening of ties to the United States disproved any notion of conquest of the now-revered homeland. In what was turning into the script of Civil War Heroics, the taking up of arms signifying loyalty, not subservience, to the American government. In a measure of impact, Sena's "stirring" Spanish-language chords were "listened to with marked attention by the large native [Nuevomexicano] population present and were cordially cheered."[120]

"Mexican" *Presente*

For all the Spanish sparkles, "Mexican" and things Mexico had their spots in the exposition. Governor Sheldon nodded "in gratitude towards and applause of the men who made the United States and Mexico republics," the "flag of the free" being "universal." Parroting Prince, Sheldon recommended that "American" and "Mexican" not be used "to denote division in sentiment and feeling. All are Americans in their devotion to the government and institutions of the nation." Nor for Sheldon's liberal taste did "Mexican" and "American" contradict mutual assimilation. "Intercourse and inter-communication" were "freer and more friendly," he avowed, "as each is learning the other's language and characteristics." Religious differences did not lead to "conflicts or ill feeling." Moreover, to be Mexican was to be white: "The facility and rapidity with which Caucasian elements fuse in America proves the great value of her institutions, and that such results are unknown in European countries must be attributed to the influence of governments not controlled by the popular voice."[121]

Accentuating the close connection in commercial relations and the growth of railroad facilities, *NM Review* editor Greene remarked on the people of "old Mexico and a large portion of our population [having] a common ancestry, common blood and kindred, and a common faith. The geographical division is an imaginary one," the governor set forth, and the inhabitants of the borders of the two countries have the same social customs and language." Yet a Creole distinction was implied: "A large portion of our citizens, those of Mexican and Spanish descent . . . bring . . . vividly before them the past glories of their race and the prowess of the men from whose loins they sprang." Sidelining New Mexicanism, Greene averred that there were "no better citizens or more law-abiding people than the inhabitants of the territory who are of Mexican descent."[122]

Nevertheless, a dissonance around lo mexicano troubled the Tertio-Millennial's harmony. Responding to an invitation to bring a crack Indian-fighting militia from Doña Ana County on the Mexican border to the Tertio-Millennial, Major Albert Fountain informed Greene that the men were reluctant to attend in uniform for they had been "abused, misconstrued, and stigmatized as the Greaser militia." Fountain regretted this prejudice splattering his Mexican men. As for the unit, the so-named Mesilla Scouts, Fountain called it "a typical Mexican company," the soldiers retaining "the same methods of drill etc. that their ancestors used two or three centuries ago." Their exercises would "be very interesting not only to strangers from the east but to military men in this territory who might get a valuable point or two about Indian fighting tactics." Fountain guided his soldiers so that they and the Doña Ana County Rangers marched in the opening procession ahead of the Laguna [Pueblo] Rifles and behind the US Infantry Regulars.[123]

Former Delegate to Congress Tranquilino Luna—remembered for his influential message during his race for delegate to Congress in 1880 in which he decried Native depredations and cited his family's historical primacy on New Mexico soil—was the Historical Society's vice president. Luna elegantly credited visitors from parts of the "great Republic" for their interest in "something nobler than the amassing of riches and the treasures of art, something on which the welfare of our great Union depends far more than upon the stoutness of our ironclads or the number of troops in the regular army." It was no less than "the love and patriotism of the people." Luna recalled the invitations to the Exposition going out, when "this love and patriotism flashed forth like an electric spark from the banks of the St. Lawrence to the Palmetto groves of the Gulf." Santa Fe was "but the capital

FIGURE 7. Major Albert J. Fountain and staff of militia, 1883. Left to right (standing): Lt. Albert Fountain, Lt. Pedro Pedragón, Lt. Maclovio Botello; (seated): Capt. Eugene Van Pattern, Maj. Albert J. Fountain, Capt. Francisco Salazar. William A. Keleher Pictorial Collection, Center for Southwest Research, University Libraries, University of New Mexico.

of the youngest Territory not yet grown old in political life, yet the first to celebrate the third century of our existence as a Christian Commonwealth." Its people were said to be "old in years but young in worldly progress." Without the "concurrence" of the people before him, New Mexico could "never develop into the grand, glorious State that nature has destined it to be."[124]

Luna then latched onto the irony of this condition. A visitor from the "centers of high culture" could well ask "how is it that a country boasting of having within its boundaries the oldest settlement in the United States is still so far behind other parts of the country with regard to its commerce, industries, arts, etc., as to be called 'the seat of the antipodes of civilization?" a phrase Governor Sheldon used to signal the cause of New Mexico's isolation. At one pole stood the "wild, untutored savage," Sheldon suggested, next to the "peaceable, somewhat industrious, uneducated and unskilled Pueblo"; at the other are the "representatives of every branch of the Caucasian family who are enterprising, courageous, educated and skilled in the trade, mechanics, science and in the theory and practice of free government."[125]

Luna understood Sheldon to place his fellow "Mexicans" right next to the Natives because they had "no civilization at all, that we are barbarians." Yet, he noted, visitors did not think themselves "surrounded by barbarians." Nevertheless, Luna had to admit, his people were "far from the summit of civilization." What "strange cause" could account for "our infancy in commerce, literature, arts, science, wealth, and prosperity, while we were already old when the Pilgrim Fathers landed at Plymouth, when the Half Moon ascended the Hudson, when [William] Penn brought brotherly love to the Delaware?"

In his modern sociology, Luna challenged the "rank, inveterate prejudice" (in New Mexicanism) that appealed "so often to the difference in race and religion to explain the differences in outward progress." In his analogy, the "supremacy of enlightenment, wealth and power" was never shared equally among all the nations of Europe, which once looked to Paris for "the spring of its motion and the principle of its life." Monarchs and princes "trembled, as it were, at what was being machinated in the Cabinet of Napoleon III and his ministers." London at the dawn of the century was "striding over Europe," striking down the colossus Napoleon at Waterloo. Where were the "mighty Republics of Venice and Genoa, once the terror of all Christendom?" Other civilizations of a single race were "scattering in a fierce struggle for supremacy, [each] nation settling in a new center of civilization." Race and religion were for none "a hindrance to grandeur and prosperity." Was it not time, Luna prompted, "to have done with prejudice and national antipathy, and to ask for a more reasonable and satisfactory answer to the question: why is New Mexico so backward in the high road of progress?"

Luna placed the Nuevomexicano nation, which he had no problem calling a Mexican regional nation, in an international-historical scheme. As he noted, outward circumstances delayed the route to civilizational brilliance in those diminished European nations. Geography was destiny. Compared to "easy circumstances with neighboring States or counties, salubrious climate, fertility of soil, friendly neighborhood"—all necessary for the success of new settlements—Santa Fe and New Mexico were unfortunate. Launching what would stand as the important script of Grueling Nuevomexicano Isolation, he noted as to how "Far from having easy communication with the civilized world, we were literally cut off from it; we were like the shipwrecked sailors thrown on a rock in the midst of the angry ocean, and this for the space of three hundred years." To the east, the nearest "ending post" was "some village on the banks of the Mississippi, with one thousand miles of desert land between us."

Faultless poblador vecinos—30,000 to 130,000 of them, according to Luna—were "scattered over an area of 121,000 square miles and struggling, most of us, for the necessities of life." Going to his favorite Indian Scourge script, the "siege" Nuevomexicanos suffered "on all sides by hostile tribes of Indians, whose methods of living were pillage and depredation," deprived the folk "of even the most necessary and common means of tilling our farms, of improving our stock, of educating our children, and above all, of deriving any benefit from the most precious and productive of our resources—our mines." Setting roots in a danger-filled landscape, "destitute of almost every means of self-defense and self-protection,

> was it even a wonder that we did not progress as other States and countries placed under circumstances a thousand times more favorable, or rather less despairing? We had just as well expected to see thriving

> cities and flourishing colonies among the victims of despotism in some province of dreary Siberia, or amid the lost explorers of the bleak Arctic Pole.

Notice the reports of officials on conditions in Spanish colonial New Mexico emphasizing the "disordered" social life on the frontier. An elite merchant class undermined the ability to develop a sound economy by keeping laborers subordinated as exploited peons; by preventing lower-class farmers from building assets out of their products, which they effected by excluding them from trade fairs to preserve their own trade monopoly; and by either refusing or not having the means to invest in advanced farming implements. Farmers dispersed their homes around far-flung fields rather than congregate to form asset-building villages.[126] Native troubles factored in, but Luna positioned himself to withhold blaming his "faultless" people. The resource patronage he appealed for would not, after all, pair up well if he overplayed the poverty of his poblador ancestors. As a result, he concluded with the wonder "under such outward circumstances . . . that there was in our forefather's energy and enough domestic economy not to become extinct."

Next from Luna's mouth came the American Saving Grace script. The "long night" of struggle passed, he hurrahed, "and the sun of enlightenment began to warm and infuse a new life into this land of brilliant prospects and expectations the realization of which is greatly dependent on you, noble friends from the East." Nothing was impossible in "Yankee land." In Luna's elegant casting of Anglo ambition, the "American genius" turned "paper into cartwheels and kitchen stores"; replaced the telegraph with the telephone using "a silk thread and a piece of an old tin can"; drove through "the bowels of mountains or over lakes and seas in palaces that defy the most sumptuous kingly residences"; and had "only to discover a faint trace of congenial elements in order to set to work and change a rock into an enrapturing garden as we see at the Las Vegas Hot Springs where but five years ago we only beheld some stray goat and some lonely woodcutter or a washer-woman."

Luna hoped that the Tertio-Millennial Exposition would fulfill its economic purpose of taking New Mexico out of its rut of sad, desolate, pre-modern isolation. In contrast to Diego Archuleta's fear of "damned Yankees," he welcomed Euro-American colonizers. "Come, then, friends from the East," he invited, "bring your capital, and exhume the wealth of the world. It is here, buried in the depths of our 'Sierras;' it will be yours, and it will be ours; for such immense treasures cannot come to the surface without starting up for us new towns, new railroads, new thoroughfares." New Mexico yearned for the touch of American genius to develop pastures for large-scale cattle and stock raising, wool for manufacture and export, farming and gardening to make arable land "as excellent as any state east of the Mississippi." Systems of irrigation and artesian wells existed for "windmills, and other hydraulic contrivances, that may refresh the thirsty plains and restore to them the luxuriant vegetation of a former period when the marauding Native could find concealment in our fields of hay or set them on fire and close his enemy in a circle of devouring flames." A well-organized militia had rid New Mexico of its "disorderly element," the restless Apache, now under control in reservations. The "intelligent, honest, energetic American patriots" coming from every state and territory for permanent settlement in a "patriotic land" offered the key to Nuevomexicano advancement.

Luna recalled the slandering of the "Mexicans" in New Mexico, as in the *New York Magazine* article that called them "aliens," not in sympathy with the government, ideas, and manners of the United States, "ready to 'return to our old allegiance [Mexico] if the chance for so doing was offered us.'" Mexicans laughed and scoffed at such "absurd, preposterous insinuations," Luna assured. "But if our fathers could rise from their graves, they would not laugh."

After obligatory proofs of Nuevomexicano allegiance to the United States, Luna concluded with an imagined blend of Mexicans and Americans. The "average Mexican" may not have been possessed with the "same amount of labor consciousness and activity shown by eastern countrymen," yet, in a script already in circulation,

> of kindness, generosity, disinterestedness, forbearance, fidelity, love of liberty and fealty to Government, the Mexican will yield the palm to no man or nation under the sun . . . What I assert, friends from all parts of the country, you will find, through self-experience to be founded upon stern fact and truth.

Thus were Luna's people "especially worthy of . . . sympathy and friendship. And bound together by the sacred ties of brotherly love, liberty and patriotism, the man of the East and the man of the Southwest will labor in an unbroken, successful harmony for the greatness and happiness of their common country."[127]

Indigenous Voices

Euro-American discourse habitually dismissed Native Americans. Sheldon, for example, sustained the myth of Natives having no history, there being no "Indian epoch." "Awkward" tribal implements, dances, and games "are sufficient to gain some idea of the habits and customs in vogue before Columbus discovered America," the governor adduced. "When and where the red man first made his appearance on this continent is not demonstrable from history, tradition or legend." After three centuries of relations with "white men," peaceful Pueblos were "non-progressive, non-assimilating, and indigestible." The Native, moreover, "whether savage or Pueblo," seemed "not to be fusible with any other race. The [P]ueblo is harmless, except as an inert substance in the social and material realms." As such, "disappearance is his destiny in the early future."[128]

After the Civil War, the myth of the "Vanishing Indian" that Sheldon promoted inhabited America's public discourses, greatly promoted by anthropologists who effectively advertised their views of evolutionary inevitability.[129] So did its natural correlate of cultural stagnation. As the *NM Review* followed up, Natives existed "with the same costumes, the same modes of life, and following the same occupations as when first discovered." It was "a curious fact that civilization has acted differently upon the Indians than upon any other race. It has compelled them to respect authority, but it has had little or no leavening influence upon their social life or their manners and customs." The occupation of Santa Fe and other cities by Mexicans, Americans, and Europeans had driven them to outlying sites "where they preserve in all of its crudity their aboriginal mode of living."[130]

It is interesting, considering such attitudes, that two Indigenous representatives were invited to address an Exposition audience. One was the Zuñi Pueblo chief Palowahtiwa (Ba:lawahdiwa).[131] Frank Cushing, at the time pioneering anthropological research on the

Zuñi,[132] translated Palowahtiwa's remarks, the chief correcting Cushing at points.[133] Clearly aware of the essentialist stereotypes circulating about Natives, Palowahtiwa in his remarks assured the audience that his people had a history. Focusing on epistemic differences in collecting knowledge, Palowahtiwa described the white man as one who uses "marks with meaning" that "preserved the words of his fathers," while Zuñi tongues served as "writing sticks." The "ears and hearts of his listeners" were their books. "Therefore, I speak straightly," he declared, "when I say that no less than the white men, our older brothers, do we, their younger brothers, the dark men of earth, know the tales of times ancient."[134]

Palowahtiwa shared the memory of how his people heard of the coming of the bearded men from "our fathers whose fathers told them as they themselves had heard from their old ones."[135] The first white man the "ancients" ever saw appeared lean, his clothes worn away, his hair and beard "long and tangled"—not noble in mien, but a rapacious stranger:

> Now whenever he saw any food on the hearth, he took it and reached for more; so that the caciques and priests who were old and wise, gathered the council and said to one another: "This man eats too much and demands more, therefore we must kill him." "No," said others, "why kill him because he eats too much?" "Because," it was answered. "No man ever lived who had not fathers and mothers and many relatives. If this man stays here, his people will come to seek him, and what will the A-shi-wi then do for food, for the men of a nation are alike?" When the sun rose one morning, Nu-we was gone and when the people asked, "Where is he?," it was replied to by the caciques and priest, "We have wrapped him in the magic matting of rush and he will awake in the land of everlasting summer, where it is said that others like him dwell."[136]

From the other side of imperialism, Palowahtiwa alluded to the arrival of the "Black Mexican with thick lips" whom the Zuñi killed (Estevan). And he conveyed the Zuñi perspective on Coronado (who

FIGURE 8. Three Zuni Pueblo men. Left to right: Palowatiwa, Nanahe, and Pedro Pino, ca. 1879–1880. John K. Hillers, photographer. Courtesy of the Palace of the Governors Photo Archives negative number 073898.

FIGURE 9. Pali-wah-ti-wa, Former Governor of Zuni Pueblo, ca. 1879–1880. Ben Wittick, photographer. Courtesy of the Palace of the Governors Photo Archives, negative number 016010.

had ravaged the Zuñi community of Hawikatuh) and his "strange people." Thinking he had come to avenge Estevan, the people "received him not gently, but with their poor weapons arrows and stones and clubs." Implying a defeated Coronado and a peace agreement, the chief reported, "But when he opened his sticks that thundered (so said our grandfathers), the war vanished as a rainstorm when the lightning flashes are forked and deadly; and we found them to be our brothers."[137]

Perhaps this was a response to the star status the Tertio-Millennial overlords accorded Coronado. If Palowahtiwa made no mention of the final conquest of New Mexico by de Vargas or of the Spanish colonial abuse of Puebloans, it may have reflected the distant location of the Zuñi homeland, making them less exploitable as vassals than the more accessible river Pueblos. There was also the accommodation that the Pueblos had worked out in the intervening 187 years with the Mexican and US regimes. In any case, the Zuñi chief gave a shout out to Jose D. Sena as an ally in his peoples' wars with the Navajo.

The reserved, impressively dignified Mescalero Apache Niit'a-héõde (known as San Juan) sat on stage with his son, fellow chiefs, representatives of the Spanish embassy to the United States, and Major Fountain.[138] As Niit'a-héõde emphasized, "We [Apaches] never were in peace with Spaniards and Mexicans." His people "never surrendered to the Mexicans like the Pueblos when our grandparents were young." Niit'a-héõde bitterly noted that the Spaniards and Mexicans "robbed us of our children and sold them into slavery."[139]

If quoted correctly,[140] both chiefs accepted the American terms of peace. Palowahtiwa understood the Tertio-Millennial Exposition as "a feast of my father [the president] in Washington," which suggested a reason for Pueblo participation in the Spanish enactments. Addressing his hearers, he said, "My friends and brothers, we are children of one father, are we not? And that father is Washington, the great chief of the land of daybreak (the east). Therefore, have I called you 'brothers,' and may we smile one upon the other, and be happy forever and through all days."[141]

Niit'a-héõde for his part observed, "We have lately been at war with Washington. But now we know better." His tribe had no quarrel with Americans; they were "great hunters like the Apache." The problem had been bad Americans, "just as there are bad Apache."

The bad Americans had Native slaves. "They murdered my people and sold their hair to the Mexicans in Chihuahua and Santa Fe. We could not forgive them." The Apache surrendered to Washington. "That is good," Niit'a-hé̃õde concluded. "We are friends, and we believe Washington is our friend." Unlike Nuevomexicano spokesmen who failed to admit their people's captivity practice, Niit'a-héõde had forbidden his young men to follow the war that the chiefs Victorio (killed in Mexico in 1880) and Naut-Chilli (members of the ladrón rogues who spiked violence with non-Natives), but they had run away, and the lodges emptied out. "They had bad counsel, but it was not mine," he emphasized.[142]

Niit'a-héõde's son wore the uniform of the government Indian School where he was learning to read. The chief proudly remarked that Apaches sent their children to school "so that they will be wise like their white brothers," a micro-cementation to American power. Glad that he attended the Exposition, he said his group was treated well. "We will return to our people," he said. "We will go home and tell our people for they thought we would never return. We have learned much."[143] After the talk, Nebraska Congressman James Laird commented that with "a little aid" the Apache "would in short time become self-sustaining," contradicting the claim of Native American disappearance. Niit'a-héõde "seemed gratified," the *NM Review* reported, and he promised that if the government supplied them with stock cattle, they would soon become self-sustaining, his ambition being "to have great herds and become rich like the Navajos."[144]

Even with the three-tiered ethno-racial stratification with Euro-Americans up top, Nuevomexicanos in the middle and Indigenous at the bottom,[145] Laird's intervention reflected early liberal aid to Natives that would grow to national prominence by the 1920s. "As Indian peoples throughout the West were defeated in battle and forced onto reservations," Charles Montgomery points out, "they reacquired in Anglo eyes the romantic qualities once depicted in American art and literature." To spectators, Natives undoubtedly appeared "as savages of noble, vigorous, and racially pure bearing. Other onlookers may have been gratified simply to see the Native Americans who had recently fought the US Army.[146] Niit'a-héõde proved a hit. At the conclusion of Fountain's tales of his former battles with the Apache chief, the crowd broke into "a grand rush for the platform [where

FIGURE 10. Three participants in the Tertio-Millennial Exposition. Left to right: Chief San Juan (Mescalero Apache), Margaret Olivia Collins, and Ralph E. Twitchell. Tertio-Millennial Exposition, Santa Fe, New Mexico, 1883. Courtesy of the Palace of the Governors Photo Archives, negative number 011241.

FIGURE 11. San Juan (Mescalero Apache Chief) and son, ca. 1880–1882. Ben Wittick, photographer. Courtesy of the Palace of the Governors Photo Archives, negative number 015894.

Niit'a-hé̃ode] and his accompanying warriors [stood] . . . [as well as] the little Indian lads [who] were all congratulated time and again by both ladies and gentlemen, not a few also presenting them with gifts of various kinds."[147]

The Tertio-Millennial Exposition proved a short-term success. The $30,000 expense that the City of Santa Fe covered brought national attention. While Greene seems to have exaggerated the extent of visitors as the Exposition wore on,[148] thousands of people who otherwise would not have come visited what public relations called "this wonderland."[149] For local entrepreneurs, however, the fair failed to reap the sought after investments.[150] A half-year later Prince still emphasized the need to induce capital to come build manufactures. Eastern investors continued to think of New Mexico as wild country with a small population and property going unprotected in a territorial polity.[151] At Chicago's 1897 Columbian Exposition, New Mexico Governor Miguel Antonio Otero described the same features of New Mexico topography that the Tertio-Millennial hosts promoted, hoping (beyond hope) for a revolution in business startups.[152]

In the key aspect of the Tertio-Millennial Exposition, Nuevomexicanos instinctively participated in this groundbreaking public stage. Euro-Americans arrogated Spanish legacies to reify the territory as a naturally endowed national treasure. Nuevomexicano legacy remembrance wielded the discursive armament of the Spanish procession, the Spanish-Pueblo embattlement, and la toma de posesión to promote cultural autonomy, epistemically leaving out any references to violations of the Church's laws prohibiting the exploitation of Indigenous nations to raise the fixtures of a positive Spanish identity inhibitively. In the time ahead, Euro-American and Nuevomexicano citizens, egged by the Tertio-Millennial Exposition, preoccupied themselves with creative Spanish-embroidered projects, setting the stage for another major construction of Nuevomexicano primacy, which comes next.

CHAPTER 3

The Realm of Spanish Memory and a People's History

AS PIERRE NORA has defined it for posterity, a "realm of memory" is "any significant entity, whether material or non-material in nature, which by dint of human will or the work of time has become a symbolic element of the memorial heritage of any community." The scales of such communities vary greatly. Nora's focus is on the monuments that have had meaning for France's community of memory.[1]

As the Tertio-Millennial Exposition expired, and to an extent because of it, a "Spanish" realm of memory sprouted about New Mexico's railroad society. Hobbies, public service displays, historical commemorations, and the like adorned New Mexico's civic field. While politically anodyne, this work sustained a field of Spanish identity for Nuevomexicanos. As an adjunct, Nuevomexicano identitarians in the 1890s whipped up a critical Spanish memory to counter damaging Euro-American notions of their people.

Civic Memory Work

In fetishizing Spanish imperial accoutrements for public consumption, L. Bradford Prince pieced much of New Mexico's realm of memory. In a keynote address at the Albuquerque Territorial Fair, for example, he spoke to the origins of New Mexico's agricultural industries: the Toltecs leaving home for the northwest to sow the very land on which the fair was happening with corn, cotton, and other plants; Cabeza de Vaca, the "first European whoever trod on New Mexican soil," inscribing in his diary about the products and livestock of the "natives"; Spaniards giving thanks "to Heaven" for the abundances provided by Natives; the priest Marcos de Niza's writing of the "long gowns of cotton worn by the people of Cíbola; Coronado's discovering domestic hens and great stores of beans and other foods, arable land for cultivation and "pastures full of flocks and sheep and goats."[2]

Other Euro-Americans jumped in. As late as 1907, Albuquerque's entirely Euro-American Elks Lodge organized a pageant for the Territorial Fair and Commemorative Convention with a portrayal of Coronado's "First Exploration."[3]

Euro-Americans enabled the everyday use of "Spanish" and "Spanish American" labeling. When Nuevomexicanos finally voted for a plan to establish a municipal government for Santa Fe after opposing it as "another scheme of Americans to drive the Mexican-speaking people out of town," Max Frost, editor of the *Santa Fe New Mexican*, congratulated the "young Spanish Americans" for showing their "true colors."[4] The bilingual Irish immigrant William McGuiness, editor of the *New Mexican Review* (not to be confused with the *New Mexico Review*) urged "Spanish American citizens" to patronize a new Spanish-language weekly.[5] Tired of seeing the ongoing political arguments between newspaper editors, the *Daily Optic* in Las Vegas queried, "Why, don't the Castilian brethren of the quill turn their aim to educate and advance their people?"[6] On the question of who would become New Mexico's federal marshal, Thomas Catron recommended Miguel Antonio Otero to the US attorney general, noting his special credential: "a descendent of one of the oldest Spanish families in New Mexico," which rendered him "a young man of fine attainments, good education, in every respect a gentleman."[7]

In an ethnic bilateralism, middle-class Euro-Americans and Nuevomexicanos cooperated in spiking Spanish memory, as in New Mexico's exhibit at the 1893 World's Columbian Exposition in Chicago. At the exposition, dedicated to the four hundredth anniversary of Columbus's "discovery of America," New Mexico contributed venerable scripts, as in the display of "an old and refined civilization that preceded by centuries the Anglo-American invasion" and brought by the "first conquistadors of these kingdoms. Hernán Cortez, Francisco Pizarro, Diego de Almagro, Fernando de Soto, Bilbao de Vargas, Espejo and others stepped on this land much before the English pilgrims landed their ships on Plymouth Rock."[8] Prince, New Mexico's governor at the time, named a Nuevomexicano, Albuquerque's T. C. Gutierres, one of two US Commissioners for the Columbian Exposition, also placing two Nuevomexicanos, Miguel Salazar of Las Vegas and E. V. Chávez of Socorro, on the four-person Columbian management committee.[9] Nuevomexicana/o residents of La Joya, a village in Valencia County, organized a delegation to visit the exposition, giving a "most cordial welcome to the most excellent Duke of Veragua," a direct descendant of "the immortal Columbus."[10]

A bilateral team also observed the three hundredth anniversary of Oñate's 1898 founding of New Mexico. The planning committee, made up of the Pioneers of New Mexico and the Historical Society of New Mexico, fashioned a who's who of the civic-commercial elite, including Prince, Territorial School Superintendent Amado Chaves, Supreme Court Clerk José D. Sena (son of the grand marshal of the Tertio-Millennial Exposition who died in 1892), *Santa Fe New Mexican* editor Max Frost, the merchant Samuel Eldodt, and Venceslao Jaramillo, a wealthy Rio Arriba County rancher businessman and assistant to Governor Miguel Antonio Otero. Predictably, the joint committee elected Prince tricentennial chair and Sena its secretary.

An impressive crew of planners and managers popularized Spanish identity far and wide. Four of the thirteen on the publicity and transportation committee were Nuevomexicanos, including Félix Martínez, owner of *La Voz del Pueblo* in the northern town of Las Vegas, and Pinito Pino, editor of *La Verdad* in the far southern town of Las Cruces. Of the twenty-six individuals on the Committee on Local Arrangements, seventeen were Nuevomexicanos. Each of New Mexico's eighteen counties had its tricentennial committee. Of the seventy-two appointees, thirty were locally prominent Nuevomexicanos. The network trafficked a Spanish imaginary across the territorial realm.[11] Its publicity hyped a multicultural, must-see parade, a commemoration "worth a trip across the continent, for few opportunities are now offered to witness the noble red man in his primitive state, and fewer yet are the scenes tending to typify and perpetuate the advent of the white man and march of progress into the trackless wilderness."[12]

The "great affair" opened at the confluence of the Chama and Rio Grande Rivers where Oñate established San Gabriel as his provincial capital. Attendees arrived at the grounds next to San Juan Pueblo (Ohkay Owingeh), forty miles north of Santa Fe, by wagon, horse, on foot, and on the Denver and Rio Grande daily special to the Chamita station, taken from there by carriage.[13]

The press billed the event as the most magnificent ever seen in New Mexico, quite the boast as the memory of Tertio-Millennial pageantry fifteen years earlier faded. An estimated thirty-five hundred persons witnessed brilliantly costumed Puebloans standing in long welcoming lines. A Pueblo honor guard escorted the governor's representative, Territorial Secretary George Wallace, to center stage. Master of Ceremonies Eldodt led the march to the ruins where Prince announced was the exact spot where Oñate founded the first European "city" three hundred years ago. After Wallace's welcoming ceremony, José María Chávez spoke on behalf of his aged father who had served in public office under three national flags.

The ever-ready Prince iterated the script of Conquistador Founders, even honoring lesser explorers such as Francisco Barrionuevo (1541) and Gaspar Castaño de Sosa (1591). Checking off the names of thirty-one of Oñate's companions, Prince dutifully noted that their descendants resided in the vicinity, blessing what had already become a permanent Nuevomexicano memory site. Former Delegate to Congress Anthony Joseph and territorial legislators Mariano Larragoite, Antonio de Vargas, and Sixto Chávez served historical bits of "patriotic fervor."

The (unnamed) governor of the host Pueblo community led the mile-long parade, followed by Secretary Wallace bearing a large American flag. Replicating the Tertio-Millennial, a cast of actors reenacted Pueblo resistance to Spanish conquest for a crowd standing on rooftops. A band of Natives performed the "dramatic dance" of the Matachines. "Gorgeous costumes," silver ornaments, and performance masks exhausted the "Kodak supplies of nearly all the picture-taking visitors." Nuevomexicano couples danced "*los bailes Franceses*," waltzes and *villancicos* presumably, in which, according to the reporter, "brilliancy of costume and grace of movement harmonized in the production of a most beautiful spectacle."[14]

In another memory project, Nuevomexicanos and Euro-Americans went on a monuments craze. It accorded with the times. In the nation-building nineteenth century, public monuments were "the foci for collective participation in the politics and public life of villages, towns [and] cities."[15] Monuments of various sorts served as important sites for representing political standpoints and promoting civic identities. When Congress appropriated $75,000 for the restoration of New Mexico's territorial capitol, *El Independiente* editor Enrique Salazar saluted the return of the building's former "splendor and beauty." Interpreting the reconstruction as a monument to honor his people, Salazar marveled at its permanence across three centuries, beginning with the privileges and rights conferred by the conquerors from Spain, confirmed by the Mexican government, and continued by the American republic when it annexed "this country."[16]

The Daughters of the American Revolution inadvertently kicked off a campaign to erect statues of New Mexico's heroes with its dedication of a stone figure in memory of Albino Pérez, the New Mexico departmental governor who was assassinated in 1837 by rebels for enforcing the central government's stringent departmental policies.[17] It inspired Enrique Salazar to contemplate tributes to Coronado, Espejo, Oñate, and Cabeza de Vaca.

In general, heroes on pedestals encouraged admirers to behold someone of their own people's character.[18] Salazar knew historians were disputing the claim of Cabeza de Vaca's "discovering" New Mexico yet was satisfied with a tribute to the hardy wanderer as one of the first Europeans to pass through the "soil of the neo-mexicanos" for he had journeyed not in a balloon but on foot, traversing the "American continent" for three years. More centrally, the people should never forget the famed re-conqueror of New Mexico, don Diego de Vargas. In the script of the Indian Scourge, he stressed how de Vargas recovered the Nuevomexicano land. Paying for the expedition out of his own pocket showed the "merits of this conquistador."[19]

The Society of First Settlers of New Mexico, *Sociedad de los Primeros Pobladores de Nuevo México*, solicited donations for Oñate and de Vargas statues on the Santa Fe Plaza, for they were the true "founders and conquerors of New Mexico." The rising Valencia County Republican politico Solomon Luna served as president of the Pioneers, banker Joshua S. Raynolds as vice president, and Prince as secretary. Other Nuevomexicanos included Amado Chaves and José D. Sena, Jr.[20]

In recycling the Conquistador Founders script, Salazar insisted on recognizing that it was Oñate and de Vargas who were the real founders of the province and therefore of the Nuevomexicano people. In New Mexico's *historia primitiva* (early history), there were no others "who occupied a more distinguished place." Salazar dedicated his journalistic skill to spotlighting Oñate as the source of Nuevomexicano autochthony, the first to conquer and establish colonization, while de Vargas recouped New Mexico in 1692 after the Pueblo Revolt. They, then, were the *padres primitivos*, forefathers of the *neo-mexicana patria*. As the territory owed its existence to their exploits, monuments to them were worthy of the support from the "entire neo-mexicano people," especially those who descended from the first settlers.[21]

Rather intrusively, Prince announced that all New Mexicans should feel proud to do their part in the "patriotic work" of donating in tribute to the "two great men connected with the early history of New Mexico." Back East, he reminded, people regularly contributed to monuments. "We certainly should not neglect the heroes of our own territory."[22] No statue came of the effort, apparently for lack of funds. Yet in the longer trajectory of Spanish identity, the impulse to monumentalize New Mexico's conquistadors would have its day.

As president of the New Mexico Historical Society, Prince alerted the membership to the immense amounts of the rarest and most valuable New Mexico relics being scooped up by outside public and private institutions. As he nudged, "one would think that the descendants of the Spanish conquerors would be eager to preserve everything connected with the prowess and gallantry of their ancestors."[23] Among the Nuevomexicano clerisy, Benjamín Read went about acquiring old Spanish and Mexican documents from public and private sources.[24] Eusebio Chacón—son of a Civil War hero, a "respected attorney and orator with literary aspirations"—collected remnants from people's homes,[25] as did Amado Chaves, the first of the territory's superintendents of public instruction.[26]

With great fanfare, Chaves and Aurelio M. Espinosa, a folklorist and graduate student at the University of Chicago, announced their resurrection of a source manuscript. The value of the equestrian play *Los Comanches*, depicting a 1774 battle between Comanches and Spanish troops in New Mexico, lay in the fact that its author was an actual participant in it. Spanish forces won the decisive encounter with the Numunuh Comanches. Chaves and Espinosa excited community interest in conquistador lore. As one researcher emphasizes, the theme in the play's outdoors performance on horseback is "unquestionably Spanish. In the name of the king of Spain and the Virgin Mary, the proud Spaniard vanquishes the heathen foe. . . . The Spaniard's patriotic and religious motives for battle are reported frequently [in the play], putting Spanish pride, patriotism, and religious zeal much in evidence."[27]

Spanish-language weeklies published scenes from the play.[28] *El Labrador* in Las Cruces called for the play to be taught in grammar and high schools to enhance its patriotic tribute to Nuevomexicano history.[29] Also enhancing circulation, the Historical Society published Chaves's account of the battle.[30] Both Chaves and Espinosa earned local fame, the former for conserving valuable manuscripts and building a repository "of folk knowledge and tradition,"[31] the latter as a budding scholar who wrote on the Comanches and edited the script of the play.[32]

With the evident growth in Spanish memory, politicians and public officials saw the advantage of emphasizing their Spanish credentials. The ancestors of candidate for delegate to Congress, Pedro Perea, were said to have come "from Spain to New Mexico with Diego de Vargas in 1693."[33] In congratulating Manuel C. de Baca for being named the territorial superintendent of public instruction, *El Independiente* emphasized that he was "descended in a direct line from the famous explorer and traveler of the sixteenth century who visited New Mexico and Arizona before any other white man and had made knowledgeable these *remotos países* (remote places) to the "civilized world." Regurgitating the common error, "the discovery and eventual conquest of New Mexico by the Spanish" was laid at the foot of Álvar Nuñez Cabeza de Baca.[34]

When Román Liberato Baca, who rode in the Spanish quatrain of the Territorial-Millennial Exposition, ran for the territorial house of representatives, he mentioned that his father and mother were "both natives of [Valencia] County and descended from families that counted among the first colonizers of central New Mexico in the seventeenth century."[35] Doña Ana County probate clerk candidate Isidoro Armijo was a reputed descendant of an "old and respectable Spanish family," his ancestors having come to New Mexico "hundreds of years before."[36] Doña Julianita Gutiérrez, the mother of Frank Hubbell, president of the Central Republican Committee of New Mexico and superintendent of the Bernalillo County Schools, prided in her descent "in a direct line from the first Spanish conquistadors."[37]

A History of One's Own

Amid the construction of a civic memory realm, a critical identitarian perspective burned. *La Voz del Pueblo,* for instance, accused Nuevomexicano politicians of betraying Spanish principles, their claiming to be descendants of Cortez, "the intrepid conquistador, but [who] sit on their Word, and mock their promises to the people, and, to top off their cup of ignominy, *voltean la espalda a su firma y rúbrica,* turn their backs on their signature and family title, which at all times has been the most sacred among men." Editor Ezequiel C. de Baca, the most likely author of those words, offered a reminder in the Spanish Discovery code: "Since the origins of our mother, Spain, the highest point of honor, from the poorest to most potent, was, and has been *la palabra del varón,* a man's Word."[38]

More pointedly, *La Voz del Pueblo* defended the Colorado State Senator Casimiro Barela, a Nuevomexicano by origin, against the false charge of a Euro-American that Barela sought to "create a base and cowardly aversion in the breast of the Anglo-Americans against their fellow citizens and neighbors of Spanish origin."[39] In another case, Enrique Salazar at *El Independiente* reacted strenuously to the idea circulating among Euro-Americans of moving New Mexico's capital to Albuquerque. Keeping it in Santa Fe, he argued, was "a guarantee of the protection of the rights of our fellow citizens of *la raza Española* who constituted four fifths of the territorial population."[40]

In the most grievous expression of resistance, an intellectual ethnonationalist sentiment arose among Nuevomexicano writers aggravated by how their people were depicted in Euro-American histories of New Mexico. As Anthony Smith discusses, "discovery and uses of a common history constitute one of the fundamental goals of the nationalist ideal."[41] Intelligentsias turned to history "for self-understanding and anchorage in a disturbing world." In their historicism, tradition was the cause of truth.[42] "Crucial events and personages in the history of the ethnic community," Smith observes, "are invested with sacred significance."[43]

The Nuevomexicano intelligentsia saw Euro-American authors hijacking their right to compose their own people's story. They never cottoned to the notion of "the People of New Mexico, Three-fold in origin and language," which Prince mounted in his *Recent Sketches of New Mexico.*[44] Nuevomexicano writers sensed distortions of their people's character in a host Euro-American authored works. Territorial Secretary William Ritch published *Illustrated New Mexico: Historical and Industrial* in 1885. The adventurist and Bandelier tagalong Hubert Howe Bancroft came out with *History of Arizona and New Mexico, 1530–1888* in 1889. Helen E. Haines, the nineteen-year-old visitor from New York, self-published *History of New Mexico from the Spanish Conquest to the Present Time, 1530–1890* (1891). In a quartet, the amateur historian and would-be anthropologist Charles F. Lummis contributed accounts of his lived experiences in Nuevomexicano villages: *A New Mexico David, and Other Stories* (1891), *Sketches of the Southwest* (1891, and *The Land of Poco Tiempo* (1893). His *The Spanish Pioneers* (1893) rendered Spanish exploration, replete with Conquistador Precedent scripts, to educate the "Anglo-Saxons" of America.

The dominance this bibliography constituted what Smith would have called "alien rule."[45] A movement to gift the Nuevomexicano people with their own history would reflect a struggle for the cultural rights of a regional nation.[46] The time had come for a monographic discourse, autogenerated to dispel Euro-American biases. As Gabriel Meléndez notes, "This generation [of Nuevomexicano writers] called for the publication of nativo history to correct misrepresentations propagated by writers from outside that community. That history, they argued, should stand against Anglo American ideations of the region."[47]

Enrique Salazar, recalled as editor of *El Independiente,* iterated the call for a "true and exact" presentation of the people's legacy, Nuevomexicano-directed. What passed for "our history," he rued, were simple copies of "primitive" texts by writers with a notable lack of information, "hardly deserving the name of history or a chronicle." Leaving the writing to persons "recently identified with the territory to pretend to monopolize the whole historical ground that corresponds to the Hispano-Americano race [would] entirely ignore the important deeds that preceded their own arrival."[48] Indeed, as one historian notes, "All the versions of Territorial history published between 1848 and 1895 were written for a Protestant public, and while the best of them do not malign the people of New Mexico, they say nothing very good about them either."[49]

As a rule, according to Smith, the ideals and values carved out of "their" histories are meant to inspire "creative action and group solidarity." Ethnohistory represents "an amalgam of selective historical truth and idealization, with varying degrees of documented fact and political myth, stressing elements of romance, heroism and the unique, to present a stirring and emotionally intimate portrait of the community's history, constructed by, and seen from the standpoint of successive generations of community members."[50]

Salazar accordingly called for a "truthful" history written by persons qualified by instructional training to avoid "errors and lies." He did not, however, mean a disinterested scholar. The job would be of little value unless written by a "legitimate son of the soil, filled with the zeal and [ethnic] patriotism essential to the enterprise." Presenting the history of one's people honored ancestors. Recounting events as they happened did justice to those who had figured in "our annals under the three different governments that have had us under their tutelage." Moreover, "To treat each epoch as it deserves to be regarded is what our history demands." The loss of an appropriate history was the disappearance of Nuevomexicanos as "a people," its educational neglect consigning the great feats and accomplishments of their ancestors "to oblivion and darkness."[51]

Salazar proffered guidelines for a proper history. A strict focus on conquistador founding was not the only way to stress Spanish belonging, he pointed out. The proper memory lens for *el pueblo* was the (familiar) Destitute Isolation script; not a sentimental pastoralism, but an existential struggle for life against the primal forces of nature, the precarity of a founding community suffering for the sake staking its soul into the soil.[52] With the uncovering of the right evidence, Salazar emphasized, the story would emerge of "our ancestors, the obstacles they overcame, and the dangers that, with great perseverance and firmness, had dogged them through three centuries."[53]

Salazar identified Anglo-American pioneers—the Pikes, the Fremonts, and the other explorers—whose journeys and explorations were magnified "by the voice of fame but who really played a children's game compared to the actions of the Spanish vecinos more than two hundred years before." The Indian Scourge script continued to operate primally in Nuevomexicano memory, comprising both long-ago and recent remembrances. Salazar's pobladores lived "isolated and withdrawn from general humanity and having to depend on themselves for their own governing, sustaining and maintaining themselves against the repeated aggressions and attacks of numerous barbarians." Revealing this travesty would show the constancy and fearlessness "of *los hombres de raza Española* in the days before the railroads when practically the whole continent went unpopulated, when they survived so long a time in a sterile and uncultured country, encircled by enemies, across a distance of two thousand miles to the nearest civilized outpost."[54]

The very esteemed Eusebio Chacón responded to the felt need for a Nuevomexicano history. Chacón represented the kind of scholar Salazar longed for, academically trained in the fine public schools of Trinidad, Colorado, at the Jesuit college in Las Vegas, New Mexico, and at Notre Dame University,[55] yet committed to the Nuevomexicano nation. Born in Peñasco, New Mexico, his sterling Spanish pedigree included a maternal line descended from Diego de Vargas's lieutenant governor, Juan Páez Hurtado de Mendoza. Eusebio's paternal great grandfather, José María Chacón, served as a colonial governor and provincial captain general. His grandfather, Albino Chacón served as a judge and member of the departmental assembly in the Mexican period. Prestige accrued through his father, Rafael Chacón, a decorated officer in the Civil War.[56] As a college student, he published essays on literature, philosophy, and history in the school magazine. The worldly Chacón taught English in Mexico and served as vice director at the Colegio Guadalupano in the city of Durango. He eventually settled in Las Vegas, NM to practice law.[57]

The thirty-two-year-old Chacón kicked off his literary career with two novellas. His commitment to Nuevomexicano nationhood appeared in his commitment to their *literatura nacional*, what Francisco Lomelí calls a "regional body of literature" based on an "autonomous cultural movement." Indeed, Chacón called his fiction his "own genuine creation . . . not stolen nor borrowed from *gabachos* [slang for Anglos] or foreigners." As he avowed, "I dare lay the foundations or the seed of an entertaining literature on New Mexican soil." Believing that "his people possessed the necessary intellectual capacity to undertake such a liberating plan to assert their sociocultural prominence in the region," he foresaw the creation "of a literature to parallel Mexico's post-Romantic literary expression at the end of the nineteenth century."[58]

While producing fiction, poetry, and prose essays, Chacón collected historical documents. On the need of a Nuevomexicano history, he "passionately" believed "that documenting and codifying was key to renewing a sense of confidence in his fellow Nuevomexicanos."[59] It meant charting a map on "the social ascendancy of his people"[60] to effect "positive change for Nuevomexicanos, at a time when their culture was under attack or when their loyalty was questioned."[61]

Chacón's "The Discovery and Conquest of New Mexico by the Spanish in 1540: Treatises on the History of the Homeland" comprised nine short installments coming out from January to July 1896 in *Las Dos Repúblicas*, a Denver journal edited by José Escobar. Chacón believed that the legend of Indigenous shock-and-awe began with meeting Spaniards, Columbus first: the "astonishment" of the Native American at "the sight of this white man so full of gentleness," his meeting them "with the greatest of pleasure, prepared with his sweet words [to have the] virgin land so that later the sublime laborers of the evangelical vineyard could come there to sow the poetic doctrines of Jesus Christ." More directly linked to New Mexico after Hernán Cortez conquered Tenochtitlán, "so much had already been said about the splendors of the North that very cowardly would have been the Spaniard who wouldn't have risked his life in that conquest, which according to popular opinion of the time, promised to eclipse those of the intrepid Cortez," and "the bloodthirsty [Francisco] Pizarro" (conqueror of Peru and the Incas).[62]

A stack of romanticism: yet, as Lomelí has noted, Chacón had a "social realist" side "driven by historical pragmatism" and the work of established historians.[63] Indeed, Chacón feared not to tread into critical assessments of Spanish explorations as in the example of Adolph Bandelier who wrote that Spanish adventurers in America were "justly charged with neglecting the true interests of colonization in their excessive greed for treasure, and thereby bringing harm to those parts of the Western Continent which they entered." Their exploits presented "the saddest pictures from the point of view of morals," yet their thirst for gold "led them into adventures which excite admiration and wonder as expressions of manly energy."[64]

Belying the Tertio-Millennial Exposition's unrestrained love of Coronado, Chacón portrayed a psychologically impaired misfit, smitten by jealousy over the loss of a woman in Mexico City, transformed from "the once prudent and courtly man he had been . . . into a person of a bitter, unpredictable, and melancholy nature." Paranoid with fears of treachery and designs on his life, he hatched "strange ideas" about equipping his troops. On expedition, he attacked and violently took the village of Cíbola (the Zuñi's Hawikatuh) without reason. In a tale that is not too different from what Palowahtiwa related at the Tertio-Millennial Exposition, Natives comprehended greed as Coronado's "dominating passion," making them distrust this latest Spaniard intrusion, fed by false and misleading stories of riches at the Grand Canyon where giants roamed.[65]

Chacón shed light on Coronado's fumbled, hapless occupations of Cicuyé [Pecos] and Tiguez [Tiguex], his undisciplined soldiers accused of rape and unjust impositions of tribute, accounts of offending chiefs, shameless thefts of buffalo hides, naive belief in a guide who lied about the location of gold, fruitless searches for Quivira, expeditionaries who suffered privations and disease in harsh weather without assistance from tribesmen, and a demoralized army demanding abandonment of the campaign. Suffering a humiliating defeat in a joust with an officer, Coronado yearned for his wife. Giving up on his "golden dreams of glory," he ordered a departure to New Spain.[66]

Tragic Coronado, Chacón related, was not exemplary of a true conquistador's soul. Why would fate not prepare for him and his men "the horn of plenty beyond those deserts full of buffalo and roving barbarians? Were they not sons of the hero of [the Battle of] Covadonga [against the Umayyard Caliphate in far northern Spain, won by King Pelagius of Asturias] and brothers of the conqueror of Guatemoczín [Aztec prince who resisted Cortez]?" Chacón beheld Coronado stripped of his command "and exiled to oblivion," dying in 1554 and buried in Mexico City. Staying with the conquest convention, however, Chacón emphasized that among the new lands he had "conquered" was the territory that encompassed what came to be his New Mexico, "without," however, "entering into the ethnological details or the reasoning by which . . . commentators arrived at the proof that our land is the one conquered by Coronado."[67] For Chacón, the twisted Coronado account fulfilled a servant's duty to provide his people with their historical memory with more reality than romance.

Chacón planned to "deal" with the entrances of Espejo and Oñate. It is to wonder how, in his hope of sustaining Nuevomexicano pride and primacy, he would have treated the violent Oñate. But he never finished. Nor is it clear why, perhaps a combination of profession, engaging in social issues, and a commitment to the literary arts.[68]

The distinction of publishing the first complete Nuevomexicano people's history in Spanish goes to Francisco de Thoma.[69] Thoma, a Spanish immigrant, editor of Albuquerque's *El Mundo*, was as Doris Meyer states a "citizen historian,"[70] suggesting someone other than Salazar's trained scholar. In *Historia Popular De Nuevo México, Desde Su Descubrimiento Hasta La Actualidad* (The Popular History of New Mexico, From its Discovery to the Present), Thoma made clear his ethnonationalist intent: "to present to our people a true story, as exact as possible, of three centuries of deeds. Its principal objective: to remind the *neo-mexicanos* of the glorious achievements and painful suffering that their heroic ancestors endured [and] to arouse pride in the souls of [Nuevomexicanos] for being part of one of the most generous, noble, and valiant races of the universe—the Spanish race."[71]

Thoma filled three-fourths of his monograph with conquistador adventures.[72] He had as his key source the Spanish king's order that the "first settlers" of Nuevo México and their legitimate descendants would earn the title *hijosdalgos de solar*, sons of nobility, recognized in all of the Indies and knights of the Castilian kingdom.[73] As he thus interpreted, after the "valiant" conquerors completed their domination of New Mexico in the eighteenth century, they turned their swords in for plows, "converting themselves into the no-less brave planter of the field." Because they retained *hidalguía*, that is, the nobility of hacienda owners, as well as the conquistador virtues of chivalry, agricultural pastoralists retained "virtudes españolas no corrumpidas por estrañas mezcolanzas" (Spanish virtues uncorrupted by strange admixtures). They took pride in their "limpia descendencia" (the pure blood of descendance) with few "casta personas de raza mesclada" [*sic*] (mixed race persons). In race and tradition, they carried on with the "duty of conserving their good customs intact."[74]

While exaggerating the extent of Spanish whiteness, Thoma crafted a subtle approach to Nuevomexicano cementation in the United States by regarding Spanish husbandry as the "solid base" on which the political state stood. The rancho class represented "la única Democracia" (the sole democracy). Channeling the latent rhetoric of Jeffersonian destiny, Thoma claimed that "All government on which the farmer rested is free and independent . . . for the reason that a free nation can only constitute itself by independent men, and no one who does not count on a secure sustenance on their real estate can be free."[75]

For the preservation of social autonomy, Thoma commanded the "native sons" of New Mexico to take pride in their ancestors, "men empowered by such name and fame." In a spirit of unassimilated loyalty, he damned "the fool" who derided

> the noble blood that circulated in [his] veins, the one who was ashamed to belong to a race that dominated the world, whose every member was a hero, a venerable Christian, that is to say, a noble Spaniard; or who vilely abjured the speaking of Spanish, the richest and most sonorous in the world, that for three centuries was the tongue of the European courts, in which poets, writers and wise men wrote, the envy of all the nations.[76]

Interestingly, the New Mexico Territorial Board of Education adopted Thoma's *Historia Popular* for school terms up to 1905, the only Spanish-language book to be so accepted.[77] The territorial superintendent of schools at the time, the former Delegate to Congress José Francisco Chaves, had a reputation of criticizing Euro-American misrule in New Mexico, and as such would have understood the rationale of providing a text to represent the people's own history.

The world explosion set off by the Spanish–American War stopped the momentum of primacy history in its tracks while shaking up its loyalty to Spanish legacy. As one historian speculated, "When the country of [New Mexican] ancestors, Spain, was fighting the nation where they lived, it must have been no easy matter to choose sides"[78]—but only for a moment.

During the saber-rattling phase of the conflict, Eusebio Chacón (going by Adelfa) witnessed a further degradation of la raza Española coming from the same prominent Americans who "mocked the tears" of the Spanish people who mourned the assassination in Madrid of Antonio Cánovas del Castillo, Spain's prime minister, two weeks previously. The "people of New Mexico too were trampled and injured," Chacón regretted, for they were "a fragment of the heroic [Spanish] race that triumphed at Lepanto [Spain's sixteenth-century war with the Ottoman Empire] and covered itself in Bailén [Spain's nineteenth-century battle with France], and [Ignacio] Zaragosa [Mexican general who beat back the French invasion of Mexico in 1862]." Spain's "grand past, like its present tribulations[,] will always touch us," Chacón memorialized. "That is why, when the criminal Anglo-Saxon insults us, we say like Cánovas del Castillo, '!Asesinos, viva España!'" (Assassins, long live Spain!).[79]

This hard siding with Spain reflected Chacón's steadfast Spanish identification and dissension with Anglo domination as we saw above. At this juncture, however, his ethno-national militancy was overshadowed by Nuevomexicano loyalty to America. Fickle intelligentsia representatives called Spain the enemy by either drawing a parallel between Cuba's plight as a colony under a corrupt Spanish empire or exercising partisan support for the expansionist policies of Theodore Roosevelt, President William McKinley's assistant secretary of the Navy.

For instance, the Territorial Assembly's joint resolution in support of Cuba's independence from Spain, called for by Roosevelt, passed without discussion or opposition. Enrique Salazar, the Republican editor of *El Independiente*, praised the act, acclaiming the men who "descended from the Spanish race [for] uniting with the enemies of Spain." Salazar noted that Anglos with a "hereditary hatred of the Spanish" likely laughed at how easily their Hispano-American colleagues denounced "la madre patria de su propia raza" (the mother country of their own race). Yet even as he had recently demanded a history for Nuevomexicanos, his loyalty to the American cause held fast—thus his patriotic cry, "!Honores á aquel que defiende a los suyos y no reniega de su propia sangre!" (Honor to those who defend their own [country] while not denying their own blood).[80]

With the sinking of the USS Maine in Havana Harbor, Salazar saw a "military fever" rising among Nuevomexicanos. As Americans grew increasingly bellicose, the journalist expressed confidence in McKinley. As consolation, he credited Spain as a proud but violent, militarily fearsome nation as it always had been. As the war flared, he ambivalently thought that it would be "deplorable if our Hispano-Americano co-citizens should be obligated to take up arms against their Spanish brothers."[81]

FIGURE 12. Enrique Salazar. This journalist, through scores of essays, may have been the most prolific Nuevomexicano writer contributing to the formation of Nuevomexicano ethnic identity at the turn of the 20th century. Unknown photographer. Author's scan from Read, *Historia Ilustrada de Nuevo México,* 540.

Nuevomexicano denial of Spain spiraled at the appearance of another New Mexicanism tract appearing in *Leslie's Weekly*. The author, John Bonner, claimed that Nuevomexicanos could never be loyal to the United States because they had "never emerged from the nursery to the school room." They were, Bonner barked, "elegantly termed greasers, that is to say, a hybrid race in whose veins Spanish, Indian and Negro blood are mixed." In classic Davis-style, "an impossible people" was said to "go to church but have a vague idea that New Mexico is ruled by one Washington who is the king of Spain"; who "see no harm in blood-letting or theft; and, when their daughters stay out over-night the truancy is condoned if they bring back a little silver in the fold of their sarape."[82] Albuquerque's *Hormiga de Oro* denounced Nuevomexicano-haters such as Bonner for using the war as an excuse to vent their inveterate antipathy and put in doubt the fidelity of nativos to the United States.[83]

Salazar fell back mightily on birthright citizenship. As confirmed in the Fourteenth Amendment of 1868, the sheer fact of being born in the United States carried fundamental rights and protections. The act has been called a "momentous turn of events by every measure," not least for the promotion of a multiethnic democracy.[84] Reflecting "constitutional patriotism," birthright citizenship sought "a reconciliation between the universalist demands of liberal principle and the need for a robust political identity, including a shared history," aiming to unite it "with the republican idea of a political life in common, an identity-conferring *patria*."[85] In the balance of regional and national homelands, Salazar leaned toward a shared US legacy, alongside contemporary citizens who by American birth were obligated to defend their country "at all times." It was, he noted, not strange for Nuevomexicano youth to feel the "bellicose ardor" in this "desperate circumstance" of war and a "true enthusiasm in taking part in the defense of the interests of their national patria,"[86] an effective override of blood-and-soil regionalism with its history of forced annexation.[87]

Ironically, Nuevomexicano enlistments fell below expectations.[88] One historian interprets it to mean working-class elements not so supportive of the war or simply indifferent.[89] Euro-American politicians in the southern part of the territory accused Nuevomexicanos of treachery and cowardice.[90] Eastern newspapers suspected New Mexico of "siding with Madrid against Washington," stating (falsely) that Spanish flags flew in Taos and in Santa Fe, the people "set to revolt against the United States at any time."[91]

Responding to the censuring of "nativos of Spanish blood," Salazar pointed out that recruitment procedures were not designed specifically for them. He offered the Civil War as an example of the right way to go about conscription, assigning Nuevomexicano officers and leaders to communities to educate young men and escort them to the enlistment station. Also serving to inhibit volunteering, a call for three regiments of cavalry came out. The requirement of experienced horsemanship meant few Nuevomexicanos qualified, a real sign of changing times. Salazar praised the Nuevomexicano youth who were scheduled for training in Texas for service to Cuba while assailing critics who challenged the loyalty of those "of Spanish blood."[92]

Answering the calumny of Nuevomexicano cowardice, Governor Miguel A. Otero II assured that New Mexico, including its citizens of "Spanish descent," was assuredly Republican and supportive of McKinley.[93] He and other defenders stressed the three Nuevomexicano companies in Roosevelt's Rough Rider regiment.[94] It became a discursive bent to emphasize that while Nuevomexicanos were Spanish, that they were fighting Spain yet were "American to the core." Newspapers burnished true patriotism by repeatedly highlighting Spanish "purity," that the New Mexicans were "of pure Spanish blood," "of pure Spanish descent."[95] Even Roosevelt himself had hailed the Nuevomexicano Maximiliano Luna, a captain who lost his life serving in the Philippines, as one who is a "representative of his race, for he was the only man of pure Spanish blood who bore a commission in the army, and he demanded the privilege of proving that his people were precisely as loyal Americans as any others."[96]

As the war waged, Salazar's disenchantment with Spain intensified. In one essay on the legacies of history, he took the temperature of Nuevomexicano remembrance. Spain, lying six thousand miles from "our territory," he rolled out, "is *only* a memory now, and something insubstantial for us" (emphasis added). It had been three-quarters of a century that Spain lost its supremacy over "old New Mexico." There was not a "single man on the surface of the territory who witnessed or had the slightest memory of the remote epoch." The Spanish language and "some customs and traditions" were all that remained. A "filial sentiment" toward her may have formed among some, but “as a political entity, Spain has disappeared from our horizon, and under no chain of circumstances could it do us good or harm.” If there were any “Neo-Mexicanos” who “still” wanted to “intercede” the past “in contraposition of the reality of the present,” they were far from the heart of the matter. “Instead of living in a place where the flag of stars and stripes flew,” Salazar bore on, “they should move to Spain or some other colony and embrace the protections of the Spanish banner.” The people “appreciate the deeds of their true valor and know that their principal duty is to sustain and defend the government of the United States with their sympathy. . . . If Spain is the enemy of our country and makes war,” Salazar invoked, “it is our enemy who looks to harm us and is not worthy of our sympathy nor our assistance. We are Americans and as such should defend our nation and our soil.”[97]

So much for imperial nostalgia. Spain may have been the “cradle of their race,” Salazar put it, but Nuevomexicanos were not obliged to grant their “eternal vassalage to an ideal sentiment not constant with the common feeling nor with their actual circumstances.” Salazar was even moved to suggest a total separation from New Mexico’s Hispanic past. Once the people voluntarily adopted the American nation, accepting its institutions and laws, it left a Spanish or Mexican colony behind. Nuevomexicanos were, Salazar indicated, neither Spanish nor Mexican but Americans by citizenship “and the majority of them by birth.” In emphasizing US birthrights over homeland rights, Salazar elevated the “peace and tranquility” that came with the ceding of the “depredations of the “barbaric Indians,” citing the emancipation of the majority of Nuevomexicanos from the semi-slavery of “odious peonage.” Blinding himself at this moment to America’s policies of Nuevomexicano exclusion, Salazar exclaimed that Nuevomexicanos had “in all respects” been treated like “natural and legitimate sons in the US, giving us the same guarantees and privileges that the rest of the habitants of the republic enjoyed.”[98]

On deeper consideration, Salazar admitted the effects of internal colonialism. Nuevomexicanos may have been reconstituted as citizens with full rights guaranteed by treaty and law, but, as he recalled, from the beginning they were denounced with lies concerning their character as humans, turned into objects of widespread disparagement and derision, put into opposition with other races in the country, denied access to education when they most needed it, and refused admission to the brotherhood of states when other territories with fewer population and resources were not denied that admission.[99]

Salazar explained it away as a national abnormality, blaming *chiflados* (ne'er-do-wells), a "sect or singular group" seen in all societies. Not bounded in permanent association or in combinations, they were found in all walks of life harboring similar ideas to realize malignant goals. Salazar represented Nuevomexicanos as fundamentally an aspirant minority group and not as a nation in search of self-determination. It justified a view of aberrant Americans causing trouble for his group, the ones to blame for having exaggerated notions of their own importance, seeking to deprive the "Hispano Americanos" of the rights guaranteed by the US government when they came into the United States. The war proved a "fecund mine" for all kinds of chiflados to do their dirty work, including those in Doña Ana and Grant Counties in southern New Mexico. Salazar fingered the district prosecutor John Bryan as one to flout New Mexicanism lies "frenetically and with violence." Such individuals had "dimmed intelligence . . . falsely calling the nativo citizens . . . traitors and disloyal," not knowing what a "solemnly ratified treaty signed by two civilized nations" meant. Making history obey his current state of mind, Salazar rhetorically asked if such persons did not know of the "value of the rights of a people that for three hundred years had enjoyed liberty and civil rights in a territory that they themselves had conquered and colonized." Leaving the matter open without suggestion of enforcement, the journalist concluded by noting that the chiflados would find it difficult to answer to the kinds of questions being put to them on the rights of Hispanos that could not be taken from them without trampling on the rectitude of the United States, racked as they were by the passion of hate.[100]

At war's end, the United States acquired Puerto Rico, Guam, and the Philippines while Cuba gained its independence. Salazar affirmed the reason why the people of New Mexico should rejoice at the admission of their "brothers of racial ancestry to the most liberal and magnanimous dominion in the universe." In a moment of true fantasy, he anticipated a day soon for New Mexico and the new possessions figuring as sovereign units within the American Union, foreseeing them as the controlling majority vote in Congress. The "citizens of Spanish race or ancestry will be the most respected and recognized," he dreamt, "and in all manner will they be able to obtain major privileges and stand equal in all things to the other classes that populate the vast dominion of the grand republic of North America."[101]

It was the ironic prayer of one of the most prolific contributors to New Mexico's realm of autonomous Spanish memory, the war demonstrating the brittleness of Spanish nostalgia. Yet, as we shall see in the next chapter, another name-orientation other than Spanish was alight, one in which other Nuevomexicanos were taking up the possibility of forging a real politics of primacy identity.

CHAPTER 4

"Hispano" Ascendant

AS WIDELY AS it had spread among Nuevomexicanos toward the end of the nineteenth century, "Spanish," I would note, was still not the hegemonic ethnic identifier it would become. Other cultural rubrics kept pace, new ones surged in support of primacy's value, and one identity-name appeared on the scene in association with a new movement of resistance to the Euro-American hierarchy.

"Mexicano" Still Placing

In 1894, the pseudonymous Un Mexicano published a poem calling for the easing of the rancor that was poisoning Nuevomexicano politics in San Miguel County.[1] Another contributor regretted how *la raza Mexicana* was losing influence and prestige in the territory's public policy arenas.[2] *El Tiempo* in Las Cruces alerted its "conciudadano mexicanos" (fellow Mexican citizens) to the *Santa Fe New Mexican* for admonishing them to step aside to learn from the way Anglo-Saxons conducted politics.[3]

"Mexican" exuded a militancy that somehow eluded Spanish identity. In response to the New Mexicanism scripts appearing in the Little Texas counties of Chávez, Eddy, and Roosevelt, *El Farol* in Capitán doubled down on the demand for Nuevomexicanos not to vote for Anglo Democratic candidates in those places "so they realize that the Mexicans know how to fight against the insults that the leaders of that party in those counties throw at them."[4]

In northern New Mexico, "Mexican" sliced into the Euro-American appropriation of Nuevomexicano land. The issue stemmed greatly from the failure in the Treaty of Guadalupe Hidalgo to provide clear-cut procedures for confirming the Spanish and Mexican *mercedes*, the communal parcels granted to groups of settler families. Congress also failed to resolve the vulnerability of communal properties in a national system of private property.[5] Both of Congress's legal procedures that were supposed to reconcile the patent petitions of land grant heirs proved dismal failures.[6] With scant natural resources available, land speculation provided the key to personal wealth. As David Caffey observes, administration in the territories often lacked the oversight of "capable, honest, and attentive federal officials" to curb the corruption, opportunism, and exploitative tendencies of newcomers and federal appointees. Unscrupulous, scheming outsiders finagled the system to acquire whole or partial grants by hook or crook.[7]

The so-called Santa Fe Ring, a loose association of lawyers, politicians, traders, investors, territorial officials, and judges exploited legal loopholes and manipulated Nuevomexicano farmers who could not always document heirship to ancestral shares. Led by Republicans mostly, the Ring became the most powerful economic and political force in the territory. Stephen B. Elkins, Thomas Catron, Max Frost, and their cronies ran the party to suit their economic strategies, including land machinations,[8] a pointed sign of internal colonialism. Certain Nuevomexicanos, themselves landholders and grant owners, collaborated with Euro-American syndicates, serving as mediators to vecino heirs.[9] For a fee, one-time Santa Fe mayor and New Mexico's first superintendent of public instruction, Amado Chaves, for instance, acted as a broker for accessing titles, "locat[ing] grant papers, or negotiat[ing] legal or purchase agreements with land grant communities."[10]

Significant loss of traditional lands "debilitated the economic viability of the Nuevomexicano majority," one historian found.[11] With the withering of subsistence farming, many Nuevomexicano workers migrated in search of employment. In urban areas, the system of paying salaries led to low or irregular wages and uncertain job availability.[12] Antonio Lucero, a coeditor of *La Voz del Pueblo*, later faulted the "practical, aggressive, feverishly ambitious" outsiders (Americanos) for the intensification of Nuevomexicano poverty in the 1890s.[13]

Nuevomexicano *herederos* (heirs) remaining on the farms resisted land theft in what Robert Rosenbaum calls a "primordial orientation."[14] Violent opposition to "foreign" squatters occurred on the original Beaubien-Miranda grant.[15] Night-riding, guerrilla fence-cutting, and barn destruction flared on the Tierra Amarilla Grant.[16] In protest gatherings, heirs and their advocates condemned Anglo cattle-ranch imperialism on the Las Vegas Grant.[17] Planks of the progressive Democratic and People's Parties challenged Republican candidates who supported land theft or schemed to gain property themselves.[18] Rio Arriba County supported herederos who defended their *derechos inherentes* (inherent rights) to the pastures, forests, and swamp lands held hostage by the conservation policies of the federal forestry.[19]

As a leading theorist generalizes, the "symbolism of land [becomes] potent in the emotional poetry of nationalism," particularly if the colonized are linked to literate advocates.[20] Of the identity referents Nuevomexicanos had to choose from, "Mexicano" punched hardest. R. M. López asked San Miguel County Republican chair Secundino Romero for assistance in combating a Euro-American maneuver to take possession of his father-in-law's property in Tierra Blanca (Quay County). As López put it, "[Usted] sabe muy bien que los gueritos siempre quieren hacerse tanto de tierra blanca como de tierra negra con todos los Mex[icanos]" (You know that the little blond ones always want to take the land of the Mexicans, be it Tierra Blanca or Tierra Negra).[21]

Allies of *La Voz del Pueblo* in Las Vegas, the largest town in railroad New Mexico, backed movement heirs with discursive fortitude, arguing that to displace herederos from their mercedes was to dispossess them of their *patrimonio*.[22] In the script of the Idyllic Past, editors incredulously wondered, "Who does not know that the mexicanos in former times [prior to US annexation] had it a thousand times better than they do today?"[23]

"Mexican"-oriented opposition to land swindlers bestirred enemy name-calling. Notable were Los caciquillos de la usurpación (the little bosses of usurpation) who in taking control of the rights of others were "becoming criminals and violators of law and rights" themselves.[24] Reputed Santa Fe Ring boss, Thomas B. Catron loomed grotesquely as the worst of land robbers. Expertly moving around property laws, lawyer Catron gained interest to seventy-five grants, making him the largest landholder in the country and the leading recipient of death threats.[25] When Delegate to Congress Antonio Joseph vowed to resolve the land grant mess through the establishment of a court of private claims,[26] an optimistic people's poet predicted, "There is no doubt whatever / [Catron] is going to die of desperate rabies / Seeing the 'Mercedes' that belong to the Mexicans / Slipping from his hands."[27]

Nuevomexicanos kept abreast of the news reporting on the Southern carpetbagger.[28] They were aware of locals in western territories calling corrupt federal appointees carpetbaggers.[29] The carpetbagger metaphor fit Catron well:

Llegó aquí el porta maletas	The carpetbagger arrived
Con el fusil en el ombro,	With a rifle on his shoulder,
Marcado con las barretas	Marked with the irons
De la traición y su escombro.	Of betrayal and its rubble.

Mixing images, the author noted how Catron betrayed *la raza*'s famed hospitality:

De trampe cayó á Doña Ana	The hobo landed in Doña Ana
Buscando quien lo acogiera.	Looking for someone to take him in.
Lo trató con cortesía	They treated him courteously
La gran bondad mexicana.	That great Mexican kindness.
Pagándoles la fineza	He paid back their grace
En arruinarles se esmera.	By striving to ruin them.

"Go back to Missouri," it was demanded of Catron, "Let us live in peace / *Cómete tu chemisturri* [Eat your own bullshit] / *Y vete, lobo rapaz* [And get out, wolf of prey]."[30]

The Land Grabber icon inspired other tags, as in "Don Tomás Borrego Catron." In the double fix, "*borrego*" (sheep) caricatured Catron's rotund build, hooking it into the stock animal traditionally cultivated by Nuevomexicano ranchers.[31] Nuevomexicanos who enabled land theft were domesticated borregos, as in the fable of a Euro-American Catronite who mistakes territorial senator Agapito Abeitia for *un borrego*, a hireling willing to lend his seat in the legislature to boost Catron's finances.[32]

His physicality also earned Catron the title *don Barriles* (barrel, cask), while his dictatorial manner made him into the "Torquemada [Grand Inquisitor] of the Santa Fe Ring." In the coupling, Catron is the *Torquemada Barriles,* who "with his gang of thieves reduced our lands" and bought off the poor people so cheaply as to send them to their "miserable ruin."[33]

FIGURE 13. Thomas B. Catron. Nuevomexicano identitarians used Catron's rotund build to caricature him as a settler-colonialist out to steal their land, ca. 1917. Wesley Bradfield, photographer. Courtesy of the Palace of the Governors Photo Archives, negative number 013309.

In *Los Americanos*, a verse of eighteen stanzas, a humble shepherd speaks for compatriot victims of land loss. In solemn and traditional Spanish literary self-deprecation, the penman concedes he is not a "consummate poet" but a "poor sheepherder / who only tends his flock." He once worked on an independent farm but now earns his keep as "a poor laborer / who lives off his salary." The gueros well knew the name of his natal county: "Guadalupe es, el firmado [Guadalupe it is, officially sealed] / por la nación mejicana [by the Mexican nation], / madre de todo lo criado [mother of all] / Virgen, Reina Soberana [Virgin, Sovereign Queen]." The intersection of Mexican state and religion reflected the sheepherder's identity as a man of the soil and victim of American predation:

> I shall speak of the foreigners,
> and what I say is true;
> they want to have us as slaves,
> but that will not do.
> Gentlemen, be careful of those
> of the American race;
> they come to possess your lands
> the ones [Mexican President Antonio López] Santa Ana granted to you.

As the verse continues, American occupiers come from Oklahoma without knowing Spanish, claiming Christianity and pretending to be "'the good stranger.'" They "make war with the world; / they come to push us out / and take over our lands." Sheepherder is not happy with how Nuevomexicanos faced the American beast with its "illustrious" agricultural and economic methods and intellectual talent. As he reprimands, laboring men "se han quedado como burros [have remained like burros] / no mas mascandose el freno [only chewing on the bridle]." The old haciendas are gone, and there is no other work except as farmhands on the ranches of the rich.[34]

"Mexican" circulated in English in New Mexico's railroad society. "The best sheep herders probably in the world are to be found in New Mexico," William McGuiness observed, "for the Mexicans are never so much at home as when they are following a herd of sheep. . . . Mexican labor can be employed profitably in this business."[35] In the campaign of 1892, George W. Gregg reported to Republican Party leader Ralph Twitchell that all candidates on the ballot in Sierra County started out by canvassing the "Mexican precincts."[36]

Of course, "Mexican" was used disparagingly. A researcher of health conditions wrote that Las Vegas contained about six thousand people, "fairly divided between 3,000 Mexicans and 3,000 Americans, for the most part living in separate portions; the former using adobe houses, and living—except as to a few better class families—with utter disregard to all sanitary laws."[37] Eugene A. Fiske, an enemy of New Mexico governor Miguel Antonio Otero,[38] wrote in favor of statehood to do away with despotic politicians, giving as a "striking illustration of this unfortunate territorial condition" Governor Otero, "the son of a Mexican father and American mother, and possessed, as those thus born are apt to be, of the worse [*sic*] qualities of both races."[39] Ironically, Otero's father, Miguel Antonio Otero I, had earlier declared his pure Spanish bloodline while challenging José Manuel Gallegos for a seat in Congress.

New Mexicanism waved the Corrupt Mexican Politician script over and again. A Chicago newspaper charged "wealthy Mexicans" with dominating New Mexico "like feudal lords." The *Denver Republican* responded that "at one time a few Mexican families controlled politics, and, to a large extent, the business of the territory, but not now." The paper noted, quite accurately, that it was "becoming less and less so every year."[40] "Mexicanos" were sometimes advised to vote for the Anglos who were their friends.[41]

"Nativo" and "native" remained firm in the railroad period from frontier days for representing primacy. Anthony Mora notes the political effectiveness of nativo in the southern part of the territory from the 1880s on, journalists using it as "the most powerful argument for ending racist policies throughout the territory." As US citizens and "the heirs of the 'first settlers'" in the region, they "resurrected claims to being colonial authorities themselves, in the process implicitly barring Indians from ever being 'first settlers,' 'Mexicans,' or even 'natives.'"[42]

Anthony Joseph, born in Santa Fe in 1846 to immigrant Azorean parents, enjoyed such popularity that supporters of his candidacy for New Mexico's delegate to Congress called him a "nativo y originario del paíz," a nativo, born in the homeland.[43] "*Acrimonia Política Entre los Nativos de Nuevo Mexico*" (Political Acrimony Among the Natives of New Mexico) appeared as the headline in a story about a rift dividing politicos.[44] *El Independiente* advised "a nuestros compatriotas que son nativos del país" (our compatriots who are natives of this countryside) to "learn to respect their own selves and make themselves respect the rest."[45]

"Nativo" and "Mexicano" sometimes intersected. "*!Comprar el voto Mejicano!*" cried the indignant Democratic editor of *El Guía de Santa Fe*, accusing Republicans of guaranteeing to beat Joseph for delegate to Congress by buying every Mexican vote at a dollar a head. "Aquí hay materia para Vds. nativos del Nuevo México" (Here is scoop for you natives of New Mexico), that is, to see how Republicans disrespected them.[46] A Republican operative reported to Ralph Twitchell in the campaign of 1892, "I received a carload of [Santa Fe Daily] *New Mexicans* [with its Republican Party propaganda] by yesterday's mail and have distributed them among the native people."[47]

The related *hijo del país* (native son) hung in. For example, in a retrospective on the first New Mexico legislative assembly in 1847, *El Independiente* pointed out that its members decreed laws that became of little interest from a legal standpoint, but were of "great, real importance" as the first pass by "our native sons" in making laws under the American regime.[48] *La Voz del Pueblo* criticized Governor Miguel A. Otero for his neglect of Nuevomexicanos, asking "'Is there any reason in the world that the native sons of New Mexico cannot have more representation in the administration of public affairs?'"[49]

The correspondent Bonafè stated that a railroad company would make sure that no *nativo del país* would be given a territorial appointment if he did not demonstrate support for policies that favored the company.[50] In support of the heirs to the highly coveted Las Vegas Land Grant,[51] *La Voz del Pueblo* claimed that they were the true "trabajadores hijos del suelo" (working sons of the soil).[52] At the opening of the 1901 legislative session, Enrique Salazar, having returned to an ethnonational frame of mind, editorialized that *legisladores nativos* needed to remember their predecessors who figured honorably for the good of the people, those who were the champions and defenders of Nuevomexicano historical *fueros* (privileges). "Remember!," he urged, "The glories of your ancestors who conquered and colonized this soil and maintained it for more than two centuries at the cost of sacrifices and untold hardships, without the help of anyone, and try to demonstrate with your acts that you and your people have not degenerated."[53]

As Euro-American power inflated well out of proportion to Euro-American numbers in the territorial population, Nuevomexicano partisans credited the candidacies of Pedro Perea and Octaviano Larrazolo for their support of Nuevomexicano belonging. *El Independiente* postulated in light of growing anti-Mexican prejudice in southeast New Mexico that the "nativo" Perea, running in 1898, was "not [the] inferior to any man in the United States" by virtue of ethnicity.[54]

As the number of Nuevomexicano assemblymen declined, Pedro G. de la Lama, editor of *La Opinión Pública*, suggested in 1895 that corruption formed a principal tool of the Euro-American takeover. Elections in the territory had become a "farse [*sic*]," he stated, from the prevalence of agents approaching poor citizens, *los hijos de Nuevo México*, with offers to purchase their votes. Unfortunately, too many poor "nativos" were more than willing to sell, a problem which only a law with severe penalties could dissolve.[55] Nuevomexicano Republicans were constrained from challenging their party for failing to give them fair representation in the high-ranking positions. Democrats in San Miguel County, where a Nuevomexicano populist movement surged, vented that the "grand bosses of the old ring" had not allowed "a single native son of New Mexico" to participate in the territorial Republican delegation to the national party convention in

Chicago, giving its favor instead to the "ambitious [Euro-American] adventurers."[56] Ranchero railed against a Republican clique causing a "plague of fawning foreigners" to come ply the administration with "voracidad canina" (canine voraciousness). New Mexico's "beautiful land" was being infested "con tus hijos por los suelos" (with your sons submerged in the ground).[57]

Manito Out of Nowhere

The diminutive *manito*, little brother from the colloquial *mano*, itself short for *hermano*, perhaps having come from Mexico, appeared as a term of endearment for the humble masses. As the headline in *La Voz del Pueblo* warned: "Malo Está el Cuento, Manitos" (It's a Bad Deal, Little Brothers), about how Republicans justified their opposition to a statehood bill.[58] "Cierto, manitos" (For sure, manitos), an unnamed contributor commented, "who really believes it?," namely, that should Félix Martínez became a Republican he would purge his weekly newspaper of its demagoguery.[59] "Manitos," another article queried, "if those guys do not want the people to know who they really are, why do they insist in forming [alternative] political parties?"[60] About its archenemy, Albuquerque's *La Opinión Pública* sarcastically and habitually belittled *La Bandera Americana* by using the sexist tag "manita."[61] "Manito" would go on to become a permanent colloquial referent for Nuevomexicanos/as specifically.[62]

Neo-Mexicano

Neo-Mexicano also began to circulate.[63] This construction evades easy translation into English. Close is "New Mexican," though the two did not match precisely: The double entendre of "neo" signified a "new" Mexican in a rapidly changing society, whereas the New of New Mexican suggested the traditional territorial figure.[64] Urbano Chacón, editor of Santa Fe's *La Aurora*, supported Anthony Joseph for delegate to Congress, proclaiming with clear nationness, "¡He aquí, oh neo-Mejicanos, un hombre que está dispuesto a derramar, gota por gota, la preciosa sangre en sus venas para hacernos grandes y felices entre todos los pueblos civilizados del Universo!" (Here is, oh Neo-Mexicanos, a man ready to shed, drop by drop, the precious blood in your veins to make us powerful and happy among all the civilized peoples of the Universe!).[65]

Spying Republican Party strength, Chacón romantically enfolded Neo-Mexicano into the classic Indian Scourge script: "El pueblo Mejicano duerme mientras que la ponzoñosa víbora del Republicanismo se arrastra sobre las inocentes margaritas que cubren el terreno salvado de las garras de los indígenas por el hidalgo noble pueblo neo-Mejicano!" (The Mexican people sleep while the poisonous snake of Republicanism sweeps over the innocent daisies that cover the land that was rescued from the claws of the indigenous by the noble Neo-Mejicano people!).[66]

Nuevomexicano progressives opposed the candidacy of railroad lawyer Frank Springer for a seat in the territorial assembly from San Miguel County because, they said, he manipulated territorial laws to deprive heirs of their shares of the Las Vegas Land Grant. *La Voz del Pueblo* accused Springer of causing "hundreds of Neo-Mexicanos" to be expelled from their homes "where they and their ancestors had lived for almost two generations, and, without a cent, have been forced to search for new homes elsewhere."[67]

The editor of the Las Vegas *Sol de Mayo* Manuel C. de Baca spoke to the worst of the ills plaguing Nuevomexicanos, the frequent "lying articles against the Neo-Mexicanos in the Eastern papers, denouncing us as a race without honor, without virtue and without decency." Displeased with Anglo culture brokers, C. de Baca portrayed offenders "showing us their teeth, a superficial smile on their lips to please us, hypocrites who, to cover the eyes of the poor Neo-Mexicanos, sign their names at the end of articles, pretending to defend us against their lies to immortalize themselves as true friends of the people from whom they hope to harvest money and honors."[68]

Organizations posted "Neo-Mexicano" on their titles. In the field of mutual aid, there was *La Sociedad Neo-Mexicana de Mútua Protección de Old Albuquerque* [*sic*][69] and in Wagon Mound *La Sociedad Neo-Mexicana.*[70] Three weeklies at least carried the label: *El Neomexicano* (n.p.), the bilingual *El Metodista Neo-Mexicano* (Las Cruces), and *El Abogado Cristiano Neo-Mexicano* (Albuquerque and Socorro), the latter two established by Euro-American missionaries.[71]

In a striking manifesto, an unknown writer employed the baroque form to link Nuevomexicanos to a classic Euro-Spanish heritage.

The ethnically patriotic "Neo-Mexicano" youth, so well-represented among their "noble people," fought against the ruthless (Santa Fe) Ring leaders, those who "most agitated the people." Every day brought news of the nativo youth, "the successors of Coronado, DeSolla, and Cabeza de Baca." The remainder of the piece presents an arresting scenario of young Neo-Mexicanos preparing for "the army of liberty, leaving behind the days when, by intimidation, the bosses of the [Republican] Inquisition submerged and oppressed their *parientes*" (relatives and guardians).[72]

"Latino" Sighting

New labels arrived from Latin America. *Latino*, which dated to the seventeenth century at least in southern countries, flourished in California's Spanish-language discourse of the late nineteenth century.[73] In El Paso, *La Sociedad Protectora de Latino-Americanos* (The Society for the Protection of Latin-Americans) combatted Texan racism.[74]

With a limited calling in New Mexico, Latino inclined toward the transregional. "The Anglo-Saxons say that God will not help he who does not help himself," *La Voz del Pueblo* reported, "And the Latinos say that after the storm comes the calm."[75] The journalist and writer Camilo Padilla congratulated Pedro Sánchez on his biography of Padre Antonio José Martínez, his archival facts being of "transcendental interest to *la raza Latina-Americana*."[76] The opening stanza in a poetic tribute to the Mexican immigrant Octaviano Larrazolo in a campaign for delegate to Congress observed, "Your very high genius / is already esteemed by the people, / *la raza latina* / judging you their champion."[77] In Las Cruces, "E." argued in a letter to *El Labrador* that the economic hardships being experienced by the people originated in "an unjust and bloody war that separated a part of la raza latina from its legitimate mother, the now flourishing Republic of Mexico."[78] *La Estrella* editor Miguel Godinez called the Spanish-speaking citizens of the United States and Mexico "hermanos de raza, los latinoamericanos."[79]

"Hispano" Rising

"Hispano" appeared in Mexico throughout the eighteenth and nineteenth centuries. Writers in the Spanish-speaking world referred to the whole of Latin America as Hispanoamérica and the people were called *Hispanos* and *Hispanas.*[80] Historian José Angel Hernández recovered an interesting usage. In 1856, Jesús Islas, a Mexican repatriation commissioner, referred to the "Hispano-Americanos" living in the former Mexican Department of Alta California ("California" as it became part of the United States). By Hispanos, Islas meant "*Californios, Mexicanos,* Chileans, Peruvians, etc. etc.," and the masses specifically. He bemoaned their "saddest of situations and lack of hope in the future" under the rule of "the Saxon race." Hispano-Americanos were abandoning their traditional agricultural pursuits, the only form of labor they knew, yet Islas said they could not compete with *los Americanos* in the new industries, made worse by their maltreatment of "*los españoles.*"[81] In 1894, Mexican American residents of Tucson formed the Alianza Hispano Americana as a fraternal benefit society. By 1906, numerous chapters appeared in New Mexico and Texas.[82]

As far as can be determined, it was in the 1870s that the earliest use of "Hispano" in New Mexico appeared, about the same time as in California.[83] In the Donaciano Vigil papers, a fragment of an 1873 unsigned letter went to an unspecified person requesting to use his name as a candidate for delegate to Congress, so as "to organize a glorious victory over the enemies of our people and of the Hispano Americano race."[84] In 1876, Methodists invoked "*Nuestra obra Hispano Americana*" (Our Hispano American work) to characterize their missionary labor among Nuevomexicanos.[85] In 1878, the Jesuit journal *La Revista Católica* condemned the laws of the assembly that were "so opposed to the feelings ingrained in the religious heart of the Hispano-Americano."[86]

"Hispano" seems to have had little, if any, use in New Mexico's public discourse of the 1880s. If so, it picked up and spread vigorously in the 1890s.[87] A weekly *El Hispano-Americano* appeared in Mora in 1890, though the editor, owner, and why it disappeared are unknown.[88] In 1890, Víctor L. Ochoa, born in Mexico and raised in Texas, moved his weekly *El Hispano-Americano* from El Paso to Socorro, a third of the way from Albuquerque to Las Cruces.[89] Two years later he took it to New Mexico's Las Vegas.[90]

Ochoa referred to New Mexico's "Hispano Americanos" so assiduously it caught on quite widely. Reporting on a patriotic event for young people in Santa Fe, *La Voz del Pueblo* called attention to the descendants of the two predominant races in New Mexico, el Hispano Americano y Anglo-Sajona, and again recommended *El Nuevo Mexicano* to los lectores hispano-americanos (Hispano-Americano readers) for its worthy literary section.[91] Albuquerque hosted the sectarian *Abogado Cristiano Hispano-Americano.*[92] An editor at *El Independiente* regretted the lack of Nuevomexicano youth in US military academies, "when in this excellent time, various Hispano-Americano youth should have a distinguished appointment as officers in the army and navy of our Nation. Not only should this be the individual ambition of our Hispano-Americano youth," Salazar recommended, "but more should be the interest, the object, and the pride of New Mexico collectively to see appropriate representation in the military arm of our government."[93]

Nuevomexicanos were struck by a Tocquevillian urge to establish voluntary associations in which "Hispano" became the neologism of choice. "When the history of our Territory is written," *La Voz del Pueblo* surmised, "the present era will be called 'Societies.' Never in our history has there been seen so much enthusiasm in the Hispano-Americano people to create societies." Whereas three years earlier only two community organizations counted on the Las Vegas Plaza, it now boasted five,[94] including *El Casino Hispano-Americano,*[95] *La Sociedad Moctezuma Hispano-Americana,*"[96] and *La Sociedad Dramático Hispano-Americana.*[97]

Anticipating what would later become the fuller merging of Hispano and Spanish names, Manuel C. de Baca, the conservative editor of *El Sol de Mayo*, condemned the climate of violence being stirred by Las Gorras Blancas—the rebel, night-riding defenders of land grants—calling on all "Hispano-Americanos . . . who still feel the blue blood flowing in their veins and the beat of the noble sentiments of chivalry in their hearts, to pull out the honor and good fame of their race to shrug off evil, unite to the good, and finally, make disappear, with their good works and acts, that black stain that [las Gorras] has wanted to throw upon the character of the Hispano-Americanos."[98] C. de Baca introduced a partner organization, *Los Caballeros de Protección*

Mutua, that would "not permit the Anglo-Saxons to disregard their brothers, the Hispano-Americanos."[99]

In critical primacy terms, *La Voz del Pueblo* proclaimed that it had been too many years that "an Hispano Americano, a native son of this soil," had not occupied the territory's gubernatorial seat, adding for emphasis, "We are Hispano Americanos and all those in whose veins runs that blood we consider brothers, as much as we would want good luck for a carnal brother."[100] A *Voz del Pueblo* correspondent alerted that the "Hispano-Americano people" had the question of their water rights pending in the territorial council. The "clamoring of the legitimate heirs of this soil, who are the descendants of those noble and brave conquistadors" was being heard all over the territory, Hispano-Americanos bearing the brunt of waterworks corporations that appropriated riverine rights "with this or that [speculative] aim," leaving farm families with insufficient irrigation water. Petitioners to the territorial council alleged that as "Hispanos" they, "the descendants of the conquistadors of this soil," had a "primordial right to the running waters."[101]

In the 1890s, *periodistas* (journalists) working for dozens of Spanish-language weeklies coalesced into a major collective force within in the Nuevomexicano discursive power niche. Like literary writers, educators, and key politicians, they were largely educated in Catholic primary and secondary schools, the well-staffed prep school in Santa Fe, St. Michael's College; St. Mary's in Las Vegas; a parochial institution in Mora; and, for girls, the Sisters of Loretto Academy.[102] Several of them had attended American colleges and universities.

In January 1891, Ochoa had proclaimed in a message to the members of the Nuevomexicano press that "unity gives power," therefore they should unite to generate power for themselves. "With rare exception," he affirmed, "all of our [newspaper] business serves to figure only as a second class means, and, notwithstanding the growth in the number of Nuevomexicano papers, we have never been able to compete with the North Americans." Ochoa envisioned an entity for making Euro-American authorities pay them heed rather than have their complaints and protests go "lost in the emptiness of official indifference." He invited the editors of Spanish-language papers in New Mexico, Arizona, Colorado, Texas, and California to join in forming an organization to serve their needs and wants.[103]

As *La Voz del Pueblo* publicized, such an organization would bring innumerable improvements for the "Latin race in general" and "facilitate great advantage for the journalists who represent that group."[104] In March 1892, in the offices of *La Voz del Pueblo*, La Prensa Asociada Hispano-Americana (The Associated Hispano-American Press) came into being. Ochoa's *Hispano Americano*, Félix Martínez's *Voz del Pueblo*, Albuquerque's *La Opinión Pública*, Socorro's *El Defensor del Pueblo*, and Mora's *El Mosquito* formed the charter group. Ochoa was understandably named president, *El Mosquito*'s Camilo Padilla vice president, and Félix Martínez treasurer.[105]

La Prensa Asociada portended an ethnonationalist organization for leading a movement for Nuevomexicano/a autonomy. As its charter mandated, members were to engage "en nuestro pueblo . . . en nuestro país" (in our community . . . in our homeland). And as one resolution declared, "nuestro linaje, our bloodline, should, of course, depend on appropriate weapons for its proper defense." The initiative would "cement the foundation on which to erect the tower of defense for our Hispano-Americano people." Another declared that "por cuanto la prensa hispano-americana es natural y por consecuencia debe ser el fideicomisario y defensor del linaje que representa" (insofar as the Hispano-American press is natural, it consequently should be the trustee and defender of the heritage that it represents). The "means and measures most appropriate and necessary for the advancement and improvement of the people" would be mobilized by the organ. All the Hispano-Americano papers were invited to join "as promptly as possible."[106]

While a movement to assail the conditions of internal colonialism seemed possible, the organization's preamble suggested a bootstraps project:

> Given the ideology of society and business that prevails in the United States of America in the present epoch, we are satisfied that to guard the standing of the rights guaranteed to us by the American Constitution, it is incumbent on us to form associations so that our forces grow to the level of the rest of our co-citizens, and with the objective of having the dignity of our ancestry and descendants be dutifully respected.[107]

Framers recognized "the impossibility of making the most of available opportunities without adhering to the system of synonymous-interest combinations in vogue throughout the United States."[108] Not to appear ideologically over the top, *El Sol de Mayo* declared that "Our race will see our associated Neo-Mexicano press taking the shield in its hand to do what needs to be done without maltreating or injuring anyone."[109]

Essentially, La Prensa Asociada became a professional guild with dues for membership, much as the ones Ochoa saw in Mexico and west Texas. Editors would benefit from standardized advertising fees and free railroad passage, free entry to theaters, access to meetings where public interest issues were debated, and better remuneration for their labors.[110] Yet the association would proceed with a reform agenda to contend with Euro-American hierarchy in the journalism profession.[111]

La Prensa Asociada met again in Albuquerque later in 1892. New associates included *El Tiempo* (Marcial Valdez, editor), the *Santa Fe Boletín Popular* (José Segura, editor), and from Los Lunas *La Crónica de Valencia* (Miguel Salazar y Otero, editor). Membership soon grew to ten New Mexico weeklies and three from Texas.[112] The board of directors emphasized the many difficulties that needed resolution to realize a "perfect and harmonious association."[113] One demand called for the territorial assembly to pass a law allowing Spanish-language presses to publish all judicial and administrative documents and territorial laws, a subsidy monopolized by the *Santa Fe New Mexican.* In the double-deck naming, the "Neo-Mexicano people, who in grand majority is composed of Hispano-Americanos" would learn and become familiar with all that concerned "their rights as citizens."[114]

However, the competition between political parties lurked dangerously. Gilded Age politics in the United States has been called "venomously partisan."[115] In proposing La Prensa Asociada, Ochoa had warned of the rancor and disagreements that tended to split his colleagues. They had to be laid aside if they were to render their work useful for improving their people's social station.[116] In fact, not even the excitement of building "societies" could head off the risk of searing factionalism. Severe mutual antagonism foregrounded *La Prensa Asociada.*[117]

Already *El Nuevo Mexicano* had begun to question La Prensa Asociada's preachments of unity while members battled one another tooth and nail. The weekly would have gladly followed the just call to harmonize but what happened in the Santa Fe municipal election had "destroyed its effect and left us with a very sour disillusion." Most Asociada members were progressive Democrats. As such, the Republican *El Nuevomexicano* pointed to Democrats quarreling among themselves, shown in the local election when Republicans swept the race for local offices.[118]

The editor of the *El Nuevo Mexicano*, the Spanish edition of the *Santa Fe New Mexican*, went unmentioned. Néstor Montoya, of *La Voz del Pueblo*, suspected a Nuevomexicano "enemy" of unity working at the direction of the Euro-American managers of the *New Mexican*. Still, Montoya, identifying with "strict exponents of the truth," admitted that the defeat of Democrats in Santa Fe was embarrassing. As he explained, "rogues who had ascended in the party for the election promoted unity and concord only to forget it within their own ranks." Insurgents put their man at the top of the ballot when by right it should have gone to the one whose family "for centuries" had "with their blood, defended the community." When time came to prove themselves, dissidents wielded promises like "a conquering sword," defeating Montoya's favorite. On the bright side, Montoya mentioned, "every day will show that stratagems of betrayal prove that the spirt of the Hispano-Americano exists for a just unity, sane and reasonable, without wanting the favor of the Anglo-Americano but rather only to maintain their rights inviolate and have them respected, as proved in the facts in Santa Fe."[119]

This soiled laundry would be taken care of within Democratic ranks, Montoya believed, but meanwhile, it was necessary to deal with the Republican *Santa Fe New Mexican*, which *La Voz del Pueblo* called "the evil spirit of our day . . . now vaunting itself as the representative exponent of the interests of the native people of New Mexico." "The native people might be poor, forsaken, and abused," *La Voz del Pueblo* shoved, "but they shall never be guilty of recognizing in the least a spurious species of humanity as their representative" (*New Mexican* editor Max Frost).[120]

The threat of an agent provocateur might have served as a point to rally around, and La Prensa Asociada called on colleagues to cool their quarrels as it insulted Hispano-Americano citizens.[121] Instead, Camilo Padilla at *El Mosquito* pitched into the cross-party fire with a discursive fusillade directed at Republican Governor L. Bradford Prince. The wizard of tricultural harmony was charged with calling Nuevomexicanos "greasers" in an interview with the *Chicago Tribune*, then tried bribing the local press to quiet the story. Prince "tiene que bailar al son del tambor de los 'greasers'" (must dance to the beat of the greasers), Padilla taunted. La Prensa Asociada resolved to censure Prince for hypocritically calling himself a friend of Nuevomexicanos.[122] Historian María Montoya is surely right in noting that critics labeled Prince a racist when he was "in actuality a Republican party man."[123] But critical Nuevomexicanos cursed the overbearing culture bear as a political animal. Padilla deemed his conduct "unworthy of a gentleman and honest man. We warn our compatriots in the territory, and beyond that he is a man who merits neither our favors nor our trust."[124]

Everyone knew that Prince yearned to own the Mora Land Grant. Padilla thus called the *Santa Fe New Mexican* "the organ of land thieves and the most servile paper that had ever seen public light in this territory, the only one to drag itself to adulation, to come out in defense of Sultan Prince."[125] *La Opinión Pública* satirized Prince as a landlord as bad as Catron, a "scourge who has come to be the curse of our co-nationals, a poisonous serpent who plants discord, rancor, and worry in peaceful peoples."[126]

The attack on the *New Mexican* would have been a worthy decolonial spar were it not for the Spanish-language section it sponsored. *El Nuevo Mexicano* thus took La Prensa Asociada to task for going after Prince, pointing to Padilla and Emilio Segura as chief perpetrators and clarifying that the *Chicago Tribune* only attributed "greaser" to Prince without quoting him directly.[127] To complicate further, Prince had the backing of the majority Nuevomexicanos in the Santa Fe County Republican Party.[128] A young (unnamed) Nuevomexicano representing *El Nuevomexicano* thus criticized La Prensa Asociada for tearing into Prince at one of its meetings. Manuel Salazar y Otero, editor of *La Crónica de Valencia* in Los Lunas south of Albuquerque, took this outlier to the shed, calling him a "mop head shield" who used the governor to cover Republican hypocrisy while wanting to swallow Nuevomexicanos "like pills."[129]

La Voz del Pueblo demanded that *El Nuevo Mexicano* not turn the "young man" into a protector of evil for the (Republican) cliques that disgraced their entire homeland. It commended Salazar y Otero for defying *El Nuevo Mexicano*, the "organ of evil." "Verdaderamente Nuevo México debe tener orgullo de un hijo tan fiel y verdadero patriota" (Truly, New Mexico should take pride in a son so loyal and patriotic), Montoya intoned, "especially when we had the daily misfortune of seeing young nativos of New Mexico who, instead of recognizing and defending the interests of their 'co-nationals' are selling themselves cuerno y alma [horn and soul] to this malvada camarilla [evil cabal] that every day is taking even the bread from the mouths of the poor Neo-Mexicanos and constantly persecuting them." Political questions were one thing, the defense of "nuestra raza" another, Montoya instructed. Yet "the day of retribution was marked and soon to be seen." Montoya pledged to march with Salazar y Otero "shoulder to shoulder, arm in arm," and he pilloried: "Understand that if there are some detestable ones who, for greedy interests, have submitted, body and soul to our enemies, those adventurers who rob and denigrate us will see that there are also many of us who will make whatever sacrifice to maintain the name of our illustrious ancestors clean" (i.e., not greasers].[130]

By 1894, La Prensa Asociada members had not learned. Camilo Padilla editorialized that "a Nuevomexicano should never feel alone in the land of his birth and among his people" and if periodistas did not "return to the unity that had been a natural part of traditional Nuevomexicano society, they would find themselves at the mercy of Americano interests."[131] Enrique Salazar founded *El Independiente* in Las Vegas to escape the discord, acrimony, and destructiveness, pledging to refrain from offensive or gratuitous attacks on persons while supporting and applauding respectable and talented colleagues.[132] Increasingly, however, *El Independiente* would be pulled into the Republican Party and into a feud with its progressive rival in Las Vega, *La Voz del Pueblo*.[133]

Back in the partisan pit, *El Boletín Popular*'s editors shook their heads over the anger *La Flor del Valle*, *El Tiempo*, and *El Sol de Mayo* launched against *La Opinión Pública* and vice-versa, the veering discord cracking old friendships.[134] Prensa Asociada leadership intervened to have parties agree to a temporary suspension of verbal war until the case could be brought before the body.[135] It is not known whether a hearing ever took place.

Ochoa, who in El Paso advocated Hispano self-protection, mutual aid, and worker rights, might have possibly repaired the ruptures by building a social movement for Nuevomexicano justice and uplift without going through electoral channels or transforming the Democratic Party into an ethnic instrument for self-determination, which would require the agreement of Euro-Americans in the party. However, Ochoa had moved to New Mexico as a political refugee. The presidency of Porfirio Díaz defined him as an enemy for aiding rebellion in northern Mexico.[136] He was arrested by US federal agents and, after getting acquitted on charges of sedition, went on to recruit for a revolutionary army on the Mexican border only to be rearrested for violating federal neutrality laws. He was convicted and sentenced to prison for two-and-a-half years and never to return to New Mexico.[137]

In 1904, *El Independiente*, now under ownership of Secundino Romero, though still edited by Enrique Salazar, regretted the years that had passed since La Prensa Asociada Hispano Americana had met. The weekly beseeched the (unknown) president to call for a reunion to reclaim its rightful and entitled role in publishing the acts of the current legislature in Spanish, critical for informing the Nuevomexicano public on matters of significance to its interests. Members of both chambers recognized the justice of bilingual publication of their business, Salazar emphasized, yet lethargic Hispano journalists did nothing. The weekly assured that it did not lobby for any "Hispano-Americano" for the job, recommending only that pressure be placed to correct the injustice.[138]

Six months later, *El Independiente* took note of the lowly condition of the territory's "Hispano-Americano press." Salazar cited the lack of patronage from the territory's "political magnates" whose contempt for the Hispano-Americano press reached such a "supreme level" that it ensured the exclusion of Spanish-language journalism from competing in public affairs and for government support. Adding insult to injury, Spanish speakers were patronizing English papers increasingly, preferring to pay "fantastic and ridiculous homage" to the papers of another language "that in most cases they do not understand, that in general has nothing to do with them nor their interests and that represents ideas and propositions different from those of the Hispano-Americanos." Not all English-language papers defamed the Spanish-speaking people, he noted, but they often followed the principle of birds of a feather flocking together, taking care of the business that pertained to them. "Native citizens" needed to do the same for the sake of the papers published in their natal tongue. Salazar called on Spanish speakers of a "generous and magnanimous sentiment" to elevate and support the papers that represented their ideas and aspirations.[139]

As Porter Stratton has pointed out, however, a high rate of illiteracy and poverty presented a perennial problem for Spanish-language journals struggling to make it.[140] Nevertheless, new Spanish-language weeklies continued to insist that the newspaper served as the principal institution for defending the interests of "El Hispano-Americano."[141] In 1908, *La Voz del Pueblo* attacked the English-language Republican papers, especially the *Santa Fe New Mexican* and the *Albuquerque Citizen*, for trying to pull the wool over the eyes of Hispano-Americano readers, as in a case concerning alleged election frauds in Valencia County.[142]

In 1909, Jesús Enrique Sosa, of the Mora *Eco del Norte*, called for a renewal of La Prensa Asociada, nominating José Montaner of *La Revista de Taos* as interim president.[143] On Miguel A. Otero's dismissal as New Mexico governor, Sosa offered a painful reminder of the effects of Nuevomexicano disunity. While the "strangers" in their midst who spoke English and "mistreated the Spanish" pressed the president to name one of their own as governor, "we remain quiet, do not recommend anyone, nor do we have the courage to tell the [Euro-Americans] 'one of ours is better than yours.'" Hispano apathy, "proverbial disunity," and "our criminal silence are the reasons why our privileges are ignored in Washington." Fearing the weakening of his people's primacy movement, Sosa said the fact that "we are natives here cuts no figure. Our suffering people [are] so accustomed to accepting without complaint all who 'Big Granpa' sends us, such that when they appoint someone passable, he seems to us like 'an angel without wings.'"[144]

Montaner likely refused the honor. In any case, Sosa nominated *La Bandera Americana*'s new editor, Néstor Montoya, as interim president.[145] Six months after that idea floated, Montaner decried the little enthusiasm that existed among the major newspapers for a press organization, commenting on how the overbearing competition for votes resulted in larger papers having an interest in smashing smaller ones.[146] Nevertheless, Montoya set October 6, 1910, for Spanish-language editors to reconvene La Prensa Asociada.[147] It appears not to have happened, and, in fact, Montoya himself soon issued a call for organizing the wholly partisan Prensa Asociada Hispano-Americano Republicana del Estado de Nuevo México.[148]

In summary, the appearance of "Hispano" contributed to the sensing among Nuevomexicano journalists of a need to combat the Euro-American forces that kept them and their people socially subjugated. However, the attempt to organize an effective decolonial force crashed on the rocks of partisan chaos. A more effective divide-and-conquer tool could not have been devised than the agonistic system for selecting government officials that the United States had come to magnify.

Already by this time, New Mexico was in a bout to win statehood. Many Nuevomexicano politicians saw in statehood the solution to their people's plight. The problem of Nuevomexicano political disunity would affect that arduous project as well, though the bulk of political dynamics would transpire within the Republican Party. Dealing with the obstacles to statehood would require the martialing of ethnic identity, and "Hispano" remained as one of the categories with which to advocate. As usual, alternative nomenclatures found their way into those discourses until the day at the climax of the statehood movement when one stood apart, as I run down in the next series of chapters.

PART II

The Statehood Accelerant

CHAPTER 5

Identity in the Starts and Fits of Statehood

AFTER LYING DORMANT for a decade, interest in New Mexico's becoming a state awakened in 1887. Proposals for attaining statehood would be generated either in New Mexico or in Congress, only to be halted by stultifying obstacles. As a consequence, acquiring statehood became a cause that ground on for two decades. Like Anglo advocates, Nuevomexicanos invested in statehood not only because it portended material benefits for all but also because it could well mean special political privileges for their beleaguered regional nation.

From start to finish, Nuevomexicano participation in the politics of statehood entailed the implementation of ethnic identity. Two springboards were involved. In one, prior expressions of American New Mexicanism were mere warm-ups for the consequential xenophobia that they weathered during the final struggle for statehood, which prompted Nuevomexicano spokespersons to swear on their people's cultural suitability for membership in the American nation. The second springboard for the launching of heritage memory involved the ways in which Nuevomexicanos campaigned for New Mexico statehood independently or under the leadership of Euroamerican advocates.

This chapter covers the first decade of the statehood movement. Ethnicity did not always surface in the political back-and-forth about the question of statehood for New Mexico. When it did, references to "Mexican" and "Spanish" followed as if on cue.

Senatorial and Presidential New Mexicanists

As strange as it may seem, the Republican Party dominated New Mexico politics, and never once did it waver in its support for statehood, yet nationally prominent Republicans too often blocked its passage. Big-name Republicans were not immune to spouting outright New Mexicanism. Things had gotten so bad that a Democrat ably and directly rebuked Republicans for their anti-Nuevomexicano attitudes in the very congressional chamber in which they wielded power.

The Outraging Struble Report

The 1888 Omnibus bill proposed making Dakota, Montana, Washington, and New Mexico states. The measure had widespread support; however, five Republicans on the House Committee on Territories dissented from admitting that "rotten borough," New Mexico.[1] In the so-called Struble Report (after Iowa Representative Isaac S. Struble), committee antagonists fully vented the Nuevomexicano Deficiency script. The extraordinary length to prove Nuevomexicano degradation involved the citing of publications, especially that New Mexicanism classic *El Gringo* by W. W. H. Davis.[2]

Vilified Nuevomexicanos challenged the committee's charges of backwardness, immorality, violence, and superstition, and the argument that the people of New Mexico would not be ready for, or entitled to, admission until they were improved by civilization, education, agricultural advancement, manufactures, and the arts. Santa Fe's *El Boletín Popular* condemned the "líbelo" as a "calumnia, ni más, ni menos," nothing more, nothing less.[3] *El Tiempo* called for public demonstrations in every county, precinct, and town "to protest . . . and demonstrate by our own actions that we are not of the caliber that our detractors say."[4] Indeed, the era of *la junta de indignación* (the irate indignation meeting) came due.[5]

At the large protest gathering in San Miguel County, Nuevomexicano citizens "without distinction as to political party, race or religious belief" bitterly attacked the Committee's "abominable lies." Félix Martínez, Benigno Romero, and Miguel Salazar condemned them in Spanish. Their set of resolutions represented a Nuevomexicano nation, assailing the unprovoked, misinformed prejudice against "our reputation as a people," deeming it unforgivable that the insults fell on "the whole" of them. Against formidable US nationalism, they could not argue that inadequacy of cultural, political, economic, or social preparedness was reason enough for denying citizens statehood.[6] Instead, they were obligated to emphasize the virtuous qualities of their people—and prove them demonstrably.

In what would become the Nuevomexicano Good Character script, advocates spoke to aspects of their admirable culture: the security of life and property it provided; the absence of violence and crime relative to any other part of the United States; the morals of the "greater mass of our people, [underscored] by their domestic virtues and purity of social customs"; all of which would render "pale the history of the same men who had vilely defiled them." The "abominable" calumniators who insulted ancestors, mothers, wives, and daughters would pay when their children discovered what they said, thereby keeping them in "perpetual detestation." The committeemen, it was charged, knew nothing of their people's precedence and duration on their homeland, that their ancestors set foot on the "north continent" before Americans had, their Roman Church having "gathered its flock before the Virginia colony even existed" and before the Pilgrims "disembarked in Massachusetts." They failed to see how their noble ancestors survived by sharing "succor, support and guidance in these valleys in the time of isolation." New Mexico therefore deserved "the praise of the good and wise ones of the land for her patience and constancy and for the success of her vigilance over the people in the practice of virtue and knowledge of God."[7]

"El pueblo americano" that loved liberty and detested lies was invited to support with "sympathy and approval those who defend their sacred communities."[8] As most of them longed for statehood as we shall see, Euro-Americans scoffed at the habitual New Mexicanism that plagued the largest portion of their territory. In a letter to the *New York Tribune*, the vigilant L. Bradford Prince pointed out that "almost every territorial paper protested that the minority report was filled with falsehoods, maintaining that New Mexico was well qualified for statehood."[9]

Not helping, a set of Albuquerque businessmen agreed with the Senate committee, stating in an open letter that New Mexico was indeed "totally unfitted for the responsibilities of statehood," the greater population being unfamiliar with the English language, and, despite "honest and . . . good intentions," formed a "class of people over whom the designing, dishonest, and untruthful politicians readily acquire a power that enables the latter to sway the former almost without limit."[10] The *Chicago Tribune* commended the "remarkable document" for confirming what it had been saying about the people under the control of "unscrupulous rings of politicians . . . whose rapacity has been the amount of money raised by taxation." The Las Vegas *Daily Optic* jumped on *Tribune* owner Joseph Medill for his "shamefully" abusing the "native-born American citizens of New Mexico." The

Santa Fe *New Mexican*, in turn, blamed it on Medill's frustration over failed investments in the territory.[11]

When New Mexico House of Representatives passed a resolution blaming Congress for the "ignorance" that insulted the Spanish-speaking natives of New Mexico,[12] the *Chicago Tribune* objected, calling Nuevomexicanos "not American, but 'Greasers,' persons ignorant of our laws, manners, customs, language, and institutions; lazy, shiftless, and 'grossly illiterate and superstitious.'"[13] Feeling much the same, the Republican majority in the US Senate dropped New Mexico from the omnibus bill. Congressman William McAdoo defended the "Spanish Americans." Nevertheless, Joseph's attempts to reconcile differences failed.[14] In the next session of Congress, President Grover Cleveland signed the Dakotas, Washington, and Montana in as states, leaving New Mexico out.

An Offensive President

In January 1892, Congressional Delegate Antonio Joseph introduced an enabling act which would give New Mexicans authority to construct a state constitution in preparation for statehood. Nuevomexicanos were enthused. The *Mora Mosquito* envisioned self-rule, "native sons instead of 'carpetbaggers'" commanding the state's higher political offices."[15] However, newly elected President Benjamin Harrison looked askance at "too many Spaniards and too few American citizens" living in the territory.[16]

The weekly *El Hispano Americano* expressed amazement at the president's disregard of un pueblo whose loyalty to the United States was unquestioned. Editor Victor Ochoa unloaded the slate of primacy scripts. "All that is lacking" he expressed, "is for us to be told that we are not sons of this land, and that our forefathers failed to gain any merit in leaving behind the posterity of a home and a patria." Waving the Indian Scourge and Civil War Hero scripts, Ochoa dared the president to "forget the disputes we endured with the barbarians, a corollary of our denial of rights to citizenship. Do not vacillate in saying that we did not take any part in the success of 1861," Ochoa continued, "when the separatists wanted to destroy the great work of the North American Confederation."[17]

Back in 1889, Territorial Councilman J. Francisco Chaves's resolution condemning the Struble Report implied birthrights for Nuevomexicanos, "born and bred under the American flag." In an era of major immigration from eastern and southern Europe, Chaves implicitly claimed that local Mexicans were more American than the immigrants arriving in eastern states.[18] In the script of Better Than Your European Immigrant, Ochoa rebuked President Harrison for not recognizing that Nuevomexicano allegiance was superior compared "to whatever other nationality, or classes that form the population of this great Republic." "Tell us, Mr. Harrison," Ochoa demanded, "if your own [white] nationals or the Germans or the English or the Poles or the Hungarians or the Jews or the French or whatever other of the nations that form the population of the United States (not to mention the tens of millions of Africans, Norwegians and Chinese) [were any] more loyal [than us] in their allegiance to the United States[?]" Despite their "patriotic virility," Nuevomexicanos were subject "without end to injuries by individuals who have never known the significance of the word patriotism." If the president refused New Mexico's admission "because of our morals and social situation," he might change his mind if he compared Neo-Mexicanos to the some of the people of Mississippi, Louisiana, and Arkansas "where many women go barefoot."[19]

Prince, who had a pipeline to American power, borrowed the script, complaining to H. O. Platt, chair of the House Committee on Territories, of the committee's looking on the people of New Mexico "as foreign and not in harmony with American institutions in a land which absorbs half a million of foreigners every year, and which manages to assimilate the very worst elements of continental Europe." Conjoining the Nuevomexicano Good Character, US Birthrights, and Competency scripts, Prince emphasized that after the United States acquired New Mexico, "all of its inhabitants except the oldest were born on American soil, and . . . its people belonged to a sister republic with institutions similar to ours and so needed no new education in free government." Quite importantly, Prince pointed out that "For over half a century they have been electing their legislatures, making their laws, and carrying on their local government under the American system."[20]

Writing in the *Kansas City Times*, a former resident of the territory liked that the enabling act failed to get out of committee, calling "ordinary Mexicans" incapable of governing a state.[21] *La Voz del Pueblo* editor Néstor Montoya wrote that such bad information came "from those who could not see beyond the point of their noses." They were "adventurer carpetbaggers," "vermin" who aimed to make fortunes "at the cost and work of others"; "liars" along with senators and representatives who "may not see us with good eyes." Not to condemn all American migrants, Montoya, "in justice," credited allies who assisted in developing New Mexico resources against those who were "too lazy and neglectful to work with others," occupying themselves "in calumniating the people, lying left and right without knowing of what they spoke."[22] Montoya, defiantly proud of the "Mexican blood" that ran through his people's veins, swore never to remain silent again in the face of such insults of "our race" from another enemy of the Mexican people.[23]

Shaming Philistine Solons

Harvey Butler Fergusson proved one of only two Democrats to win delegate to Congress from New Mexico in the railroad era. A devotee of the Progressive William Jennings Bryan, Fergusson proudly wore the badge of Republican old guard enemy.[24]

Enrique Salazar liked Fergusson's ideas on statehood. As he told him, his policies demonstrated "a desire to protect the interests of the Neo-Mexicano people and particularly native citizens." In the "talented and reasoned" Fergusson, Salazar saw the quality of respect for his people that was demanded of Euro-American leadership. Fergusson thanked Salazar for his nonpartisan "gentlemanly" message, especially because press attention to his work tended to be injurious. He did not hesitate to call "hispano-americano" claims for civil rights acts of justice.[25]

Fergusson answered Salazar's questions with flattering scripts. On the sixty-day residency requirement to vote, which would permit Euro-American strangers to diminish Hispano participation in the writing of a state constitution, he said that reducing Nuevomexicano influence was the last thing he wanted since "Hispanos" were the "first inhabitants" in New Mexico (undermining the claim of disenfranchised

Native Americans) and should therefore retain "in great part" the power that they originally possessed. They were citizens of the United States "in the plainest and truest sense of the word," and for that he did not enter into any agreement that would in the least go against them. Fergusson promised to give them proper consideration and rights by going with the waiting period to vote so that "Hispano-Americans" would have "their" legislature.[26]

Fergusson sustained Nuevomexicano identity when he stood on the floor of the House in support of his bill for leasable public lands so New Mexico could advance public education in preparation for statehood. José Segura at *El Boletín Popular* urged the support of Fergusson, calling his public lands measure "an act of justice to the people of this territory."[27] In a striking oration before the Committee of the Whole on why New Mexico was entitled to statehood, Fergusson joined those who recoiled at American New Mexicanism. In unprecedented remarks he charged directly at Republicans for denying full citizenship to Nuevomexicanos, denouncing the taunting of the "native or Spanish American people of New Mexico" with the insult of "an alien population," a people whom he was proud to be "their representative and their defender." Fergusson accused Republicans of partisan cynicism in unjustly assailing "Hispanos," cruelly seeking excuses "for what party necessity seemed to demand—the continued exclusion of New Mexico from the Union" so as not to have to approve the admission of a Democratic territory.[28]

Nuevomexicanos, Fergusson contended, had long been deprived of their right to admission under the Treaty of Guadalupe Hidalgo and congressional policy regarding the territories. He also fumed that this "long-suffering people" had been the victims of falsehood and slander and that "the illegal, unconstitutional, unjust, and oppressive course of the Republican Party toward New Mexico" was proof of that. The delegate bitterly recalled the infamous Republican Struble Report, citing slurs from Davis's *El Gringo*, calling the "shameless libel difficult to properly characterize . . . in parliamentary language." The characterizations were "wholly, wickedly, injuriously and recklessly false," written by an "irresponsible scribbler, who hoped to sell his book by the very exaggeration of histories, or who had been kicked out of some virtuous Spanish-American home . . . for conduct unbecoming a gentleman."

Fergusson laid the blame for the "vicious mouthings" squarely onto Republican chests, their "deadly work" now permanently taking its place in the records of the Congress. New Mexico's delegates had the duty to denounce the "terrible calumny" until "these [Nuevomexicano] people finally get justice at the hands of Congress." Speaking personally, Fergusson remarked, "I have known Spanish-American citizens of New Mexico for fifteen years, and I tell you, Mr. Chairman, it is utterly impossible that their mothers and fathers were the moral lepers pictured in that minority report." Channeling Prince's version of the Good Character script, he added that the insult filled him with "hot indignation" and that

> to contrast those words with what I have learned these good people to be when I remember the Christian home of our Spanish-American citizens, the dignity, the piety, the loving charity, and the lofty virtue of their matrons, and the modesty, the innocence, and the purity of their maidens. The very stones in the floors of their churches, hundreds of years old, bear witness against these base charges; the dents in the stone floors where they perform, and have for hundreds of years performed, their daily devotions are silent but eloquent and convincing proof that they are, and always have been, a most devout and Christian people.

Fergusson closed denouncing the monied oligarchy that "prostituted the powers of government to serve its own selfish and avaricious ends." While the Republican Party was "ostensibly performing on the stage, we can plainly hear the prompter behind the scenes, and the money power, or the Republican Party, whoever you will, is intolerant, tyrannical, and un-American in its treatment of New Mexico."[29]

Fergusson's public lands bill sailed through. Unfazed at being called bigots, House Speaker Thomas Reed and his Republican colleagues likely felt that expanding education resources would remedy the deficiencies their impassive minds beheld in alien Nuevomexicanos. The law, according to one historian, "probably did more than any other one thing to promote education and prepare the people of New Mexico for statehood."[30]

"Mexican," a Partisan Tool

In 1890, friends in Washington advised New Mexicans to form a constitution to show Congress their readiness to become a state.[31] Governor L. B. Prince and the territorial assembly passed a measure to convene a constitutional convention. Democrats, however, refused to participate in a project it said would privilege the Santa Fe Ring and business interests with special provisions including low corporate taxes.[32] While Democrats urged voters to invalidate the constitution,[33] *La Voz del Pueblo*, which at this early date leaned Republican, called it the opportunity to have "our" senators and representatives confirmed as intelligent entrepreneurs, capable of self-government. Editor Néstor Montoya warned of the "public shame" to be cast on the Neo-Mexicanos who opposed statehood, preferring to "leave us in oppression."[34]

Nuevomexicano Republicans authored two propaganda columns in support of the constitution, both employing a "Mexican" identity. José D. Sena, a delegate to the Constitutional Convention and son of the late José D. Sena who played chief marshal in the Tertio-Millennial Spanish Pageant, penned *Veinte y Cuatro Razones Porque los Nativos de Nuevo Mexico—o sea los Mexicanos como los llaman—Deben Votar por la Constitución y Erigirse en Estado* (Twenty-Four Reasons Why the Nativos of New Mexico—or the Mexicans as they are called—Should Vote for the Constitution and Establish a State). Reason One declared that it was time to demand that the government fully comply with "its promises to incorporate us into the brotherhood of the States of the Union as stipulated in the Treaty of Guadalupe Hidalgo, which was the greatest inducement that could have been offered to us to embrace the rights of citizenship in the United States and renounce those of the citizens of the Republic of Mexico."[35]

Reason Three mixed the Nuevomexicano Good Character and US Cementation scripts, holding that America knew "when it received us in its bosom and established us in a system of territorial government in plain compliance and entire confidence, that, while of Mexican nationality, we possessed all the qualifications necessary—fidelity, valor, obedience, capacity, honor, and integrity—to become complete citizens of the United States." Better yet, the Good Character script in Reason Twenty referred to "the Mexican sustenance of love and respect, [which] by virtue and national honor was transmitted [to us] by our ancestors [and] had no recognized rival."

Reason Seven merged the rare Mexican Founders script and US Cementation, declaring that Nativos deserved statehood because the "Sons" of Mexican heroes Hidalgo, Morelos and Iturbide were "just like the Sons of Washington, [who] had never been slaves, but were simply free and independent." Reason Five assured that the people were capable of self-government because for thirty years they had passed "their own laws" and their leaders were "talented Mexicans, born, raised and nurtured on their own land . . . whose laws the Congress of the United States had sanctioned without exception." Reason Six denounced the "whole bunch of impostors, who with private protests, denied the Mexicans their rights, who tried to denigrate them, and would submerge them to a despicable state of not being able to govern themselves." Here readers would have known that Sena meant Democrats pretending to be friends. Related to Reason Twenty-Three—that the people supported the draft constitution because they "detested all impostors who, with a smile on their lips tried to use them as instruments for their own aggrandizement"—would appear more explicitly later in the campaign.

Reason Seventeen linked "Mexican" to the problem of land usurpation, claiming that the "mexicanos"

> deserve quick approval of the mercedes legitimately granted to their ancestors by the governments of Spain and Mexico to prevent the multitude of *tropelías* [outrages] that are committed on their lands, by the negligence of the government in holding up their settlement, and their removal to the public domain.

Such a Land Grant script on behalf of farmers of humble means flew in the face of the fact that the charge of land theft was commonly put to alleged Republican land-grabbers.[36]

Recalling the Traitorous Nuevomexicano script that had been so harshly lodged against Senator Jacinto Armijo in the public education battle in the 1870s, Sena commented,

> I would say that my opinion has always been and still is today that the Mexican who votes against the constitution for political motives, hatred, or personal vengeance so as to gain some personal advantage or the hopes of one, is a spurious son of New Mexico, a traitor of the same, disloyal to his country, and a murderer of the most sacred interests of all the New Mexico community.

Sena closed with a resounding duality:

> Viva the native New Mexicans, noble children of Hidalgo, the glorious father of their independence! Adopted children of the immortal Washington who, with ballot in hand, will march to the voting booths on October 7, 1890, and will vote for the constitution at once to assert for all time that they are worthy of the sovereignty they strive for, and that they themselves are capable of self-government and amply responsible for sustaining a state government.

The other Nuevomexicano-directed propaganda document took the fight directly to the Democrats. The unnamed author used a traditional allegorical *diálogo* to turn the table on the actual terms of the partisan conflict, portraying Democratic Party Euro-Americans as exploitative settler colonials and Republicans as the princes of liberty. The piece in a Spanish-language weekly carried the byline Argus. In Greek mythology, Argus Panoptes is an alert creature with many watchful and vigilant eyes. Typical in the Nuevomexicano diálogo, two paisanos cross paths on the road to Taos. Juan de los Reyes (John of the Wise Kings) engages the humble voter, José Alamitos (Joseph of the Hinterlands).[37]

The Republican Juan begins assertively: "How happy I am to see you," immediately probing with, "I wanted to know how you felt about the state constitution." There follows:

> José: "What? What? I am against it, as are all the poor people. Alejandro says it will be our ruin, that taxes will be too *crudo* [harsh] and that the territory is too poor, and he who feels sorry for the people and who loves them is working against it until he can no more, and you will see how well he says it.

"Alejandro" implicated the Democrat Alexander Gusdorf who settled his family in Taos from Germany in the 1870s. A member of the territorial council, he signed on to the Taos County Democratic Party's refusal to sanction the Constitutional Convention because of its pro-corporate bias.[38] Juan speaks of Alejandro as a self-interested intruder:

> Well, [Alejandro] says wrongly, because you cannot ruin someone who is ruined. Now, what tax are the poor going to pay when they do not have anything to give; you well know that the remainder of nothing is nothing. If the territory is poor, it's precisely because of its inferior condition before the general government. A territory is not appreciated, not respected, does not have voice nor vote in national issues, and the president of the United States is a monarch over the territories because they were not consulted in his election. Now, insofar as Alejandro loves us, for what does a man come here but to enrich himself, who, after his pockets are filled, will return to his country laughing at those whom he betrays in different ways?

Pinning Gusdorf like this flipped the Democratic Party's usual impeachment of rich land-hungry Republicans, based on the fact that Gusdorf had, as one historian notes, acquired "considerable land" in Taos County.[39] Moreover, Albuquerque Jewish businessmen had signed a petition against statehood, arguing that business would not be served until Congress provided "some convenient, speedy, inexpensive, and certain method to settle the present anomalous condition of title to the vast area of our most valuable lands, which are now claimed largely by unscrupulous and designing persons"—implying the Santa Fe Ring.[40]

Juan faults José for not seeing how the more outsiders praised him and smiled, "so much more they hate and deprecate you." The further claim, that they were "hypocrites by instinct, sagacious by calculation, always betraying us," was suggested in José D. Sena's twenty-four reasons. "Is it possible," Juan surmises, "that we believe in those of our enemies who are sneakier and closer?" José innocently wonders whom, then, to believe. "In our fellow citizens," Juan responds (given that most Nuevomexicanos were Republicans) "those who are honest and illustrious," whose "blood" is, "as General Riva Palacios said,"

> our blood, their flesh our flesh, their bones our bones; in those who have their temporal home here, and who consider this country as their only patria and the place where they would live until they repose in the cemetery, and who, living and dying here leave their assets here to their children and the example of their virtues to form, with our children, *la patria* that should serve the future generations on this soil on which we now pass.

Mexican politician, military officer, jurist, diplomat, and writer Vicente Florencio Carlos Riva Palacio Guerrero had recently visited Santa Fe. A rare treat for educated Nuevomexicanos, *El Boletín Popular* commemorated his visit by publishing his poetry.[41] Exploiting Riva Palacio's prestige, Juan links statehood to the value of homeland primacy as the Mexican guest had imparted it.

"But Juan," a quaking José begs," the people are so poor here that in order to gain a dollar the men have to look for work in Colorado." As Juan shoots back: "And they always will be, for every day *gambusinos* [gold diggers] and *pelados* [shiftless ones] come in." Reflecting Mark Suzman's point about nationalist movements longing for "national integration . . . a vision of economic power and the development of the area's natural resources,"[42] Juan sounds the Economic Development script that Republicans had been repeating since the Tertio-Millennial Exposition. As he explains, capitalists would only invest in states where they believed they could safely form companies. Should New Mexico become one, "we will not need to go to Colorado nor any other state to look for work, since here we would have jobs because capitalists would come just as they have gone to California, Texas and Colorado after they became states, and set up factories to work the wool."

A transformed New Mexico would produce "an abundance of what is necessary for life, adding to the benign and salubrious climate under that pure, blue, and serene sky." In Juan's ethnonationalist romance, "We and our children would form one of the happiest, most prosperous, and advanced peoples in North America."

As former delegate to Congress Harvey Fergusson had amply demonstrated, Democrats actually condemned national Republicans for hurling New Mexicanisms, but Juan draws José into seeing Alejandro and his Democratic pals saying that Nuevomexicanos were incapable of governing themselves and insulting their [Republican] legislature. What they really meant, but dared not say, is that "the people of the land [are] very inferior and not worth anything." As sly Juan ventures:

> Well, tell them that the transportation facilities are very easy now, so from Africa we will order a boat full of Anthonies [pluralizing the Azorean delegate to Congress Anthony Joseph], another bunch of Alexanders from Germany [pluralizing Gusdorf], and from back east a carload of Rosses, Gildersleeves, Longs, Smiths and Johnsons [names of known Democrats], and we can leave fast.

Talking like an anticolonial rebel, Juan has Nuevomexicanos overriding imported bosses with self-rule:

> ¡Ah, José! That is the true cause for why Alejandro and others like him oppose a state government so much, because they would see, in rage and envy, our compatriots exercising high and honorable posts. They would have to be governed by a race they consider inferior and which they are accustomed to denigrating,

> those who have always seen the Mexican (no matter how intelligent he be) with the dejected aspect of the oppressed, feeling threatened, with his sombrero in his hand, arms crossed before the ever-imported federal employees, with that sad and humble frown on their lips: "Your majesty, have pity on the poor Mexicans. . . ." Oh, how sour and painful it would be then to see the Mexican with a proud and peaceful face as governor, senator in the great Congress of the nation, judge, prosecutor, marshal, presidential elector, exercising the wisdom, the power, and the right of all American citizens.

Alejandro and friends did not want the people's destitution to end so they could treat them like "instruments and not men, leaving our children abject, deprecated, defamed, without a future for anything, always humiliated, asking measly favors from those adventurers. How is it possible," Juan poses, "that they, our enemies, would accept the change that would venerate, honor, and elevate us?"

José trembles at the thought of self-rule getting tripped up. "But if I don't know how to read, and if I'm ignorant," he implores, "and most of the vecinos are just as backward, when will we have those high positions?" Juan responds adroitly: "Oh! Almost all the youth know how to read and write, and they even talk in American." We detect the script of Imminent Advancement as Juan continues: People in the states suffer from ignorance by "living in submission and slavery," but not for that

> do men fail to work for the progress, betterment, and advancement of the human family. The race to honor and glory is open to all citizens. For that reason, we should all work for it. If we do not find ourselves in high positions in society, we work for our children to have it; and if we don't find it, we help our compatriots, not letting the feeling of patriotism extinguish itself.

Juan also mixes the scripts of Poblador Primacy and (a qualified) Future Self-Rule:

> The honor that our compatriots want is honor for our patria, of which we are a part. Among our paisanos are many men of talent and honor who would be able to take charge of state government and we are the ones who choose and elect at our desire and contentment. Finally, we shall take advantage of this opportunity to enter at once into the true camp of liberty, wisdom and right.

The two friends part ways, promising to meet again. Argus, in turn, forwards a transcript of the dialogue from Fernando de Taos in the Nuevomexicano heartland to the *Santa Fe New Mexican.*[43]

As popular literature, the diálogo would have been a lively gift to the community. As propaganda, it was a creative way to make the case for one party's policies on an important issue. However, it likely failed to gaslight voters into believing the ruse of Republicans as boss-free humanitarians. Quite likely, Néstor Montoya—who had just established *La Bandera Americana* in Albuquerque, was a member of the territorial house, and, as we saw above, preferred to call Nuevomexicanos "Mexicans"—authored the piece.[44] The Argus byline, however, seems to have harbored someone else as well. Key correspondence suggests that in sketching the dialogue, Montoya utilized talking points provided by Tom Catron of all people, the greatest land-grabbing villain who used the territory's Republican Party to maintain control of Nuevomexicano politicians.

Badly wanting Nuevomexicanos to support the constitution, Catron offered cash and advice to Nuevomexicano subalterns to translate and distribute drafts of his campaign broadsheets, including J. Francisco Chaves, who presided over the Constitutional Convention, and quite likely José D. Sena who in his Twenty-Four Reasons used ploys that appeared in the diálogo. As the crafty Catron conveyed to Montoya:

> If we are admitted, you will see good times. Immigration and capital will come into New Mexico, and everyone will receive good wages. As long as we are kept in the condition of a territory, foreign money will be excluded under the law of the United States, and money from the states, not having any competition,

> will not be brought here. We will be forced to sell our property at a sacrifice, and people will be without wages or with insufficient wages. There is nothing in the world which will be of such benefit to the laboring classes as an influx of immigration and foreign capital. The immigrants who will come to this country will all bring some means. Foreign capital is compelled to employ labor in the mines and on the lands in order to make it productive. You can readily see the advantages and place them before the people. See that every voter in the state is turned out and votes.[45]

Catron's points regarding the material benefits of the constitution and Nuevomexicanos not knowledgeable about statehood form important allusions in the dialogue. His letter, dated September 20, was followed by the diálogo a week later.[46] However, a gap appears in Catron's expropriation of Nuevomexicano identity: It is likely that Montoya slipped in the business about Nuevomexicano self-rule. That Catron, who pined for a seat in the US Senate, would encourage Nuevomexicanos to monopolize state offices fails to ring true.[47] He wanted Montoya to believe that the Democrats provided the "great opposition" to the constitution because they were "afraid of the Mexican people" eager to control the state "to the injury of the Americans." "You and I know [it] is not true," Catron conveyed. "The Mexicans have always divided up the offices fairer with the Americans, and they are divided in politics just the same as the Americans." As such, he said, "it would be impossible" for the Mexicans "to get together to control the state exclusively in their own interest and against the interests of the Americans. Besides, they have no disposition to do so."[48] As a Nuevomexicano identitarian, Montoya would not have agreed, and he knew where the threat to Nuevomexicano self-determination came from, including key Republicans.

Disappointing Republicans, the constitution lost out by 8,687 votes.[49] Nuevomexicanos rejected it soundly.[50] One historian doubts that the masses of people wanted the admission of New Mexico into the union.[51] The constitution included a secular school system and so priests likely spoke against it from their pulpits. Traditionalists still wanted morality-based classes for their children.[52] For posterity, the diálogo reveals one of the ways that the rhetorical terms of ethnic nationalism had shaped the territory's political discourse.

Spanish Identity Erupts

A discursive "Spanish" heritage burst when an accessible Euro-American used "Mexican" derogatorily against Nuevomexicanos. In 1895, the Denver priest Thomas H. Malone attended the conferral of pallium on New Mexico Archbishop Plácido L. Chappelle. Cardinal James Gibbons of the senior US Catholic archdiocese in Baltimore officiated the placement of vestments on Chappelle's shoulders. Bishops from two states and another territory graced the ceremony. A resplendent jubilee lit up the Santa Fe Plaza.[53]

On his return home, Malone published an account of his visit in his own *Colorado Catholic* journal. While in Santa Fe, he wrote, he heard a certain regret: Chapelle, he of "such force of character and superior intellectual attainments, banished to such a limited field." As he explained:

> The Mexican, in our opinion, is doomed and destined to disappear like the Indian. An indolent people, they seem to have neither the energy of the Indian nor the intellectual life of the Spaniard, these two natures and characters having seemly suffered by the mixture and making a result inferior in some respects to the Indian and in all respects to the Spaniard. Hence, we do not believe it possible for the church, even under the guidance of such will as strong, or an intellect as brilliant as Archbishop Chapelle's, to build up a Mexican population that will be able to hold its own with the Americans of that territory.

The poor archbishop was consigned to a place and a people, Malone regretted, "where, and among whom, the good resulting is so comparatively less than in other parts of the country where the good would be measured at the maximum."[54]

Leading Nuevomexicanos blasted Malone reflexively and prodigiously. Two indignation meetings rocked Santa Fe, one orchestrated by La Sociedad Literaria y de Debates (Literary and Debating Society), the other roused by former Territorial School Superintendent Amado Chaves, historian Benjamín Read, Valencia County rancher/political boss Solomon Luna, former Delegate to Congress José Francisco Chaves, José D. Sena, and nineteen others. Each event produced a manifesto and ordered that it be published in Albuquerque's *La Bandera Americana* with a call for all newspapers in New Mexico, Colorado, and Arizona to do the same. A copy went to Archbishop Chapelle.[55]

As one resolution logged, Malone conducted "a cowardly attack, unjustified and malicious." He erred in not recognizing that the "majority of the population of New Mexico is Hispano-Americano" (as opposed to Mexican). Not only was the reverend "not familiar with the native population," had "never associated with it, knew nothing of its habits and customs"—he was "not motivated by the doctrine of charity of Our Father Jesus Christ for all men." "Hispanos" were wholly in the Church's tent virtually by definition, explained *El Nuevo Mexicano*, nine-tenths of them being "loyal Catholics."[56]

Malone's insults called for a penetratingly sharp religious primacy. As Amado Chaves charged, Malone hypocritically usurped the "sacred name Catholic" to "satiate the inclinations of his depravity." As part of the Founding Church script, used in the 1870s secular school controversy, the "cheeky propagandist" was accused of failing to realize that

> centuries before he knew the world, those "Mexicans" had planted the Cross and established the faith, constructed churches and educational facilities at the cost of their lives and, [Indian Scourge ablaze,] defended their religious credo with their blood against the barbarities of the energized Indians whom Mr. Malone laments had not been extinguished.[57]

Had Malone said that the Mexicans were "too kind-hearted and tolerant to permit the systematic exploitation of many adventurers of his own gumption, and, instead of giving them the boot, opened their arms the more to fatten them up," *La Voz del Pueblo* exhaled, "in that case he would have spoken the truth." In his Nuevomexicano Deficiency script, Malone displayed low character, ingratitude, and hypocrisy. A man with noble sentiments would not rely on "vainglory in depreciating what in his eyes appears humble, nor does he throw out insults like a shyster, hurting the sentiments of his fellow creatures." Proof of true Catholicism lay in the "hundreds of priests who have lived among us. Therefore, the assertions of the pretentious Malone leave the titles of impostor, traitor of the religion he professes, and Judas Iscariot upon his forehead."[58]

La Voz del Pueblo editors were reminded of settler colonial "scoundrels" who came from the East "to live among us with the malformed opinion that the Mexican is very inferior to the rest of the races of mankind when many of them received our greatest favors." Others were the "dregs of the American population who acquire their false information in taverns or places of deprivation, few of them having been seen in this land until the railroad brought them from the east, putting on airs of importance [by] lying about the people of New Mexico until they fall down." The lawyer Octaviano Larrazolo stood as a prime example of a true "Mexican" who consistently surprised "Anglo-Saxons" with his "emphatic talent."[59]

Malone committed the normative sin of tearing down social boundaries. As one M. Rivera intoned, Nuevomexicanos were "superior to the Indian and equal to the intrepid *español,*" indicated by the very "energetic and intelligent" condemnation of the "famous and gratuitous calumniator of the neo-mexicano people."[60] Malone's claim of Mexicans "condemned and destined to disappear like the Indian" made no sense, one critic said, proof lying in "crass ignorance of the statistics of a population of this country." Although borne of a tough Destitute Isolation, as the familiar script went, Hispanos sat at the pinnacle of Western civilization:

> That the Hispano-Americanos of this territory are equal to any other civilized people in their loyalty to their country, in education and learning, and more advanced than other peoples, considering that for three hundred years they were continually attacked by the savages, thousands of miles from the mother country, lacking protection, without schools, without means, and that owing solely to their natural valor and patriotism are still a people today.[61]

In this ethnonationalist refrain, the "natural valor and patriotism" of such an experience had formed "a people."[62]

In recent editorial essays, Enrique Salazar had been mulling Nuevomexicano historical isolation and here it helped him lay out an elaborate primacy account. "Perhaps we could contest his reverence that the Neo-Mexicanos during three hundred years have lived in this sterile and unproductive country," he expressed,

> protecting themselves against enemies that at every pass threatened their lives, and that during all this time survived without any help, and at a cost of occupations provided for their own necessities without asking for charity and without needing the help of anyone outside of what divine providence dispensed, and without dying off for fault of nourishment.[63]

Much as Tranquilino Luna did at the Tertio-Millennial Exposition twelve years earlier, Salazar recognized historical destitution and the "defects" it left in the people. But while Malone detected vestiges of deficiency, "as a preacher of the gospel," he was not perspicacious enough to perceive their true meaning. "Dressed in the character of priest," he could not let the moment pass without denigrating "the poor mexicanos who had the misfortune of sparking his hate and bad faith." Indeed, their character shortcomings were no different than "all the nations, races and peoples that have been, and are, and will be since the world is world and until it ends." The reverend might have commented similarly about *his* Irish compatriots, in misery since before the nineteenth century, "dying of hunger by the thousands," "a great number" of them dependent on "public charity to survive"[64] (recalling the Better than Your European Immigrants script).

"Deficiency" in the "Spanish race in New Mexico" was, in a word, beyond the capacity of a "malignant calumniator" to understand. The 150,000 citizens who were descendientes de espanoles . . . acreedores al título de hispano-americanos (descendants of the Spaniards accorded the title of Hispano-Americano) followed the uses and customs that were transmitted "since the age of the Reconquest of Diego de Vargas close to 300 years ago by the first settlers and ancestors of the actual residents." Plying the scripts of Destitute Isolation and the Derelict

Mexican and American Governments, Salazar arrived at the Past Living in the Present script, what Benedict Anderson identifies in nationalist rhetoric as "a simultaneity of past and future in an instantaneous present."[65] The people could not, Salazar explained, "deflect the natural consequences that invariably impact communities that for a long period are not in intimate contact with the rest of the world and the civilization of the age." Reflecting an abiding nation, "we suffered delays, and we could not advance so much as we could have done because of a lack of protection that the governments of Spain and Mexico did not give us, and for this reason the generality of our people did not obtain the advantages of education that we would have obtained if we had found more happy circumstances."[66]

Insofar as Malone represented US New Mexicanism, Salazar argued that "perhaps more than any other nationality would have done if they would have been in our situation," the "Spaniards" did what was necessary to survive. Hitching Indian Scourge to the Nuevomexicano Good Character script, he offered,

> Our ancestors amply verified, with the nobility of their blood and the clarity of their talent, the sustenance of themselves against the innumerable hordes of savage Indians that continually besieged and attacked without forcing them to belie their valor and without obligating them to cede an inch of the land they had acquired with the power of their arms, which they watered with their blood.[67]

Dispelling any sense of mestizaje in this community's coherence, the understanding was that all settlers were born of pure Spanish blood.

Reinforming the Salubrious Annexation script, Salazar relished that after thirty years of test and crisis, the American government adopted "our sufferings and placed a perpetual respite to them," subjugating the hostile tribes that had spilled "so much of our blood for more than two and a half centuries. Then our people could breathe and go along in tranquility and without worry to carry on with their industries and ordinary occupations, depending as they always had on the sweat of their face and the light of their intelligence for planning each day and looking toward the education that they missed so much."

In a qualification of the rescue, however, this same government failed to show its "usual liberality," withholding the means Nuevomexicanos needed to develop their "illustrious skills."

Twentieth-century critics such as George A. Sánchez would denounce the United States for neglecting a people it forcibly annexed.[68] Instead, Salazar meekly conjectured that it may not have been without reason that America did not provide adequate assistance. After all, "the descendants of the Españoles who discovered and conquered the new world did not need charity; they could depend on themselves as they had done since the era of the conquest of their land." In this script of Poblador Hardiness, Salazar maintained that it was a "very prudent and sensible determination to leave us to our own resources and efforts." The policy proved itself by the "great advance" the people made in the previous twenty-five years. Refracting the Ethnonationalist Competency script, "We have been in good times y en los dones mas apreciables de la civilización" (and in the most appreciable blessings of civilization). Most of "our people realized the necessities of the age, and they would unite and make some sacrifices if asked to do so to get the lights of education extended to them in all the fields of the territory."[69]

In time and on a "right" road, "we will [Salazar plodded on] be able to realize so many hopes that we have conceived for our race to be at the level as the Anglo-Americans who arrived to colonize our territory and establish their residence in our midst." As it followed, the "sinister prophecies of our [New Mexicanist] enemies inspired by the invincible antipathy felt against our people, were not founded on any reason or tangible act." Yet, in the script of Virtual Self-blame, there were "everyday lessons of great utility for our advancement, wrought by [American] men who had great knowledge of ourselves, wiser in the arts and worldly business, who naturally knew how to exploit our innocence, taking advantage of our riches because we had our eyes closed, knowing little of the tricks and cunning snares practiced in the more advanced countries."[70]

It cost his people that they spoke a "foreign language," making it necessary to depend on men who knew the laws and practices of the country. Consequently, "our native co-citizens . . . had to content themselves with the role of pupils and submit to the direction of individuals who knew the depth of the government system and by their nationality had the influence and consideration that we lacked." Yet the "lights of education" were not "generalized among our people so that they be placed at the foot of equality with the experts who have manipulated [things] until now." It was "very natural" with no embarrassment, "being that our country, conquered by a foreign nation" should bring the men of that nationality to constitute "our tutors or directors until our people knew their rights and learned the art of acquiring and conserving them."[71]

It had not been easy. Yet in defiance of Malone, "Our race will NOT be extinguished; on the contrary it will grow in number, riches, and influence and will always be an important factor in the business of New Mexico." Like the people

> of the great nation we belong to, we will never count as isolated in the American hemisphere because in the New World there are innumerable peoples of their race and language who differ with the Anglo Saxons, including the imperium of the continent in possession of Mexico and Central America and the Hispano-Americanos that occupy almost all of South America.

Making up four-fifths of the settled territory, Nuevomexicanos and their descendants would maintain themselves as its "actual possessors . . . without danger of extinction, with all prospects of acquiring major importance every day as we go advancing in the arts and industries of civilization even with the fiction of the inferiority of our race with which so many of our enemies brand us." The absurdity in the accusation of their inferiority was proved by the "phalange of illustrious men of our race, who have fulfilled a great role in the affairs of New Mexico since the fortunate American annexation of these parts, showing that we do not cede even one point in intelligence, energy and instruction to the most illustrated of other races that are found in our midst."[72]

It all pointed in the direction of self-rule but in an informal or naturalistic manner, for "little by little," the honors and positions of authority would go to those with qualifications, "without placing attention on race or origin," for "of course the Hispano-Americano people will make the necessary distinctions, giving preference to their friends and the citizens who, by their talents and instruction, are deserved of their confidence and suffrage." The people, "who naturally love work, will know how to make a place for themselves in the struggle for existence and will acquire a position so honorable and advantageous among the elements that we will come to form the future population of New Mexico. Nothing can disturb this, nor can the privileges that assure us of our position be yanked away."[73]

Calming the turbulence of Nuevomexicano wrath, Archbishop Chappelle called Malone's characterizations "unfortunate." A French national who came to New Mexico in 1891,[74] Chappelle knew a thing or two of Nuevomexicano scripts. While ignoring the good qualities of the "Mexican population," he acknowledged this "race" whose strength survived in the "vast territory" under adverse circumstances and whose intelligence was above question. The "lovely Spanish language" was still one to admire after a "long separation from the mother country." Flagging a key criterion of nationness, the people preserved the faith of their ancestors while appreciating "our American institutions," a blessing he would seek to preserve while procuring their well-being. With the help of a devoted clergy, the deacon of Santa Fe declared, "splendid results will be obtained for the Mexican people, in both religious and social life."[75]

The Nuevomexicano backlash seems to have really stung Malone. In the *Daily New Mexican*, he spoke with humbled remorse to the "Spanish-Americans of New Mexico." He had been "exasperatingly misunderstood," he grieved, and it was with regret that "our Spanish-American friends in our neighboring territory have taken offense where none was intended." His paper had, he emphasized, "printed countless articles in defense of the Spanish Americans against their unjust critics." A bit queasily he claimed never to have been "among those that have made use of the disdainful epithet 'Mexican' to denote the people of Spanish blood in New Mexico."[76]

In a strange third-person plural, Malone contorted what he meant by the "Mexicans." As opposed to the "native population," it referred

> only [to] the habitants of the Pueblos—some twenty in number—the half-breeds who associate with them, and their immediate followers: to these and these only

> did he intend references; to these and these only was his article, in justice applicable, and any other construction he now repudiates and insists that to give his article the construction which has been given by it, in certain [circles], is both an injustice and a wrong.

Switching to first-person plural, Malone conceded:

> We perhaps made a mistake in using the term "Mexican," but, as we have said, it never entered our mind, in view of the vulgar use of the word in the western countryside, to apply it to others than the inhabitants of the Pueblos and the [half-breed] others mentioned above. [It was the] reclamation of these very people that the church is directing, through a zealous and self-sacrificing clergy... And our opinion was and still is that this people is destined to disappear and become forgotten; that it is an impossible task to ever elevate them to the plane of the American character, and by Americans we include all—the Spanish Americans, as well as the Irish-Americans, German-Americans, etc.[77]

Throwing the Puebloans under the train, so to speak, Malone conceded Nuevomexicano primacy with its Historical Destitution script. "Spanish Americans" had "to contend against great odds in the struggle for supremacy in New Mexico—a supremacy we are happy to say they have attained in every walk of life, and which we trust they will maintain for all time." In the context of the statehood issue, he hoped that New Mexico would soon "add another star to Old Glory and may her Spanish-American sons soon be heard in the halls of the nation's Congress." Such was the "wish of the *Colorado Catholic*, an accomplishment which its editor will do his share to bring about."[78]

El Boletín Popular and *La Voz del Pueblo* translated Malone's "Spanish-American" to "Hispano-Americano."[79] In place of "half-breed," *El Boletín Popular* inserted "mestizo."[80] Nuevomexicano leaders seem not to have objected to the claim that Puebloans and mestizos were destined to disappear, but if Malone's "half-breed" signified lower class, it was clearly wrong to suppose that they were beyond the clutch of the church, for just recently the leading parishioners of Our Lady of Guadalupe Church reported to Archbishop Chapelle that the poor families had made sufficient contributions of five and ten *centavos* to begin the reconstruction of their church and monsignor's residence.[81]

The unrelenting *Revista de Taos* could not believe Malone had made a mistake in repeatedly using "the word 'mexicano'" in referring to the "Mexican descendants of the Spanish." It was one thing for him to feel bad about insulting them and quite another to say that Mexicanos were those who hauled wood while "Hispano-Americanos" wore watches, smoked cigars, and spoke English. "We are all Hispano-Americanos," it was emphasized enthusiastically, "wood carriers or no, and this paper as a defender of the people, never will let pass the distinction between the poor class and the rich, calling the latter Hispano-Americanos and the others Indians, or rather 'Mexicans' in the mocking meaning of the word used by strangers." Ill-equipped to accept the claim of a coherent people, Malone stayed true to that feature of his character at the festivities in Santa Fe where, as he reported, "there had not been any Pueblo Indians present, and if there had been it would have been easy to understand that they are never called Mexicans." The charity Malone refused others was the charity refused to him, his self-serving apology taken "for what it was worth."[82]

As the snapshots in this chapter show, Nuevomexicanos were moved to express their primacy identity on the early platform of the statehood movement, and a Euro-American delegate to Congress memorably answered the slings of American New Mexicanism to Congressional colleagues. Nuevomexicanos were not averse to employing "Mexican" as their ethnic rubric if they could control its meaning. However, derogations of "Mexican" in the homeland called for a hard-hitting "Spanish" identification. As the movement for statehood slogged on, a tendency of name heritages to narrow emerged, as the next chapter illustrates.

CHAPTER 6

Down the Stretch, the Uneven Resort to "Spanish"

AS THE NEW millennium dawned and the movement for statehood assumed what historian Marion Dargan calls "a real boom,"[1] Enrique Salazar announced that Neo-Mexicano honor demanded that leaders "persist and persevere" in the push for statehood, there being no other way to "liberate our people" from the "disqualification, indifference and disdain" they suffered. Because ancestors "colonized and redeemed this grand territory at the cost of great sacrifices and penalties, Neo-Mexicanos" were worthy of good fortune and deserving of better treatment than what they had been given "at the hands of the obsessive antipathy so many have professed." With statehood, the "monumental pyramid of calumny and falsehoods" that damaged the Neo-Mexicano people would crumble "before the light of truth." Salazar perceived the enemies of his people becoming "everyday more impotent" while the "number of our [Euro-American] friends who defend and protect us with sincerity and energy grows."[2]

While the prospects of gaining statehood seemed brighter than ever, Salazar and his compatriots would continue to experience frustration. Before long, another local scandal similar to the Malone fiasco drove Nuevomexicanos to another Spanish fit. Then two congressional policy roadblocks rolled out of Washington, one to destroy New Mexico's Spanish language, the other to conjoin New Mexico and Arizona. A more optimistic scenario intersecting the Spanish heritage and statehood emanated out of the governor's office.

A Hapless Missionary

In 1901, Nuevomexicanos thought they took care of Anglo Christian meddling in their people's cultural and racial integrity back in the Father Malone affair. But it returned with even greater force when Methodist Missionary Nellie Snider published an essay entitled "The Spanish American" in the *Las Vegas Sunday Morning Review* (hereafter,

Review). That edition of the *Review* has since gone missing. However, many of the passages quoted by critics reveal the gist of Snider's messaging, which was originally meant for the eyes of Eastern donors on the difficulties of proselytizing among Nuevomexicano families.[3] There was, for example the description of the elderly as so illiterate they did not know how old they were; their being "as ignorant as the Hottentots of Africa"; missionary work being "as foreign as that in China or Japan"; the ignorance being due to the Catholic Church where they were groomed by superstition and crime, never hearing the "sweet word of the Gospel."[4]

Review editor J. F. Manning had been out of town and could not review the piece in time, but when he returned he immediately sensed the danger. In the four years he had lived in New Mexico, he had never seen such distortions. Among other things in his apology, he credited Catholics for bringing education to remote New Mexico.[5] The regrets fell flat and heritage scripts flew like bats out of a cavern at sundown.

Again, the wrenching of Nuevomexicano faith. "The Hispano-Americano people have never needed anyone, and much less people of her stripe to show us religion, morality or civilization," Enrique Salazar scowled in Spanish.[6] To *La Voz del Pueblo* the issue betrayed territorial primacy. As it commented:

> The most beautiful and most glorious pages of our history are those that inform the world how the Catholic priests, the pure apostles of Our Señor Cristo, in the times of the conquest of this continent, poured their blood for the faith. Listen to history; there the willing reader finds page after page of touching renderings of the martyrs who suffered the apostles of the faith on this continent when, for the time, they embarked on the noble work of disseminating the teachings of Christ among the indigenous.[7]

Much more than Father Malone's gaffes, Snider's offenses motivated Nuevomexicanos to conjure what the sociologist of religion Emile Durkheim would have called the human totems of their clan-nation's religion.[8] The Coronado Franciscans Marcos de Niza, Juan de

Padilla, and Juan de la Cruz were the first to bring the Gospel. The latter two were martyred at Quivira and Tiguex and Fray Marcos returned to Mexico a broken man. Yet somehow Catholics and "not Snider nor any other Methodist . . . initiated Christianity in these far off lands."[9]

It was, moreover, a shame that everyone did not know about Father Antonio José Martínez and his founding of the first schools in New Mexico. Unlike the privileged Snider, the first Sisters of Loretto did not come across the plains by train in comfort. They found themselves "subject to all kinds of privations and dangers, of being killed by Indians." Heroically, they established convent schools in San José, Taos, Mora, Albuquerque, Las Vegas, and Las Cruces. "Again," Salazar hectored, "it was the Archbishop Lamy and not the Nellie Methodist [*sic*] who brought the Christian Sisters to New Mexico to educate our youth." From the lens of the Average European Immigrant script it appeared that Snider had the slums of American cities in mind where the poor people "lived as if they were beasts," for she knew nothing of New Mexico.[10]

Some six hundred indignant souls packed the San Miguel County courthouse. The illustrious Eusebio Chacón, whom we last saw scribing a history for his people, consented to address avid protestors.[11] Chacón drew a resounding masterpiece of Nuevomexicano nationhood, a thematically rich sketch of blood, community, family, conquistador founding, isolated destitution, and Indian Scourge.

Chacón took Snider to say that "the Spanish American or Mexican" was held back by the lack of an "evangelical light" because he "is part Spanish and part Indian." In what Nieto-Phillips calls the "language of blood"[12] and just as Nuevomexicano identitarians upbraided Father Malone, Chacón issued a strict correction:

> I am a Spanish American like those who are listening to me. No other blood runs in my veins than the one brought over by don Juan de Oñate and later by the renowned ancestors bearing my name. If there is any place in the Spanish Americas, or what was once under Spain's rule, where the purity of physical features of the conquerors ha[s] been preserved, it has been in New Mexico. Some mixture has occurred, of

> course, only slightly and rarely, but to claim that we are a community of mixed peoples does not stand up to historical fact or scientific analysis.[13]

At the same time, however, Chacón refused to rank order the races. Betraying classic Creole distinctions and US New Mexicanism, he saw no disgrace in being of "mixed race." As he assured, race mixture reflected "a renewed nobleness similar to how the Romans were enhanced by the Goths or the Normans by the inhabitants of Albion during feudal times." Nor did he discredit western-hemisphere Native Americans. The "so-called Germanic or Saxon races in the period of human development which amalgamated the European peoples," he extolled, "did not possess either the temperament, intellectual prowess, or anything that would be considered superior to the indigenous peoples of the Americas when our forefathers conquered them."

Chacón iterated this positivity against two major developments occurring in the social background. First, many Nuevomexicano growled about the *peones* they saw flowing into New Mexico and other places in the United States since the 1890s when an economic recession drove them out of Mexico. In a context in which too many Nuevomexicanos lost work, some Nuevomexicanos blamed the migrants as outsiders in their heritage territory who were taking jobs from them.[14] In patently bad behavior, Nuevomexicanos derided the mestizo laborers, cutting them down as *surumatos*, that is, boors, paupers, country bumpkins. Professional Mexicans were not immune either. Manuel Sariñana, a journalist from Mexico, penned a picaresque novella to parody the maltreatment he received at the hands of pretentious "Spaniards." Chácon considered himself a Spanish American, yet in his speech he implied disagreement with the Mexican dissociation his fellow ethnics expressed. Spanish brethren were better served directing their passions of pride to offending Euro-Americans.

Chacón's remarks were also backed by the news reaching New Mexico of prominent commentators damning the human consequences of the European "discovery" of America. Philosophers, writers, and journalists called the effects of Western imperialism a social evil with no redeeming good, having shed voluminous blood, caused the extermination of millions of inoffensive and innocent Indigenous people, leaving excessive, superfluous waste behind. Henry Vignaud, a Franco-American writer living in Paris, charged in his book that the documentary evidence of Columbus's accomplishments was fraudulent.[15]

In two thoughtful editorials, Enrique Salazar credited Native land precedence, stressing how the Indigenes established legitimate sovereign ownership rights to both North and South America centuries before the European incursion. Salazar also honored the "tenacious resistance" of Natives, their defense "inch by inch" of the territory that they occupied and the implacable war they waged against the European invaders. While Salazar found it impossible to deny the purchase that his legacy intelligentsia had paid to the "immortal" rewards that Columbus's mission delivered in the name of civilization, he appreciated the importance of prior Indigenous presence with its culture of courage in America.[16] Chacón surely agreed.

In a virtual domestic nationalism, Chacón scolded Snider for her visits to humble Nuevomexicana homes. The missionary intruded with the "vulgar curiosity of someone who possesses considerable animal instinct, and ignorant of the most elementary rules of urban etiquette," sticking her nose into everything, "even into the ovens and chicken coops." Chacón's verbal diorama of the typical vecino family idealized the nobility of the classic European peasantry. In the old hunchbacked woman weaving petticoats "with a very pious needle," Snider thought she "found the prototype of the elderly among her people in that ragged beggar" when she did not know "the typical Spanish American motherly figure" and failed to understand the "scullery maid's instinct." "Spanish American" women washing their clothes in a thermal stream spoke to "the immortal scene of Homer's or L'Assomoir's washer lady." Snider may have known "one or another poor young woman educated in sectarian schools" but who, "thanks to the religious reformations among us, eventually graduates as a chambermaid or maid servant at the home of some American lady." Snider blinded herself to the "spiritual young woman who dreams of our people, nor does she know, nor will she ever get to know the true Spanish American who is imprudent, bold, but proud of his home and deeply fond of his family."

Snider allegedly derided dirt-floored adobe homes with broken chairs, "old rags and pieces of carpet in a corner," a single room, she apparently beheld, with "up to seven people with children born and growing up in poverty, ignorance, superstition, and deprivation." As Chacón responded, "I confess that [my home], although partly made out of adobe, doesn't come close to the one the excitable writer saw. Neither do your homes look like that," he reminded his hearers. In his many travels throughout the territory, "those wilting flowers dying in the little windows as described by the author seem to me healthy and robust, a sure sign of a delicate artistic temperament among the people who cultivate them." Neither he nor his country folk had ever seen an evangelical missionary, proving Snider's disqualification to offer assessments of the house's interior. Had "this lady" seen one of "our houses from the inside, she would have noted [how] our children grow up surrounded by all the amenities that love can lavishly provide."

In a strategic comparison with domestic Anglo whiteness, Chacón observed how in his people's homes, "where the necessities of life are simpler than in the city, there are no alabaster lamps nor white velvet sofas that make our homes look like miniature palaces. But," he proceeded,

> where there is a good-sized table, hospitality sweetens the stay of the traveler because Christian charity never denies a resting place for the fatigued traveler to recline his head. Oh, such soft and delicate beds created by the peasant's poverty and his small savings for which he never expects any kind of acknowledgment. It is a lie that his beds are dirty rags.

Chacón's strategic anthropology presented homelife as sublime as anyone could find. "I have frequently come across those humble huts," he testified. "I have spent long nights hearing simple stories told there; I have come down from the high position of my ideals to share with them, being human and happy. I have reclined my forehead on their poor pillows: poor but white like the spotlessness of their souls, perfumed with the mystical aroma of their kindness."

In the first-person plural, Chacón painted a satisfying domestic nation. The missionary, he claimed,

FIGURE 14. (*above*) Eusebio Chacón. As an accomplished novelist, public servant, and historian, the Notre Dame University alum authored some of the most creative narratives for the construction of Nuevomexicano ethnic identity. Unknown photographer. Author's scan from Read, *Historia Ilustrada de Nuevo Mexico*, 460.

FIGURE 15. Family outside residence. Santa Fe, New Mexico, ca. 1884–1892. Showing the sort of "humble hut" Eusebio Chacón knew, visited in Santa Fe at least, and used to inform part of his response to Nellie Snider's account of poverty-stricken homes she claimed to have witnessed. D. B. Chase photographer. Courtesy of the Palace of the Governors Photo Archives, negative number 031644

> never set foot on the carpet where our small children push their toys. She will never know the moral side of our existence because she doesn't sit down to read with us by the tepid lamplight those delightful and profound works of the Dantes, the Victor Hugos, and the Walter Scotts that have ennobled the world. Never will her voice desecrate the space where we go in the evenings to share our anxieties, where the rhythm of our chants awaits us along with the sweet lifelong companions evoking melodies of love on the piano keyboard. No, those angular and hypocritical faces, those people with yardsticks in their hands and numbers in their heads, those who judge religion by the criteria of the merchant—those will never enter our homes.

Snider simply did not know the people she aimed at for conversion, though she may "indeed know some other unfortunate person who forgets his origins and his feelings as a man in exchange for supporting him and his family, while denying his faith."

As Chacón recalled, this was not the first time his people served as the target of "gratuitous as well as unjustified attacks." It was fruitless trying to find the cause in "rational reasoning." The passions of prejudice, he reflected, "always remained veiled in mystery ever since our forefathers came from Spain and have occupied this land, laying claims to it through our labor and populating it for our posterity." We also hear the Grueling Isolation script when he summons earlier times: "Without resources, and surrounded by brave and warlike tribes, the life of the people of the Territory during the domination by Spain and Mexico was a continuous struggle. Under such circumstances, our own educational institutions, had we any to speak of, could hardly prosper."[17]

Chacón worked the script of his people's educational loss in a smooth ideological transmission. It was "our crime along with having colonized the New World," he put it. "If we are attacked for such a crime with uncouth acrimony [as Snider's], we need to lower our heads and confess our guilt." Time had changed, indicated by the disappearance of the "immense buffalo herds" and the bellowing train overcoming the heavy wagons "with determination." While the "entire face of the Territory" was transformed, Nuevomexicano luck had not. Representing the US Colonial Neglect script, Chacón chided "the government that today boasts so much of educating Cubans, Puerto Ricans, and Filipinos hasn't done anything to spread education among us. The few educational institutions that exist among us are the product of our own labor, raised from our savings and supported at our expense." The government failed to give a "single cent" for Nuevomexicano development. We pick up echoes of Tranquilino Luna and Enrique Salazar: that there were no "talented writers, erudite statesmen, or economists should not have surprised anyone."

In the late Spanish colonial period, Father Morfí noted the lack of clerical support to adequately minister the far-flung settlements in the New Mexico province. As a consequence, a "great many" of the people died without the benefit of the Sacraments and throughout their lives they had known "less about religion than the Indians themselves."[18] No matter. In a lapse of heritage memory, a spiritually assured Chacón insisted that Nuevomexicanos were "not as abandoned by God as some writers [believe] who pass in our midst like apocalyptic horsemen with the cup of bile in one hand and the scythe of hate in the other."

In a significant reputational point, Chacón emphasized, "Indeed, we have suffered and waited the hour of our redemption with patience, but that redemption is certainly not brought by those who insult our homes and our beliefs." Snider's character assassination could not have "any other effect than to ridicule and to humiliate us in the eyes of the government and the good American people who have yet to know us." Those before him needed to ward off the malice expressed in that "defamation which is a ploy intended to frustrate our political aspirations." Self-determination was at stake above all:

> We return today with the zeal of those who know no other homeland nor banner than the American to petition, perhaps for the twentieth time, that overly desired admission to the sovereignty of Statehood to prove that we are worthy of republican liberties and capable of assuming the responsibilities which they bring with them.

To an extreme, "everywhere and from all political parties, all that one hears is the popular voice which calls for this change," yet "in our midst, there rises an unknown, stifling, and oppressive voice that denounces our native people. Could this be with the hope that our petition be ignored so that we continue in the precarious state of national pariahs?"

Chacón, smitten by the colonial oppression of it all, concluded with a vision of irredentism as an option. If the nativos could serve only as "beasts of burden," if they were to remain "in the sad tutelage of the government" as they had thus far, "if you do not partake in the public affairs of this nation which is yours," and "if your Anglo American brothers see you with mistrust and . . . envy the small bliss that you can reach by governing yourself, then it is time for you to pack up your goods and take them with your ancestors' remains to another more hospitable country." His people's talent and vigor drew from the inheritances of their Iberian ancestry: "The same initiatives that illuminated the journey of [Portuguese nobleman Pedro Álvares] Cabral and [the Spanish writer and politician Pedro Antonio] Alarcón," Chacón heralded, "light up the night sky in the same place they saw them." In the finale:

> Men who think like you and who speak like you and who embrace your same beliefs have raised wonderful cities at the foot of the Chimborazo Volcano [Ecuador] and on the banks of the Paraná [Brazil]. If the country where your Diego de Vargas sleeps no longer has hope for his offspring, take note that the world is large, the world is good, the world is generous. Look for a country where you may become the master of your destiny.

The discourse rallied the ranks. As Francisco Lomelí notes, Chacón's printed speech produced among Nuevomexicanos "a wave of cultural nationalism . . . against the onslaughts of attacks by outsiders."[19]

But would it truly assist the movement for statehood? The mass meeting's bipartisan Committee on Resolutions—consisting of Republicans Chacón, Enrique Salazar, and Patricio Gonzales; Democrats Demetrio Silva and Serapio Romero; and Union Partyites Antonio

Lucero and Juan José Herrera—hoped it would. In their resolutions, the deputized keepers of la patria branded Snider "an adventurer, an ingrate, a hypocrite and a demagogue, who after partaking of the hospitality of our kind people, has reciprocated with infamy and repeated insults." Shaming her gender, Snider was arraigned for having dishonored the name of a classic "'cultured [American] miss,' back of which she would hide from our just indignation." Because of her "criminal" characterizations, this stranger was "unworthy of living in our community."[20] Would the manifesto bulk up the Nuevomexicano demand for statehood?

Senatorial Interjections

The Nellie Snider brouhaha pumped Spanish identity mightily among Nuevomexicanos. At the same time, however, it hardly rippled the larger politics of statehood. In short order, a US senator made a shocking move to block New Mexico statehood and after that another solon launched an outrageous proviso in the name of statehood. Both initiatives threatened to upend the meaning of Nuevomexicano territorial primacy. This is why they are tended to here, although, it bears mentioning, neither controversy compelled Nuevomexicanos to unfold the Spanish heritage to the same exuberant extent that the Snider episode did.

The Primacy of Language and a Primacy Language

Nation-states have often granted formal language rights to minorities whose land base they have brought under their control. Such rights afford the protection of "institutional forms, structures and processes through which speech occurs." Appearing mostly in multicultural countries where the language group is demographically concentrated, they are meant to protect the participation of linguistic minorities in the "machinery of government, in broadcasting in the media, in schools, in the public and private workplace."[21]

The linguistics scholar David Marshall argues that since Nuevomexicanos formed a "conquered culture," they constituted a linguistic majority in their territory, a status shared by the French in Quebec for whom language rights were installed in Canada's constitution. However, the Treaty of Guadalupe Hidalgo made no mention of language rights for Nuevomexicanos and Californios.[22] At best, Congress funded translators in 1853, and in 1884 supported publication of territorial and federal proceedings while permitting either Spanish or English for school instruction.[23]

Like many dominant nationalisms, the one in the United States upheld a single language after Independence, English serving as a quasi-official tongue. English Americans, asserting their "political superiority" in the Continental Congress, consolidated English as the language of official documents, ceasing to issue proclamations that had appeared under other languages, especially German. "Throughout the early decades of the 19th Century," a researcher found, "attempts to obtain minority language rights met with stiff resistance, mostly in reaction to new immigrations, especially of Irish and German Catholics."[24]

In former Mexican lands, federal appointees used English.[25] As colonial policy, English-only represented "vernacular languages-of-state," pushing out a language if it differed by region, much like the English banning Gaelic in most of Ireland, the French pressuring Breton "to the wall," and the Castilian regime reduc[ing] Catalan to marginality."[26] The New Mexico territory brought the matter to Congress's attention. Euro-American Republicans thus harangued Nuevomexicanos. In 1874, for instance, New York Congressman Clarkson N. Potter judged New Mexico undeserving of statehood not only because of its slow development but also because the people there were "mainly of descendants from Mexicans" who did not speak the English language and for whom territorial legislation and court business was conducted largely by means of an interpreter.[27]

Nuevomexicanos intuited a right to the protection of their legacy language. In 1895, Enrique Salazar called for the statehood act then in play in Congress to proscribe the right to use Spanish in the public schools, in the judiciary, in government proceedings, and in managing counties. While "Hispano-Americanos" desired to learn English, Salazar swore that "they will never again consent to having their native language prohibited and suppressed in the areas where it prevailed."[28] This linguistic identification formed an element of Nuevomexicano nationness since Spanish operated in public functions, speeches, newspapers, electoral campaigns, and households.[29] On precisely this condition, the new chair of the Senate Committee on Territories, Indiana's Albert Beveridge, mounted a campaign to prevent New Mexico from becoming a state.

The 1902 Knox Omnibus Bill, named for Massachusetts Representative William Knox, proposed the simultaneous admissions of Oklahoma, the Indian Territory, Arizona, and New Mexico. The bill passed the House but stalled in the Senate when Beveridge held up Pennsylvania Senator Matthew Quay's attempt to take an immediate vote on it. Beveridge deemed Oklahoma fit for statehood if it took in the Indian Territory but balked at Arizona and New Mexico.[30]

Beveridge followed up by organizing a subcommittee investigation of each territory. In New Mexico, the group visited Las Cruces, Las Vegas, Santa Fe, Albuquerque, and Carlsbad, observing conditions and taking testimony from Delegate Rodey, teachers, school superintendents, newspaper editors, census enumerators, justices of the peace, postmasters, ranchers, interpreters, and working citizens. The committee took special interest in how much Spanish was spoken in schools, the courts, political campaigns, and at home—of course finding a unique prevalence.[31]

The so-called Beveridge Report, released in early December 1902, proposed a substitute bill recommending that Oklahoma and the Indian Territory be combined into one state and leaving New Mexico and Arizona out for reasons of inadequate population volume, population-to-land ratio, low economic development, low value of natural resources,[32] and most centrally the "educational, moral and other elements of citizenship," which rendered the people unequal "with the remainder of the people of the Nation." The committee censured the "native New Mexicans of Spanish and mixed Spanish and Indian descent" because their "institutionalized" Spanish language obtained in American-run schools, conducted as they were exclusively in Spanish because the students had to understand that language for the "active affairs of daily life." In addition, when children were taught English, they often relapsed into Spanish. As the report concluded, "If the test of illiteracy were confined to the English language only, the committee is of the opinion that the percentage of illiterates would be much more than doubled."[33]

Beveridge's investigation turned into a campaign to beat the Spanish language out of the Nuevomexicano social body. That it had voted for statehood only meant that docile people could always be made to vote for anything if told it would help them. The committee looked to the time when education and an increase in the Anglo population would perform its "modifying work with the 'Mexican' element." Only then would "this mass of people, unlike us in race, language, and social customs" come to form "a creditable portion of American citizenship."[34]

Once again, New Mexico opinion exploded. Politicians, the English and Spanish press, regular citizens, and businessmen condemned the report as a sham.[35] Both parties rallied in Washington to undo the damage.[36] Local organizations held urgent meetings. Going to the heart of the question of whether the American nation could accommodate a foreign language group, the Mesilla Valley Chamber of Commerce in Las Cruces noted that thousands of people along the east coast of the country spoke a language other than English without being denied equality as citizens of a state.[37] Chiming in this vein, the Central Labor Union in Albuquerque resented "the stigma . . . that the American born and naturalized people of New Mexico are not as fit to become full-fledged sovereign citizens of this great republic as are the aborigines and government wards of the Indian Territory."[38]

Albuquerque hosted two protest gatherings. Befitting their ethnic segregation, Euro-Americans in New Town railed against Beveridge's "unfair methods" for intentionally looking to craft a "hostile" report even as the Treaty of Guadalupe Hidalgo guaranteed that New Mexico would become incorporated as a state. Citizens were urged to unite and by appropriate action express "our common indignation."[39]

Old Town Nuevomexicanos elected Jesús Romero chair and the bi-ethnic Thomas Werner secretary. The majority Nuevomexicanos on the Resolutions Committee included Néstor Montoya, Jesús Romero, Modesto Ortiz, T. C. Montoya, Desiderio Montoya, and Vivián Perea, together with H. K. Quinney, S. Crollett, and R. Springer. They chiefly complained about Beveridge and his committee remaining "but a few hours in each of our cities trying to obtain only damaging evidence against our people, especially upon the subject of the Spanish language." One resolution repeated what was now the Spanish War Dividend Denied script, the "paternal" US Government sending shiploads of teachers to Puerto Rico and the Philippines to teach the "young bolo men how to shoot in English," though nothing comparable was ever offered to Nuevomexicanos who were forced to do the best they could "by [their] own unaided efforts" (in Destitute Isolation). The gathering resolved to "refute the slanders placed upon a loyal people by a prejudiced senator, one who has shown himself to be narrow-minded and fanatical."[40]

El Independiente pointed to the need to defend "justice and the truth," which would prevail "when a community defends its purposes with valor and energy every time that circumstances demand that it should." Accordingly, juntas de indignación in Doña Ana, Bernalillo, and Valencia Counties passed resolutions defending nativos against the "calumnies," "denigrations," and "slanders" cast by "the enemies of the people of New Mexico."[41]

Speaking to the issue of the deep rootedness of Spanish, *El Combate* editor Patricio Gonzales called "our beautiful language, originating in Castilian," essential for the people's success. "Our natural dialect has been used in New Mexico before and after the government's new territorial acquisitions," Gonzales emphasized, "and every day it has become more necessary and important among us, and it would be a major obstacle to our well-being to make it disappear in the form that many on the American continent want." However, in this early era of the modern resistance to colonialism, this was about as far as a demand for respect of Spanish-language rights went. Perhaps legal counsel would have helped. Activists were left in any event to a discourse of hope. Because the Beveridge report came from a minority on the Senate Committee on Territories, Gonzales felt certain that Beveridge's assault would prove of no account, the Democratic Congress sure to admit New Mexico as a state, leaving the people's use of Spanish alone.[42] *La Voz del Pueblo* opined similarly, that because Beveridge was a Republican he naturally promoted "lies and calumnies," and the lobby delegation slated for Washington would soon prove him wrong.[43]

In lieu of demanding language rights, Nuevomexicanos took the common sense route, insisting that their people made progress in learning English. Superintendent of Territorial Schools José Francisco Chaves announced that only teachers capable of instructing in English would be hired, a policy, it was believed, to put New Mexico on par with the "most cultured" states. At the same time, it was not meant to have pupils forget the "mellifluous language of Cervantes that our ancestors brought as they settled this land with their blood."[44]

The normally partisan Democratic *Voz del Pueblo* patted the Republican Chaves on the back, calling him a true liberator and the planter of a "pure and healthy seed with the aim of the proper cultivation of good and beneficent results." Chaves's "love of the soil where he was born, could never be bested," it was said. "Without doubt, he has realized that the hatred against the Hispano-Americano people that exists in the east, will not disappear until the teaching of English among the people is generalized, and until then, we can never admit that we have the aptitudes to be admitted as a state."[45] It seemed like a capitulation to Beveridge's campaign to wipe out Nuevomexicano Spanish. To offset it, the editor fell back on the corruption of the territory's Republican bosses and their nativo lackeys who "dominated and dominate the territorial government for their themselves." While school laws were good, political hacks played favoritism in the appointment of unqualified teachers and district administrators through a system of patronage designed for partisan support;[46] in practice, that would ensure that the education of Nuevomexicano youth had little chance of fulfillment.

Proving Republican dereliction, *La Voz del Pueblo* noted that President Theodore Roosevelt backed the Beveridge investigation and report. Delegate Rodey, Governor Otero, and other Republicans supported Roosevelt's renomination for the presidency instead of passing resolutions at its convention proscribing all who were against the people of the territory and sending a delegation to oppose Washington Republicans. In sounding the fantasy, the weekly made the point that territorial Republicans could never force recognition of Nuevomexicano rights so long as their national party bosses believed they were purchasable with a few appointments.[47] This certainty deflated the potential of standing strong on an ethnonational support for the Spanish language, especially in this early modern period and the absence of a general language rights movement. At least Republican Senator Quay led a formidable challenge to the Beveridge Report. Beveridge filibustered and the Knox Bill died. Quay's challenge was a sign of an undercurrent in the Republican Party starting to look well on New Mexico statehood, though how to make it come about was the question.

Michigan Representative Edward L. Hamilton, a Republican, postured to resolve the long-standing statehood debate for New Mexico and Arizona by combining them into a single state. It would be called Arizona with Santa Fe as its capital for five years after which residents would vote to keep or change the capital's location. When Arizona reached two hundred thousand in population and New Mexico eight hundred thousand, they would be separated and turned into individual states with their original names. Significant inducements were offered in cash, public lands, and two federal districts each if the territories accepted the offer.[48]

White Arizonans, dismayed that New Mexico Democrats viewed this as the only way for their territory to gain statehood, made their absolute opposition to the notion of joining so many Mexicans clear, while in New Mexico almost nothing could have threatened the Nuevomexicano stake in belonging in the territory more than this jointure proposal. At the Republican *El Independiente* editor Enrique Salazar had met influential "Neo-Mexicanos" who opposed it. Reasoning from the Spanish Settlement script, Salazar, who was backed by *El Independiente*'s powerful owner Secundino Romero, emphasized that to have Nuevomexicanos so absorbed without consultation denied what had belonged to them from the time their homeland "was colonized by civilized people in the sixteenth century." Jointure thus portended their "political and mortal ruination and destruction."[49]

Indeed, worries over primacy and nomenclature emerged. New Mexico had the same right as Virginia, New York, Massachusetts, and other "ancient communities" to have their own name.[50] Salazar rapped about the meaningless of names that did not correspond to their circumstances and, worse, did not befit a populace.[51] If a name change was legacy erasure, making Santa Fe a temporary capital spelled geopolitical dismemberment, a "betrayal and a trap" that hid insidious, if not sinister plans against the ancient capital. If it went through, "discord and confusion" in the administration of justice would follow. Harm and prejudices would principally befall nativos. New Mexico was better off as a territory indefinitely than submitting to this.[52]

The Conquistador Founding script had its place here. *Nuevo México* was the name given by the "first discoverers and conquerors to this land," and as such it was important to have it remain "until the very end of the last chapter of the capital." Salazar reserved special invective for Anglo settlers who "for whatever bastard interest were ready to sacrifice even the most sacred privileges of our people, and under that footing admit, without care, the abolition of a name so dear to the hearts of the people of New Mexico." They and Washington officials insulted the name that "for more than three hundred years the territory had carried," advancing the most "absurd and outrageous reasons," the "true significance being the pure and implacable hatred that they harbor toward the nativos of this locality, which impels them to extend their disdain toward the name that our territory has had for such a long series of years." Because so-called friends had become enemies over this "repugnant and inadmissible" idea, nativos must openly fight.[53] Doing away with New Mexico reflected an "inveterate hatred" of its original settlers and their descendants, Salazar stormed. The Americanos calling themselves friends, who went along with it, could simply leave for more agreeable places to suit their "aesthetic preferences."[54]

Salazar pounced on Arizona's extreme white supremacy. At least powerful Euro-Americans in New Mexico expressed inclusion values whether sincere or not. In Arizona, they excluded Mexicans "specifically with regard to their race and class" to keep their economy and government from being dominated by "greasers."[55] Salazar scorned their "fumes of superiority and contempt." Nuevomexicanos had never harmed them, nor did they have the "most minimum desire to be with them. Our citizens, far from desiring such an alliance, repudiate and reject with all their might what they see as the worst calamity that could come their way."[56]

A bard calling himself Alarí from Galisteo in lower Santa Fe County, claimed to be a "statist" (*estadista*) in tribute to the land of his birth. He did not like that both parties in the lower Pecos Valley urged Congress to make New Mexico and Arizona a state. Under a representative democracy, how, Alarí wondered, could three hundred fifty "brutes" pretend to exercise more power directly to Congress than the rest of the territory's population through their elected representatives? In a verse of five dizain stanzas ending with a quatrain, Alarí swore that he and his people were prepared to beat back such an insolent move to preserve their "beloved federation."[57]

Alarí landed another dizain, this one chocked with primacy. Metaphorically it called out, the idea of marrying Arizona "*con el Viejo Territorio*" (with the old Territory) sunk, for Arizona was the original child of New Mexico. It was not right to bind the two, even if mandated by Congress. Arizona is a "*muchachita*" (a little girl), New Mexico the "*anciano*" (the elder). "*!Pueblo!*" (My People!), Alarí, commanded, "*reboza su dona*" (cover her [Arizona's] trousseau). A ten-million-dollar subsidy for jointure was quite the prize, the scribe understood, yet the people did not want "to have it said that we were bought." Questions of the spiritual and of existence were aroused:

También sabemos sentir	We also know how to feel
Y hacen fuerza hasta el morir	And it gives us strength to the death[.]
Por conservar nuestro nombre	In keeping our name
Dejémonos de aplaudir	Let us applaud no more[.]
!Viva Dios, !que viva el hombre!	Long live God! Long live mankind!
Nos están metiendo miedo	They are making us afraid
Que si no es estado este año	That if [New Mex.] not be a state this year
Quedará el neo-mexicano	The Neo-Mexicano will be left
Nomás chupandose el dedo.	To suckle his thumb.
Pero en visto yo no puedo	Yet as I see it
La cosa profetizar	I cannot prophesy
Si el territorio ha de estar	If the territory should remain
Territorio para siempre	A territory forever
Aunque haya un millón de gente	Even with a million people[,]
Escuelas y educación.	Schools and education.

The poet understood the sacrifices of machinery, construction, manufactures, and buildings in not being a state. "*!Oh! que injusto fué el congreso!*" (How unjustly did Congress act!). Such were the questions that were compelled in Alarí's heart, and if his people tended to them, blessed would he be.[58]

Alarí was Jesús María Hilario Alarid, a former assemblyman who earlier composed poetry decrying the erosion of the Spanish language.[59] Soon after these verses appeared, Alarid noted in a letter to *El Independiente* that everyone knew him personally "as in my loyalty to my friends and the fatherland that I defend." Since his "tender infancy," he knew he was born in New Mexico's capital. Taking to the Salubrious Annexation script, he ruminated on the day in 1846 when the tricolor flag of the United States flew in the Santa Fe Plaza. When he was eight, his loving mother warned him not to approach, for the huge horses bearing soldiers might trample him. They were there to hoist the flag of the United States on the long pole in the middle of the plaza. The child asks why. As his mother explains, the soldiers were "sons of the American government" because Santa Fe no longer belonged to Mexico. But, she cautions, "who knows how the foreign government will treat us?" She recounts how New Mexico's governor abandoned the people's defenses when Americans invaded, leaving the people with the only choice of swearing loyalty to the new government, "to love that flag like it is our own mother." Never tiring of seeing it wave, she supplicates: "Come son; from now on you are free and independent."[60]

This Romantic Cementation script justified Alarid's right to ask why Congress would give New Mexico ten million dollars to be joined with Arizona but not use it for an independent New Mexico state. "Why not five million for New Mexico and five million for Arizona, two more stars shining "on our Glorious Banner?" Ten million would not suffice to purchase him or cause him to change one word of the "heartfelt sentiments" he harbored for the "neo-mexicanos." It was enough to recall *Vox Populi—Vox Dei*, the voice of the people is the voice of God.[61]

The Republican majority on the House Committee on Territories introduced the Hamilton bill on April 19, 1904. In the partisan carve, it brought Oklahoma in as a Democratic state and made Arizona-New Mexico Republican.[62] Salazar scorched congressional Republicans for violating their national party's policy of having New Mexico and Arizona admitted separately. The worst were those who without authority tried convincing Republican Congressmen of the "notoriously false" assertion that New Mexicans liked jointure. Such a constitution "could only be approved by fraudulent means."[63] It was not just a case of New Mexico's losing statehood but being turned into something that did not exist, "nor had a place among the independent and sovereign communities of the Union." Hope lay in Neo-Mexicanos voting against the constitution. Then would those with ambitious and malevolent views of submersing the "Neo-Mexicano people in the depths of the sea of political slavery" find their mockery.[64]

Giving the managers of *El Independiente* hope, Republicans found Nuevomexicanos in the Taos, San Miguel, and Rio Arriba County districts polling against jointure.[65] Republican Party chief Holm Bursum saw that "outside of Bernalillo, Valencia and Socorro, no 'Mexican counties'" were in favor.[66] Salazar called on the other counties and the upcoming Territorial Republican Convention to repudiate consolidation,[67] and he sent the negative resolutions of San Miguel County Republicans to Congressional Delegate Bernard S. Rodey.[68]

The jointure bill passed in the House. The Senate now needed to heed the unequivocal, virtually unanimous objections of the people of New Mexico and Arizona. Salazar saw future Congresses better disposed to give New Mexico and the other territories their statehood justice.[69] However, pundits saw strong prospects for passage in the Senate, neither dissident Democrats nor Republicans putting up an effective fight against Beveridge, the chair of the Senate Committee on Territories.[70]

The denouement of the Hamilton dynamic is legendary. In summary, the bill looked good in the Senate, but dissident senators won a requirement that the final decision be decided by the voters in both territories. President Roosevelt, now supporting the bill, twisted the arms of bosses in both territories to persuade their constituencies to go for it. New Mexico executive Republican Holm Bursum calculated that statehood would look good for the territory's statehood chances should it vote for the measure and Arizona did not. The territorial Republican party was induced to endorse passage, reversing their opposition.[71] Should Arizona decline as predicted, a plank provided that New Mexico would immediately elect delegates to construct a state constitution for submission to Congress with a petition for immediate admission.[72]

In a rare agreement, the Territorial Democratic Party appealed to the people to vote yes based on Roosevelt's warning that it would take years before New Mexico could expect another statehood bill.[73] Salazar saw the gap that jointure was opening between the bosses of the territorial Republican Party and the "immense majority" of the voting members who stood "irrevocably" opposed. The people would never agree to the sacrifice of the name and identity of New Mexico, he railed, "on the whims of bastard ambitions and utilitarian plots for personal and political aggrandizement."[74] Flipping a hundred eighty degrees, Delegate Rodey gave a "grand speech" in the House for jointure. "Too bad," Salazar commented; "the majority of his constituents did not agree with him."[75]

Republicans flooded the northern districts with Spanish handbills supporting jointure.[76] Bursum and Andrews lent a hand to Eugenio Romero, Secundino's father who arranged a trip around San Miguel County. Bursum told the *New Mexican*'s Max Frost, "I feel that San Miguel County will come in all right." He worked the party leaders in Mora County so that they, too, seemed to be "all right on statehood."[77] It worked famously. Nuevomexicano weeklies came to believe that statehood even in this form would "improve the conditions of all" and give the "Spanish-Americans" a strong enough vote to ensure protection of their rights.[78] As historian John Braeman found, the Republican machine in New Mexico delivered the promised vote, joint statehood carrying 26,195 to 14,735 while Arizona rejected by a five-to-one margin. "More than corporate influence and political manipulation was responsible for the outcome in Arizona. So lopsided a vote reflected the popular antipathy felt by Arizona's Anglo-Americans against New Mexico's Spanish-speaking population."[79]

Later that year, New Mexico legislators scheduled a bipartisan convention for delegates to write a state constitution. Sixty-six delegates were elected, and the convention convened on the first Monday of January 1907.[80] However, not all delegates could attend. A committee representing all counties planned to confer with the territorial assembly on the best time and means of reconvening. Members set February 5, when representatives would be in session, as the day to meet.[81] At the request of delegates, House Speaker R. L. Baca introduced a bill to sponsor an official constitutional convention in August. Due to "some adverse influence," the bill never reported out of committee.[82]

Nuevomexicano exasperation at another statehood failure had a voice in a balladeer with the call name Pero Grullo.[83] Pero Grullo's verse, "When will New Mexico become a state?" was a *cuando*, a way of literarily asking, "When?" as if statehood was forever in stall mode.[84] Perhaps, the lines sighed,

> When the frog grows hair / And when mules have sires / And the burros know how to read / And can explicate the catechism; / When the wolf becomes honest / And follows good principles / And the chicken-eating coyote / No longer takes without permission; / When the cat no longer scratches / and the dog does not growl / And the ox is no longer famous / As a consummate politician; / When the serpent / Has no poison in its fangs / And the scorpion / Flatters and shows kindness; / Then the day will come / Happy and Joyful / As statehood arrives / A prize so deserved. / No one will speak Spanish / For its abolishment, / And all vecino burros / Will bray in English.[85]

A Governor Invigorates the Spanish Heritage

As he assumed the New Mexico governor's seat in 1907, George Curry, the Lincoln County veteran of Theodore Roosevelt's Rough Riders, made statehood the centerpiece of his administration, and in generating support for it, he relied heavily on the promotion of the territory's Spanish heritage.[86] Ralph Emerson Twitchell, the former Santa Fe Railroad agent who had witnessed the Tertio-Millennial pageant and had since ranged into writing New Mexico history, influenced the governor to go in this direction.[87] Twitchell had recently created the Coronado Memorial Association in part to campaign for a monument dedicated to Coronado to be placed on the spot where it was said he "discovered" Las Vegas. The territorial assembly appropriated $5,000 for the project contingent on the Association providing an equal amount.[88]

Signing off on the fund, Curry announced the Coronado Commemorative Convention to be held at Albuquerque's territorial fair. As the governor proclaimed somewhat offbeat, "History, too often negligent, has but grudgingly recognized the wonderful and heroic efforts of the early Spanish pioneers in the exploration and colonization of the Great Southwest." The most "vitally interested" people of New Mexico, he emphasized, should lead in recognizing the debt owed to the memory of those "brave pathfinders of nearly four centuries ago, and by a concerted effort take what steps are proper to perpetuate and to preserve to posterity for all time, by organization, by monument and by enacted law, the traditions, the memories and the words of our first pioneers."[89]

Curry appointed Solomon Luna—the Valencia County kingpin and Republican Party National Committeeman whom many regarded as the most distinguished Nuevomexicano statesman—as director of the convention. The only other Nuevomexicano on the Convention organizing committee of six was Miguel Otero, whom Curry had just replaced as governor.[90] In calling in his inaugural address on the Twenty-Seventh Territorial Fair to advance New Mexico's goal of becoming a state, Curry predicted that the one next year would be the "first annual fair of the State of New Mexico."[91] The crowd roared.

Curry believed that an official endorsement of the Spanish Heritage would strengthen New Mexico's hand in the pursuit of statehood. The Coronado Commemorative Convention (CCC) opened the Fair to "perpetuate the name and fame" of Francisco Vasquez de Coronado who "paved the way for the Latin civilization in New Mexico," the *Albuquerque Journal* tacking on, "who founded what is soon to be one of the richest and most progressive states in the Union." Joining special guest Brigadier General E. D. Thomas, commander of the Colorado District of the US Army, on stage were "the men most prominent in the civil, political, and religious life of the territory," among them Chairman Luna, Master of Ceremonies Otero, Octaviano Larrazolo, and *La Bandera Americana* editor Néstor Montoya. No other Nuevomexicano sat on the executive committee.[92]

Former Delegate to Congress Harvey Fergusson opened the program with the signature "Spanish Pioneers" theme. Fergusson cloyingly played to the redoubtable trope of the "splendid progress toward a common destiny [being] made by the Spaniard and the American side by side in New Mexico." As he proposed, "Let us bend every effort and consecrate every energy, toward demonstrating what the two great civilizations united can do toward making New Mexico one great, splendid, enlightened civilization and Christian state." In reaching the word "state," as the *Albuquerque Journal* cooed, the "magnetic and eloquent orator" was "followed by deafening applause."[93]

Larrazolo followed Fergusson. Besides his Democratic Party credential—running against Bull Andrews for delegate to Congress the previous year—Larrazolo was a practiced promoter of New Mexico's

Spanish identity.[94] As if to fix any lingering Euro-American doubts concerning the Nuevomexicano's honorable religious legacy, Larrazolo was given the task of speaking on the topic of the "Mission Fathers" in colonial New Mexico.

Ever the iconoclast, Larrazolo in his 3,481-word heritage account altered Spanish identity's tendency to idealize a unified conquest by splitting the holy scriptural arm off from violent military, focusing on "that silent group of unpretentious and humble soldiers whose uniform was the loose cassock, whose only weapon was the emblem of our redemption, which they carried in one hand while in the other they held the message of the Martyr of Golgotha [Calvary] to mankind." Friars in this imaginary were the soldiers of the Cross, immortal benefactors of humanity who "in all ages and among all peoples, have ever sought to introduce God and a Godly morality and purity in the home, which, in turn is the cornerstone of the social and political organizations among men." Larrazolo's friars heroically competed with the "helmeted campaigns," as right followed wrong, laboring to work *with*, not against, the "good Indians" with the "burning love of humanity . . . with no weapon but the crucifix, with no shield but their unfaltering faith in God, with no hope of earthly reward."[95]

This humane slant, founded on Spain's commitment to the "gentle influence of religion," resembled the one Charles Lummis gave in his reissued *The Spanish Pioneers*, mourning the "gentle zeal" of the missionaries whom rebel Native Americans had "martyred."[96] An Indigenous author recently contradicted the theme: The Catholic missionary project in New Spain involved the "militarization of Jesus," integral in the conquest of Native lands for church and state.[97] Standing on his generation's Spanish platform, though, Larrazolo lit the Indian Scourge script, hailing colonizers under the burden of suppressing "the blind superstition, the unbridled fury and the uncontrolled passions of those savage tribes."

Touching on the Christian conquest of the Pueblos, Larrazolo bypassed the toma de posesión. Missionaries in his account "lost no time grappling with the work before them" and carried it out "with difficulties." Conquest "was easy enough by the use of superior force to bring the Indians to accept or submit to a foreign domination"; it was "quite another thing to persuade them by a process of reasoning, to forsake their religious creed, to abandon their traditions and to adopt a new faith." Friars visited every pueblo, "teaching and instructing the Indians who everywhere flocked around them and treated them with reverent respect." This was a "class of men who by reason of their association and calling . . . exercised great power and influence" over the sorcerers and medicine men who (in blaming the victim) "saw their own prestige diminished among their countrymen in proportion as the popularity of the missionaries increased."[98]

Significant for the founding of the New Mexico church in Larrazolo's narrative, friars completed and dedicated the chapel at San Juan de los Caballeros by September 1598, "the first Spanish colony in New Mexico." Missionaries had by the end of the year poured the water of baptism on the converts, as they had established churches in ten pueblos and eighty-three towns or villages with more than forty-five thousand duly converted. "Those zealous men created permanent schools in the principal settlements where reading, writing, vocal music and useful trades were taught." With no hint of missionaries quick to appropriate Pueblo lands or demand exorbitant tribute, the Church grew in "beneficent influence."

Larrazolo offered two reasons for the Pueblo Revolt. *Invidia*—jealousy, that favorite emotion in Latin American accountability—led sorcerers to decree the destruction of the missionaries and carrying out "murderous designs" against the "soldiers of God." Also significant, and apparently not defining conquistador heraldry as a necessity for statehood, the Revolt burst from the "many abuses and arbitrary rule of the Spanish authorities in the year 1680." Churchmen persevered in the long run. Denying indigeneity its time-honored temporal precedence, Larrazolo emphasized how, "in earnest, the virgin soil had been broken, the sod had been turned over and the seed had only been scattered, because it is true that the blood of martyrs is the seed of the Church."

Having related his legend, Larrazolo shifted gears: The appeal from the "native people" of New Mexico "to the people of this great nation" requested that they kindly convey to friends and neighbors that "we are very unfavorably known, and this through the ignorant or willful misinterpretations of others." Larrazolo decried the stereotype of nativos as "pathetic" simply because the United States had conquered them. For that, he was "forcefully" reminded "of the truism that, the ingratitude of princes is proverbial, and unfortunately, that is but too often true also of nations." His present audience could serve as a vehicle for putting Congress on notice: "Hispanos" were among the most civilized Christians in the world. It proved the ability to self-govern, shown somehow by Nuevomexicano ancestors founding New Mexico before Sir Walter Raleigh's Roanoke laid the foundations of English power in America, and before the founders of Plymouth Rock "listened to the invocation of the Pilgrim Fathers." The people had the courage to sustain the province despite their "abandonment" by Spain, Mexico, and the United States, which had them rely on "their own resources in a land separated from any other center of civilization" (Tranquilino Luna).

"Tell them," Larrazolo ordered,

> that we are not a race of degenerate and ignorant people, but that we are fully abreast of our time; that we have colleges, universities, schools, private and public, and a system of public education second to none in the country; tell them not to be afraid to trust us, and to remove the hand of tutelage that so long and so unjustly has been kept over us; that the native people of New Mexico have ever been true to themselves and to their sacred duties.

Enhancing the Spanish realm of memory and fortifying Nuevomexicano identity, the *Albuquerque Journal* published Larrazolo's talk in its entirety.

Soon after the Convention, Curry hosted a statehood strategy session to support Congressional Delegate William Andrews's statehood bill.[99] Euro-Americans formed the majority of the hundred-plus delegation named to the lobbying team.[100] At least Roman L. Baca served as secretary, José D. Sena as treasurer, Eugenio Romero as vice chairman, and Venceslao Jaramillo as one of six district vice chairmen,[101] with Luna himself taken into the governor's inner circle. Some thirty Nuevomexicano county representatives received certificates of appointment.[102] Like the many that came before, the Andrews statehood bill died, but Curry's demonstrative cultural policy formed a major step on the road to pinning things Spanish to the struggle for statehood.

CHAPTER 7

Subnational Constitutionalism and the Privileging of "Spanish American"

IN 1908, OUTGOING President Theodore Roosevelt, newly elected President William H. Taft, and the national Republican Party called for the granting of statehood to New Mexico and Arizona.[1] In 1910, then, Michigan Congressman Edward Hamilton introduced an enabling act giving each territory the opportunity to craft a state constitution. Senator Albert Beveridge, still chair of the Senate Committee on Territories, had the measure pigeonholed, but Vermont Senator William P. Dillingham successfully submitted an alternate enabling bill when Beveridge was absent from the Senate floor.[2] However, Beveridge, known as New Mexico's "worst enemy" in Congress,[3] would not quit troubling the statehood cause. As chair of the Senate Committee on Territories, he still had some power to wield and something to say about the enabling act.

The issues raised in the New Mexico portion of the hearings concerned nothing more than the territory's indebtedness and railroad provisions.[4] The wider discussion on Arizona dealt with matters of critical interest to Nuevomexicanas/os. On point was the law that Arizona passed requiring citizens to know English and have a primary education to be able to vote. At the poll station, the voter would prove his qualifications by reading from the US Constitution to a county inspector. No election had been held in the territory since the law passed, but it was on the books and so the Committee discussed whether it should be kept and how it might affect New Mexico.[5]

All seven Arizona witnesses coming before the Committee opposed the voting law. They agreed: Its real purpose was to prevent the local Spanish-speaking citizens from exercising their franchise. Arizona Governor Richard Sloan called it "not so much an education as a racial qualification."[6] Committee members revealed how the Nuevomexicano claim to deep primacy in their territory was far from a shibboleth but the key for comprehending the injustice of the voting law. As Sloan put it, the ancestors of these people had "lived here long before any American ever visited the Territory or dreamed that it should become at any time one of the United States, who know no other home or country."[7] To the self-identified "native" merchant and former assemblyman J. Lorenzo Hubbell, the Mexicans were "'to the manor born,' born right there, and were there before we acquired the Territory."[8] The Reverend William H. Ketcham, director of the Bureau of Catholic Indian Missions, acknowledged the "natives of the soil, speaking Spanish not through any particular fault of their own, if it be a fault. They are born to it, native to the soil."[9]

As Sloan explained, the settling of the Arizona portion of New Mexico formed the central reason for doing away with the law because the people in question were the "'best element' in the Mexican population who resided in the farms, ranches, and country communities" where they reared families and "who, by every consideration, are entitled to all the rights and privileges of citizenship."[10] Sloan equated the Arizona law to the "dominancy of the white race" that disqualified Negroes with education requirements.[11] Hubbell, claiming to speak "on behalf of the Mexican people of the Territory," framed the objection to the law in terms of an offshoot of territorial primacy, the historic membership of Nuevomexicanos in the Republican Party. Two hundred fifty or more of the three hundred Republicans in his county alone were Mexicanos and they voted a Republican into office as Arizona's delegate to Congress. As a result, Democrats in the territorial council felt the need of having "some means" to curtail the Mexican influence in their affairs; thus the restrictive voting law.[12]

Beveridge understood the importance of historical primacy as well, noting the need to preserve the right to vote for what he now sympathetically called the "old Spanish families." Nevertheless, nothing could deter him from his deep aversion to the Spanish language. When former Arizona Delegate to Congress Ralph H. Cameron proposed that in the constitution English be stipulated as the "primary language" in public school instruction with the clause, "*Provided* [*sic*], nothing in this act shall preclude the teaching of other languages in said public schools," Beveridge assured that the committee would consider it in executive session, but, "I will say right now that so far as I am concerned, I should never consent to that under any possible circumstances."[13]

Committee member Senator Charles Hughes asked Cameron, "You mean teaching Spanish, do you not?" Before Cameron could reply, Beveridge interjected: "Why certainly. It means that New Mexico and Arizona," at which point Cameron broke him off to say it covered "Latin, French, etc." As Cameron continued, "I suppose that the wording as it now stands would preclude the teaching of anything but the English language." Beveridge grew impatient:

> No; it says the schools shall always be conducted in English. There is not any use in going into refinements. The purpose of that [other languages] provision, both with reference to New Mexico and Arizona, and particularly the former, is to continue the thing that has kept back the speaking of English and the learning of English, to wit: That because they may conduct the schools in other languages, in many of those Spanish speaking communities, particularly in New Mexico, they will do so.
>
> Senator Dillingham: And they have done so.[14]

As Cameron, Piles, and Hughes reinforced, the teaching of any other language than English simply meant the learning of a second language.

Beveridge, however, refused to entertain even this pedagogical advantage. As a result, the Senate committee's amendments to the Enabling Act eliminated the language and education requirements for voting but struck the "teaching of other languages" in the schools from the New Mexico and Arizona constitutions. Forcing the repression of Spanish by other means, Beveridge instituted the requirement that state legislators and state officials "read, write, and understand the English language sufficiently well to conduct the duties of office without the aid of an interpreter."[15]

On the floor of Congress, Beveridge revealed his intent to smash vecino nationness as glued together by the Spanish language:

> Everybody knows, one of the difficulties of the situation down there, particularly in New Mexico, is the curious continuance of the solidarity of the

> Spanish-speaking people, the people of Mexican descent. These people have kept together in a most amazing way and have maintained not only their social relations, living close together and not scattering out and mingling with other people, but they have maintained also a remarkable tenacity to the tongue of their fathers. It would be well, of course, if at least the men who make the laws could speak the language which all the rest of us speak. . . . Our bill does not require anybody else shall do so [*sic*], but certainly the legislators should. That will be one of the first things that will break up that condition, which has been for a long time a serious problem before Congress and before the better people down there. The whole subject is a profound ethnological and sociological question. Our bill begins its solution.[16]

Beveridge believed that the retention of Spanish prevented Nuevomexicanos/as from assimilating America's dominant tongue. But what *La Voz del Pueblo* feared was the denial of a right to bilingualism. What Washington solons needed to realize was that the Spanish-speaking of New Mexico had always desired to learn English, indeed, were prepared to learn it once an adequate public school system could be put together. More than likely, the principal problem had been Congress's refusal to provide sufficient funding for schools. However, once again, the Democratic weekly blamed local Republican misuse of monies slated for rural schools for the committee's "stupid" language provision. New Mexico had teachers aplenty, the paper reported, and it was ready to instruct in the districts outside the towns to enable the children to learn English. The Enabling Act would not be worth a "firecracker" without an adequate system of education with well-paid teachers offering classes six months of the year. *La Voz* editors saw congressional approval of the act coming out of the fear of (New Mexicanism) Eastern newspapers holding Republican feet to the fire that it be done.[17]

The young Isabel Tenorio inscribed the Defense of Language script in poetry. Translated from the Spanish, it reads:

If [George] Washington lived

The American People would
Now proclaim with enthusiasm
"Do Not Forget Castilian!
Language is Sovereign"
And now on this continent
Should the government
Keep the franchise uppermost
With malice toward none
Nor disrespect for our people.[18]

Nuevomexicano Representation in the Constitutional Convention

The Senate Enabling Act passed in both chambers on June 20, 1910, and Taft signed it forthwith. New Mexico had sixty-six days to elect one hundred delegates from throughout the territory with the duty of drawing up a state constitution.[19] The campaign for delegates was heavily partisan. Democrats and Republicans wrangled over apportionment for making election procedures fair. Democrats and progressive Republicans warned of conservative Republicans ramming through pro-corporate provisions and therefore called on candidates to commit to "the people" by favoring reforms such as the referendum, the initiative, recall, and primary elections. According to Nuevomexicano Democrats Ezequiel C. de Baca and Antonio Lucero, such protections were tailored for vulnerable nativos.[20]

In the campaign, Nuevomexicano Republicans turned to the tactic of appropriating homeland primacy in its Spanish heritage vernacular. As posted by *El Eco del Norte*, after three centuries of struggle against all manner of obstacles, the present triumph owed a great deal to "Castilian reinforcements of intelligence, energy, and resources that have instilled new life and valor to the civilization brought here originally by the Spanish explorers and conquistadors." Their meritorious labor and sacrifices were not in vain for descendants of the first settlers finally had the shelter and the refuge under the American flag that for so long eluded them.[21] In addition to competence and practical experience in public business, those selected as convention delegates, the paper propounded, should be "amantes del pueblo neo-mexicano" (lovers of the Neo-Mexicano people).[22]

Nuevomexicanos were still the majority in New Mexico's population. Still, the Euro-American electorate had increased markedly since 1900,[23] and so old-hand Euro-Americans won two-thirds of the convention's hundred delegates. At 33 percent, Nuevomexicano representation fell below demographic parity.[24] Yet, a third was not nothing, especially when, in a convention with Republicans holding a commanding seventy-one seats out of a hundred, all but one of the Nuevomexicanos was a Republican.[25]

At least Tom Catron lost his bid for convention president.[26] Satisfied, the progressive *Voz del Pueblo* declared that the men who had been the cause of the "descendants of the original settlers of this territory losing their legitimate [land] inheritances should not receive, for anything, the vote of any man in whose breast beats an independent heart."[27] Yet what progressives feared happened, a convention dominated by a close-knit team of conservative Republicans—Charles Spiess as president, together with delegates Catron, Fall, Bursum, Luna, Spiess, Charles Springer, Malaquías Montoya, Eugenio Romero, and Victor Ortega. Regular Republicans served as chairs of all standing committees save one.[28]

In a saving grace, Nuevomexicanos formed a power niche. On the Committee of 21, said by one historian to have "dictated all policies and practically wrote the constitution," sat eight Nuevomexicanos, including Eugenio Romero (San Miguel County), Malaquías Martínez (Taos), and Victor Ortega (Santa Fe).[29] Nuevomexicanos made it to all twenty-seven standing committees, chairing nine, Luna heading the powerful Committee on Committees.[30] The group became what another historian called "a formidable force at the convention."[31] Still another described a "comparatively solid block welded by common interest."[32]

That common interest was constitutional. The principal product of the arrangement brought about subnational constitutionalism specifically in a set of civil rights provisions for both the protection and participation rights of Nuevomexicanos/as.[33] As political scientist Jack Holmes puts it, the provisions appeared "because Hispanic leaders"—bound by the "camaraderie of political fellowship and many lasting personal attachments"—knew their interests well enough to insist on their inclusion.[34]

Nuevomexicano delegates shared a people's identity, some more than others. Bernalillo County delegate Antonio A. Sedillo, José D. Sena, and former territorial legislator and editor of *La Bandera Americana* Néstor Montoya[35] had identitarian experience. Larrazolo lost his race for delegate, but since gallery members could participate in sidebar discussions,[36] he consulted with delegates during sessions, including the fiscal conservative Solomon Luna.[37] At the same time, it made for a consociational process writ small that Euro-American delegates supported the program of civil rights, commentators noting how readily they accepted what the "natives" wanted.[38]

Because of the costs involved, conventioneers decided against the recording of minutes.[39] A catalogue of enactments, press reports and other sources reveal Nuevomexicanos leading the way in the composing of the "Spanish bill of rights." Key provisions contravened the oppressive enactments in Beveridge's Enabling Act, the entrenched discrimination in and outside the territory, and the constitutional stipulation for "mak[ing] no distinction in civil or political rights on account of race or color."[40] In an implied allusion to colonialism, Section 5 of Article II of the Bill of Rights provided that "The rights, privileges, and immunities, civil, political, and religious guaranteed to the people of New Mexico by the Treaty of Guadalupe Hidalgo shall be preserved inviolate."[41] Introduced by Néstor Montoya, it met the requirement of not being repugnant to the US Constitution at the same time it addressed the rights of "the inhabitants of the proposed state." Reference to "the people of New Mexico" implicated the civil and political rights of the "Mexicans" that were under consideration in Articles VIII and IX of the Treaty of Guadalupe Hidalgo. The provision passed unanimously.[42]

The objection to what Erlinda Gonzales-Berry calls Beveridge's "opposition to inclusion of native language rights"[43] came at the reading of the Compact with the United States (the necessary arrangement of relations between a state and the federal government), one press column reporting "a wave of indignation . . . spread[ing] over the convention. Democrats and Republicans alike denounced the language in the Enabling Act which, while purporting to be for the purpose of admitting New Mexico into the Union on an equality with the other states, surrounds her with conditions hitherto unheard of in laws of this character."[44] As Committee Chair Springer began reading the committee's report to the Committee as a Whole, the convention, by "unanimous consent . . . voiced its protest at the unnecessary and humiliating provision of the enabling act which requires the incorporation into the fundamental law of various and sundry matters which Senator Beveridge thought necessary for the government of what that eminent statesman presumably considers a semi-barbarous people."[45]

Section 5 of the Enabling Act mandated that the State "shall never enact any law restricting or abridging the right of suffrage on account of race, color, or previous condition of servitude." Of course, the convention had no choice but to obey Beveridge's mandate that the "ability to read, write, speak, and understand the English language sufficiently well to conduct the duties of the office without the aid of an interpreter shall be a necessary qualification for all State officers and members of the State legislature."[46] Delegates greatly resented the coercion. Quoting the US Constitution and the Treaty of Guadalupe Hidalgo, Springer called the requirement "unfair and a violation of pledges made to the people of New Mexico when this country was first occupied by the American military forces."[47]

Delegate Fall moved that the section be preceded by the phrase "and in compliance with the provisions of the enabling act, it is provided . . . " etc., notifying Congress and the president that the people of New Mexico did not adopt the provision "of their own free will but do so under compulsion." With New Mexico's gaining admittance as a state, its representatives in Washington could then demonstrate "the injustice of these restrictions."[48]

C. M. Compton, Democrat from Roosevelt County where Spanish-speakers formed a minority, seconded Fall, calling the amendment "a proper protest against an unnecessary and unjust restriction" while giving the "native people" the right to "take care of themselves." Delegate E. S. Stover quoted the Enabling Act and the US Constitution to prove the unconstitutionality and injustice of the language requirement. The Act's purpose in admitting New Mexico on an equal footing with the other states of the Union meant the people had the right "to elect whom they please for their state officers and legislators, and so long as this state is restricted in this manner, she is not on an equal footing with the other states of the Union." Sena oddly answered Beveridge with the point that "for forty years, there had never been a territorial officer in New Mexico unable to conduct business in the English language."[49]

Catron read from the Treaty of Guadalupe Hidalgo the promise to honor "them who did not retain their identity as Mexican citizens . . . all the rights and privileges of American citizens." Fall's amendment, emphasizing that treaty rights were "higher law than that of any state constitution" and enabling the State of New Mexico to bring the language issue up in court "with a view to securing justice for her people" received unanimous approval.[50] According to the *Albuquerque Journal*, the convention acted "within perfect reason, voicing a protest" against unfair provisions in the Enabling Act. Compelling fluency in English to hold office could "scarcely be construed otherwise than as a 'slap.'"[51]

That the editorial replicated arguments from Spanish identity indicated the sway of Spanish language discourse on mainstream politics. In telling nomenclature, for example, it agreed with what *La Voz del Pueblo* had argued, that "Our Spanish-American citizenship [*sic*] . . . has been ambitious to master the English language." That Spanish, "a language of history and romance," was "more beautiful than the English," resonated with the Defense of Language script. Moreover, "The fact that a man speaks it is fully as creditable as that he speaks English." The language restriction thus misrepresented the sentiment of New Mexicans, the column continued, leading to the conclusion among outsiders "that New Mexico is not an English-speaking state." Such a restriction was "not in accord with the rights accorded New Mexico when she became a territory of the United States," and as it did not fulfill the expressed intent of admitting New Mexico on an equal footing with the other states, it was "unnecessary and uncalled for."[52]

As the editorial continued to state, the language proviso "may go far toward removing an objection which has been made much of by the enemies of New Mexico. If nothing else it will assure them that we don't plan a Castilian monarchy down here; it is just as well to humor them and let it go at that." The convention had not to go further "than the polite explanation appended to the constitution, for New Mexico is proud of her Spanish-American citizenship and the progress it has made, shown nowhere more clearly than by the native delegates to the Constitutional Convention who are working harmoniously with their brethren for the best and most up to date and thoroughly American constitution possible to frame."[53]

With its capacity for biting sarcasm, *La Voz del Pueblo* marveled at the unity unfolding in the appreciation of the beauty of the "Castilian" language. Contrary to what anyone might say regarding the lack of peace and harmony at the convention,

> after the blustery scenes typically triggered in the constitutional hall, many times a sweet and gentle calm arrives; at these moments, the white dove of peace takes advantage of the opportunity to extend and spread its lovely wings over the gentlemen delegates. Rubbing their eyes and raising their right hand over their heads to put in order their bristly hair, made so by their [political] battles, return so sweetly, one with the other, as if nothing bellicose had occurred between them.

As *La Voz* further marveled: Had Republicans awakened from their lethargy? Even Catron argued with the Democrats over who would have the privilege of registering the most energetic protest over congressional action in general and Beveridge for having gratuitously insulted the "Hispano-American people" with their ungentlemanly demand. However, the cynics at the paper opined that the language restriction was adopted in the state constitution only because there was no alternative. Still, in the name of the "Hispano-Americano people," *La Voz* thanked the delegates for the "mournful orations" they had pronounced in the name of the "Spanish-speaking mortals" of New Mexico.[54]

If Fall's "polite" protest would fail to give Congress pause, at least the convention's Committee on the Elective Franchise rejected the Beveridge requirement, to wit:

> The right of any citizen of the state to vote, hold office or sit upon juries, shall never be restricted, abridged, or impaired, on account of religion, race, language or color, or inability to speak, read or write the English

or Spanish languages except as may be otherwise provided in this constitution.[55]

Néstor Montoya chaired the Committee, which included Eufracio F. Gallegos, Atanacio Roibal, and Venceslao Jaramillo.[56] Their makeover of the clause rebuffed Beveridge's Spanish language bias and answered anti-staters who deemed Nuevomexicanos unqualified for state citizenship due to their traditional language. As Holmes noted, such provisions "did not occur spontaneously or unheralded in the brief span of the constitutional convention of 1910. They had precedent, and one found its way into the constitution in the face of a congressional stricture to the contrary."[57] The legacy of Nuevomexicano primacy and nationness formed the principal precedents. The convention recognized a right to exercise the subnational powers of the state to face federal dictation.

The Enabling Act required that the public schools not only be free from sectarian control but "shall always be conducted in English."[58] Nuevomexicano delegates did not balk at introducing English in the schools, which, according to historian Lynne Getz, suggests that "they foresaw the addition of English, rather than the loss of Spanish, in popular usage."[59] They addressed this issue in much the way the Nuevomexicano intelligentsia had been demanding for a decade. Sedillo introduced the measure that became Sec. 8 of Article XII Education, which stipulated as follows:[60]

> The legislature shall provide for the training of teachers in the normal schools or otherwise so that they may become proficient in both the English and Spanish languages, to qualify them to teach Spanish-speaking pupils and students in the public schools and educational institutions of the state and shall provide proper means and methods to facilitate the teaching of the English language and other branches of learning to such pupils and students.[61]

Getz sees this and other language provisions steering a middle course between the demands of the Enabling Act and the wishes of the Nuevomexicano delegates. As a participation right, it allowed for the assumption of English as a temporal benefit for Nuevomexicano youth to assimilate the English language, an otherwise important point given that contemporary America discriminated against foreign languages, including German.[62] Gonzales-Berry interprets the section as a "subversive maneuver meant to create a space, albeit an ambiguous one, for the inclusion of Spanish in the classroom."[63] She agrees as well with Robert Moyers's conclusion that it was an attempt "to get around these requirements by providing for the employment of teachers who could speak Spanish in Spanish-speaking communities and by providing that Spanish might be used to explain to children the meaning of their English textbooks."[64]

Another language right in Sec. 12 of Article XX provided that for the first twenty years "all laws passed by the legislature shall be published in both the English and Spanish languages and thereafter such publication shall be made as the legislature may provide."[65] Gonzales-Berry calls it "no less than a coup against the national mandate" that prohibited the use of Spanish in government transactions. The time limit of twenty years "suggests that Nuevomexicano legislators expected that the subsequent generation would be totally bilingual and that there might not be a need for printing laws in Spanish after 1931."[66]

Another participation right turned on preemption, which addressed the problem in the southeastern quadrant of the territory where schools were segregated by race. Sec. 10 of Article XII provided in terms of the commanding ethnic nomen, that the

> Children of Spanish descent in the state of New Mexico shall never be denied the right and privilege of admission and attendance in the public schools or other public educational institutions of the state, and they shall never be classed in separate schools, but shall forever enjoy perfect equality with other children in all public schools and educational institutions of the state, and the legislature shall provide penalties for the violation of this section.[67]

The important provision would require policy monitoring for enforcement of the general clause that mandated "a uniform system of free public schools sufficient for the education of, and open to, all the children of school age in the state."[68]

In calling the constitutional convention to order, Catron had said that the constitution would "invite immigration," a matter pertinent to Nuevomexicano rights.[69] It made *La Voz del Pueblo* and others cringe about future immigrant "Americans" further overshadowing Nuevomexicanos politically and economically. Accordingly, Sedillo introduced the proviso that would "Prohibit the Creation of a Bureau of Immigration.'"[70] It failed to make it into the constitution, but it is notable that no such bureau was established after New Mexico became a state.

Of final significance, the Nuevomexicano constitutional safeguards were made virtually impossible to amend. Three-fourths of the members of each house would be required to propose any change, and for ratification, at least three-fourths of the electorate in the "'whole state[,]' and not less than two-thirds of those voting in each county."[71] According to Holmes, the "absolute" strictness of the standard barred "other groups or those in control of the formal agencies of government from undertakings which would denigrate [the] political capacity [of the Hispano Americans]."[72]

On the final day of the convention over three-fourths of the delegates (seventy-nine) voted to confirm the constitution. Eighteen voted against and four abstained. All Nuevomexicano delegates approved except one, and the exception, the independent Jacobo Aragón (Lincoln County) did not vote.[73]

At the closing of the convention, Néstor Montoya proposed a salute. "In the name of the Spanish-American members of the Convention," he pronounced, "all delegates here have, as one man, helped to safeguard the rights of the two hundred thousand people of that blood in this Territory, as loyal a people as is to be found in any State of the Union."[74] It was a declaration of triumph not only for subnational constitutionalism but also for the title of "Spanish American" as the term of art for the whole of the Nuevomexicano people.

Next came the referendum to confirm or deny the constitution.[75] The Nuevomexicano electorate formed a crucial body and so it mattered what their leaders had to say about the constitution. The day after the convention's adjournment, Octaviano Larrazolo joined Governor Mills and his entourage of pro-constitution figures on a speaking tour through counties with the greatest number of Nuevomexicanos: San Miguel, Mora, Taos, Rio Arriba, Santa Fe, Bernalillo, and Doña Ana.[76] Forty-two thousand copies of the translated constitution were disseminated in coordination with the Larrazolo stops.[77]

If ever a moment had come for Nuevomexicano primacy to vindicate itself, that moment had arrived—and Larrazolo sensed it. At Santa Fe he proclaimed, "If you want to acquire your freedom and transmit this sacred heritage in the land hallowed by the blood of your fathers who fought to protect it, [then] seize your opportunity, and do not let it slip through your hands to your lasting regret and that of your descendants." A burst of applause and a rush to the stage reportedly adulated the "silver tongued orator."[78] Delivered at the Albuquerque courthouse before the largest of crowds, Larrazolo's "forceful and convincing speech" reportedly paid "eloquent tribute to the native people."[79]

With over a hundred newspapers editorializing in favor of statehood (sixteen opposed), 70 percent of the electorate (31,742 to 13,399) passed the constitution. It went over in all but four of New Mexico's twenty-six counties. In those where it didn't—Roosevelt, Lincoln, San Juan, and Sierra—Euro-American Democrats ruled, yet in each the measure barely lost.[80]

Jubilant Identity

The voices of the Nuevomexicano/a intelligentsia rejoiced in voluminous editorials, poetry, speeches, and public proclamations.[81] As Luis Tafoya gushed, approval came not because of politicians' prophecies but by "the conviction harbored in the good sense of the people, who were never dumb-witted, realizing it would be the depth of stupidity to squander the opportunity to obtain essential privileges and advantages."[82] In the triumph over the New Mexicanism Alien narratives, Tafoya hailed the greatest majorities in the northern counties as enhancing "Hispano Americano" patriotism and public spirit, making the calumnies and vituperations of fanatics and hypocrites laughable. Poetically he affirmed, "No need to shrink back / Noble ones / We are worth a great deal / More than what they say of us."[83]

Scripts of Nuevomexicano Self-Determination and State Ownership waved in abundance. *La Revista de Taos* claimed just reason for

"Neo-Mexicano citizens" to be proud of proving "to the whole world their supreme desire, equal to all the cultured and civilized people of the earth, to acquire its complete autonomy as a Free State, Sovereign and Independent, with all the splendor of the sun of liberty to which for a thousand reasons the people of New Mexico deserved."[84]

Considerable joy rode in a "Spanish" carriage. In a sense it reflected the informal imprimatur of the Constitutional Convention in which "Spanish," "Spanish American," and "of Spanish descent" prevailed as the principal name of the Nuevomexicano people.[85] *La Voz del Pueblo* translated the phrase "Children of Spanish descent" in the Constitution as *los niños de la descendencia española.*[86] The *Washington Post* reported that "some 135,000 inhabitants of Spanish-American descent demanded protection of their equality before the law and retention of their ancient rights and privileges."[87]

The prize of statehood commanded Spanish primacy accounts. Benjamín Read—writing in *La Revista de Taos*, the major weekly in the far northern counties—heralded the people's justice following the "long, painful, at times humiliating struggle" of "the sons of New Mexico, descendants of the Intrepid Spaniards who more than three hundred years ago implanted Christianity and civilization on the virgin soil of New Mexico, their sealing the grand episode with their blood. Now we have entered in the complete possession of the inestimable inheritance bequeathed to us by our parents, the liberty that had cost them so much."[88] Inscribing further, Read proclaimed that the people's determination had forged "the Brooch of Gold connecting the memorable day of 21 January of 1911 with the glorious 30 of April of 1598 when Oñate nailed the cross with his own hands and unfurled the royal Banner to take solemn possession of New Mexico close to the Pueblo of San Juan."[89]

Read marked the "brilliant" conquering milestones between two liberatory dates. On the 15th of December 1693, don Diego de Vargas consummated the reconquest of New Mexico. The other "no less memorable" event came on the 18th of August 1846,

> the day destiny decreed would begin the regeneration of the people of New Mexico with the spontaneous annexation of the territory to the American government, which ended the sufferings that had for centuries

> affected the isolated Territory, [and made] the impossibility of receiving the opportunistic assistance of the Central Government, given the great distances between Santa Fe and the City of Mexico and the lack of transportation means, the stagnation of industry caused by the perpetual raiding of savage Indians that marauded everywhere, and the fault of not educating the masses.[90]

Further in the script of Ethnonational Liberation, Nuevomexicano patriotism drove "our loyal citizens to valiantly engage the many efforts to deprive us of our autonomy." Hard struggles turned on

> the magnificent spectacle of good Nuevo Mexicano sons, converting themselves into true patriots and into patriotic orators, all speaking with an eloquence possible only at moments in which the life or liberty of an entire people are in danger! The eloquence of the citizens that, inspired by pure patriotic love, fights for their liberty, and for those of his fellow citizens came from the soul; it is the eloquence that convinces, that moves, that terrorizes enemies.[91]

In a Roman allegory, Read shared the patriotic love of the Nuevomexicano heart, captured by the "sublime" eloquence of that ardent patriot, Cicero, as he reflected on national patriotism:

Morir por la patria,	To die for the nation
Dulce morir;	What Sweet death;
Vivir sin patria,	To live without a homeland,
Triste vivir	Such a sad life.[92]

Before a large audience at the fiftieth anniversary of St. Michael's College, Larrazolo communicated an artful yet more sobering message. He launched his epideictic imaginary evocatively:

> In realizing the contrast between the New Mexico of today and the land originally encountered and

> conquered by those intrepid men, in measuring the progress made by their descendants across the centuries of labors, one's enthusiasm is overwhelming.
>
> And, if but for a moment we could revive the buried ashes of those illustrious forerunners of civilization, so that they might witness the fruit of their labors, they would doubtlessly consider themselves engulfed in [unbelievable] illusions at witnessing so different a sight.

Larrazolo wedged in the rhetorical question of whether his community had prepared itself for statehood. Just imagine, he begs of his audience, the return of the glorious conquistadors to New Mexico today, setting their sights on a ramshackle site: "Where we today find ourselves, they would discover and cement themselves to the soil but now see with disbelief the dilapidated and faltering walls of this partially reconstructed [New Mexico] temple." A bereft people had been too shy for their own good:

> And, recognizing it to be the product of their own hands of yesteryear, overcome with pressing memories of the long ago, [they] would inquire of it, "What justifies your presence here in this scarred and dismembered ruin of the centuries?" In what manner have you weathered the destructive arrogance of time? And how have you caressed the hand of that cruel destroyer which, with such respect and tenderness, has seen you observe the constant ebb and flow of the centuries, generation after generation? And you stand here! Can't you see that at your side rises a majestic and imposing cathedral and superb buildings [in America proper] which appear to ridicule your old age? "But no," they would say, "Be not ashamed in the presence of such luxury about you, and do not be disturbed at all by this progress surrounding you."

US New Mexicanism inspired Larrazolo to drive home his point concerning Nuevomexicano preparedness, implying that recognition of their historical heritage would guide them to success:

> Should someone mock you as to who you are, tell them you are the cradle which for the first time tenderly rocked the birth of Christianity in this great republic; and should inquiry be made of your mission, answer them that in your venerable and ancient breast are kept fresh and unblemished memories of the glories as well as of the misfortunes of these colonizers of New Mexico in their centuries of struggles; tell them you are the mystic ladder of progress whose foundations are secured by the first annals of the seventeenth century, and that you have remained as a messenger from those people and those times, extending to the children of today greetings from the conquistadors who wish them further success in their efforts towards greater and greater progress.[93]

Larrazolo in the grandeur of his oratory realized how his people needed to know that New Mexico would not have been anywhere near ready for statehood had the Nuevomexicano nation not laid down a Christian foundation.

Benjamín Read did not mention Larrazolo or his piece, but he clearly responded to them in an account that encapsulated the scripts of a half century. As he hyped, don Diego de Vargas had "forever" set down the "banner of Christianity, symbol of temporal liberty and sure compass to the door of ETERNAL happiness," but neither he nor his predecessors "in the glorious business of discovery, colonization and the civilizing of this far away province" could have imagined "the fruits of their fearlessness and incomparable valor." For Read, "Never would they return [in apparent answer to Larrazolo's conquest ghosts] to see how they had overreached the sovereignty of the King's Laws of Spain."[94]

With erudition to rival Larrazolo's, Read escorted other historical legends in with presumptions behind the Doctrine of Discovery. "Just like Moctezuma and his predecessors" who would never have imagined,

> no matter the fateful tradition of respecting the prognostications of Huemac and Quetzalcoatl [Toltec priests] who announced the destruction of Imperial

> Mexico, that from Iberia there should come, "with their clean hands," Cortez and his band to snatch his [Moctezuma's] reins, destroy his Government, idols and human sacrifices, instead, giving them new faith and civilization, taking them out of a state of semi barbarism, in which they were unfortunately locked, elevating them to the dignity of Christian beings. Notwithstanding, the Eternal finger had marked the hour for the consummation of the terrible and cruel evolution.[95]

The change took effect, the imperium of Moctezuma disappeared, "and on top of the rubble was raised a new civilization with the banner of Christ for support and guidance." The powers of the kings of Castilla lasted three hundred years, Read imparted, "civilization in its marvelous march" reaching the "zenith of its development, in those ages lighting in the hearts of the sons of Moctezuma and the descendants of the Great Cortez the flame of absolute liberty and on 16 of September of 1810, Hidalgo saluted the morning aurora with the famous shout, ¡Viva Méjico!"[96]

Destitute Isolation had removed New Mexico from the center of government, leaving it "forgotten, isolated and virtually unprotected." The people had made "frequent pleas and pathetic messages." Representing two generations of a regional intelligentsia's historical epistemic, Read had Pedro Bautista Pino, New Mexico's first deputy to the Spanish Cortes, and Governor Pedro Fermín de Mendinueta going to the Spanish court to petition for support, Mendinueta hoping that the viceroy would see how eighty soldiers could not guard "nor succor" the settlements. With Mexico's independence, the "sons of New Mexico" had reason to hope for the assistance and protection that the colonial governments had denied them. It was "mere illusion; the poor people kept suffering, even more than before."[97]

In Read's third evolutionary phase, the "noble and suffering sons of New Mexico" pined for the American flag, the "symbol of true liberty," only to have the promise of privileges under equal citizenship that Kearny had "solemnly" pledged turn into "another illusion." At least the people were more protected from Natives and had acquired the enjoyment of "almost complete civil rights." With that small autonomy granted—the right to legislate and have a delegate in Congress—room had been made for the people to demand complete citizenship. After sixty-three years of constant battles, "we have chosen to savor the desired morsel. Soon, then," Read proclaimed, "we shall become a federal entity."[98]

Read agreed with Larrazolo: For the "young Hispano Americanos" and their successors, the "adversities and responsibilities" of change awaited. There were problems in the "science of government" that his own generation was incapable of addressing. Critical self-rule awaited. Youth must take an active part in politics at home and in the country, and if not, the assuredly stolid government would "remain in the scary hands of the stranger." Study the federal and state constitutions well, Read counselled, "read a book on political economy." After a good education, only the ambition of being a good citizen was more important "for the sons of New Mexico." Beware the lure and "twisted intentions" of dishonest politicians. A man could be political and not dishonest, which would "redound in his honor, to the benefit of his co-citizens and that of society."[99]

The writings of the Nuevomexicano intelligentsia had long riveted patriarchal imaginaries. Among the Nuevomexicanas beginning to break through their gendered walls,[100] eighteen-year-old Aurora Lucero made a popular contribution to the discourses of statehood. The daughter of the venerable coeditor of *La Voz del Pueblo*, Antonio Lucero, Aurora delivered a speech at an event at the Normal University in Las Vegas, New Mexico, that took off on the wings of Spanish Discovery and Indian Scourge. The descendants of the conquistadors "ripped the veil of mystery off the seas and gave to the world a new continent," she pronounced. They fought gallantly [in the Pueblo Revolt] "for the preservation of their homes and defended their lives at the blade of their swords." Spanish settlements, overwhelmed by the "tremendous numerical superiority of Indians in 1680," forcibly moved to El Paso del Norte. Far from an embarrassed retreat, their actions were "sublime in heroism, equal only to the retreat of the Ten Thousand in beloved Greek history" (in the Battle of Cunaxa, 401–399 BCE, the march back to Greece from the Persian Empire).[101]

And now, anticipating statehood, Aurora worried about the descendants of the "conquistadors of this soil," those who came in the fifteenth century obligated in a new order to fight "for the prestige of their race . . . dearer than life itself." Leaving indigeneity in the dust, Lucero put the "two classes of people" facing the future, "the descendants of the mighty races which were different one from the other in language, origin, and customs, even more in their economic conditions." Old cultural differences threatened harmonious union, and "It is an absurdity to think that this obstacle could be removed by renouncing one's blood, tongue, or our customs! How could this be done?" She refined the problem of interethnic adjustment, the masses of both nationalities being "not educated in a way that one and the other know and appreciate the other more intimately." Ever the traditionalist, she favored education "sustained on the base of a Christian civilization" to inculcate "the spirit of love of neighbor, the only way to harmonize the discordant elements of our civilization."[102]

Heir to primacy's religious colonization, Lucero located her people's cultural primacy in Santa Fe's Christian community, home of the churches, chapels, educational institutions, and "grand and glorious traditions." In them the people would thrive "while the dust between Colorado and California is found mixed with the bones of the founders and their subsequent defenders and will remain there forever. Their descendants, the Hispano Americanos, while remaining in the new state and while stricken by adversity, still are, and for always will be the marvelous link in the chain of time that forever will connect the history of the old world with that of the new." Now that they had "possession of what is ours, the grace of a state," it promised a partnership with Anglo Americans to make New Mexico "the most fluorescent community of all that have formed in this glorious American union."[103]

Lucero protested the imputation "often thrown out" that her people displayed indifference to the benefits of modern progress. "The facts prove the contrary," she argued, shown by regular school attendance. Still, US colonialization and the federal government's refusal to provide the necessities to sustain life had left "Hispano-Americanos" to fight "hand in hand to defend their homes from the incursions of the savage Indians" without reliance on other than their "perseverance and indomitable valor." The exigencies of a new state made it necessary for all to recognize her people's "long residence in this soil" and the "glorious feats of their relevant elders." Their fundamental need was for "that most powerful arm of the times . . . which is intellectual development." The US government denied them "this grace"; indeed, in the Spanish War Penalty Denied script, more educational resources went to the Filipinos in one year than were provided to the 'Hispano Americanos' in seventy.[104]

Lucero called on all patriotic citizens to encourage the betterment of the Hispano Americano children in rural districts if they "sincerely" desired that they take active and prominent parts in public issues. "Peasant farmworkers" needed to understand what was "owed to society, what it is to have rights from that society." All other reforms should be set aside until the day they understood that there was no more important task than to make the new state march "toward the unknown horizon and future." Still, while acknowledging the importance of scientific knowledge, she was invested in the classic pedagogical question of morals. All over the country, "the public schools are rapidly [becoming] the new religious temples. This new religion (if atheism can be called a religion) consists of no religion completely, because it enables the negation of the Supreme God." In the rich literary style of religious traditionalists heard in the 1870s,[105] Lucero deplored the prevalence of the profane in the chaos of modern life. The absence of religious instruction in the public schools produced "waterfalls of crime" in the large cities. Immorality arose from "loose reins in towns, villas and cities, defiling the atmosphere we breath and the land we walk on." Scholars proved that "a people without God has to fall; that Greece fell when its gods became allegories; that Rome lost its valor when its people had lost its faith; and that dead nations dissolved after the people lost their foundational faith."[106]

As New Mexico "pour[ed] in the cement" for a state, Lucero called for religious diversity "so that all the religious divisions can stand . . . without being concerned, and so deeply set in all the eternal Principles of Justice that they be lasting." Marrying the Enlightenment and tradition, she called for a law to declare "in truth, as equally as in Words, that religious liberty, just like civil liberty, remain[s] here plainly guaranteed for all men; that all men are in fact free and able to enjoy the blessings of that liberty that is founded in the right to do well, with the rights of all as its base and with the light of reason as its guide." As much as Lucero respected the liberal emphasis on education, she insisted that it must also be moral. Accordingly, and "in the name of Justice," she naively advised the people of their new state to construct what would become their wholly secular system of public education and, in doing that, to make sure that their "spiritual and material potentials," as well as the "rectitude of their consciences," remain firm. Assuring that this new voice would make its mark on the consciousness of New Mexicans, her words appeared in at least three Spanish-language newspapers, as well as the *Santa Fe New Mexican*, and produced an outpouring of plaudits.[107]

For two-thirds of a century the Nuevomexicano populace maintained life in a colonial ward. Adjusting to the institutions of a foreign sovereign, an imposed settler colonial hierarchy, sustained competition with Indigenous nations, and the aggravations of US nationalism, educated Nuevomexicanos clamored for political dignity and self-determination—and at every turn compelled an identification with the regional homeland under various names until subnational constitutionalism whittled the options down to "Spanish American." But now, with a dominant Spanish identity in hand, what fate awaited Nuevomexicanos/as in their glorified state?

PART III

"Spanish"

DOMINANT AND FRAGILE

CHAPTER 8

The Heyday of Spanish Identity

ON JANUARY 6, 1912, President Taft signed New Mexico into the company of American states.[1] At last, New Mexicans were taken into "an active and coordinated compliance with the ongoing activities and objectives of the dominant group in society."[2] Another celebratory spree broke out, rife with primacy scripts and conquest heraldry. In the decades that followed, two major results of statehood would prove consequential, one disappointingly ethnopolitical, the other affirmatively ethnocultural.

Constitutional Letdown

Nuevomexicano politicos had gone to the Constitutional Convention of 1910 determined to gain subnational constitutional advantages for their people. G. Alan Tarr checks for subnational constitutional successes in the United States and fails to find permanent minority protections in any of the fifty states. Montana and New Mexico's constitutions recognized obligations to Native Americans and "Americans of Spanish ancestry" respectively, yet they failed to become important independent protections for minority rights. In New Mexico, Tarr writes, "courts have ruled that neither the recognition of rights under the Treaty of Guadalupe Hidalgo . . . nor the protection against discrimination for children of Spanish descent conferred a right to have the Spanish language and culture preserved and continued in public schools."[3]

In essence, the battery of protection and participation rights amounted to little. It did not help that Nuevomexicano protocols came in an era in which the liberal ideal of civil rights was vested in the individual as opposed to the post-Civil Rights focus on collective rights.[4] Regarding the "self-understanding of most states," constitutional expert Nicole Töpperwien notes that it was "of and for one nation and the definition of the nation as being composed of equal individuals or as a culturally homogeneous entity without subgroups. This understanding of the nation-state limit[ed] the legitimacy of participation rights at the very outset."[5]

Sec. 10, Article XII, The Educational Rights of Children of Spanish Descent, included not only the prohibition of separate schools by race but also a guarantee of "perfect equality with other children in all public schools and educational institutions of the state." Yet educational inequality became a perennial issue, indicated by subpar scholastic performances and disproportionate dropout rates. It was confirmed by the research associated with a 2018 district court ruling that decreed in favor of Hispanic and Native American plaintiffs who sued the state of New Mexico for denying low-income and English-language learner students their constitutional right to a "uniform and sufficient education." The judge in that case mandated that the state provide the resources to bring Native American and Hispanic education to the adequacy criterion in the constitution.[6] The state has found it impossible to meet the standard.

The equal education provision intersected with the Beveridge requirement that public school instruction be conducted only in English. Constitution makers realized the difficulties it would produce. Sec. 8 of Article XII Education, which provided for the training of teachers in the normal schools to the point of proficiency in both the English and Spanish languages, suggested it was possible to create an effective bilingual education program.[7] But when educators attempted to establish bilingual education in the decades after statehood to have Spanish-speaking students improve in the schools, business interests fought tooth and nail against state funds going for that purpose.[8]

Although New Mexico's subnational constitutionalism addressed problems of internal colonialism by ensuring the right to vote, it could not guarantee fair or equitable electoral representation, much less nativo self-rule, which the primacy movement had no power to explicitly demand. As legal scholars point out, the problem with the bill of rights approach (as well as judicial review) is that it only provides for negative rights that protect individuals against discrimination but is insufficient, especially for territorially concentrated groups with "deep historical roots in the subnational unit in which they are living" that desire powers allowing them to "participate in the management of the constituent units. They demand the provision of mechanisms for political participation and representation." To emphasize that further, a bill of rights is "incapable of ensuring a fair distributional allocation of goods or of providing affirmative benefits to minority groups." Nor does it fully respond "to the expressive demands for recognition that are so often central to ethnic minorities and to the legitimacy and stability of democratic institutions across ethnic groups."[9]

The question of Nuevomexicano participation in politics formed a case in point. Some attempted to remove Beveridge's rule that knowing English was required to hold public office, but without success. In urging people to vote for the change, *La Bandera Americana* unambiguously called the proposed restrictive amendment an insult and used typical primacy terms to level its opposition: "those who settled and began the first eras in these lands, to the noble and hospitable sons of New Mexico, the Hispano Americanos." When the amendment lost, the *Albuquerque Morning Journal* explained that that was due "largely to a failure of those voting to fully understand it, hundreds of voting against it largely through a mistaken conception of its meaning." In addition, the Nuevomexicano vote was seriously low, forty thousand versus sixty-nine thousand in the first state referendum.[10] Another effort two years later succeeded in removing the language restriction,[11] but it would not take long for the restriction to lose its relevance among an increasingly bilingual populace and English-speaking Nuevomexicano professionals.

As a result, Euro-American ambitions for federal and state office-holding undercut the Nuevomexicano goal of Nuevomexicano self-rule on the basis of a Nuevomexicano majority in the electorate. At the opening address of the first state convention of the Republican Party, L. B. Prince cynically recalled in front of partyites New Mexico's long, arduous struggle to achieve statehood, casting it in the shadow of its "heritage of glory." The Coronado expedition with "its spirit of venturesome bravery and gallantry"; the conquests of Oñate and de Vargas; the martyred priests who brought Christianity to the region; and two hundred years of families in the Rio Grande Valley who fought for civilization: The allusions represented Prince's[12] slap in the face of Spanish identity for in the first election of state offices, the Republican Party callously failed to nominate a single Nuevomexicano for major state office. Prince himself would go on to scramble for a US senator's seat. It was a betrayal of the decades in which Nuevomexicanos served as the rank and file in the Party of Lincoln and of the encouragement Euro-American politicos offered Nuevomexicanos to push for statehood only to have it benefit themselves.

While episodes of this sort would seem to have vindicated the Democratic Party's constant slam at the top leaders of the Republican Party for their self-interested policies, Democrats did no better, nominating a Euro-American for governor and Congress.[13] Moreover, both Thomas Catron and Albert Fall horse traded to snag the Nuevomexicano majority state legislature to elect them New Mexico's first US Senators.[14] Up until 1940, Nuevomexicanos represented 38 percent of the New Mexico state senate and 22 percent of the state house of representatives, though those numbers fell well below the proportion of Nuevomexicanos in the New Mexico population.[15]

Compensative Spanish Identity

In the early 1920s, the writer Elizabeth Shepley Sergeant moved to Taos to recover from injuries she suffered as a Great War correspondent in France. In an article in a national magazine, Sergeant noted that the new visitor to New Mexico "does not at first realize the degree to which what may be called the Spanish complex influences the conscious and unconscious mind of the state."[16] It was the Spanish Realm of Memory, matured by the achievement of statehood, that had moved her. On one level of the complex Sergeant referred to, Euro-American culturalists monumentalized Spanish colonial legacies with ornaments on and in public and commercial buildings, historical museums, the canvases of the Santa Fe and Taos artistic communities, books on "Spanish folklore," tourist routes, and entertainment venues.[17]

In the Nuevomexicano community, Spanish identity flourished into its own golden era. In a way, it helped resolve the problem of first-class citizenship for the Nuevomexicano populace, for as social change theory points out, the enhancement of cultural pluralism can be an important offsetting response to the challenges that internal colonialism and ethnic nationalism pose.[18] In this sense, the boom in Spanish identity at this time symbolized a rightful, if not righteous belonging to a valid piece of America that Nuevomexicanos/as had claimed as their right since their annexation by the United States.[19]

Spanish/Hispano identity continued to click in the Spanish language. *La Revista de Taos*, for example, praised *La Voz del Pueblo*'s twenty-ninth anniversary edition as the "most extraordinary" ever published in New Mexico *en el dulce idioma de cervantes* (in the sweet language of Cervantes), "indubitably showing the highest level of culture that New Mexico has ever acquired, and particularly among the descendants of the Spanish conquistadors who know how to appreciate in all its valor the language of their ancestors."[20]

Spanish identity pulsed in a new generation of Nuevomexicano families. The marriage of Lea Sandoval and Damián C. de Baca in Bernalillo regally represented the uniting of "two of the oldest Spanish families in the state . . . establishing their record as one of the oldest families of Spanish American aristocracy."[21] Obituaries blessed departed ones with Spanish and conquistador ancestries and Native-fighting prowess, among them Pedro Perea, Rafael Romero, Ezequiel C. de Baca, Alejandro Sandoval, Ambrosio Ortiz, José Francisco Chaves, and Nestor C. de Baca.[22] A consolidating Nuevomexicano middle class styled their organizations with titles like the Spanish American Society, the Spanish American Mutual Protection Association, and the Spanish American Alliance.[23] In the field of popular culture, *El Nuevo Mexicano* editor Benigno Muñiz organized the *Villeros Alegres* (Happy Villagers), a musical group that sang the traditional folk ballads of the wood haulers and sheepherders "of the 'Spanish hinterland."[24]

At the start of World War I, *La Voz del Pueblo* praised "*nuestra gente de raza Española*" (our people of the Spanish race) for their patriotic volunteering.[25] Leaders called for the quartering of Nuevomexicano soldiers in their own unit, for, Octaviano Larrazolo pronounced, the "Spanish-Americans," a "distinctly home-loving people," would be more comforted if they were "banded together in one regiment, speaking one language, carrying out many of the customs of their people and sharing memories that are dear to their race."[26]

Santa Fe, long defined as a Spanish culture harbor, radiated Spanish identity, investing Spanish Americans with a special status in the city, one destined to last for a long time. Not least, the annual founder's Fiesta de Santa Fe (Fiesta) churned out Spanish identity like a new mechanical engine. As historians emphasize, Euro-American businessmen, merchants, and directors of the state-museum-controlled Fiesta for twenty years. Yet, from the start, Nuevomexicanos had a subaltern but solid stake in the event just as they had in the Tertio-Millennial Exposition. In the inaugural (actually the centerpiece of Santa Fe's 1911 Fourth of July), they hauled out la toma de posesión.

George Washington Armijo—hailed as a "descendant of one of the oldest and most prominent families in the Southwest" and a "leader of his people"—proved the "fitting" choice for the role of de Vargas, for he carried out the part with "stature and bearing."[27] Other Nuevomexicanos with main roles in the "resplendently" attired troupe[28] included County Treasurer Celso López, City Marshal Nicolás Sena, and Supreme Court Clerk José Sena, Jr., with the Euro-American businessmen James Seligman and Samuel Cartwright playing side parts. López acted as the "mainstay of the movement" that made the de Vargas pageant "such a success."[29]

The following year, the throng attending what was now called De Vargas Day was estimated at eight thousand coming from Española, Estancia, and Albuquerque. Also splashed with extensive Spanish glory were Nuevomexicano readers of the reports of the celebration in the daily *Santa Fe New Mexican.*[30]

The progeny of the chief conqueror's "heroic band," it was reported, conducted the honors. Moreover, the "direct descendant of the Indian who met De Vargas in the old plaza of Santa Fe performed in [the portrayal of] the compact made those centuries ago when his forefather pledged allegiance to the colors of a Spanish king." Armijo recounted the story of de Vargas, his company of clergy, forty soldiers and fifty mexicano and Native friends marching in to take possession of "*La Villa de Santa Fe*" for the King of Spain. Finding that the Tanos have fortified their village for resistance to his occupation, de Vargas informs them that the King of Spain would pardon them if they immediately obeyed his orders. They come back with word that the disturbed people would not go quietly but would allow only de Vargas, his main priest, and six disarmed soldiers to enter. The conqueror reaches the point where the Tanos erected a cross, kneeling to kiss it.[31]

Under a stiff sword properly raised, de Vargas's proclamation affirms, even more piercingly than the staging of la toma in the Tertio-Millennial Exposition, that King Charles had forgiven their heresy of "renounc[ing] the Catholic religion":

> [for] the sacrilege by which you have deprived the clergy of their lives; the desecration of the churches, and the smashing of images and contamination of sacred vases; the cowardice with which you have knifed

> the Spanish inhabitants without pity for women and children; the barbarity with which you have burned their ranches and the consequences that have followed such abominations; it has been ordered by the clear authority of His Majesty to pardon you without other conditions than that you return to the flock of the Holy Church, which is prepared to receive you like a pious mother if you beg for forgiveness with penitence and tears and swear obedience to Her Catholic Majesty like our legitimate King.[32]

Compliant Native Americans order that the Royal Standard be raised. "Resonantly and intelligibly," de Vargas declares the Villa de Santa Fe the Capital of the New Mexico Kingdom, now taken in the name of Sir Carlos II. Soldiers shout three "Long Live the Kings" to enable them to serve the people as they should. He and the other Spaniards kneel before the Holy Cross as the priest chants the "Te Deum Laudamus."[33] Two famous photos of Armijo as de Vargas in conquistador regalia circulated widely in the pages of *El Nuevomexicano.*[34]

In 1919, Edgar L. Hewett, director of the New Mexico Museum, together with Sheriff George W. Armijo, José D. Sena, Jr. (whose father scripted and starred in the Coronado pageant of the Tertio-Millennial Exposition), Augustín Durán, and Adjutant General James Baca persuaded business interests to make Santa Fe Fiesta, as it was now called, an annual commemoration.[35] In that year's pageant, Armijo appeared as "De Vargas the Conqueror" on the front page of the *Santa Fe New Mexican* (see Fig. 16) just as he did in 1912.[36]

In 1920, the Fiesta so entranced the editor of Albuquerque's *La Bandera Americana* that he hailed to no end the memory of Santa Fe as "the capital of this kingdom during the dominion of Spain and Mexico." The glory scripts of Nuevomexicano belonging ruled stronger than ever. No other state of the Union could "with greater glory celebrate the discovery and conquest of these lands of the American continent discovered by Columbus," editor Néstor Montoya rang out, much like he did at the conclusion of the 1910 constitutional convention, because New Mexico has been "the theater of the great processions and sufferings of the first Spanish Conquistadors and the martyred missionaries; the Catholic fathers of the Order of San Francisco

FIGURE 16. George Washington Armijo as Don Diego de Vargas. A Rough Rider under Theodore Roosevelt, Armijo earned a Purple Heart in Cuba, later serving as chief clerk of the New Mexico House of Representatives, vice president of the Santa Fe City School Board, Santa Fe alderman, Santa Fe probate clerk and recorder, secretary of the 1910 Constitutional Convention, and secretary of the New Mexico Corporation Commission. Unknown photographer. Author's scan from *Santa Fe New Mexican,* September 12, 1919, 1.

watered this soil with their blood." Combining Indian Scourge and Santa Fe Precedence, Montoya highlighted the taking of New Mexico from the hands of "the savage Indian tribes for civilization and Christianity, more than a year before the first English colonies to the north and east of us, and where there lie their descendants of Spanish ancestry, contented American citizens [they are], happy and prosperous under the starry flag of the United States."[37] Fiesta promoters encouraged Nuevomexicano nativos throughout the state to bring their families to Santa Fe every year to preserve their historical memory of the time when it was "under dominion of Spain, the national mother of Mexico after its independence, and of the American state to present times."[38]

In 1929, the Euro-American Fiesta Council turned the Fiesta de Santa Fe over to Spanish Americans. From then on, a Nuevomexicano played de Vargas and only Nuevomexicanas were entitled to serve as *Fiesta reina* (the event's queen). Not until 1945, however, would the Fiesta Council presidency go only to Nuevomexicanos,[39] making the Fiesta more of a Nuevomexicano cultural possession.

In the early 1930s, Spanish fiestas sprouted in other sites.[40] While Santa Fe ennobled de Vargas, the Española Valley (twenty-six miles northward) laid festive claim to Oñate. The annual summer Fiesta del Valle de Española began in 1933 when Nuevomexicano legislators from the Valley introduced a House resolution to set aside July 11 as a state holiday "in honor of the first permanent settlement in the entire Southwest," a settlement which "should have been recognized more generally" for it was "one of the great events in the history of the United States."[41] In the press report of the proposed resolution there appeared a history of Oñate's planting of the Spanish flag and the Christian cross, establishing New Mexico's first capital at San Gabriel, the "first settlement of a civilized people." It referenced New Mexico's "First Lady, the wife of Don Juan de Oñate," lauded as "no ordinary person, this original First Lady, being the great-granddaughter of Cortez, the greatest explorer of this continent." As it was further noted, the poet Villagrá documented the "well equipped . . . gentlemen soldiers who accompanied Oñate."[42] The first Oñate Fiesta Royal Court in full costume was held that year. Delfín Salazar played Oñate and Siria Lucero "Mrs. Oñate."[43]

The descendants of Old Town Albuquerque's original families had long promoted the occasion of its community founding with an annual procession. In 1988, they erected a bronze statue of its founding hero, don Francisco Cuervo y Valdés, astride a raised stallion.[44]

Golden Era Scribes

In the decades after statehood, a generation of Nuevomexicano/a writers published books and articles on the Spanish heritage they claimed as theirs.[45] The older members of this sector carried over from the pre-statehood era of primacy identity. Benjamín M. Read, the son of a Euro-American father and a Nuevomexicana and a lawyer, sallied on with the identitarian yearning "to provide histories "'*por un hijo nativo de Nuevo México*'" (by a native son of New Mexico) to balance the biased and inaccurate stories about the territory."[46]

Read's *An Histórico-Synoptical Sketch of the Mexico-American War* (*Guerra Mexico-Americana*) came out in 1910, and his *Illustrated History of New Mexico* (*Historia Ilustrada de Nuevo México*) in 1912. Community of memory authors congratulated Read. One, Isidoro Armijo, praised Read's "literary gem, which will shine in all the ways it treats of our rich, historic, and romantic New Mexico."[47] Aurelio Espinosa heaped a "thousand commendations" on Read's history of the Mexican-American War for its erudite exposition and the "valor and weight that you give to our race in the conquest, colonization and social organization of the territory." The chapter treating the historical events since 1846 to the present, Espinosa related, "should make the enemies of our race and of our people blush."[48]

Reciprocating, Read called on compatriots to heed the young Espinosa, "the honor of our race and the pride of New Mexico." Read saw in Espinosa the weight of a new generation of the Nuevomexicano intelligentsia. "With our cooperation," he put it, "we shall give him encouragement, demonstrate to the world that we know how to appreciate the true sons of New Mexico in their just valor, and the excellence of those of our brothers who, owing to their constancy, energy and legitimate ambitions have distinguished themselves in the world of letters, redounding their praise-worthy efforts and interesting

FIGURE 17. Aurelio Espinosa, ca. 1902. The young Espinosa established a reputation as an up-and-coming scholar of the Spanish language and Spanish literature and went on to become a key academic figure for his articulations of the historic claims of Spanish identity. Unknown photographer. Author's scan from Read, *Historia Ilustrada de Nuevo México,* 466.

works to the benefit of humanity and the honor and glory of New Mexico and the race of our ancestors."[49]

Aurelio Macedonio Espinosa, born and raised in a village in the far northern Nuevomexicano culture region of southern Colorado, graduated from the University of Colorado and the University of Chicago. He earned a PhD in 1909, going on to carve a noted career at Stanford in folklore studies. His local fame took off while he studied for his advanced degrees. In 1904, while working on his master's degree, he taught at the University of New Mexico (UNM), where he caught the attention of *La Bandera Americana.* Néstor Montoya praised Espinosa as "el erúdito catedrático" for his delving into modern languages, pedagogy, and philosophy; for his teaching; for annotating a classic Spanish drama, *El Gran Galeoto*, for English speakers; and for promoting UNM's Spanish language and drama program.[50] *La Voz del Pueblo* heralded this "nativo of our soil" for embarking on a study of the Spanish spoken in New Mexico. It "bespoke of those who he calls the *español neo-mexicanos.*" His "honorific" hiring as a Stanford professor "indicated what all the neo-mexicano youth can accomplish with perseverance in their studies."[51] The correspondent *El Corresponsal* laid an homage "to the young man who is doing great studies."[52]

The Espinosa legacy ultimately derived from the research he conducted on Nuevomexicano folk culture. While claiming scientific precision, Espinosa, according to Chris Wilson, "saw what he was prepared by his background to see. His heritage as a son of Spanish hidalgos and the academic pursuit of pure stocks of folklore combined to send him on a self-fulfilling search for pure Spanish culture."[53] Indeed, his grandparents had instilled in him key legends about their lineage as "descendants of Spanish families who had come from Spain to the viceroyalty of New Mexico in the 16th and 17th centuries, among the first settlers of upper New Mexico" and of his father's origins traceable to Captain Marcelo Espinosa, a member of Oñate's 1598 colonizing party.[54]

Rather than pioneering Spanish identity for New Mexico, as many have said, Espinosa took the reins of and refined the ideological primacy that a nineteenth-century Nuevomexicano intelligentsia laid down decades earlier. The Romantic movement's daze over the "archaic, the traditional (or pseudo-traditional), and the peasant," often for high culture tastes,"[55] worked in his favor of centering Nuevomexicano pobladores as the heart of the Nuevomexicano nation. In arguing that vecino language, folk culture, and (eventually) race reflected "pure Spanish," Espinosa put the finishing touches on Nuevomexicano ethnonationalism. In a clean, simple script of the Past Living in the Present, he argued that elements of rural culture were brought to the region by the Spanish settlers and there they remained intact. In the classic formulation, the native language, an old, pure dialect, evaded Native influences and added few Euro-Americanisms. All the myths, superstitions, tales, proverbs, riddles, children's games, and ballads commonly heard in the families of northern New Mexico and southern Colorado represented the age of Cervantes, which, for Espinosa, defined "Spanish" culture for the region.[56]

In this isolation thesis, Spanish settler culture remained pristine through centuries of remote geographic and historical life.[57] In a published letter to Read, Espinosa enforced the American Settler Colonial script, noting how in 1846–1848, Nuevomexicanos "were generous and gentlemen with their [American] equals, but did not know how to tolerate insults like those that had never been hurled to the sons of Spain."[58]

Yet, Euro-American locals relished Espinosa's work.[59] At the request of "many of his New Mexico friends" and the president of New Mexico Historical Society, Espinosa authored a monograph "for a popular presentation" on "the Spanish language as spoken to-day by nearly one quarter of a million people in New Mexico and Colorado, . . . a rich archaic Spanish dialect, largely Castilian in source."[60] Policy-wise, Espinosa called for the public schools of the Southwest to make the study of Spanish possible "for the benefit of the Spanish-speaking children of these regions who have no opportunity to learn to read their native tongue." The scientific and "compressive study of New Mexican Spanish folklore should be encouraged in every legitimate way," he called out, "by the learned Societies and educational institutions of New Mexico."[61] In the 1930s, Espinosa wrote a school primer stressing that "New Mexico is still an integral part of Spain."[62]

A spate of authors followed Espinosa's calling with reminiscences of their childhoods in northern New Mexico villages. Cleofas Jaramillo, Nina Otero-Warren, Fabiola Cabeza de Baca Gilbert, Aurora Lucero, and others did their part to disseminate the word of the "pure," "uncontaminated" Spanish customs they grew up with.

L. B. Prince's "Three Cultures in Harmony" theme survived as a public relations gimmick. However, tensions and civic conflict characterized relations among Nuevomexicanos and Euro-Americans. Accordingly, not all Spanish identity manifested itself romantically, nor did a Spanish heritage, embellished with New Mexican overtones, pacify Nuevomexicanos when it came to continued evidence of old-style discrimination at work. As in other attempts at fulfilling subnational constitutionalism, meaningful integration needed to be "constantly won."[63]

Statehood represented a vindication of nineteenth-century New Mexicanism, yet vestiges of the orientalist-style prejudice persisted.[64] As such, Jesús María Alarid, a former territorial government administrator, wrote to Néstor Montoya in 1913 of the pride he felt in "los patricios hijos de este suelo de Nuevo México" (the patrician native sons of this New Mexican soil). Alarid's pride extended to the forceful way New Mexico *hijos* openly challenged those newspaper editors of the eastern United States who stereotyped the "Hispano-Americanos" as incompetent in professional and business matters. He added praise for the exemplars of professional rank, the "gentlemen" who were associated with the weekly newspaper *La Voz del Pueblo*—don Ezequiel C. de Baca, don Antonio Lucero, and don Félix Martínez. For anyone to deny Martínez's avocation as a "true diplomat," Alarid maintained, was to deny "the light of day." Others included Secundino Romero, chair of San Miguel County's Republican Executive Committee and owner of *El Independiente*; Benjamín Read; and Montoya himself. They often fought among themselves politically, Alarid noted, yet they acted as one in defending against the animus of "enemies" who scorned "los hijos nativos del país," striking back at Euro-Americans who claimed that Nuevomexicanos engaged in politics only as pretenders to obtain *papa* (the dole) but whose abilities (in terms of the Good Character script) reflected their very "nobleza de alma y aptitudes" (nobility of soul and fitness).[65]

Illustrating Alarid's point, Secretary of State Antonio Lucero went after Euro-American dominance on New Mexico ground. In a speech delivered in 1914 before the state Archaeology Association, Lucero complained of how the "Spanish Americans of New Mexico" contended with "the race problem," a "most pathetic" problem, not quite like the African American question in the South or the "Asiatic" issue, but close. It was because of Anglo disdain and a "racial preoccupation" that inadequate attention was being paid to the education of Nuevomexicano children and the consequent poverty it engendered. It was therefore the duty "of all loyal Neo-Mexicanos . . . to yank out the root of this preoccupation." With his experience at the forefront of Nuevomexicano leadership, Lucero spoke "not from hearsay" but from his own "intimate knowledge."[66]

Lucero had what he called a "long cherished desire" to "give some facts about the Spanish Americans, their history, their origin and the language they speak in the home, in order that they may be better known by the new settlers of this state and to show, also, how unjust and how cruel it is for anybody to look down upon them." Innovating a race script, he emphasized that his people were "not only Caucasians; we belong to that branch of the white race, the Aryans, which more than all the others has made the history of the world." Nuevomexicano whiteness equaled and, in some ways, excelled that of northern Europe. "The Spaniard has a past as proud in its deeds of valor," Lucero preferred, "as haughty in its intellectual attainments, as pure in language, as advanced in its laws, and as glorious in its achievements as that of the Anglo Saxon race. Ours is a past that can take its place in that grand procession of greatness that is part of history," Lucero bragged, "a past that should be admired, honored and never ended."[67]

It was a false equivalence, yet Lucero, like his daughter Aurora years before, saw the discrepancy in the Caucasian distinction as a bridge to bring about "the cultivation of a better acquaintance, one with the other—the Anglo-Saxon with the Spanish American." As he saw it, "How to remove this obstacle is the question which should engage the attention of every person having the best interests of the state at heart." One part required the realization that Nuevomexicanos were not "an inferior race or the dregs of Europe." Upgrading his Destitute Isolation script with equal parts masculinity, Lucero charged that, like Anglos, Nuevomexicanos were "descendants of men who did not flinch at dangers—men who, cut off from the rest of the world, in the midst of a hostile land, kept alive the fires of civilization for nearly three hundred years—until the Americans came." Respect for the right of Nuevomexicanos to belong to New Mexico required respect for the language handed to them "by the discoverers of this new world." Nuevomexicanos were American citizens, yet "they do not need on that account to deny either [their] origin or . . . race or language or . . . traditions or . . . history or . . . ancestry, because [they] are not ashamed of them and [they] will not do it because [they are] proud of them."[68]

Separately, Malaquías Martínez at *La Revista de Taos* asked readers whether the people who descended from the conquistadors and colonized Neo-Mexicano land three hundred years ago "had no inter-linked rights that deserved respect and consideration and not be trampled or annulled?" "Last[-]minute" Anglo arrivals would surely hold the people down by the neck, relegating them to political nothings in violation of American laws and rights guaranteed to all citizens of various origins. Martínez was at a loss for how to register claims for equal participation in civic honors and the state's administration of public affairs. He also wanted to know what obligation the people were under to submit to the exorbitant taxes that benefitted others. He concluded that no such obligation existed. With a majority of votes, the Nuevomexicano policy should work to gain that portion of resources that "corresponded to the heritage of our forefathers."[69]

Because of the disappointing results in the first state elections, Octaviano Larrazolo launched the Native Son Movement. This initiative represented the sort of problem newly incorporated ethnic groups inherit "to gain the capacity to increase their political leverage."[70] As Larrazolo exhorted, Hispanos needed "to seek their freedom in the land hallowed by the blood of [their] forefathers."[71] The Native Son Movement for political inclusion deserves a major scholarly study. Basically, members of the Native Son campaign pressured the Democratic and Republican Parties to have Nuevomexicanos make up half of their state and federal ballots.[72]As a result, four late nineteenth-century identitarians were elected to state office, three of them former editors of Spanish-language weeklies. From *La Voz del Pueblo*, Antonio Lucero was elected secretary of state in 1911 and Ezequiel C. de Baca governor in 1916. Néstor Montoya of *La Bandera Americana* went to Congress in 1920. Other cases included Benigno Hernández, elected to Congress in 1915, Larrazolo as governor in 1918, and Dionisio "Dennis" Chávez to Congress in 1931. Despite these successes, inequality continued to affect Nuevomexicano political representation at higher levels.

The state's institutions of higher education formed a whole other issue. It came to a head in the early 1930s with the accusation that the University of New Mexico in Albuquerque was failing to respond to the educational needs of Nuevomexicano/a youth. The blame for campus discrimination fell on the Euro-American fraternities. A lobby of students and community members urged the state legislature to abolish the Greek societies. The bill for this purpose was submitted by Senator Juan Sedillo, the chair of the Senate Education Committee, whose father, Antonio, served as a delegate to the state Constitutional Convention of 1910. Primacy scripts born in the nineteenth century fortified criticism of the university. The Independent Club of Bernalillo County commended Sedillo's stand against "those usurpers which come into our beloved land of our inheritance with their prejudiced minds, pretending to be superior in class to our ancestors." Whipping out the old script of Nuevomexicano Chivalry, a citizen noted that "If anyone has the right of way concerning the state University [of] New Mexico, it is certainly the children, grandchildren and the great-grandchildren of the families of New Mexico who extended a welcoming hand and gave hostage."[73] The anti-fraternity bill did not pass, and resentful Spanish Americans went on to a larger protest, charging a psychology professor at the university with attempting to foment racism against high school students with his psychology research.[74]

In 1921, a working-class group also protested under Spanish identity. Seventy men "of Spanish descent" in Deming, in the far southwestern part of the state, filed a petition to Governor Mechem and Congressman Néstor Montoya in which they accused the contractors or foremen in charge of hiring workers at a road construction camp with "openly" declaring that they would "hire no 'Mexicans.'" Nuevomexicanos were clearly turned away. As the petition emphasized, they were "American citizens of Spanish ancestry," some veterans of the World War. The petition forwarded by La Liga Protectora de Obreros Hispanos Americana (The Protective League of Hispano Americano Workers) affirmed that such discrimination was "unjust and disgraceful." Investigations to substantiate the assertions were demanded, as well as such actions as necessary to "terminate a condition that is subversive of the best interests of the state." Three men were identified as company culprits.[75] However, the company was federally contracted and so the state of New Mexico had no jurisdiction in the matter. Governor Edwin Mechem agreed that such discrimination should not be tolerated under his watch. Knowing as much, State Highway Engineer L.A. Gillett informed the governor that he would try to change the attitude of the contractors "by suggestion."[76]

The Supplementary Rubrics

While "Spanish American" dominated the name field, "native" and "nativo" stayed fast. In 1926, the local social scientist Paul A. F. Walter wrote at the request of the federal Food Administration descriptions and photographs "of native and Indian methods of drying food."[77] The use of Indian Scourge had declined by that point, yet in 1916 one Isaac Montoya expressed support for Ezequiel C. de Baca for governor, calling him one of "natural law's" principal heirs, like one of "our own people who first irrigated our land with their blessed blood, battling the savage Indians, until conquering and converting it into a fruitful country?"[78] If anything, Nuevomexicanos at the pinnacle of Spanish identity were more apt to envy the "great benefits and guarantees" that they said the federal government bestowed on Native Americans. One editor observed Nuevomexicanos doing poorly in the party nominations for state office, fearing that their domination by Anglos was near complete, their only hope lying in gaining the sort of privilege Washington bestowed on Cherokees, Sioux, Utes, Cheyenne, Navajos, Pápagos and other successful tribes.[79]

"Neo-mexicano" had decreasing utility. In one early instance, the Las Cruces journalist and public servant Isidoro Armijo glowingly endorsed Elfego Baca's challenge to Harvey Fergusson's seat in the US Congress, painting him as a hero among the legions of Nuevomexicano statesmen. As he raved in glowing Spanish, "In the beautiful heavens of neo-mejicano constellations, multiple stars illuminate the history of our race because they have been stars that have figured well, because they have been constellations that have shined, like the sun on every page of parchment in the historical romance of their feats, like intellectual lights that highlight the pages written in a history more than romantic, true and written with a pen of gold."[80] Armijo's primacy made trial balloons of various nomenclatures. "There has been, and, thanks to our noble race, there are men, in whose veins run the blood of their Spanish, Mexican, and Aztec ancestors in our homeland of New Mexico, who made, and are making the history of their natal land—of their country."[81]

The Contradictions of "Mexican"

One effect of the Mexican Revolution was to harden the Nuevomexicano-Mexican distinction, in the extreme "Spanish American" meaning of "not Mexican." The Lourdsburg *Western Liberal*, responding to the charge that the "native people of New Mexico" were in sympathy with the Mexican Republic, said it couldn't be true as they not only had been a part of the United States for seventy years but also were "thorough Americans." In fact, "anyone well acquainted with them knows that our people of Spanish descent are much superior to the average of the people in the Republic of Mexico and that they do not look with favor upon them but there exists here a considerable prejudice against the people from the Republic. In part this has been due to the fact that many who have come to live in New Mexico have been fugitives from justice and of a bad class of people."[82]

Pancho Villa personified a "bad class" of Mexican, not least for his invasion of Columbus, New Mexico.[83] New Mexico Congressman Benigno Hernández aggressively called for action against "the recent raid and outrage committed by a marauding band of Mexicans from Mexico in our State."[84] In Tierra Amarilla, *El Nuevo Estado* noticed "very ignorant" persons of Mexican origin who saw the paisanos of Texas, New Mexico, Arizona, and California ripe for recruitment to a revolt against the United States. Defending los Neo-Mexicanos against the "unfair" suggestion, the editor launched into US Cementation, citing their unflagging loyalty to the American flag, their love for the homeland, which "we would defend with our lives and honor." Although of "Hispanic blood," the Neo-Mexicanos were American citizens "in every sense of the word and to use our name in connection with rebellion incited by irresponsible, hallucinatory and ignorant persons does much harm to us."[85]

As in the Spanish-American War, cementation heuristics also appeared in El Corresponsal's discussion of the possibility of the United States and Mexico's going to war because of President Wilson's refusal to recognize the presidency of Victoriano Huerta, his having played a role in the assassination of President Francisco Madero. What position would Nuevomexicanos take?, the weekly queried. Since their American annexation, the people of New Mexico were "grateful for their liberal gifts," such as inclusion on an equal footing with the general citizenry, a rise in prosperity and well-being, and beneficent laws and institutions. Neo-Mexicanos had been effectively separated and distanced themselves from the central authority that once included them in the Mexican Republic—or, in the venerable Civil War script, Hispano Americans who displayed their loyalty and adhesion to the United States with their arms to defend the national cause.[86] *Revista de Taos* editor José Montaner assured that when the president asked for volunteers, "the youth from all parts of New Mexico will, with prompt enthusiasm, enlist in the phalanx that New Mexico will organize. Such cooperation will silence the detractors who would calumniate them."[87]

What can be detected, then, is how the history of keeping Nuevomexicano identity apart from Mexico stressed both belonging to New Mexico exclusively while preserving loyalty to the United States, a move that helped steer Nuevomexicanos away from possible confusions and entanglements that could have arisen from the tensions of the Mexican Revolution.

However, just how fanatically the distinction between "Spanish/Hispano" and "Mexican" could hold was shown in 1921 when feathers flew after an Anglo called a Nuevomexicano "Mexican" without any ill intent. In the incident, Antoinette Hanna Baca resigned as assistant adjunct general of the National Guard over an evaluation of a Nuevomexicano second lieutenant by one of her charges, National Guard Inspector Col. J. J. Boniface. "Personal observation and questioning of this officer by me," Boniface innocently reported, lead "me to believe that this officer is a factor in this troop, which can benefit with proper study and application. He is a Mexican. He is well liked by the Mexicans in this troop and should serve to keep them together."[88]

Important to note, Assistant Adjutant General Baca was a Euro-American. Furthermore, the officer who was evaluated, Jesús M. Baca, was her brother-in-law, brother of her husband, former National Guard Adjutant General James Baca.[89] It is not known how much influence the men exercised over General Baca, if any. However, she forwarded her resignation to Governor Edwin Mechem in indignant protest over Boniface's report.[90]

General Baca began her resignation letter with an expanded military service script, noting that the "Americans of Spanish descent served with distinction in the Civil, Indian, Spanish-American and World Wars, and I consider the insinuation that it is necessary to ride herd on any group of American soldiers a most unique and insulting one." In recommending the dismissal of Boniface, she told her superior National Guard Adjutant General Henry Brown, it was "just such statements as this, by just such tactless blockheads, that have caused so much racial prejudice in this state." She came to "more fully realize and more keenly appreciate the loyalty to America of Americans of Spanish descent than does the average citizen of New Mexico. I am also fully aware of the vast amount of crass ignorance displayed by newcomers into the state regarding the difference between Spanish-Americans and Mexicans."[91]

In General Baca's memory, this was the first time since her service in the office in which an insult of this nature failed to be addressed "with promptness, directness and courage." She emphasized how Lieutenant Baca had enlisted "at the age of 17 in Company E, 1st [R]regiment, [I]nfantry . . . when the [National] Guard was called to federal service and sent to the Mexican border . . . and saw practically continuous service through the Mexican border campaign and the World War," before his discharge on returning from active service overseas.[92] Boniface testified that he used the word "Mexican" inadvertently. As one "unused to the custom of the country," he gave no offensive meaning to it.[93]

His explanation went nowhere. In praising Baca's "attitude," the editors at *La Voz del Pueblo* doubted that Boniface would convince anyone, indeed doubted that he himself believed it. And so they posed: "How could [General] Brown believe in a National Guard in our state when it intrudes to denigrate the majority of the people in the state?" They recommended that rather than accept his explanation, the military should hold Boniface responsible for the "most crass ignorance." The writers agreed with Baca about the scope of the problem, which implicated the "menguados ignorantes" (lesser ignoramuses)

> who come from the East to make a big splash among us, thinking themselves as "white" Americans and superior to the nativo people of New Mexico whose *histórico abolengo* [historic lineage] is certainly superior in many respect to theirs, and as long as they are the "white men," the Hispano Americanos are the "Mexicans" and "greasers," and when they come across one of us with skin the color of milk diminishing its *blancura* [whiteness] calling them "white" Mexican, because according to their caliber it can never happen that they be their equal, much less their superior as it happens in most cases, in education, in gentlemanliness and level of ability.[94]

It all had to end, the editor forewarned, if outsiders wanted to live here "in peace and harmony," especially in official spheres.[95]

As late as 1931, the Club Latino Coronado de Colorado objected to an editorial in the *Brighton Register* insinuating that "los ciudadanos Americanos de descendencia española, a los que con toda ignorancia llaman 'mexicanos'" (the American citizens of Spanish descent who in total ignorance are called "Mexicans") were living off county funds, unjustly blaming them for pushing the county to the brink of bankruptcy.[96]

Striking, however, are Nuevomexicanos who readily accepted "Mexican" as the right label for themselves at the apex of Spanish identity. Among a host of examples that could be cited, Leopoldo, the correspondent for *El Nuevo Estado*, consistently referred to *la raza Mexicana*.[97] In the election of 1914, he called the nativo Alcario Montoya the greatest agitator on behalf of "los intereses del Mexicano" (the interests of the Mexican) and "los intereses del pueblo mexicano" (the interests of the Mexican people).[98] Also generalizing "Mexican," a T. A. Bernal complained in 1919 that no state law that could benefit the worker and sheepherder would come as long as los mexicanos remained owners of small properties with small herds of sheep.[99] *La Voz del Pueblo* featured a column with the title *El Obrero Mexicano* (The Mexican Worker) that advised fellow laborers on how to present one's self to the boss to gain negotiating leverage.[100]

José Sotero Durán recorded in his discourse a fascinating Chicanoesque complaint against a federal department in the name of classic Nuevomexicano primacy while rejecting "Spanish." In an open letter to US Senators Lynn J. Frasier and Burton K. Wheeler, Durán emphasized his "sacred duty" to highlight the "misery and poverty that weighed on the shoulders of those original sons of this continent erroneously called 'Spanish Americans,' who ended up as subjects of this government as a result of the shameful invasion of our national territories and citizens by the hordes of Anglo-Saxons" (translated in La *Bandera Americana* as "llegaron a ser subditos de este gobierno como resultado de la vergonzosa invasión de nuestros territories nacionales y naturales por los hordas anglo-sajones"). Durán decried the many promises that had been made and betrayed to "our ancestors by the Anglo-Saxon wave." He called the Treaty of Guadalupe Hidalgo the last, desperate, and supreme effort by "Mexicans" to gain protections "for our beloved children with no results." The most important articles of the treaty were suppressed by the "unmerciful invader, revealing his sinister intentions. By design and natural will, this entire continent is ours [i.e., the Nuevomexicanos/as], nonetheless we are orphans in our own home, although our motherland still exists."[101]

Durán cited, as one example, the denial of rights to the land grants that Mexican and Spanish governments ceded to el mexicano, the snatching "de nosotros" (from us) of those properties, along with other rights, "por el más 'fiero' despotismo" (by the fiercest despotism). Other than "a few Mexican traitors who are used by some Anglo Saxon elements as instruments

> to betray my people on election day, the rest of my people, as a general rule, are paid badly in all senses of the word; poverty forces them to live in the sub urban areas, on the edges of the most undesirable cities where we dream of happiness to dissipate our desperation, where we live in the outer spheres and die of misery. The cold tomb offers the only solution to our misfortune, affectionately offering us the asylum of its breast to dull our pain.[102]

Durán challenged the senators to see the Veterans Bureau as the latest of the institutional oppressors to maltreat those who were taken in the European war "to assassinate and be assassinated." He asked (fruitlessly) for a few minutes to convince them of the urgency of an investigation into these charges.[103]

Some Nuevomexicanos held on to "Mexican" even when Euro-Americans called them Mexican pejoratively. In 1929, Colorado resident Refugio B. y García warned about the abuse and disrespect *la gente blanca* (the white people) in Otero County in far southern New Mexico used to treat "us los hispano-americanos o ya seamos mexicanos" (us Hispano-Americanos or in other words us Mexicans). Not a single public office was filled by a mexicano, García complained, for "the white ones" had "little use for us." A Club Hispano-Americano was just established, García noticed. It helped, but not enough. In the latest issue, the schools separated "los mejicanitos de los blancos" (the little Mexicans from the white kids). The Mexicans were put in one room and the "hueros" (light ones) in another. More had to be done about such race issues "para el bien de nuestra raza" (for the good of our race).[104]

Betraying the aim of Spanish American identitarians to have their ethnic label universalized among the Spanish-surnamed, Anglo political operatives found it "second nature" to call Nuevomexicanos "Mexicans," just as it was, according to Carey McWilliams, among the Anglo-Americans with respect to the Californios who considered themselves "Spanish."[105] In 1916, for example, a Republican field lieutenant reported that Frank Hubbell might, in his race for Congress, have a chance to win Socorro County if he could "get enough Mexican votes to see him through [and] if he will get on the ground and make a precinct campaign for them."[106] In 1918, A. A. Hine informed Arthur Seligman, president of the Democratic State Central Committee, that it would be "almost impossible to revise the pool of his county "as most of the precincts has a [M]exican chairman and one year they are Democrats and the next Republican."[107] In a 1920 campaign, Earl Wilson advised Seligman to have congressional candidate Richard Hanna tour Monticello, "a large Mexican precinct with almost 150 registrations two years ago."[108]

The Discursive Complexities of "Hispano"

For the most part, "Hispano" and "Spanish" were interchangeable. *La Voz del Pueblo,* for example, referred to the pride of "aquellos hispano americanos—de origen español nacidos en Nuevo México" (those Hispano Americans of Spanish origin born in New Mexico) in an editorial that praised Ezequiel C. de Baca, the weekly's own former editor, whose "direct descendance [was] from conquistadors and first settlers of New Mexico," who had begun to serve as New Mexico governor. That was proof enough of his "enthusiastic and able defense of the interests of the Hispano race in the important and rich state that they gave birth to."[109]

For the first time the 1930 Census included "Mexican" as a race exclusive of those who were denominated "white" or another racial category. *El Nuevo Mexicano* editor José Antonio Martínez conjured the confusion it would likely cause in New Mexico. Martínez believed that Nuevomexicanos had an appreciation for their neighbors on the other side of the Rio Bravo. No one more than they realized "that deep down we are even brothers of blood, that through our veins runs the same blood as that of the Mexican citizen." Yet Nuevomexicanos were "subject citizens of Uncle Sam, whether by voluntary choice or by Divine Providence," and so it was incumbent that they obtain recognition of their numbers in the mass of the American citizenry. In classic script form, Martínez advised his people to let the polltakers know that they were "sons of the descendants of the immortal conquistadors that settled these lands, insist that the enumerators register your name with the notation that you are Hispano-Americano." Otherwise, they would be classified as "Mexican," and the (local conservative enemy) Charles Springer would take total control of New Mexico and decide to "round up yours [of your element] who move about these domains, more than a quarter of yourselves, the descendants of Padre [Antonio José] Martínez [an ancestor of the editor], with the risk of being summarily returned to the other side of the Bravo and then to the Mariana Islands."[110]

However, some citizens justified "Hispano" as a stand-alone designation for a Nuevomexicano territorial nation, and it is worthwhile to contemplate the logics. One L. E. Bernal, for example, was moved by the Nuevomexicano increase in public affairs to pen a thoughtful essay on the proper name for Nuevomexicanos, flatly declaring "Hispano-Americano" as the correct term to the clear exclusion of "Spanish and Mexican." Nor did "Hispano" include Spanish speakers in Florida, Georgia, Louisiana, New York, or Chicago, in Bernal's view, but rather the former Mexican lands of "Texas, Arizona, California, and especially New Mexico and Colorado." Bernal acknowledged that all the countries south of the border were called Hispano América and their inhabitants Hispano-Americanos, which, he said, caused confusion in the minds of many who did not know of the different connections the label signified in Latin America. "American," he urged, related to political geography and had nothing to do with one's race or ancestors. The African American was an American, same as descendants of the Puritans or of those of Iberian or Scandinavian blood. "No other element in particular should monopolize the name 'American' for itself to the exclusion of [the others]." Native Americans, strictly speaking, were the "first possessors of this continent hundreds, and probably thousands, of years before any European planted themselves on these shores for the first time." They were undoubtedly the most entitled to carry the name 'American.'" If time had reserved "American" for all who were allied with the United States, it was probably the most appropriate for the first builders and founders of the Southwest settlements.[111]

As such, Nuevomexicanos had logical reasons for distancing themselves from Mexican identity. As Bernal saw it, "mexicano" applied to those who brought the first European language to the Southwest. Ill-informed writers treated the Mexican people as if they were foreigners with foreign customs and foreign relations, inevitably and erroneously relating the word "Mexican" to Mexico. Only those "who had lived for many years in one of the Southwestern states and who had taken sufficient interest to investigate the first settlers 'in our Hispano Southwest'" could properly distinguish the uses of "Mexican . . . among the native sons of the United States and Mexico." There was "no erasing, forgetting, or taking the 'adjective Mexican' for granted." No one could set aside "Mexican traditional influences and past contributions as related to the ancient settlers in the history of some states." The names of "meritorious heroes, of world fame," would have to be erased from memory. The names of families that still existed revealed the past and explained the presence "of this race in the states of the Southwest." Regardless of their first national flag, "their connection to their first patria remained from the moment in which a new [US] flag was opened and took possession of their lands." What changed? Mexico and the United States became "entirely foreign, one from the other, in the last two generations in the lives of the people of New Mexico, and of the surrounding states. Neither the name 'Spaniard' nor 'Mexican' could be put to the Spanish speaking constituency," Bernal argued.[112]

"Not one of the thousands of Mexican inhabitants would ever think to go to Spain in search of faraway relatives, and the same thing could be said [among Nuevomexicanos] with respect to Mexico." To Bernal, the name least apposite for Nuevomexicanos was "Mexican." Because the citizens of the neighboring country were known in all parts of the world as "Mexicans," it was a name that corresponded to them "by right of the country they live in." The Hispano Americanos were the Southwest Hispanos. "Everyone can understand this," Bernal noted. He advised Hispano Americanos to let travelers and tourists, "with their curious ignorance," know that "neither Mexico nor any other foreign country claims the adhesion of this people." As a sign of their Americanism, none had ever expressed "any opposition to learning English, and it will not take long to see all the Hispano Americanos able to take great advantage of it. Destiny has decreed that we live in the United States and we feel proud of it; we are proud of our citizenry. We are Hispano Americanos or better said, Americans always!"[113]

Someone going by the name Roux was, in his humble opinion, pleased to beg, without presuming to "correct, teach, much less polemicize for the opportunity," to contemplate the right "formula" to distinguish "the conglomeration of persons born in this land and in whose veins ran, among some in mixed and in others pure form, the blood called Spanish." "Americano" did not work because it referred to all those who were born in any country of the Great Continent from Canada to Patagonia. "Hispanoamericano" signified the "immense territory conquered by powerful Iberia "from the California peninsulas, the elevated Santa Fe plains, to the extensions of the Argentinian Pampas" that "received from generous Spain its language, religion, science and even blood. All persons, being mestizos or criollos, born in any Spanish-speaking nation or state of the continent Columbus discovered are Hispanoamericanos." "North American" did not identify "this society . . . because Canadians and Mexicans are also North Americans. The correct name is "of a proximate genus and reflect[s] proper difference." That would be, as the pedant Roux awkwardly concluded, "*Hispano-Estado-Unidense* (Hispano-United States)."[114]

In conclusion, statehood made for a qualified "Spanish American" dominance in the field of Nuevomexicano/a ethnic identity. However, Spanish identity and New Mexico's realm of Spanish memory, as the majority of Nuevomexicanos and Nuevomexicanas clung to them, turned into brittle constructions. With the passage of time and the accumulation of social changes, hegemonic culture formations often lose their luster. Spanish identity proved no exception.

CHAPTER 9

The Means of Attack

AS SPANISH IDENTITY flourished in the decades after New Mexico became a state, it harbored two ideological vulnerabilities. One concerned the truth value in the essential claim that Nuevomexicanos/as constituted an unimpeachable Spanish people. The other tied into the morality of that identity's conquest legacy. Inevitably, each saw a discursive challenge coming after it. The first stigmatized the notion of the Spanish heritage as the lodestar of Nuevomexicano ethnicity, even as Spanish identity started to weaken on its own. The other hacked at Spanish imperialism, shifting popular knowledge by redeeming Pueblo Native standing in New Mexico history.

Reactive Mexican Americans and Chicanos

Only Mexican Americans were positioned with the rightful sensitivity and legitimacy to pose a socially significant challenge to the idea that their ethnic heritage was defined by Spanish culture, race, and history. In an article he published in 1932, the UNM folklorist Arthur Campa—who was born in Mexico but raised in Albuquerque—did not name Aurelio Espinosa but clearly had him in mind when he shamed "charlatan and quack scholars induced to break out into print with everything that has a Spanish semblance. . . . Even noted folklorists," he added, "have fallen under the spell."[1] In 1939, Campa ramped up in the pages of *El Nuevomexicano*—at the time, the state's most widely read Spanish weekly—belittling the tendency to ascribe "grandeur" to being Spanish. Historically, Campa argued, that attribution did not match "the sort of Spaniards our ancestors were, and how we inherited their blood." To call oneself "Spanish" did not "guarantee a clear ancestry and distinguished lineage." Crafty Romantics lay behind the self-identifier intent on "making us nobles so they c[ould] exploit our lineage afterwards while boasting of the purity of our true blood."[2]

Highly sensitive to that duplicity, Campa launched a guerrilla challenge to Spanish identity. It came in the glow of the work that Mexican intellectuals such as José Vasconcelos and artists such as the muralists Diego Rivera, José Clemente Orozco, Jean Charlot, and others conducted to reinvigorate Indigenous and mestizo nationalism during the Mexican Revolution,[3] and the Mexican state's promotion of "mestizo" as the "quintessential Mexican" citizen.[4] Consistently with these trends, Campa argued that Diego de Vargas did not restart a pure Spanish community after the Pueblo Revolt. Instead, a mixed Spanish-Native presence grew "to such a degree that . . . 2400 'mestizo children' [were] baptized by the clergy." Responding to Spanish identity's immutable social boundaries with Native Americans, Campa held absolutely that in the mestizo process, "racial distinctions are lost, but civilization gains strength through continued contact with the native culture. Today, there are people who claim pure blood lines—nonsense before the facts which history presents."[5]

In a technique Octaviano Larrazolo had perfected, Campa wondered if Coronado and Oñate were to appear, "would they recognize their own people? What vestiges of the colonies created by Conquistadores would they find? What would they say of that riotous preoccupation about Spanish origins, recalling, with a smile, that none of the great leaders brought a wife or family with him?"[6] Nevertheless, bowing to territorial primacy, Campa proposed "Nuevomexicano" as a faithful title, taking off from the Spanish pride of birthplace, their "identification with the soil, and adapting it until one can no longer break away from it. From this emerges the 'adopted fatherland.'" It was not true, he pronounced (somewhat blind to Creole legacies), "that in one place or another there were only Spaniards who never mixed with the Indians." As he claimed, "today we are blind and cannot see the mixture of Indian and 'Hispano' [because now] the person who is the least Spanish is the one who tries the hardest to be so."[7]

Initiating what would crystallize as the "Where's the Mexican in New Mexican" motif, Campa asked about where the people got the name "New Mexican"? "The name says it all," he affirmed. "To become New Mexican [they] first had to be Mexican." There was nothing denigrating about this, Campa stressed, shown in the "enchantment" people around the globe felt about Mexico. Using a phrase that could have only appeared in a shifting cultural zeitgeist in Mexican American circles, Campa presciently stated: "We become a laughingstock if we do not accept reality." As such, "We cannot lose time on foolishness and preoccupations which make us the mockery of everyone else. By being New Mexican, we will be Mexican because of our undeniable culture and for never having denied ourselves."[8] In a glint of Spanish identity slippage in the community, Campa pointed to an educated generation rising "without the stupid preoccupation of whether one is or is not a true Spaniard." This "new aristocracy," with knowledge and ability, did not seek "refuge in the myth of pure Spanishness, or of being real Spaniards." The "generality of Mexicans" attaining the merits of professions were out to "learn how to channel their abilities through the path of greatest advantage for their own culture."[9]

Slippage also appeared in the 1940 Coronado Cuarto Centennial Commemoration, which the government sponsored to celebrate the four hundredth anniversary of Francisco Vásquez de Coronado's explorations. But mere celebration did not tell the whole story. The state pined to boost tourism against a backdrop that had "a Spanish colonial past still liv[ing] on the narrow streets of Santa Fe, Truchas, and Taos."[10] However, former Congressman Benigno Hernández, who helped obtain funding for the project, grew dissatisfied with the Hispano participation. "We have to do something," he asserted, "to stir those people." Not that long ago there would have been no problem recruiting Nuevomexicanos to make outsiders "know or understand the importance to the native element of this historic celebration."[11] Yet only two Nuevomexicanos sat on the eight-member Coronado Cuarto Centennial Commission, Hernández and Aurelio Espinosa's brother Gilberto.[12] Moreover, no tributes to the descendants of conquistadors occurred. As Charles Montgomery noted, the Spanish theme was but "incidental to interests of Anglo cattle ranchers, farm, railroad, and mine owners, and real estate developers. Even Anglos who bowed politely to a Spanish inheritance looked forward to a very different future."[13]

The so-called Mexican American Generation established civil rights organizations in California and Texas[14] to challenge racial segregation in the Southwest and promote the rights of World War II veterans and their families.[15] New Mexico was the second state to start a chapter of the important League of United Latin American Citizens

(LULAC). LULAC "men's councils" formed in Las Vegas, Santa Fe, Albuquerque, Taos, La Mesilla, Parkview, Socorro, Valencia, Belen, Questa, Santa Rosa, Roswell, Española, Las Cruces, and Bernalillo. Ladies LULAC councils appeared in Albuquerque, Santa Fe, and Las Vegas. Nuevomexicanas served on LULAC national boards. The Albuquerque men's council became the largest in the nation at one point. Breaking down Nuevomexicano/a isolation, New Mexico councils developed extensive networks with Texas counterparts. Four of its decidedly middle-class members served as national president of the organization, and a LULAC national conference convened in Santa Fe. LULAC appealed to Nuevomexicanas/os alike who witnessed inequality deepening in their communities as their representation in the state legislature decreased.[16]

Historian Cynthia Orozco finds New Mexico LULACers using "Hispano," "Spanish," and "Spanish American" to identify themselves.[17] Yet "Mexican" identity got wedged in. US Senator Dennis Chávez was himself a LULAC member. His membership in the Mexican American Generation was reinforced by the role he assumed as head of President Franklin Roosevelt's Fair Employment Rights Commission, which made Chávez a hero to Mexican immigrants who appealed to him for support.[18] As such, Chávez, a nativo who had politically apprenticed in the Spanish golden era, called his Nuevomexicano constituency "Mexicans" who, in the name of "fair play" and devotion to the Democratic Party, needed more appointments to state agencies.[19]

In the 1960s and 1970s, the Chicano Chicana Movement (CCM) challenged and ended up overshadowing "Spanish" and "Mexican American" identities. A term that came from urban Mexican American argot, "Chicano" appealed as a political name from barrio antipathy to authority and rejection of staid middle-class values. Chicano activists incorporated elements of Mexico's revolutionary nationalism. The appropriation of the Aztec legend of Aztlán embodied the Chicano homeland in the Southwest.[20] Aztlán for the CCM paralleled what New Mexico was for nineteenth- and early twentieth-century Nuevomexicano identitarians. While elements of the CCM aimed for social reform and the promotion of upward mobility for Mexican American youth, radical CCM ideology delegitimated the American colonization of Aztlán.[21]

CCM historians, anthropologists, and sociologists followed Campa's lead, severely rebutting Espinosa's heritage scripts, fantasy heritage narratives, and alleged slanted history.[22] Spanish Americans from the golden era who wrote romantic remembrances of their "Spanish" past came in for it. The work of Cleofas Jaramillo was dinged, for example, for reifying history "out of the need for a simpler story of Spanish adventure, conquest, settlement, isolation . . . and its adjunct 'purity.'"[23]

Chicano/a college students were strategic identitarians. E. A. Mares recalled that "our elders almost desperately insisted we were Spanish, not Mexican."[24] The proposal for a Chicano studies program that the United Mexican American Students submitted to the administration of the University New Mexico called Spanish identity an anachronistic carryover. The organization of mostly Nuevomexicanos burst the bounds of New Mexico-specific belonging, declaring that so-called "Spanish Americans" should "look into history" and face the fact that "the Chicano" had his origins in Mexico, "whether he now lives in Chihuahua, Taos, San Antonio, Pueblo, or San Diego."[25]

In reaction to the assault on Spanish identity, Fray Angélico Chávez went on a mission to rescue Spanish primacy from the clutches of Chicanismo.[26] At the 1970 inauguration of the New Mexico State University president, Chávez elevated the "inordinately proud" Spanish "pastoralists of the north." Chávez's "shepherd *ganadero*" was "proudly individualistic," the opposite of Mexico's farm peasant, ever "industrious and plodding, unimaginative and subdued in spirit." Nuevomexicanos did not identify with the Mexican Revolution, Chávez maintained. "This is why, for example, New Mexicans as a whole have not risen to the call of people like the [land grant activist Reies Lopez] Tijerinas, who are of Mexican origin with an inborn hate of the Colossus of the North."[27]

Chávez issued this claim even though legacy Nuevomexicanos/as most assuredly joined the Chicano/a movement in substantial numbers.[28] Nuevomexicano Professor Ricardo Griego thus took Chávez on at a community event where he inverted the US Cementation script, offering that the 1847 Taos Revolt and the assassination of Charles Bent represented the honest Nuevomexicano response to New Mexico's conquest. Griego believed that the people of New Mexico would preserve their culture that was "founded on a socio-political consciousness of the realities of oppression and domination."[29]

The winds of Chicano-Mexican identity also blew against the community structures that Spanish Americans laid claim to. In 1983, the renowned Chicano artist Luis Jimenez won a commission to create a sculpture for a park in Albuquerque's Old Town district. Jimenez said his piece, titled "Southwest Pietá," represented a New Mexican Native man cradling a wounded Native woman. Spanish American critics, however, saw in the image the classic Mexican legend of Ixtaccihuatl and Popcatepetl, an Aztec warrior holding a maiden who has been raped by Spanish conquistadors. Spanish American residents who defined Old Town as Spanish colonial territory, called for the scrapping of the project for being "too Mexican" and failing to represent New Mexico's true Spanish culture. Citizens debated heritage in letters to newspapers and at community meetings; critics recited statistics of Spanish atrocities against New Mexico Natives; and Spanish Americans assigned significance to the fact that the Spanish flag had flown over New Mexico for four hundred years, which overpowered in symbolic significance the mere twenty-four years under the Mexican banner. As the Anglo community "listened in somewhat befuddled silence," the city arts board capitulated to Spanish American demands, finding another location to place the sculpture.[30]

A Chicano versus Spanish American confrontation spilled onto the pages of a popular Albuquerque alternative newspaper in 2010. It began with the interview that columnist Joseph Baca conducted with Gustavo Arellano who ran his syndicated "Ask the Mexican" column in southern California. Suddenly Arellano asks: "Are there still people who call themselves Hispanos, or is that some Chicano myth?" Baca replied: "The folklore of Hispanos of Spanish descent is alive and well." Santa Fe was "the Mecca of this mixed-up mythology," Baca clarified, but it was accepted in the towns of Las Vegas, Taos, and Española. Confused "Hispanos" used the fact that many of them are "light-skinned with blue eyes to advance their claims." Reflecting the epistemic of the academic canon on Spanish identity, Baca related how "Much of this lore really came about as a form of self-preservation among Mexicans when faced with strong tides of overt racism from whites." And so, "Suddenly, every wire-broom mustachioed Mexican became a pure-blood Castilian-speaking Spaniard, purged of any

Tapatío sauce in his veins. So, when you hear that Castilian lisp being used by a Northerner," Baca summed up, "you may want to beat them like a piñata for their confusion."[31]

In response to Baca's remarks, one Michael Martínez bristled at the idea of Hispanos as "'wannabe Europeans' who believe we are 'descendants of the Spanish royal court.'" Martínez resented Baca's implication that "we [Nuevomexicanos] are really Mexicans pretending not to be Mexicans." Calling such views fiction, he had his historical account so readers could "better understand and appreciate modern Hispano culture." That history began in 1598,

> when the Spanish, our ancestors, arrived here under the leadership of Don Juan de Oñate. This was the beginning of the Hispano society of New Mexico. From 1598 until 1821, New Mexico was part of Spain, except for 12 years from 1680 to 1692 during the Pueblo Revolt, when the Hispanos lived in exile in the El Paso area before returning. Santa Fe was established as our capital in 1610. New Mexico was part of Mexico for only 25 years, from 1821 to 1846. New Mexico has been part of the United States for the past 164 years, since 1846. We were part of Spain for 211 years."[32]

For Martínez, this homogeneous people, a nation in effect, surviving across centuries was well documented by the "very good records" kept by the Spanish. "Any armchair historian could make whatever claims they wanted"; what they could not do was "change history." Hispanos today, Martínez pressed on, "come from the old Spanish families who first settled here starting in 1598. We do not want to be Europeans, we are Europeans. We do not call ourselves Mexicans because we are not Mexicans (sorry Gustavo). And as for claiming to be part of the Spanish royal court, I agree that the vast majority of us are not. But nearly all real historians agree that the Hispanos of New Mexico are our own distinct society or subculture within the greater Latin culture." Baca, Martínez claimed, failed to appreciate how the Chicano movement "of the '70s made us all generic 'Hispanics.'" Modern-day Hispanos were a "testament to our Spanish ancestors and we are proud of our culture, traditions, our Spanish language and our many contributions to our state."[33] Martínez remained true to classic Spanish identity, but times had changed, and the fact that he debated against another Nuevomexicano identitarian represented the extent to which Spanish identity was being pushed against the wall.

"Hispanic" did indeed erode Spanish identity. As Cristina Mora documents, this label spread powerfully out of the efforts of federal census officials who wanted a term to collapse Latino nationalities. To instruct people on how to identify as "Hispanic" on census forms, they enlisted the help of Spanish-language media marketers and executives as well as Mexican American, Puerto Rican and Cuban leaders who had their reasons for wanting such a category. The ambiguous name without specific heritage associations became increasingly popular as more influencers entered the field to achieve their organizational goals. Once institutionalized, it was assumed "to have always existed."[34] As the notion of a Spanish heritage grew ambiguous or marginal, "Hispanic" served as a handy option, effectively suggested in qualitative (nonstatistical) surveys of Nuevomexicano/a samples in Santa Fe and Albuquerque that found overwhelming preferences for "Hispanic" self-labeling over "Spanish."[35]

Also shaving Spanish identity were the essentialist subidentities that appeared like schismatic formations. In the 1980s, a striking Jewish identity movement sprung among Nuevomexicanos and Nuevomexicanas based on the claim of descendance from crypto Jews in New Mexico who hid from the Spanish Inquisition in the seventeenth and eighteenth centuries.[36] Two other schismatic identities founded themselves on Indigeneity. An Aztec/*mexica* dedication spun out of the Chicana/o Movement, one of its aims being to accelerate the demise of the myth of "pure" Spanish culture in New Mexico.[37] Genízaro identity represents the legacy of Indigenous captives, eschewing acknowledgement of how this process helped define New Mexico's mestizaje in favor of a definition of Genízaros as a distinct ethnic group meriting its own rights and recognitions.[38] These manifestations, though they contain their own truths, have reflected the lack of a central Nuevomexicano identity system. For as Edward H. Spicer generalized in relation to pluralism in the Southwest, the "content or meaning, of a set of terms is by no means uniform for those who use them, because their experience of ethnic relations is not identical, and intensity of common identification and sense of distinctiveness varies."[39]

Native Americans cared little about the validity of Spanish identity per se. They zeroed in on key depictions encoded in that identity's symbolic structure: the emblems put in public spaces to honor Spanish figures and their conquest exploits in New Mexico.

In the 1960s and '70s, the slogan Red Power represented an increase in Native voices contributing to the realm of social discourse. The American Indian Movement (AIM) produced "a significant realignment in the historical narrative of colonization and the location of Native Americans within that narrative."[40] A First Nations power identity artfully captured the moral high ground of indigenous history.[41] In what Native scholar Michael Wilcox called "repatriating history,"[42] it negated the legacy of Christopher Columbus. Supplanting the classic idealization of the "discoverer" of America, the image of the initiator of European colonization, genocide, and land theft came into sharp focus, producing a movement to demolish Columbus Day and Columbus statues.

If Nuevomexicanos and Euro-Americans in centuries past constructed *indios bárbaros* to their satisfaction and rendered "savage" into a legitimate category, First Nation memory defined them as instruments of symbolic violence. A key instance involved the Soldiers Monument on the Santa Fe Plaza.[43] A Nuevomexicano-dominant legislature established the cenotaph in the session of 1866–1867, recognizing "the heroes who have fallen in the various battles with the savage Indians of the Territory of New Mexico."[44] In 1974, AIM formally requested that the obelisk be taken down. When the mayor demurred, someone secretly chiseled off "savage,"[45] a clear act of "symbolic vandalism," unambiguously representing "semiotic disobedience."[46]

Soon, the sites, monuments, and rituals portraying Spanish conquest were drawing the attention of the national #LandBack organization. Two historically resonant representations generated emotive resistance: la toma de posesión, enacted annually in both the Fiesta de Santa Fe and the Fiesta de Española Valley; and the bronze portraits of the leading New Mexico conquistadors, Juan de Oñate and Diego de Vargas.

These sites cast the sense of Spanish identity as a dominant ethnic nationalism. The nonprofit Caballeros de Vargas and the Nuevomexicano-dominated Fiesta Council sponsored la toma de posesión in the Fiesta de Santa Fe. The wholly Nuevomexicano city council of Española supervised the Española Valley Fiesta. Nuevomexicano groups commissioned the Oñate and de Vargas statues in Santa Fe, Alcalde, and Albuquerque, and a Nuevomexicano artist created the Oñate figures. Each emblem reflected "the context and totemic meaning from which collective identity emerges."[47]

The contention that flared between Native critics and Spanish defenders represented a battle of identities in an era of recognition movements. A recognition movement, Jürgen Habermas notes, includes categories from "formerly colonized regions" demanding guarantees of the status, survival, and equality of their adherents' "cultural forms of life and traditions."[48] Recognition movements demand that authorities and lateral groups "actually demonstrate respect" for cultural formations.[49] Native assaults on Spanish icons represented an attack on the civic recognition that Spanish adherents had built up in their status struggles in New Mexico's past. In the eyes of Native Pueblos, conquest representations were instruments in the continued denial of their right to respectful recognition. Native resistance fought to have the Spanish conquest *de*recognized, while Spanish identifiers experienced an assault on their hard-earned historical recognition. The remarkable battle of identity epistemics formed what James Brooks calls "that peculiar alchemy that binds 'history as social process' to 'history as knowledge.'"[50] A discursive proxy war relit the passions of the violent embattlements of the past. Presentist survivors with well-equipped scripts and accounts prepared to take up where the physical encounters left off in the nineteenth century.[51]

The Pueblo challenge to the Fiesta de Santa Fe that rippled in the late 1970s[52] exploded into a momentous public debate. In 1992, rapidly gathering Native memory was fostered by a documentary film that captured the emotional strains and contradictions of Puebloans participating in an insensitively organized Fiesta when non-Pueblo and whites enacted Native roles. Puebloans and Native allies saw La Entrada—an armored conquistador company riding into the Plaza on horses to enact la toma de posesión—"smacking of oppression."[53]

The Fiesta Council adjusted the portrayal so as to depict Spanish and Natives living in harmony "as a direct result of the re-conquest." The de Vargas player bore a crucifix rather than a sword. Archbishop Robert Sánchez guided a Mass of Reconciliation to help heal old wounds. Conquest now meant "to unify through the conquest of love." In portraying a kinder, gentler conquest, Los Caballeros de Vargas, in consultation with the governor of Tesuque Pueblo and the Archbishop, revised the Entrada script. To deflect the appearance of glorifying the defeat of Puebloans, the Fiesta highlighted intercultural cooperation. Nevertheless, some Puebloans continued to demand the removal of the Entrada.[54]

Coincidentally, the 1990s presented a time for Spanish identitarians to realize what had eluded late nineteenth-century Nuevomexicanos, the casting of ancestral heroes in bold statuary. The Nuevomexicano artist Reynaldo "Sonny" Rivera emerged as a key figure for projecting Spanish memory. The brilliant sculptor had created small-scale works of Nuevomexicanos/as, both regular folks and iconic figures. The New Mexican Hispanic Culture Preservation League, a leading Spanish-American organization, recognized Rivera, who was born on his family's farm in Mesquite "along the Camino Real near Las Cruces," as a cultural treasure for directing his "talents toward a part of his heritage."[55]

In his first monument, Rivera produced the stunningly chivalric Equestrian Juan de Oñate. Installed in 1993 at the opening of the Oñate Monument Resource and Visitors Center in Alcalde north of Española, Oñate, astride a spirited horse and "clad in full battle armor," struck a pose, as Erika Doss has noticed, "modeled after the bronze equestrian statue of Marcus Aurelius in the Piazza del Campidoglio in Rome."[56] At that, its overriding aspect, not least the conqueror's facial gesture, envisaged an avenging knight (see Fig. 18).

Commemorative statues are commonly defined as offerings to history, but as art professor Erin L. Thompson notes, "monuments aren't history lessons—they're pledges of allegiance."[57] At the unveiling of the Equestrian Oñate, state Senator Emilio Naranjo, who caucused legislative colleagues to pass the bill to fund the monument, proclaimed, "in northern New Mexico and the United States of America it is a great honor to give thanks to Juan de Oñate." Television news video

FIGURE 18. Equestrian Juan de Oñate. Oñate Monument Center, Alcalde, NM, 1993. Reynaldo Rivera, sculptor. Advanced Source Productions, photographer. Source: Wikimedia. CC BY 2.0, no changes. https://creativecommons.org/licenses/by/2.0/.

showed the crowd cheering and chanting, "Viva Don Juan de Oñate. Viva Emilio Naranjo."[58]

In the same esprit at the four hundredth anniversary of New Mexico's "founding," Spanish Americans in Albuquerque Old Town petitioned the City's One Percent for the Arts program to support the acquisition of a bust of Oñate to be carved by Rivera. Before the City could render a decision, Pueblo leaders mobilized to defeat the proposal. City council meetings, the press, and the streets formed the memory battlegrounds for Natives and allies to defame Oñate and Spanish Americans to defend him with all the passion possible.

In one discursive bombardment, Puebloans hit on the Nuevomexicano conception of "founding." "Honoring the so-called colonizers is an insult to the scores of Pueblos that already existed in New Mexico at the time the Europeans arrived," Puebloan leader Conroy Chino denounced. "Native people had settled this land hundreds, perhaps thousands of years before any Spanish colonist set foot here." Clearly, the Doctrine of Discovery no longer held the practical power it once did, and Spanish Americans could not contest the literal question of settlement precedence as they had with the title of nativo in the nineteenth century.[59] As the indomitable Old Town activist Millie Santillanes conceded, "no one is denying that the Indians were here first."[60] In the one founding peg to stand on, a Spanish American queried, "How is it possible to have a New Mexico without its founding governor. If you kill Governor Oñate, you kill New Mexico, for without him there is no New Mexico."[61] The lawyer John Salazar called Oñate a George Washington, the "European founder and first governor of New Mexico, a new kingdom within the Spanish empire." The sculptor Sonny Rivera thought Oñate "a hell of a man" for being the "father of New Mexico." The families and clergy who came with Oñate were infused with founding primacy, and about them the social activist Gene Hill observed that "they established and founded our great State as the farthest outpost of Spain's Kingdom."[62]

Such an argument assumed a consensus of devotion to the value of "New Mexico." Natives, however, claimed that their people would have been better off without that invention. As the controversy raged, underground vandals, driven by lex talionis, surreptitiously sawed off a foot of Equestrian Oñate since, as history tells, he ordered the same punishment for captured Acoma men in 1598. Claiming retaliation on behalf of "brothers and sisters of Acoma" while helped by saws and an armed vision,[63] they scoffed at the idea of positive Spanish institutions. In their memory of vassalage, Natives were "forced to work in the mines, plant crops and build Roman Catholic missions."[64]

The discursive storm barreled on like this for weeks before compromise agents got in on the action. A nonprofit team of UNESCO-esque intermediaries whose modus operandi promoted multicultural peace, reconciliation, and resolution, diplomatically ruled the war of memory a draw. At a price of $600,000 and a corner of the art garden fronting the Albuquerque History Museum, Spanish Americans gained a grandiose statuary called La Jornada (The Journey) while Pueblo artist Nora Naranjo-Norse created Numbe Whageh, a landscape artwork signifying territorial purity.

In La Jornada, Rivera and his collaborator Betty Sabo produced a unique ensemble of memory nation that could have arrived directly from a nineteenth-century imaginary. In his right hand, the noble Oñate determinedly holds the scrolled Requerimiento authorizing the official taking of the New Mexico province for Spain. Slightly behind, a Tlascalan guide scopes the way ahead. Representing a founder of the colony's own holy Church, a sandaled Franciscan kneels on his staff hopefully. Two helmeted conquistador soldiers are on guard, one bearing the banner of Spain on a pole with a crucifix at its tip. A mother on a burro cradles an infant, the visage of Virgin and Child. A humble sheepman bears a lamb about his shoulders, a Jesus-type of the Good Shepherd. Hacienda aristocrats ride with the herd, feathers upright on the cover of one. Pobladores lend their shoulders to oxen hauling a supply *carreta* out of a rut, signaling the rugged terrain of lore that they are to about settle and tame.

As Sonny Rivera, one of the artists of La Jornada hoped beyond hope, the resolution was "going to be for everybody concerned, a kind of understanding."[65]

La Jornada misleads history somewhat. On crossing the river into New Mexico, Oñate forged ahead with a guard to meet with leaders of the Pueblo communities who lived in the area. The large contingent of families, ranchers, laborers, carts, livestock, domestic implements, and farm tools took two months to catch up with the expedition's leader.[66] Once again, the precise truth cared for naught. For the New Mexican Hispanic Culture Preservation League, portraying the

FIGURE 19. (*above*) La Jornada, front view, 2005. Reynaldo Rivera, sculptor. Albuquerque History Museum. Ewald Judt, photographer. Courtesy of the photographer.

FIGURE 20. (*left*) La Jornada, right-side view, 2005. Reynaldo Rivera, sculptor. 2005. Albuquerque History Museum. Philip B. Gonzales, photographer.

FIGURE 21. (*right*) La Jornada, rear view, 2005. Reynaldo Rivera, sculptor. Albuquerque History Museum. Philip B. Gonzales, photographer.

trudge upriver satisfied "our deep desire to acknowledge our Spanish Colonial roots."[67]

The pause of the contention over La Fiesta de Santa Fe ended in 2016 when organizers once again staged the conquistador Entrada and Pueblo submission. Fifty resisting Natives crowded the stage in front of the *toma de tierra* with tape over their mouths to represent the silencing of their voices. Placards and circulars cited the number of Puebloans killed during the Spanish occupation, each demanding an end to Fiesta Court visits to the schools, calling for the teaching of alternative perspectives on the Pueblo Revolt, and petitioning the City of Santa Fe to stop funding the Fiesta because its religious feature violated the separation of church and state as inscribed in the US Constitution.[68]

Mayor Javier González encouraged Indigenous and Fiesta leaders to work together. Hesitant about changing tradition, he suggested an Indigenous Peoples Day for Santa Fe in place of Columbus Day. He scripted de Vargas as "a gentleman who was very religious, who was very worried about the conflict [with the Pueblos], who struggled with questions of the sort, 'When do I use force? Can I do this without using force? What is our community going to look like afterwards?'"[69] In counterpoint, Natives emphasized that "this is indigenous land, and the fact that it's indigenous land that has been occupied violently is a historical fact and [the Entrada is] an ongoing condition that's a violation of fundamental human rights." In the volley, a Spanish American shouted, "Viva la Fiesta!" and Natives answered, "Abolish the Entrada!" "Never," Gloria Mendoza yelled. Interviewed later, Mendoza addressed the divisions being caused by the protest with her memory script: "We were the first ones to assimilate with Native Americans . . . That's what Santa Fe is all about—assimilation, and [in an establishmentarian's voice] we accept any culture that comes here."[70]

Similarly, another Spanish American declared that de Vargas "protected Puebloan kiva [sacred chamber] faith," following up idealistically with, "I think when people really take some time to learn the history of New Mexico, they would have a little different attitude than these anti-de Vargas protesters. When de Vargas came back, yes, it was a military takeover. He wanted it peaceful. Didn't turn out entirely that way when he returned . . . a year and a half later, but many of the Pueblo people did welcome his return because of the beginning of the incursion of the people from the plains, the Navajo and Apache people."[71] Another qualified the glory of de Vargas as the "agent of conquest" with the claim that it didn't matter

> whether or not people consider [him] to be peaceful or violent; it was colonialism and it was conquest and it was a much larger process of eliminating native people, dispossessing them of their land, killing them and making it so that they could not live their sacred way of life anymore, and [so Natives are] rising up and saying "No more." It's really simple. There's evidence of Native people in this land for 25,000 years.

In a kind of capstone, an Indigenous voice stressed historical trauma, proof lying in the tragic rates of alcoholism, liver disease, drug abuse, and suicide among Native Americans young and old.[72]

While Mayor González meant to mitigate conquest in 2017, the Fiesta Council decided to stage a traditional Entrada after all. As a caution, Los Caballeros de Vargas President Manuel García, seeing Natives preparing for protest and fearing disruption, changed the time of the de Vargas procession to an earlier hour. Entrada players did not enter on horse, nor did they don the accustomed armor, yet as they stepped onto the stage, "the pageant's script still emphasized subjugation," the *Santa Fe Reporter* noted. "De Vargas tells the man playing the part of the Tesuque Pueblo cacique [not a Puebloan] that the Spanish king will grant them a full pardon for the Pueblo rebellion in return for their conversion to Catholicism."[73]

The rescheduling plan meant to cool things down; instead it steamed Natives. Pueblo leader Elena Ortiz bitingly called members of Los Caballeros de Vargas "spineless" for moving the time of the Entrada without notice, which proved for her "beyond a shadow of a doubt that [officials] and the Fiesta Council are deathly afraid of us." The Fiesta Council and Los Caballeros made their decision, Elena charged, "behind closed doors in the dead of night" because "they're cowards, and [in a sharp rebuke of classic Nuevomexicano memory], they're liars just like their ancestors."[74] "In a deadly mistrust of the other," a Native told the *Reporter* "a lot of lies are being told. The truth is a lot of people were massacred; they think this celebration is a reconquest. We don't want it anymore."[75] The Entrada "is very much a celebration of genocide," a Diné ally proclaimed. "All we want is truth."[76] Middle fingers and curses crossed directions. From the stage, the de Vargas procession chanted, "'Que Viva La Fiesta!'" Two teenagers were "visibly enraged" as they shouted in support of the Entrada and Fiesta before exiting the stage.[77] A Spanish American took advantage of the occasion to taunt two anti-Entrada white women who, they said, had profited off the African slave trade.[78]

Police tried moving demonstrators to the free speech zone, but when Natives balked, police pushed and protestors formed a human chain, which led to the arrest of eight. Over a hundred protestors from Albuquerque went around police barricades to enter the Plaza, their signs honoring Po' Pay and the Pueblo Revolt and decrying the ongoing slow genocide of Native people. The front-page photo of San Ildefonso Puebloan Jennifer Marley getting arrested after she and a police officer had physical contact iconicized righteous Native resistance. Protesters pushed on to City Hall and then back to the Plaza, banging drums and yelling at tourists to go back to Europe.[79]

Los Caballeros President García apologized for changing the start time. Hoping for a cessation of hostilities, he pledged to meet with conventional Native leaders—not with protestors whom he said represented a "fraction" of Pueblo communities—to bring it about.[80] The new president of Los Caballeros de Vargas, Thomas Baca, a bus driver who played de Vargas in 2014, tellingly said the decision produced heated debate in his family, many relatives opposing attempts to cut Hispano traditions. In the spirit of reconciliation, he contended, "We can't forget our Spanish ancestors but we also need to understand the reaction that some traditions generate."[81]

A former state historian, Estevan Rael-Gálvez witnessed the tumult. After returning to New Mexico from Washington, DC, where he had served as senior vice president at the National Trust for Historic Preservation, he launched his work as a consultant—an endeavor reflected in the founding of his firm, Creative Strategies 360°. Dedicated to "Illuminating and Inspiring Creativity, Consciousness & Community," the project engaged in research, public education, cultural advocacy, and exhibit design, while collaborating with communities, governments, universities, and cultural organizations on transformative initiatives aimed at collective healing and long-term sustainability.[82] In the years that followed, this work—grounded in deep research and sustained community engagement—laid the foundation for truthful racial healing and transformation in New Mexico, culminating in the creation of *Decolonizing New Mexico*, an online platform dedicated to reframing the region's complex past.[83]

Rael-Gálvez contracted with the City of Santa Fe to work with a team under the city's Arts Commission to develop a long-term plan called "Culture Connects Santa Fe."[84] While on this project, he witnessed what he called the "growing voices that gathered in protest, particularly around the ritual of the Entrada that depicts a very particular version of the late 17th century 'reconquest' of the region by Spanish authorities following the 1680 Pueblo Revolt." Rael-Gálvez recognized both the challenge and opportunity "before us."[85]

Rael-Gálvez revealed a fascinating philosophical perspective in his PhD dissertation on Native captivity and slavery in northern New Mexico from the Spanish colonial era to US annexation. He harbored a deep aversion to the notion of Spanish blood purity, backing it with personal and professional knowledge. The Nuevomexicano populace was produced and reproduced, he held, through the mixing of Spanish and Native elements in "generations of racial and cultural mixture realized and defined as much by amicable unions as by coercive relations." Rael-Gálvez rejected ethnic categorization on principle, grudgingly referencing "Nuevomexicanos." This name and "Hispano/a, Indo-Hispano/a, Spanish, manito, Spanish-American, Mexican-American, Spanish-speaking, Raza, Mexican, mexicana/o and Chicano/a," he declared, failed to "describe the tensions of the multiple and contested categories of identity." Out of his deeply human mission of breaking down artificial boundaries, he hoped to "bring all of these terms and the 'identities' and pasts that they allegedly describe to internal crisis." It reflected Rael-Gálvez's early life, "raised in part by grandmothers, each born in the late . . . nineteenth century and carrying in their blood this storied legacy of indigenous captivity."[86]

Nor were monuments of any worth, "particularly those that glorify, even if symbolically, the violence of conquest and imperialism, and that perpetuate false narratives based on forgetting history more than remembering it whole, here or anywhere in the world."[87] Rather than doing away with the Fiesta, Rael-Gálvez proposed interrogating

La Entrada, having the community recognize that it had been justified in the name of tradition "though it is not actually grounded in the full history and wisdom of the people it allegedly represents."[88]

Rael-Gálvez stepped onto the scene as a tailor-made conquistador slayer. After 137 years in which the Spanish identity scripts, accounts, and narratives of de Vargas's reconquest had barely changed, he would put in motion what Lawrence Kritzman calls "a form of genealogical revisionism," a "metamorphosis" in the "recycling of knowledge through associations and new symbolic representations."[89] Under his guidance, the metamorphosis would give canonical recognition to how the Fiesta has evolved over time, "reflecting less accurately the period of history it aims to depict and more the period in which it was invented." Rael-Gálvez argued that Spanish identity misconstrued the original 1712 proclamation establishing the Fiesta de Santa Fe. It did not commemorate conquest, but rather, a peaceful gathering "with vespers, mass, sermon and a procession through the Main Plaza." Accordingly, the reigning interpretations had to be reexamined, "for they obscure and erase, and harm." Those individuals who witnessed or participated in conquest rituals did not contribute "in any meaningful way to deeper historical understanding."[90]

In the tectonic epistemic shift Rael-Gálvez pushed, a "calming effect" would result from the elimination of imperialist artifices like "*celebration, bloodless, reconquest,*" language that failed to accurately recognize the "contours of colonialism and its effects." Equally troubling, he noted,

> is the stereotypical representation of *both* Hispanic and Native Americans in which people are depicted as static and frozen in time. These offensive portrayals erase entire cultures, collapse others, and fail to account for the ethnic mixtures resulting from indigenous, European, and African cultural convergence in New Mexico history.

A sense of "being proud of a cultural and ethnic background" did not, in Rael-Gálvez's mind, depend on "a story of domination." "For the Hispanos of New Mexico, there is a wealth of legacy from which

FIGURE 22. Estevan Rael-Gálvez. Replica of Oñate's Foot, installation view. SITElines: Casa Tomada, 2018, SITE SANTA FE. Courtesy of Estevan Rael-Gálvez.

to draw that includes great beauty and profound wisdom reflected in centuries of art, literature, agriculture, philosophy, and architecture."[91]

Rael-Gálvez's elegant articulation coincided with the aims of a major collaboration being formed by former governor of Cochiti Pueblo Regis Pecos, Mayor González, Archbishop John Wester, and the All Pueblo Council of Governors. Their deliberations in 2018 culminated in a resolution founded on Rael-Gálvez's program. Forwarded to Santa Fe Mayor Alan Weber, the resolution acknowledged that the Entrada had deviated from the original intent of the Fiesta, a religious event "honoring the Virgin Mary." Its usual enactment perpetuated colonialism "and less than the truth that it was a tumultuous time [during Vargas's return to New Mexico], leading to great suffering, trauma, and pain for the Pueblo people . . . everything that a peaceful and bloodless re-entry as revisionist history inaccurately reflected."[92] Following up, the All Pueblo Council of Governors affirmed how recent events had compelled a need for principled dialogue to restore "the integrity and dignity of relations built over many years by our respective leaders guided by core values that reflect our collective resilience and perseverance despite the tragic events that reflect the dark side but rising above to deal with the truth and reality of our history."[93]

The Council called for a meeting to include the mayor, the archbishop, and the Fiesta personnel to define a process for "genuine reconciliation to heal the wounds of the past and celebrate the beauty of our respectful cultures, traditions and peoples." Its five-point plan called for discontinuance of the Entrada; an apology from the Church for "the historic injustices it inflicted"; an articulation of "the beauty of the transformation of the Pueblos celebrating the union of Pueblo way of life and Catholicism"; a Truth and Reconciliation Commission to plan and redesign a "more inclusive and celebratory commemoration"; and the commissioning of a piece of art "that commemorates the reconciliation and the truth of past atrocities to learn from and that the commemorative piece of art reflect the spirit of peace as a gift to all future generations and be placed in the Santa Fe Plaza."[94]

The Mandelaesque Truth and Reconciliation Commission had representatives from the Pueblo Governor's Council, the Fiesta Council, Caballeros de Vargas, Archbishop John Wester, and new Santa Fe mayor Alan Webber. The Commission followed Rael-Gálvez's prescription for human convergence. La Entrada would be retired so that "all cultures be united, in honor of the peace that was achieved through Our Lady of Peace, La Conquistadora," the saint that de Vargas honored to bring about peace in the war with the Pueblos. In 1693 "and for some years after," the Commission's historical message noted, "there was hostility and resentment between the Native and Spanish cultures," but since then relations had softened. Fiesta Council president Melissa Mascareñas said it was the first of many steps "that will allow generations of Santafecinos to set aside painful actions while affording us an opportunity to focus wholeheartedly on the original intent of the 1712 proclamation, which called for masses, sermon, vespers and procession through the Plaza." Nevertheless, Los Caballeros declared its intent to continue perpetuating the memory of de Vargas in some form.[95]

The reconciliation document did not mention the Fiesta or de Vargas, nor did it include an apology from the archbishop. It did present a remarkable peace entreaty for public consumption. Employing meanings from the Council's Resolution and Rael-Gálvez's proposal, it included an official acknowledgement of "trauma, tragedy and sorrow," an understanding of its legacy "in the present," and recognition "of wounds older and deeper than any on this continent."[96]

In addition to E. Paul Torres (chair of the All Pueblo Council of Governors), Mayor Webber, and Archbishop Wester, the document was signed by the president of the Caballeros de Vargas Thomas Baca, Manuel García, and president of the Fiesta Council Melissa Cardenas. It signified a virtual surrender of classic Nuevomexicano ethnonationalism founded on hierarchy and social boundaries with los indios. Instead, a breathtaking Pueblo-Hispano unity acknowledged "the ties that bind us together in an unbreakable bond of solidarity with each other, our Creator and the land we all love." The needed healing for a "genuine reconciliation" would prove "challenging and complex," would "test our resilience," would therefore require "honest and compassionate engagement no matter how hard, no matter how long." Together, all would make an offering of peace and resolve to move forward as one. "Let us release our burdens," the call went. "Let us unlearn and relearn. Let us walk together, one step and then another, that we may speak truth, that we may be transformed, that we may heal, that we may become kin."[97]

Such an amalgamation, if it was that, portended a collapse of the ideological pluralism that had long undergirded the region's politics, attested to by the rise of Native American power itself, perhaps incompatible with a merger with Nuevomexicanos or any other ethnic group in the age of recognition politics. Thus, as no Native demonstrator was appointed to the Truth and Reconciliation Commission, the populist Elena Ortiz declared the victory belonging "to the people on the ground . . . who put their bodies on the ground." Implying the maintenance of ethnic boundaries, Ortiz emphasized that restoration was "by the Pueblo people for the Pueblo people. And make no mistake, the Pueblo leadership, in this instance, followed our lead. They followed the women and the youth into this fight. They supported and defended us. And they acted on our behalf to restore justice and dignity to what is supposed to be a community celebration. I am grateful and humbled."[98]

Per official proclamation, a mindful "multidenominational prayer gathering" opened the 2018 Fiesta de Santa Fe. Natives recited prayers in Keres and Tewa Pueblo languages. A Catholic priest gave a homily in Spanish and Latin. A rabbi from Santa Fe's Interfaith Leadership Alliance spoke to reconciliation. Regis Pecos pointed to the opportunity Hispanics had "to be frank and earnest about their ancestry," specifically, "to focus less on Spain and more on their ties to indigenous cultures," to the revelations that many of them had "forebears who were Genízaros . . . Native American slaves sold to Hispanic families from the 16th to the 19th centuries." A handful in the crowd expressed subdued resistance. Going against the grain, local historian Richard Polese held a sign proclaiming "De Vargas Protected Pueblos' Kiva Faith," and "Viva la Fiesta!" In a revised Spanish identity script, Polese claimed that de Vargas "offered genuine respect for Native faith practices."[99]

Traditional Spanish Americans mourned the loss of a key symbol in their memory store. "What happened to our city?," a former City Council member asked on Facebook. "It's so easy to say any event does not conform to your thinking." A warehouse manager fretted about the simplification of history "at the expense of Hispanics in a state where genealogy holds considerable importance to many families. Some of my ancestors were beheaded during the Pueblo Revolt. . . . War is war and there's nothing we can do about the past but learn from it." In the sense of separate nations, the commentator riffed: "We don't go to the Pueblos and protest on their land against their traditions."[100]

As *New York Times* correspondent Simón Romero observed, the Entrada's cancellation was "emblematic of the many ways in which Hispanics have ceded economic and political power in Santa Fe to Anglos in recent years, to the point that many families who have hewed for generations to the city's Hispanic traditions can no longer afford to live here." More to the point of the moment, in the culturally strategic shift in political balance, tribes were asserting greater economic power due to the proliferation of Pueblo reservation casinos.[101] Left out was the trend of Spanish American cultural power steadily giving way.

In addition to steering the Santa Fe Fiesta negotiations, Rael-Gálvez connected with Javier Sánchez, the Yale/Notre Dame-educated mayor of Española,[102] about his city's upcoming Fiesta de Española Valley. This annual event commemorated Oñate's 1598 occupation and establishment of the first provincial capital at nearby San Gabriel, which was, as noted above, first commemorated in 1898. Consistent with wording in the Fiesta bylaws, the official theme of the 2017 Fiesta was "Where Cultures Unite." Where or how went undefined, and so critics were left unsure about what it meant. In any case, to open the Fiesta, Oñate and his *cuadrilla* pulled an Entrada, filing in on horseback and in Spanish period costumes, flashing victory salutes.[103]

News to many Españoleños, recently elected Mayor Sánchez announced plans to change the pageant.[104] Following the recommendation in Rael-Gálvez's assessment of the Fiesta de Española Valley, Sánchez created a Community Relations Commission to replace the Fiesta Council so it could rewrite its bylaws and remove "harmful symbols."[105]

Rael-Gálvez's report, which went to the city council, included a brilliant sketch of what historical conquest meant for territorially dispossessed inhabitants. Titled "Reimagining the Española Fiesta," it sought to "creatively raise consciousness toward the work of fortifying the community of Española." In critiquing the Fiesta bylaws, the report also deconstructed the prime scripts of nineteenth-century Nuevomexicano ethnonationalism as in the notion of "first families" brought by Oñate, which "fore-fronted *población*, or the peopling of this area." That "peopling," however, went "hand in hand with *despoblación*, the dis-peopling of an area,"[106] that is, the reduction of the total number of Puebloans because of Spanish colonial rule.

Echoing the inclusionary epistemic, "Reimagining" made the case that "Community" comprised more than Spanish Americans. Indeed, the very idea of "honoring only one set of forebears in a very particular period, 1598 for example," helped to perpetuate the falsehood "that ancestry is a singular linear structure that follows one patriarch," a smashing of nineteenth-century epistemic Creole pride.[107] Moreover, history's pobladores, "imagined to be of pure Spanish blood who arrived to the region with Oñate and, about a century later, de Vargas," belied the "actual changing and mixing of people that has occurred in the region over the last 300 to 400 years,"[108] putting the lie to the nineteenth-century construction of poblador homogeneity. The work to "recover and transcend" what the Fiesta had been for almost a century would require not only "decolonization,"ˊ came the forewarning, "but a more imaginative remembering the health, wellbeing, and vibrancy of all of its residents." Implementing a Truth, Racial Healing and Transformation initiative would require "an assessment of the viability of removing harmful elements and replacing them with authentic commemorations of a legacy that truthfully defines the complexity of the people of the Española Valley."[109]

Based on Rael-Gálvez's short- and long-term plans, the mayor hoped to inspire his city to reimagine the Fiesta along the lines of "living traditions" to spur dialogue and conversation "around the story of dominance." Mayor Sánchez approached the City Council with a request to approve the appointment of a Community Relations Commission to include women from nearby Santa Clara and Ohkay Owingeh Pueblos.[110]

Resistant City Council members called the changes "a form of ancestral discrimination." Speaking like a legacy member of Nuevomexicano intelligentsia, Councilor John Ramón Vigil emphasized, "We're not proud of what happened and transpired at Acoma, but I think we need to recognize the positive aspects of Oñate. . . . I'd like to highlight that he brought Christianity" (as if it would pacify protestors). Another wrangle over Spanish identity broke. Porter Swentzell, a history professor at the Institute of American Indian Arts and member of Santa Clara Pueblo, said that the "havoc at Acoma has overshadowed evidence of famine at Native American communities as

Oñate and Spanish soldiers requisitioned food reserves." Breaking off a piece of Spanish Americanism, Oñate was called "not necessary" for a successful Fiesta. Maurus Chino, an artist from Acoma Pueblo, felt, however, that it was not possible for Española to change the Fiesta, even those elements he found humiliating. "We've been in this mode of thinking for 400 years," Chino pointedly observed. "It's something that is going to be very hard to change."[111]

Mayor Sánchez successfully overrode Councilman Vigil's attempt to block the new appointments to the Fiesta's organizing committee. Vigil stated that many citizens were very angry to see the changes to the Fiesta, "and unfortunately this is their culture, they're very proud of it here." A month later, Vigil's measure to remove the Fiesta from City authority passed unanimously. Española would have nothing more than a "co-sponsorship role" in its operation. To ease tensions, Mayor Sánchez agreed to sign.[112]

In a situation of uneasy tension, Vigil explained that the shift in Fiesta administration was needed to avoid an effort to "redact history and make the decades-old festival 'politically correct.'" Most citizens he had spoken with wanted to keep Oñate because of his historical significance to the Valley "and because the parade itself has sentimental value for long-time residents. It's about their culture, and it's about their history." In a bit of accommodation, Vigil acknowledged the need for "trailblazing a new path," which called for community input. Meanwhile, due to the time it would take to form a new nonprofit, the Fiesta for 2018 was cancelled.[113]

The COVID-19 shutdown extended the hiatus of the Española Valley Fiesta and Santa Fe's another year. In 2020, the killing of George Floyd brought on a movement to topple hundreds of statues of Confederate officers and Columbus in the South and elsewhere.[114] In this climate, an angry crowd accosted the Oñate figure in Albuquerque's La Jornada, brandishing a chain to crash it down.[115] President Donald Trump swore punishment for anyone indiscriminately destroying "anything that honors our past."[116] Oñate defenders included a right-wing militia. The Albuquerque Department of Cultural Affairs collected public opinions on the appropriate disposition of the statue. In the hope that such situations familiarly occasion, one commentator called it a "watershed" moment that could finally set the community on a "healing process" over New Mexico's conquistador legacy.[117] La

Jornada sculptor Reynaldo Rivera, however, fumed. "Sure, [Oñate] wasn't a saint," the artist accepted, "but you can't put aside what the Spanish brought—you know, the horse, the pig, the sheep, the cow, the wine and the mining industry. . . . Indian lives matter, but also, you know, my people—Hispanic lives matter. I matter. My art matters. I'm pissed."[118]

In Santa Fe, Native Americans moved against the de Vargas statue that stood in a park next to the Cathedral Basilica of St. Francis of Assisi.[119] A multicultural crowd also attacked the Civil War and Indian War cenotaph and a monument devoted to the famed/infamous Native-fighter Kit Carson. As in the case of Albuquerque's Oñate, Mayor Alan Webber removed the Santa Fe tributes. Recognizing the moment of "moral truth," it was, Webber emphasized, "long overdue."[120]

Virgil Vigil, president of La Unión Protectiva de Santa Fe, Nuevo Méjico—a fraternal organization dedicated to preserving the language, traditions, history, arts and culture of "our descendants of the original Spanish colonists of Santa Fe, New Mexico"[121]—sued the City of Santa Fe for the damage done to the Soldier's Monument because Webber approved the noninterference of police as protestors damaged the obelisk. Vigil accused Webber of unleashing an "angry, violent mob" to attack police and bystanders, which created chaos and misinformation. While Webber's action served the city's Culture, History, Art, Reconciliation and Truth project, Vigil called it a violation of New Mexico's Prehistoric and Historic Sites Preservation Act because it altered and dishonored the service of "Hispanic veterans."[122] When Webber announced his run for reelection, Vigil took out an ad in a Santa Fe alternative newspaper telling of the "dark reasons" why he should not be supported, his: removing Diego de Vargas; aligning with "anti-Hispanic" Native groups not recognized by the "eight North Pueblo brothers and sisters"; and discounting the attacks on "our religion."[123]

The Unión Protectiva de Santa Fe's website provided space for Spanish Americans to vent. One contributor was "just sick over the many attacks on my daughter's heritage and on the unique peace Santa Fe enjoyed before these past few years." Another complained of the losses: "First our Entrada, then our Plaza, now our Fiestas??" Still another wondered, "Mayor Alan Webber, why do you hate

Hispanics and our culture?" Someone posted, "Look. Let's just take down everything that is Hispanic since that's the problem. . . . Change the city's name to an indigenous name. Let's get rid of the churches too—they're too Spanish. Let's replace all the churches with indigenous churches. Yes, let's clean and scrub SF until there's no more Spanish remnants."[124]

A fifth generation Santa Fean "of Spanish descent" expressed her angst at losing an identity foothold in the city, informing Webber that his "white liberalism" divided the community and "erased" her heritage. Reacting to the refurbished Fiesta, she recalled from her family's participation in the Entrada "a celebration in which both Native Americans and Hispanics came together to commemorate peace between the two groups." She would not apologize for her father's portrayal of de Vargas, and she did not recognize the narratives of dominance and submission in the Entrada, remembering that there had never been any racial division "between us."[125]

North of Santa Fe, Ohkay Owingeh Pueblos planned on converging around Rivera's Equestrian Oñate in Alcalde. Rio Arriba County Commissioner Leo Jaramillo indicated that the statue would likely be removed for safekeeping. Supporters of the statue reacted in the comments section of the online press story. "First the statues come down," one alarmist said. "Then the [Spanish] society comes down. Hispanics of New Mexico, be warned. The statue destroyers are coming for YOU next. Prepare your families and yourself. War is coming." As another contributed, "if WE want to move forward in unity and peace WE must bring Popay's statue down,"[126] that is, from Statuary Hall in Washington, DC, which was installed with great fanfare as an exemplification of a "social and symbolic presence [of Native Americans] within contemporary American society."[127] New Mexico's US Senators had him put there, the comment complained, "without reconciling the genocide he committed against the Spanish community. I'm sick and tired of politicians (including some [Spanish American] Norteño's) caving to pueblo demands," the critic cried out. In addition,

> If Jaramillo or any other Rio Arriba Commissioner loses their spine and has Oñate removed, they have no business in their elected offices. . . . Pueblos do

> not pay property tax, so them having an opinion over the matter is mute. Respect is a two way street, stop making demands and start making more concessions. Po'pay next to civil rights pioneer Dennis Chaves [represented in Statuary Hall as well] is a "slap in the face."[128]

Another, affirming that he was a Spaniard whose ancestors came with Oñate from Valverde de Llerena, Extremadura, Spain, wrote that the

> false narrative being spread by some in the Native American community is offensive to me. Moreover, my great great grandfather was dragged out of his home and shot with a bow and arrow in the back while running for his life - leaving my great great grandmother screaming and hiding her only child under a bed mattress in order to try to save her life. Oñate's statues in Alcalde, Albuquerque and everywhere else in New Mexico need to remain standing and Spanish New Mexicans need to stand up to this bullying by some in the Native American Community. Our Spanish heritage needs to be preserved, if not, all the sacrifices and suffering our Spanish ancestors went through will be destroyed and forgotten. Enough is enough![129]

Nonetheless, the county stored the statue for safekeeping (where it remains as of this writing). In the demonstration, red handprints appeared stamped on the pedestal where Equestrian Oñate formerly stood and a young Ohkay Owingeh warrior performed a victory dance on it (see Fig. 24). Offended Spanish Americans confronted the celebrant threateningly.[130] For Red Nation leader Elena Ortiz, Oñate no longer haunted the region. In her sigh of relief, "For the first time in many years, we don't have to stare at Oñate. . . . The presence of that statue was an act of violence upon Pueblo people from the moment it was put up and now, finally, it's gone."[131]

Both leading Fiestas were cancelled due to COVID-19 in 2021. In the 2022 Fiesta de Santa Fe, the message of Native American *princesa*,

FIGURE 23. Pueblo Native American on pedestal. Alcalde, New Mexico. Molly Montgomery, photographer. Source: Randall Balmer, "A Spanish Conquistador Gets Pushed Off His Pedestal," *Rio Grande Sun*, September 10, 2020. Courtesy of Harvey Yates.

Leslie Talache of Ohkay Owingeh, signaled the revamped program of bringing unity "between local Hispanic and Native people." Talache pledged to show children that Native Americans and Hispanics could be one. Deactivating collective memory, she declared, "Whatever happened in history is just that, it's history, and we can't change it, so we need to move forward."[132]

Oñate's Entrada returned to the Fiesta del Valle de Española in 2022 with an indoor program titled "Juan de Oñate Replies to Accusations." In costume and in character, the Oñate player Ray Griego and the chair of the Fiesta Speaker's Committee, Robert Valdez, considered it a final say in the debates that Oñate was "absolved" of eighteen of thirty criminal charges that were filed against him by the Spanish government over his treatment of Indigenous people while the rest were judged "difficult to prove." However, *The Source NM* called it an attempt to "downplay" Oñate's crimes and "polish his legacy," as it clung to a "false retelling" of a "war criminal." Oñate was, the outlet noted, "exiled in 1614 by the Spanish government and found guilty of cruelty and excessive force, according to Spanish journals and testimonials, and a tradition of oral histories maintained by the people of Acoma Pueblo." Critics hit on the historical presentations for having "no women, no Pueblo historians, nor any of the numerous local scholars critical of the pageantry." Matthew Martínez, a former lieutenant governor of Ohkay Owingeh and Pueblo scholar, noted that speakers "were very much along the same theoretical practice of . . . idolizing a particular figurehead that his own people ostracized and exiled."[133]

In 2023, Native Americans in Santa Fe demanded stoppage of Fiesta Court visits to school history classes where they performed and gave history lessons of de Vargas's reclaiming Santa Fe. The Santa Fe County School Board had limited these, but the all-Nuevomexicano school board in the Pojoaque district voted to have the Court meet with students.[134] Again, Natives and Spanish Americans packed a school board meeting, and again tempers "boiled over as the board wrestled with the latest chapter in the city's conflict over historical narratives, the religious affiliation of Fiestas and present-day racial tensions." As the meeting devolved into repeated shouts, a Spanish American grieved over the assault on her people's history and a Native mourned the "continuation of celebrating violence and racism and colonization." The "anti-Indigeneity here today," the Indigenous voice declared, was "really disheartening and it really hurts."[135]

The Board denied the proposal to discontinue Court visits but directed School Superintendent Hilario Chávez to meet with Fiesta and Indigenous representatives to work out a compromise. Chávez suggested scheduling visits after school hours, not only to make for a more effective parental "opt-in, opt-out" but also to "potentially attract a larger audience and create more vibrant celebrations in [the schools], as we talk about larger, more inclusive celebrations that would bring many more cultures to our district." Fiesta devotees objected to the tearing down of cultural boundaries and the Board rejected it three to two.[136]

A month later, a young Nuevomexicano wearing a red Make America Great Again cap shot and seriously wounded a Native American activist as he participated in a celebration of the Rio Arriba County Commission decision to withdraw a plan to place Equestrian Oñate on a pedestal in Española. Opponents of Oñate mourned the violence and the historical roots of the near tragedy.[137]

In June 2024, a sense of calm had descended over the public discourses of ethnic identity in northern New Mexico when Santa Fe Mayor Alan Webber, in his authoritative role of democracy's conduit, announced a plan to put two statuaries on display. The one of Diego de Vargas was slated for the New Mexico History Museum; the other, consisting of two figures, the Tesuque Pueblo Runners Catua and Umtua, who "ignited the Pueblo Revolt of 1680," for installation at the Santa Fe Convention Center.[138]

Smarting over the culture contentions wracking his administration, Webber in his press conference made it a point to disown the "two small vocal minorities," one of which did not want Native runners put on display because the "Pueblo Uprising was a bloody revolt that took the lives of hundreds of Spanish priests, women, men, and children,"[139] the other objecting to de Vargas representing the return to Santa Fe of European colonizers who "perpetrated genocide on the indigenous Native American people." The "shouters" of both factions overshadowed what should be a "constructive, positive, and significant moment for Santa Fe," the keeper of law and order maintained while claiming that the tactic of weaponizing history was "not Santa Fe." Webber convened the governor of Tesuque Pueblo, leaders of the Caballeros de Vargas and Fiesta Council, chair of the All Pueblo Council of Governors, and the executive director of the New Mexico History Museum. Serving as backup for the mayor, they declared agreement with the purpose of honoring Spanish and Pueblo traditions by making the artwork accessible to public viewing in indoor venues where they could be protected. This "small step" would not "do away with divisions," the mayor conceded, yet it showed that progress was possible "when people of goodwill and good hearts work together. Here in Santa Fe, we can show respect for each and respect for all. And that's no small thing."[140]

It was "wishful thinking," a *Santa Fe New Mexican* reporter observed. A bulldog in defense of his Spanish heritage, Virgil Vigil of La Unión Protectíva assailed the mayor for again attacking the people of "Spanish descent" in Santa Fe. It was, he contended, "totally disrespectful" to Spanish history, culture, traditions "and our Catholic Faith." Vigil re-presented the familiar script of the Spanish "natives" as those slaughtered in the Pueblo Revolt at the rate of over four hundred men, women, and children, twenty-one Catholic priests dragged by horses "along the street until they died," one taken to Tesuque Pueblo and stoned to death. "Now, they publicly celebrate this!" Vigil decried.[141]

In August 2024, the installation of each work of art came about. The Pueblo piece by Pojoaque Pueblo sculptor George Rivera went to a corner of the Convention's Center's free and open front lobby. Vigil had charged that the de Vargas statue was destined to be placed "in the cellar," that is, the New Mexico History Museum's permanent below-ground Southwest history display. That it would not be visible to the public Vigil called unequal treatment, a "double anti-Spanish standard."[142] Vigil's point must have been taken seriously, for de Vargas got a spot on the Museum's first floor. However, rather than in the Museum's entrance lobby, it stands by itself just outdoors in a narrow, barren walkway between buildings, hardly obvious even to paying patrons. In the agreement that was struck with Los Caballeros de Vargas, which had donated the artwork to the city in the first place, it would remain in the Museum until 2028 and, after that, returned to the nonprofit. At that time, it could reclaim its significance as a token of Spanish heritage memory—likely off the beaten path of civic central.[143]

FIGURE 24. Diego de Vargas at New Mexico History Museum, 2025. Donna Quasthoff, sculptor. Robert Otto Valdez, photographer. Courtesy of Robert Otto Valdez.

Coda

CLEARLY, MANY IN the state of New Mexico and southern Colorado continue to call themselves "Spanish"; Spanish memory remains an important component of Santa Fe's cultural identity; and Spanish identitarians stand at the ready to defend their right to uphold and celebrate their Spanish forebearers.

Nevertheless, the decline of classic Spanish / Spanish American identity is in clear evidence. As one critical commentator accurately observes, dwindling numbers of people are any more "aroused with pride" by representations of Spanish conquerors.[1] Even the formidable Millie Santillanes, a die-hard Spanish advocate, admitted that in a survey she checked off "Hispanic/American." "If I wanted to think old," she noted, "I would have written 'Spanish/American'—but today, though I am of the Hispanic culture, my nationality is American!" While continuing to deny "Mexican/Mexican-American/Chicano,"[2] Santillanes tipped her identity's classic balance between regional and federal loyalties to the side of Americanism.

Significantly, moreover, Spanish emblems have been disappearing from the public square. The University of New Mexico, for example, submitted to Native American pressure to remove its institutional seal that sported a conquistador and a Manifest Destiny pioneer (a design from the Spanish golden era[3]). What was once the Spanish Colonial Arts Museum in Santa Fe is now the Nuevomexicano Heritage Arts Museum. Oñate High School in Las Cruces, in turn, became Organ Mountains High School. Still standing but not in use is the former Oñate Monument Resource and Visitor Center in Alcalde where Reynaldo Rivera's Equestrian Oñate once stood. The facility on Rio Arriba County property was dedicated with appropriate fanfare by Nuevomexicano and Euro-American politicians to promote the Española Valley and Rio Arriba County with cultural exhibits and research projects to impart a "thorough knowledge and appreciation of the origins of the Hispano culture, its social systems and institutions."[4]

However, the project soon lost its state funding and after offering the space for a string of community programs, the county abandoned the 7,500-square-foot building.[5] With "Oñate Monument Center"

FIGURE 25. (*above*) Oñate Monument and Visitor Center, front, 2025. Alcalde, New Mexico. Robert Otto Valdez, photographer. Courtesy of Robert Otto Valdez.

FIGURE 26. (*below*) Oñate Monument and Visitor Center, rear, 2025. Alcalde, New Mexico. Robert Otto Valdez, photographer. Courtesy of Robert Otto Valdez.

embossed over the front and rear doorways, the aging pink structure stands on the country highway as an imposing if dilapidated and anachronistic monument to Spanish heraldries past.[6]

Today, *querencia* is the term for encoding a politics of territorial primacy. Querencia in Spanish means a deep affection for one's place.[7] Nuevomexicano and Nuevomexicana adherents call it "love of home, love of place," an "aware[ness] of the [New Mexican] landscape which carries the memory of those who came before."[8] Rural querencia rests on the survival of vecino life and townships dating to Spanish colonial times. The material structures of old Spanish/Mexican land grants, ancient irrigation *acequias*, and idiosyncratic culture forms are querencia's monuments.[9] Quite markedly, the querencia trend steers far from of any Spanish connotation, implicitly signaled in its association with the antithetical identities of *la raza*, "mestiza consciousness," "Chicana/Chicano," and "Genízaro."[10] Aficionados of the regional linguistic vernacular labor to protect their homeland "dialect" dating to the 1500s from erosion or disappearance without for a moment adopting Aurelio Espinosa's stamp of a "rich archaic Castilian language," or even suggesting that it once may have been such. Instead they favor a script of linguistic intermixture reflecting the cultural diversity that defined the New Mexico frontier from the beginning.[11]

Intriguingly, a Nuevomexicano graduate student in history prominently submitted a call in Albuquerque's newspaper for the erection of monuments to honor the Nuevomexicano heroes of New Mexico's Mexican period, said to be "seriously lacking." Now that the over-represented era of Spanish monuments, which meant to claim that "we are Spaniards in the flesh" but only for "tourism and to 'whiten' the image of New Mexico history," was at its end, Raúl Montaño Ayala proposed that New Mexico "honor the Mexicans who fought in the Mexican-American War, arguably the first Mexican-Americans/Chicanos." Perhaps reflecting the rise of another phase of Nuevomexicano identity construction, he noted that it had been over sixty years since the Chicano Movement, "and collective pride in our Mexican heritage has never been so ingrained and widespread."[12]

Conclusion

THERE IS THE sense in which the study of Spanish identity in New Mexico belongs to the history of ideas, to the knowledge that "ideas matter," which they do in multiple ways in society. The ideas that serve as the content of ethnic identity are designed to conjoin select elements of a population and slicing out others. Ideas have the power to motivate action but also to generate opposition. It is from this broad perspective that we've come to grasp what Spanish identity has meant for New Mexico. In an important interpretive realization, the ideas that have comprised Spanish identity have followed the winds that have shaped Nuevomexicano/Nuevomexicana history. By now, the rise of Spanish identity should seem less anomalous and irrational than what conventional wisdom has tended to decree.

Spanish identity rode in on the route from Spain's sixteenth-century monarchy to New Spain, landing in the territory being defined as the imperial post of *Nuevo México.* There it remained, firmly planted by Spanish officials. Creole descendants kept it alive during New Mexico's tenure in the Republic of Mexico when imperial New Spain no longer existed. It moved next into the US New Mexico territory where legacy Creoles persevered in keeping Spanish identity going clear into the twentieth century.

A Nuevomexicano intelligentsia sustained a stubborn identity of belonging to New Mexico to deal with the social, political and economic complexities that US annexation laid on them. It was a system of internal colonialism, as I have deemed it, which makes the Nuevo Mexicano tendency to push their territorial primacy a general manifestation born of forced annexation.

The economics of annexing frontier New Mexico played a major part in the sustenance and promotion of Nuevomexicano primacy. It was a perennially underdeveloped land without the requisite natural riches to forge an advanced economy. The feeble economic modernization of New Mexico was unable to draw cultural forces formidable enough to roll over the conventions of Nuevomexicano/a tradition. Thus, while Texas and California also manifested Spanish identity before their US annexations, both of theirs remained stunted or disappeared under the weight of overwhelming capitalism and the attending conversions of them into states of the Union. In contrast, New Mexico's Spanish identity flourished as long as Euro-Americans remained a small minority of the population hoping for the resources with which to build a powerful economy. This helps us see how Spanish identity was less of an anomaly and more an instantiation for Nuevomexicano social evolution.

Still, between the two formal heritage options, "Spanish" and "Mexican," it is imperative to clarify why the former fared better in the nineteenth and early twentieth centuries. In addition to staking their blood deep into New Mexico's soil, establishing their rooted autochthony as a central and originating presence in its past and present, the process of forging an ethnic nationalism called for the claim that their birthrights coalesced to form a "nation" (Latin, *nascere*, *natus*). The Nuevomexicano irredenta—of a territory historically or ethnically related to a political unit but under the political control of another—played on the notion of a single ethnic people to advocate for its right to sociocultural fulfillment on land it claimed as theirs by settlement rights. Although now irredentas with cultural differences sharp enough to matter under the sovereign jurisdiction of the United States, Nuevomexicanos advanced the notion that their people merited first-class incorporation into the social, political, and cultural body of that national state based in significant part on the pluralistic principles ingrained in its own Constitution.

Insofar as a politicized heritage is artfully constructed (as opposed to flowing naturally from the depths of a culture), in the final analysis, a hale Spanish heritage more effectively postulated an integrated people than did a Mexican legacy. In the Mexican period, the claim of Spanish descendance continued from colonial times as a property of partisan Creoles who upheld limpieza de sangre and high culture to disassociate from the mestizo and indigenous portions of the population. In little more than a decade after American annexation, identitarians began stipulating a holistic nation by bringing into the fold the entirety of the Spanish-speaking populace. The "Mexican" referent also served at certain moments to emphasize primacy and convey nationness, as we saw, but as a culturally effective heritage, it had its limits. Ethnic identity tends to impress by wielding a substantial memory bouquet involving ancient origins, bedrock institutions, and signifying life experiences. As such, a Spanish coherence offered greater intricacy than a bare Mexican identity, which, in recognizing internal sociocultural diversity suggested social segmentation.

Reusable heritage scripts powered the notion of a people, even for a culturally diverse Nuevomexicano populace. In the imaginary, Spanish colonial markers—the noble discovery of a special land, a heroic settler community, a pure bloodline at a time when race distinction counted as a criterion of worth, a venerable spiritual base, and the conquering of aggravating enemies—presented the stuff of nationness. The suggestion of "founding" took memory further back and more romantically than the recently independent "Mexico" for suggesting the birthing of an ancient homeland and for painting a portrait of a courageous people. A swashbuckling conquistador legacy quickened attention to origin stories, a critical factor in the lore of all nations, while providing the scripts to espouse indigeneity on a rationally defined homeland. The legend of hardy poblador ancestors, the lasting basis of community, heroically struggling to survive, ran in the scripts of determined opposition to inveterately scourging Natives, an ideological piece that emanated from the experience of violence on the frontier even as it masked imperialism's inbred aggressions.

Limpieza de sangre, which Creole liberals originally claimed for themselves, was mythologized to cover all Nuevomexicanos. It elided the significant mixed-blood reality in the populace while ideationally mortaring social boundaries with Native Americans (and increasingly Mexican nationals) while claiming equality with or superiority over Euro-American heritage. Adopting the global spread of Spain's civilization and Christianity gave the Nuevomexicano "nation" standing when international norms recognized nonstate cultural nations. In contrast, the etymologically indigenous root *mexica*, which in theory could have evolved out of Hidalgo Guadalupe identity, could not quite excel for a sharp nation value, held back by Mexico's neglect of their former paisanos, and pushed back by America's xenophobic ranking of Mexicans to the low end of humanity's evolutionary scale.

The discursive handling of regionalism by Nuevomexicanos represented another instance of ethnic-based mobilization tapping into "deep-seated, historical, social, and cultural ties, creating a sense of collective identity that political leaders can manipulate to enhance loyalty and participation."[7] Spanish identity served to address both local and national problems. At home, a discursive nationalism around territorial primacy and a bona fide people bolstered the contentions aimed at a territorial hierarchy manned by "strangers," "foreigners," and "carpetbaggers." Misruling governors, territorial secretaries, supreme court justices, stationed military officers, ambitious settler citizens, venturing capitalists, political party honchos, and, in their own way, liberal culture brokers stirred the pot of internal colonialism, encouraging a Nuevomexicano intelligentsia to struggle for their privileged share of what New Mexico and America had to offer.

At the national level, Nuevomexicanos ran with the offer of US citizenship, legitimating the conquest of their homeland and patriotically committing to a standard of belonging to the US sovereign. Yet the normative requirements of dominant US nationalism were littered with obstacles that blocked Nuevomexicanos and Nuevomexicanas from full inclusion in American society.

Not many Americans saw the merit of the Nuevomexicano autochthony argument, if they ever encountered it, in the statehood cause. Rather, they othered the territory's Mexicans as culturally and racially degraded, and therefore antithetical to the haughty American nation. Certain Nuevomexicano spokespersons willingly acknowledged the shortcomings in the people's background compared to America's high-flying civilization. They faced the incoming ideological storm by insisting on their people's worthiness, demonstrated by the heroic struggle their ancestors undertook in an inhospitable landscape to preserve the Christian integrity of New Mexico. However, strong-armed injustice depends on preserving the gross inequalities and socioeconomic disparities between the powerful and the subaltern, so that when Nuevomexicanos and Euro-Americans repeatedly negated the disparagements by pointing to the good character of the irredentas, those who pulled the strings found little to respect.

This very New Mexicanism spurred the movement to inscribe the New Mexico Constitution with a bill of ethnic rights, priming the virtuous "Spanish American people" for civic protections and political participation in their longed-for state. However, in a regrettable state of affairs, they did not have the political capital to make the state of New Mexico enforce the educational, language, and voting rights encoded in the constitution, much less fulfill the dream of self-rule. At the least, the celebratory lauding of their Spanish roots represented their satisfactory standing of their rightful place in New Mexico, the United States, and the world, quite as they transformed from a colonized to an aspirant minority group.

Chicano historians have cast Spanish identity overboard for not staying true to Mexican nationality and Mexican-oriented politics. Yet, insofar as they challenged Euro-American hierarchy, the epistemics and purposes of Spanish identity can be judged as "progressive" according to today's currency of standing for justice and against the subjugation of peoples. However, as Nuevomexicanos who considered themselves Spanish turned to face both Mexican nationals and Native Americans, their memory subjectivities demonized these social others as only ethnic nationalism can. It was a bleak negativity that Spain had long spun for posterity, and the bill for it came as postmodern forces hastened to fell the anachronisms of Spanish identity.

The potential always existed for "Spanish" and "Mexican" self-denotations to conflict. They opposed one another in the Mexican period and in the early years of the US territory. From the 1860s to the late 1880s, they seemed to coexist, as reflected in Antonio Gonzales's primacy disquisition in calling for statehood in the 1870s, Tranquilino Luna's remarks at the Tertio-Millennial Exposition in the 1880s, and in the 1890s when land grant defenders discoursed against Euro-American land grabbers in the frame "Mexican" identification. However, the "surumato" malediction hurled at Mexican peasants in the 1890s–1910s (alluded to in chapter 5), marked the start of Spanish identity hardening a disaffiliation with people from Mexico, a bias that was amplified by the Mexican Revolution. It is significant that this scandalous identity reaction was prompted by a combination of significant immigration from Mexico and tensions between Mexican and US governments, which, for Spanish Americans, only reinforced American patriotism.

It was a strange parallel with US New Mexicanism for Spanish Americans to stigmatize the status of being Mexican. Yet, by the time the golden era of Spanish identity had ripened, Spanish dissociation from lo mexicano was set in stone, which prompted Mexican Americans and Chicanos to actively oppose Spanish identity. As the geographic separation of Nuevomexicanos/as and other Mexican Americans in the Southwest broke down, the former loosened their attachment to Spanish identity. Hitching their wagons to out-of-state Mexican

Americans and Chicanos/Chicanas, they rattled the cage of a Spanish colonial heritage, favoring the artifices of Mexicanness instead. As they did, they chipped at the wall of the Spanish imaginary.

In Castile's monarchical cause of planetary expansion, the countenance of the Native American haunted Spanish identity. For centuries, the locutions *¡Viva España!* and *La Conquista* interlocked. As a defined Spanish kingdom, the New Mexico province inherited Spain's official call for demolishing inevitable challengers to its absolutist control of acquired lands. As a consequence, the put-down of Pueblo and Plains Natives permanently stained Nuevomexicano Spanish identity, which never saw rhyme nor reason to scrap it from its doctrinaires until it became too late. As the politics and discourses of identity jetted across civic America, the Spanish proclivity for actual and symbolic supremacy over Native Americans molded into an Achilles' heel. #LandBack retribution—history's moral fiber riding high on its back—effectuated an exclamation for the decline of New Mexico's Spanish identity.

En fin, it's the complexity of Spanish identity that stands out, by turns, an instance of sociological generality, a sacred attachment to hearth and home, a shield to ward off the blows of would-be masters, an axe to clamber for safety, a cudgel to effect unjustifiable preoccupations, and a shamanic rattle for survival's sake. Such have been the functions, furies, tragedies, and contradictions of Spanish identity as we have witnessed its manifestation in New Mexico.

Notes

Preface

1. Simmons, *People of the Sun*, 57.

2. This account of the Espinosa-Bloom correspondence is adapted from Gonzales, "'A Perfect Furor of Indignation.'"

3. See Gonzales, *Forced Sacrifice as Ethnic Protest*, 125–50.

Introduction

1. In the most important of the surveys, Hunley, et al. ("Social Identity in New Mexicans") sampled 507 descendants of Spanish-speaking background for their first, second, third, and fourth choices in classifying their ethnicity. In the range of nomenclatures that appeared, "Hispanic" was selected first 44 percent of the time while "Spanish" was first at a 12 percent rate. However, 72 percent of the first-choice "Hispanics" gave "Spanish" as their second choice. Contributing to the suggestion that the bland "Hispanic" category functioned as a proxy for "Spanish," 72 percent of the first-choice "Spanish" identifiers denoted "Hispanic" as their second. In a parallel, "Nuevomexicano/a" was selected first 15 percent of the time with 72 percent of its selectors marking "Spanish" as their second. None of those who made "Spanish" first had "Mexican" as their second, and only 2 percent marked "Mexican American" second (220).

2. Campa, *Spanish Folk-Poetry in New Mexico*, 12, 13, 15.

3. Austin, "Mexicans and New Mexico," 142–43.

4. Wilson, *Myth of Santa Fe*, 148–49, 75–76.

5. Zeleny, "Relations between the Spanish-Americans and Anglo-Americans," 307–40.

6. Montgomery, *Spanish Redemption*, 13, 64. See Gonzales's review in the *New Mexico Historical Review*, 329–37.

7. Manifest Destiny was "a cluster of ideas that relied on racism to justify a war of aggression against Mexico"; Gómez, *Manifest Destinies*, 64–71, 81; quote, 86.

8. Gómez-Quiñones, *Roots of Chicano Politics*, 298–99; also, Valdez, "Insurrection in New Mexico," 18; Acuña, *Occupied America*, 76–77.

9. Gómez-Quiñones and Vásquez, *Making Aztlán*, x.

10. Gómez-Quiñones, *Roots of Chicano Politics*, 194–95, 308.

11. Nieto-Phillips, *Language of Blood*, 51–53, 81–82.

12. Mora, *Border Dilemmas*: "members of," 224, 9–19.

13. Gonzales, "'History Hits the Heart'" and "Political Construction of Latino Nomenclatures in Twentieth-Century New Mexico"; Horton, *Santa Fe Fiesta Re-Invented*, passim.

14. Smith, "Ethnic Cores and Dominant Ethnies," 16.

15. Calhoun, *Nationalism*, 70, 9.

16. See, e.g., Shils, "Primordial, Personal, Sacred and Civil Ties." For discussions of the constructivist-primordial debate, see Calhoun, *Nationalism*, 30–36; Norval, "Thinking Identities," 59–70.

17. Smith, *Theories of Nationalism*, 187–89; "Introduction: "The Formation of Nationalist Movements," 5; "'Ideas' and 'Structure' in the Formation of Independence Ideals," 36; *Myths and Memories of the Nation*, 9.

18. Connor, *Ethnonationalism*, xi; also, Smith, *Ethnic Revival*, 66.

19. Seton-Watson, *Nations and States*, 5.

20. Anderson, *Imagined Communities*, 4.

21. McCrone, *Sociology of Nationalism*, 6. Scholars working in the history of nationalism in Latin America challenge Anderson's "imagined community," e.g., Lomnitz, "Nationalism as a Practical System."

22. Connor, *Ethnonationalism*, 205, 40–41.

23. E.g., Doob, *Patriotism and Nationalism*, 188.

24. Wirth, "Types of Nationalism," 723.

25. See Barth, "Introduction," esp. 32–38; Erikson, *Ethnicity & Nationalism*, 12.

26. Suzman, *Ethnic Nationalism and State Power*, 12; Royce, *Ethnic Identity*, 6.

27. Bruner, *Strategies of Remembrance*, 1, 2–3; quotes, 7.

28. Martin, "From Negro to Black to African American," 83.

29. Preucel and Matero, "Placemaking on the Northern Rio Grande," 85.

30. Wallerstein, "The Construction of Peoplehood," 78.

31. Such ideological identity systems arose in the Garvey Movement, the Civil Rights Movement, and the Sixties-Seventies Chicano and Red Power Movements; see, Breton, *Governance of Ethnic Communities*, 157–58.

32. Although it can be created or shaped by state policy. For the discussion of state and organic identitarian intellectuals, see Malešević, *Identity as Ideology*, 185–88, 196.

33. That is, beyond the allusion to members of extreme right-wing political movements in Europe who oppose immigration and multiculturalism. For example, Malešević critiques the study of ethnonationalism from an identitarian perspective (4, 30, 121).

34. Yack, *Nationalism and the Moral Psychology of Community*, 57, 60.

35. Breuilly, *Nationalism and the State*, 404.

36. Kaufmann, "Introduction," 1.

37. Wimmer, "Dominant Ethnicity and Dominant Nationhood," 36.

38. E.g., Harvard political scientist Huntington (*Who Are We?*) tied the US's core culture to Anglo-Saxon virtues and political principles. As state nationalism, Huntington exaggerated fears of people of Mexican descent, both Mexican Americans and immigrants, who were rapidly increasing in the US but continued

to hold on to their traditions, incapable of fulfilling such core Anglo-Saxon concepts as democracy.

39. Schermerhorn, *Comparative*, 96–97. Minorities are also incorporated into nation-states through the emergence of pariahs, the integration of indigenous isolates, and because of migration.

40. Schermerhorn, *Comparative*, 106–7, 192–97; also, Gonzales, *Política,* 2–4, 16–18, 34. On the meaning of annexation tied to the case of Texas, see Montejano, *Anglos and Mexicans in the Making of Texas*, 309–12;

41. Hechter, *Internal Colonialism*, 96–97, 106–7, 192–97. For an earlier formulation of internal colonialism, see González, *Internal Colonialism and National Development.*

42. Schermerhorn, Comparative, 96–97, 106–7, 192–97. On the changing conditions of regionalism, see Connor Ethnonationalism, 178.

43. Peckham, "Internal Colonialism," 41–59; Doob, *Patriotism and Nationalism*, 184.

44. Coakley, "Introduction," 2; Tuan, *Space and Place*, 154.

45. Keating, *State and Regional Nationalism*, 20–22.

46. Smith, *Nationalism in the Twentieth Century*, 52; also, Smith, "Introduction," 1.

47. Young, *Politics in the Congo*, quoted in Smith, "Theories and Types of Nationalism," 121.

48. Smith, "Towards a Theory of Ethnic Separatism," 21; also, Smith, *Theories of Nationalism*, 216. Such movements occurred against the colonial regimes in Britain, France, Spain, and Canada; Smith, *Nationalism in the Twentieth Century*, 21.

49. Gellner, *Nations and Nationalism*, 45.

50. Olzak, *Global Dynamics of Racial and Ethnic Mobilization*, 48; Kaufmann, "Introduction," 1.

51. See Cronin, "Ideology of the IRA."

52. Shoup, "Foreword," ix; Ambrosio, *Irredentism*, 2; Schermerhorn, *Comparative Ethnic Relations*, 134.

53. Smith, *Nationalism in the Twentieth Century*, 19.

54. On consociational democracy, see Lijphart, *Democracy in Plural Societies*, 1, 25; Spencer and Wollman, *Nationalism*, 186–87.

55. Enloe, *Ethnic Conflict and Political Development*, 84. Some systems are wholly organized on cultural diversity, others may reflect an ethnic and purely sectional federalism. For general treatments of ethnic federalism, see Enloe, "Internal Colonialism, Federalism and Alternative State Development Strategies"; Olzak, *Global Dynamics of Racial and Ethnic Mobilization*; Horowitz, *Ethnic Groups in Conflict*; Nielson, "Flemish Movement in Belgium after World War II"; Olzak, "Ethnic Mobilization in Quebec."

56. Kelly, "Political Downsizing," 211–12.

57. Williams and Tarr, "Subnational Constitutional Space," 3–4, 15.

58. Toepperwein, "Participation in the Decision-Making," 42. Interestingly, the resolution of irredentism in the Irish Republican Army that came out of the 1998 Good Friday Agreement resulted in a power-sharing arrangement in the Northern Ireland Assembly among Unionist and Republican/nationalist

parties; see, Patterson, *Ireland Since 1939*, 331–43; Jarrett, *Peace and Ethnic Identity in Northern Ireland.*

59. Smith, *Nationalism in the Twentieth Century*, 173.

60. Gonzales, *Política*, 199–201.

61. Williams, "Liberalism, Colonialism and Liberal Imperialism," 63 and passim.

62. Gonzales, *Política*, 98–99.

63. See Gonzales, "Mexican Party, American Party, Democratic Party," 260–61.

64. "Official Public Proclamation Regarding Insurrection, Records War Department," *Santa Fe New Mexican*, February 15, 1846, 24–26; *Insurrection*, esp. 24; Sterling Report, *Insurrection*, 8; Twitchell, *Leading Facts of New Mexico History*, 233–34.

65. On the Taos Revolt, see Crutchfield, *Tragedy at Taos.*

66. McNierney, *Taos 1847*, 83–86.

67. "Nuevo México al Frente," *El Independiente*, May 5, 1898, 1.

68. E.g., Gómez, *Manifest Destinies*, 42–43.

69. Montejano, *Anglos and Mexicans*, 310.

70. Gonzales, *Política*, 43–46; Lozano, *American Language*, 7.

71. Alarid, "Hispano Bastion."

72. Translator was a necessary profession for political proceedings and in private enterprise. Jesús M. Sena y Baca's business translated official documents from English to Spanish and vice versa. "Anuncios," *La Gaceta Semanaria de Santa Fe*, July 17, 1869, 3.

73. Hechter, "Dynamics of Secession," 269–75.

74. For a review of the literature, see Guardino, *Dead March*, 14–15.

75. E.g., "Call," *Republican Review*, June 28, 1873, 2; for evidence, see Gonzales, *Política*, 207–49, passim.

76. Kaplan, *Politics and the American Press*, 1.

77. "Don Tomas C. Gutiérrez," *El Nuevo Mexicano*, November 21, 1864, 2.

78. Kellas, *Politics of Nationalism and Ethnicity*, 218.

79. Johannsen, *To the Halls of the Montezumas*, 13; also, Gómez, *Manifest Destinies*, 21.

80. "Local News: The Festivities," *Republican Review*, June 8, 1872, 2.

81. Glenn, Unequal Freedom, 54.

82. Thompson, "Brave Christian Soldiers," 270, 265–66, 267–68, 270–71, 277–87; Anderson, History of New Mexico, 817.

83. Thompson, "Brave Christian Soldiers," 266–67, 290, 291, 292–96.

84. "¡Honrad a el que lo Merece!," *La Gaceta de Santa Fe*, April 26, 1862, 2.

85. "The State Question," *Weekly New Mexican*, March 23, 1872, repr. April 2, 1872, 1.

86. Blackhawk, *Rediscovery of America*, 215.

87. Gonzales, *Política*, 28.

88. Lee, Blood in the Sands, 160.

89. Mora, *Border Dilemmas*, 11–12, passim.

90. Weber, "'Scarce more than apes,'" 300.

91. Gómez, *Manifest Destinies*, 64–84.

92. For the same pattern involving Mexicans in the annexation of Texas, see Montejano, *Anglos and Mexicans*, 37.

93. Blackhawk, *Rediscovery of America*, 220.

94. Calhoun, *Nationalism*, 23.

95. Members would have had access to classic and widely distributed publications on the foundational histories of Spanish New Mexico, e.g., Villagrá, *Historia de la Nueva Mexico* (1630) and Sigüenza Y Góngora, *Mercurio Volante*, 1692.

96. On community of memory, see Nora, *Realms of Memory*, vol. 1.

97. On the history of black nationalism addressing a white power structure with proof of a black noble tradition, see Lind, *Next American Nation*, 272–73.

98. For an account of what he independently called the "Neo-Mexicano intelligentsia" in the late nineteenth century, see LeFebre, "Pedagogies of Resistance and Self-Preservation," 75–103.

99. On the importance of individual and collective "life-scripts" utilized by US Blacks to sustain their ethnoracial identity in a context of anti-Black racism, see Appiah, "Identity, Authenticity, Survival," 159–61.

100. See, e.g., Anonymous to Editor ("Greasers as Citizens"), *New York Times*, February 6, 1882, 2; Mora, *Border Dilemmas*, 112; Lee, "The Manliness to Defend Themselves," 168–73, 191–92. Reflecting the structural possibilities of forced annexation, the August 29th Movement, a Marxist-Leninist Chicano organization in the 1970s, argued that its appropriation by US capitalist imperialism made secession necessary for New Mexico; August 29th Movement, *Fan the Flames*.

101. Hechter, "Dynamics of Secession," 270; Olzak, "Ethnic Protest in Core and Periphery States," 35; Hechter, "Dynamics of Secession," 269–75.

102. Kaplan, *Politics and the American Press*, 1.

103. Esp. in charges of corruption, e.g., Un Mejicano to *Santa Fe Weekly Gazette*, August 8, 1868, 2; Otro Corresponsal to Editor ("Respuesta"), *El Monito*, November 1, 1890, 2.

104. "A Remediar el Mal," *La Bandera Americana*, 2.

105. In 1875, the Republican County Convention of San Miguel County endorsed Stephen Elkins for reelection as delegate to Congress; "Convención Republicana del Condado de San Miguel," *La Beliota*, May 25, 1875, 2.

106. Karst, *Belonging to America*, 30–31.

107. Glazer, "Federalism and Ethnicity," 72–73, 81.

108. "Policies and Problems of the Confederation Government," Library of Congress.

109. Stratton, *Territorial Press of New Mexico*, 98.

110. Lamar, *Far Southwest*, 62, 127, 143.

111. Lamar, *Far*, 62, 127, 143. On the early statehood movements, see Gonzales, *Política*, 393–95, 356–57, 399–400, 501.

112. The shifts in acceptance and popularity associated with "Negro," "black," and "African American" nomenclatures illustrate the rise and decline of collective complexes of ethno-racial identity; see Martin, "From Negro to Black to African American."

Chapter 1

1. A substantial literature attests to the Spanish colonial roots of New Mexico's social differentiation and diversity. For a comprehensive review, see Sunseri, *Situational Identities,* 9–38. For a schematic account of Nuevomexicano differentiation in Mexican New Mexico, see Gonzales, *Política,* 66–69.

2. On the etymology of criollo, see Schwaller, *Géneros de Gente in Early Colonial Mexico,* 41–44.

3. Twitchell, *Spanish Colonial Lives,* 250. Vigil, Kaye, and Wunder (*Spain and the Plains,* 152) deny the scholarly consensus of a Creole grouping, claiming it was impossible to estimate their proportion "because social distinctions were blurred, so over a period of time all colonists professed allegiance to the group that defended the colony and upheld Spanish traditions on the frontier."

4. Kessell, *Spain in the Southwest,* 111.

5. Scholes, "Civil Government and Society in New Mexico," 98.

6. Frank, *From Settlers to Citizens,* 111–12.

7. Galgano, *Feast of Souls,* 152; Chávez, *But Time and Chance,* 20.

8. Hale, *Mexican Liberalism in the Age of Mora,* 217.

9. Chávez, *Très Macho,* 2; Frank, *From Settler to Citizen,* 152.

10. *Vecino* "refers to the non-Indian settlers of New Mexico." Literally "neighbor," its meaning included "a sense of belonging to the province in the late colonial New Mexican documents. Settlers were commonly referred to by Franciscans or provincial officials as 'vecinos' as distinct from 'Indios,' the inhabitants of the pueblos who represented another kind of neighbor"; Frank, *From Settler to Citizen,* 1.

11. Pino, *Exposición de la Provincia del Nuevo México,* 241

12. Galgano, *Feast of Souls,* 152. On Creoles struggling against gachupín accusations that they were too lazy and unfit to rule, see Vallen, "Conqueror and the Archive," 31.

13. Gutiérrez, *When Jesus Came,* 150–55; quote, Kiser, "The Politics of Slavery and Social Hierarchies," 292; also, Delay, *War of a Thousand Deserts,* 158.

14. Brading, *Origins of Mexican Nationalism,* 56; 31; also, Weber, *Mexican Frontier,* 35–42; Sánchez, *Between Two Rivers,* 100–1; Harper, "Juan Bautista," 20, 23.

15. Simmons, Spanish Government in New Mexico, 205–6.

16. Brading, *Origins of Mexican Nationalism,* 70, 72, 73–74.

17. Hale, *Mexican Liberalism in the Age of Mora,* 39, 42–43, 125–41: quote, 216; Brading, *Origins,* 70, 72, 73–74; Fowler, "Valentín Gómez Farías," 40–41. The protocols for legitimate participation in the "Spanish community" of New Spain required a genealogical certificate attesting to blood purity. As a result, "whites were mainly Creoles," and they considered themselves "of European" extraction; Mignolo, *Idea of Latin America,* 73–74.

18. Simmons, Spanish Government in New Mexico, 205.

19. See the short biographies in List of Mexican Governors of New Mexico, Wikipedia.

20. William G. Ritch to Epifanio Vigil, December 1, 1877; Donaciano Vigil Papers. State Archives of New Mexico Collection 1961–003; Biographical and Autobiographical Notes. Box 8487, folder 308; 1800s.

21. Donaciano Vigil to Honorable Assembly," June 18, 1846, in Vigil and Weber, *Arms, Indians and the Mismanagement*, 3.

22. Vigil and Boudreau, *Donaciano Vigil*: "Vigil's family tree," "Donaciano was a militia officer," "In a society of low literacy," 14–38; "Creole families typically," 45.

23. Vigil and Boudreau, *Donaciano Vigil*: "travels they conducted," 36; "Antonio Barreiro," 41–43.

24. Weber, *The Mexican Frontier*, 19.

25. Donaciano Vigil, autobiographical note, Donaciano Vigil Papers, State Archives of New Mexico; quoted also in Tórrez, "'El primer y principal ramo,'" 149. On New Mexico's state-supported church, see Perrigo, "New Mexico in the Mexican Period," 36–37.

26. Netanyahu, *Origins of the Inquisition*, 980.

27. Economic and ecclesiastical subjugation in New Spain resulted in eleven million Indigenous losing their lives in the eighty years after the Spanish invasion; Cocker, *Rivers of Blood*, 5.

28. Kiser, "The Politics of Slavery and Social Hierarchies," 287.

29. Montejano, *Anglos and Mexicans in the Making of Texas*, 35.

30. Gonzales, *Política*, 67–68; cf. Gregg, Commerce of the Prairies, 76; Horgan, Lamy of Santa Fe, 234.

31. For details, see Krauze, *Mexico*, 92–117.

32. Villoro, *Los Grandes Momentos Del Indigenismo En México*; re. Clavijero, 95–133; re. Mier, 137–147.

33. Brading, *Origins*: "welding together," 25; "historical indigenismo," 81, 32; 82–83, 84; Krauze, *Mexico*, 81, 79.

34. Mora, *Border Dilemmas*, 105–6.

35. Brading, *Origins*: "priest's consciousness," 23; "Creole priesthood," 83.

36. In his memoir; Romero, "Apología of Presbyter," 329; Chávez, *But Time and Chance*, 14–15.

37. Francis, "Padre Martinez," 267–68; Chávez, *Très Macho*, 8, 12.

38. Chávez, *Très Macho*, 12; Chávez and Chávez, *Wake for a Fat Vicar*, 39.

39. Chávez, *But Time and Chance*, 22–24.

40. "Obituario," El Nuevo-Mejicano, August 17, 1867, 1.

41. Chávez and Chávez, *Wake for a Fat Vicar*, 28.

42. Tórrez, ""El primer y principal ramo,'" 141.

43. Romero and Sandoval, *Reluctant Dawn*, 25; also, Chávez, *But Time and Chance*, 41; Mares, "Padre Martínez and Mexican New Mexico," 115.

44. Francis, "Padre Martinez," 158; Beck, *New Mexico*, 121. For the majority castas in the Nuevomexicano populace, see Frank, *From Settler to Citizen*, 177; Aragón, "People of Santa Fe," 397, 402–03; Gutiérrez, *When Jesus Came*, 196, 206.

45. Beck, *New Mexico*: "deprived of their rights," 121; Romero and Sandoval, *Reluctant Dawn*, 15.

46. Romero, "Apologia of Presbyter," 340.

47. Boyle, *Los Capitalistas.*

48. Martínez, *Esposición que el presbítero*, 5, 6, 7 (unnumbered), 269; Francis, "Padre Martinez," 158.

49. While leading insurgency, Morelos designed a program for establishing the Mexican nation and convened the Congress of Anáhuac for declaring Mexico's independence from Spain.

50. Chávez, *Très Macho*, 12; "Mexican patriotism and," Chávez and Chávez, *Wake for a Fat Vicar*: "Mexican patriotism," 39.

51. Chávez, *But Time and Chance*, 66, 68–69, 76–77; Chávez, *Très Macho*, 12. New Mexico Governor Antonio Narbona asked Martínez to spy on the illegitimate Manifest Destiny activities of the Americans; Mares, "Many Faces of Padre Antonio," 24.

52. Hale, *Mexican Liberalism*, 217.

53. In various proclamations; Twitchell, *History of the Military Occupation*, 221–22.

54. Quoted in Bloom, "New Mexico Under Mexican Administration 1821-1846: III," 41.

55. Warner, *Archbishop Lamy*, 108–9.

56. Chávez and Chávez, *Wake for a Fat Vicar*, 79; Warner, *Archbishop Lamy*, 109; Twitchell, *History of the Military Occupation*, 221.

57. Twitchell, *History of the Military Conquest*, 220.

58. Simmons, Spanish Government in New Mexico, 173.

59. For the details, see Gonzales, *Política*, 142.

60. Chávez, *But Time and Chance*, as its president, 86–90.

61. Pope Pius IX acceded to a synod of American archbishops and bishops for a vicariate apostolic for New Mexico, naming Lamy as its prelate; Bridgers, *Death's Deceiver*, 72.

62. Bridgers, *Death's*, 81–141; Francis, "Padre Martínez"; Chávez, *But Time and Chance*, 92–150; Chávez, *Très Macho*, 25–92; Chávez and Chávez, *Wake for a Fat Vicar*, 31–167; Aragón, *Padre Martínez and Bishop Lamy*, including an extensive bibliography, 133–41.

63. Chávez, *But Time and Chance*, 95; Mares, "Many Faces of Padre Martínez," 26; Bridgers, *Death's Deceivers*, 136–37.

64. In their "good cop, bad cop" routine, Machebeuf served as "hatchet man . . . so that the saintly Bishop Lamy could remain unsoiled by the dirty work of direct confrontation"; Bridgers, *Death's Deceiver*, 108.

65. Francis, "Padre Martínez," 265.

66. Chávez, *Très Macho*, 47–52; Chávez, *But Time and Chance*, 110–12; Mora, *Border Dilemmas*, 107.

67. For Gallegos's Creole lineage, see Chávez, *Très Macho*, 3–6; for his preparation for seminary, 9.

68. Chávez, *Très Macho*, 41–46, 52–62. In his experience, Gallegos participated in the selection of the equivalent representative from New Mexico to the Mexican Congress; Chávez, *Très Macho*, 17.

69. Gonzales, "Mexican Party, American Party," 263-67; Chávez, *Três Macho*, 63-65, 65-66, 70, 77-80.

70. Chávez and Chávez, *Wake for a Fat Vicar*, 95.

71. Otero's charges included: citizens of Mexico allowed to vote; judges of election, including a priest, telling Otero voters their votes could not be counted at the poll; keeping polls open after legal hours for pro-Gallegos voters while hindering Otero voters; more votes submitted for counting than there were names on the poll books, all of them pro-Gallegos; votes for Otero not counted by precinct judges; minors voting for Gallegos; a priest interfering with the submission of the poll book in a precinct; one poll book used in a precinct when two were required; votes for Otero left in the ballot box uncounted; judges of election not sworn in according to law; refusal of the Territorial Secretary to count legal votes for Otero; see United States, Papers and testimony in the case of Miguel A. Otero, contesting the seat of Jose M. Gallegos (5–7).

72. Warner, *Archbishop Lamy*, 94–95; Chávez, Três Macho, 89–90; Gonzales, *Política*, 309–10, 312–16.

73. Gamio, *Mexican Immigration to the United States*, 54.

74. "Contested Election—New Mexico," May 10, 1856, in Cong. Rec., House of Representatives, Misc. Report 90, 1–3; cf. Chávez, *Três Macho*, 90. For a detailed account of the election, including the candidate's appearance before Congress, see Gonzales, *Política*, 300–16.

75. "Contested Election—New Mexico," May 10, 1856, in Cong. Rec., House of Representatives, Misc. Report 90, 1–3; cf. Chávez, *Três Macho*, 90.

76. Chávez, *Três Macho*, 91.

77. Miguel A. Otero to the Editor of the Washington (DC) *Constitution*, January 5, 1861, in Stegmaier, "New Mexico's Delegate in the Secession Winter Congress, Part 2," 515–21.

78. Kiser, "The Politics of Slavery and Social Hierarchies," 293.

79. Bridgers, *Death's Deceiver*, 134–37.

80. Montejano, *Anglos and Mexicans*, 309.

81. For the detailed background on these problems, see Gonzales, *Política*, 252–53; also, Lee, "The Manliness to Defend Themselves,"167–70.

82. These developments are detailed and documented in Gonzales, *Política*, 252–53.

83. Gonzales, *Política*, 253.

84. Mantena, "The Crisis of Liberal Imperialism," 130–31 and passim.

85. Williams, "Liberalism, Colonialism and Liberal Imperialism," 101, 104, 107, 109, 112.

86. "Our Territory," *Santa Fe Weekly* Gazette, February 12, 1853; Gonzales, *Política*, 255.

87. Benedict, "Anniversary Address Delivered Before the Historical Society of New Mexico," 8.

88. Ritch, *Inaugural Address of Hon. W. G. Ritch, President*, 7, 8.

89. Whiting, "Minutes of the Historical Society of New Mexico," 259–308; Meketa, *Louis Felsenthal*, 20–22; Hunt, *Kirby Benedict*, 173–74.

90. Suggested in Lamar, *Far Southwest*, 146. On the definition of subaltern and its application to native elites in Latin America, see Reeves, *Ladinos with Ladinos, Indians with Indians*, 168.

91. Bushman, *America Discovers Columbus*, 45.

92. See Bushman, *America Discovers*, 8, for how American nationalists invented the myth of Columbus as the father of the United States.

93. Bushman, *America Discovers*, 107.

94. Williams, "Liberalism, Colonialism and Liberal Imperialism," 96.

95. Benedict, "Anniversary Address Delivered Before the Historical Society of New Mexico," 8, 9. For the speech, see Hunt, *Kirby Benedict*, 174–75.

96. Benedict, "Anniversary Address," 9.

97. Diffie, "Ideology of *Hispanidad*," 457. On *Hispanismo* nationally, internationally, and in New Mexico, see Nieto-Phillips, *Language of Blood*, 176–87.

98. Fisher-Onar, "Remembering Empires," 5.

99. Benedict, "Anniversary Address," 9.

100. See Bandelier and Rodack, *Discovery of New Mexico*, 43–44; also, Krieger, et al., *We Came Naked and Barefoot*, 7-20. For the authoritative Cabeza de Vaca story, see Reséndez, *Land So Strange*.

101. Benedict, "Anniversary Address Delivered Before the Historical Society of New Mexico," 10.

102. Benedict, "Anniversary," 11.

103. "When asymmetric power relations are inscribed in situations of cultural difference, the oppressors, like the oppressed, often inhabit the alien discourse of the opposing 'other,' building up hybrid representations that become the basis of much colonial practice"; Levin Rojo, *Return to Aztlan*, 11.

104. Benedict, "Anniversary": "no common," 8; "men and women," 11; "at the base," 13; "instructed," 15.

105. Benedict, "Anniversary," 15, 16–17.

106. Weber, "Scarce More Than Apes," 299; also, Resendez, *A Land so Strange*, 10.

107. Bushman, *America Discovers*, 10.

108. Benedict, "Anniversary": "descendants of," 5; "purely Spanish blood," 16–17.

109. "Revolution of 1837," Santa Fe New Mexican, December 24, 1863, 1.

110. Whiting, "Minutes of the Regular Meeting of the New Mexico Historical Society, December 31, 1860," microform, frames 165, 284, 289–90, 294, 300.

111. Facundo Pino and J. M. Gallegos, "Preamble and Resolutions of the Council and House of Representatives of the Legislative Assembly of the Territory of New Mexico, in Relation to the Hon. Kirby Benedict, Chief Justice." *Santa Fe Weekly Gazette*, February 1, 1862," 2.

112. Mora, *Border Dilemmas*, 27; Waldstreicher, In the Midst of Perpetual Fetes, 327.

113. General G. A. Smith speech at Fourth of July Commemoration, in "94th Independence Day, a Successful Celebration," *Santa Fe Weekly Post*, July 9, 1870, 1.

114. Cervantes, *Raíces del Periodismo Hispano*, 46.

115. Tránsito Mata, "Discurso," *La Revista de Alburquerque*, July 22, 1876, 3–4.

116. Mata, "Discurso."

117. DeLay, "Blood Talk," 246.

118. New Mexico. Legislative Assembly. Address of the Legislative Assembly of New Mexico. Three and a half months earlier, New Mexico Governor Henry Connelly put out his call for citizen mobilization that addressed some of the homeland notions Nuevomexicano lawmakers aggrandized into more a suggestive notion of nationhood. See Henry Connelly, "Proclamation by the Governor, 9 September 1861. Territorial Archives of New Mexico: Governor's Papers, Henry Connelly 1861–66, microform, reel 1, frame 343.

119. "La Fraternidad Piadosa del Condado de Taos," *El Nuevo-Mejicano*, April 6, 1867, 3–4.

120. New Mexico, Journals of the Legislative Assembly, December 4, 1865–February 1, 1866, microfilm, reel 3, frames 1 and 128.

121. Weigle, *Brothers of Light*, 63, 75.

122. "La Fraternidad Piadosa del Condado de Taos."

123. See Weigle, *Penitentes of the Southwest*, 5–13.

124. Some researchers favor a Third Order of St. Francis explanation, others a diffusion from Latin America, or an indigenous innovation. On the debate, see Florescano, Étnia, *Estado y Nación*, 314; Weigle, *Brothers of Light*, 142. On the literature on the Hermanos, see Pulido, *Sacred World of the Penitentes*, 53–56.

125. Knaut, *Pueblo Revolt of 1680*, 73.

126. Papers in the Case of J. Francisco Chaves vs. Charles P. Clever, Delegate from the Territory of New Mexico, 40th Congress, misc. doc. no. 154, 98.

127. Untitled, *Daily New Mexican*, August 26, 1868, 3.

128. Ambrosio Armijo to C. P. Clever ("Judge Armijo's Letter"), March 15, 1864, in *Rio Abajo Weekly Press*, May 3, 1864, 1.

129. "Antipatía de Raza," *Estafeta de Las Vegas*, in *Revista Republicana*, November 11, 1871, 3. Unless otherwise indicated, all translations from Spanish are mine.

130. Miguel E. Pino, Samuel Ellison, "Joint Resolution of the Legislative Assembly," *Weekly Gazette*, December 30, 1865, 2.

131. Antonio Gonzales, "Manifiesto Dirigido a los Mejicanos de Nuevo Mejico," in *El Nuevo Mexicano*, April 16, 1872, 4.

132. Williams, "Liberalism, Colonialism and Liberal Imperialism," esp. 99–103.

133. Williams, "Liberalism."

134. Donnelly, "Making of the New Mexico Constitution, Part 1," 462; Anonymous, "For the Constitution and a State."

135. Ting, "Social Construction of Nation," 454.

136. Keating, "Regionalism and Regionalization," n. p.

137. Doob, *Patriotism and Nationalism*, 229; Gans, *Limits of Nationalism*, 2, 97.

138. Keating, "Regionalism and Regionalization," n.p. On liberal nationalism among the Quebecois, see Bélanger, "Quebec Nationalism."

139. Fukuyama, *End of History and the Last Man*, 116; Deutsch, *Nationalism and its Alternatives*, 82.

140. Report of the Governor of New Mexico to the Secretary of the Interior, 1901, 59; Vaughn, *New Mexico History and Government*, 213. For an examination of

schooling in New Mexico prior to its US annexation, see Torrez, "El primer y principal ramo." Torrez has reason for thinking that the illiteracy rate may have been considerably lower, 148.

141. Williams, "Liberalism, Colonialism and Liberal Imperialism," 103. On civilizing missions in European colonialism, see Stoler and Cooper, "Modernizing Colonialism," 3–4.

142. "Escuelas," *Santa Fe Republican*, September 10, 1847, 3.

143. Oliverio, "El Educado y el Ignorante," *La Estafeta de Las Vegas*, repr. *La Revista Republicana*, October 7, 1871, 3; also, Oliverio, untitled, *La Estafeta de Las Vegas*, repr. in *Republican Review*, February 21, 1872, 3. Oliverio was a Euro-American, going in English by Oliver.

144. Bullis, "Brief History of Education," n.p.; "Governor Lane," *Gazette*, August 20, 1853, 2.

145. Laws of the Territory of New Mexico: passed by the Legislative Assembly, 1857–1858, 86–87.

146. Hills, "New-Mexican Spanish," 707; Ogden, *Historical Sketch of St. Michael's College*, 87–88; Demetrio Perez testimony, Chaves vs. Clever, House of Representatives, 40th Congress, 3rd session, misc. doc. no. 14, 3.

147. Lamar, *Far Southwest*, 144.

148. W. A. Clark to Editor, *Advertiser*, July 12, 1873, 1.

149. "Governor's Message," *Republican Review*, January 13, 1872, 1; New Mexico, *Laws of the Territory of New Mexico Enacted by the Legislative Assembly of 1871–1872*, 42.

150. "Governor's Message"; New Mexico, *Laws of the Territory of New Mexico Enacted by the Legislative Assembly of 1871–1872*, 42.

151. George G. Smith, "Ought New Mexico to be Admitted to the Union?," *Republican Review*, March 11, 1876, 1.

152. Lamar, *Far Southwest*, 145; Everett, "The Public School Debate in New Mexico," 115–16; C. R. to Editor, *Revista Católica*, in "Ese Proyecto de Escuela, "*Revista Republicana*, January 8, 1876, 3; Untitled, *Santa Fe Weekly New Mexican*, in *Republican Review*, January 15, 1876, 2.

153. C. R. to Editor, *Revista Católica*, in "Ese Proyecto de Escuela," *Revista Republicana*, January 8, 1876, 3.

154. Smith, "Protestant Schooling," 671; "Protestant consensus," 684, 685; "vital to the highest," 687, 690.

155. C. R. to Editor.

156. "The Jesuits and the School Law," *Republican Review*, March 4, 1876, 2.

157. J. A. Truchard, "The Answer," *Republican Review*, April 8, 1876, 1–2.

158. Truchard was one of six young priests brought to Santa Fe from France in 1856; Salpointe, *Soldiers of the Cross*, 208.

159. Salpointe, *Soldiers of the Cross*.

160. "La Vigesima-tercera Legislatura," *Revista Católica*, in *Revista de Albuquerque*, February 2, 1878, 3.

161. "La Vigesima-tercera."

162. "La Vigesima-tercera."

163. Quoted in Stratton, *Territorial Press of New Mexico*, 138–39.

164. *Territorial Press.*

165. Report of the Governor of New Mexico to the Secretary of the Interior, 62.

166. *País* connoting a "'region, kingdom, or province'"; Coronado, *World Not to Come,* 68.

167. José Francisco Chaves to Diego Archuleta, January 27, 1866, trans. in "That Terrible Scheme," *Weekly Gazette,* September 22, 1866, 2; Spanish extracts in "Aquel atentado Terrible," *Gazeta Semanaria de Santa Fe,* September 29, 1866, 3.

168. Un Observador to *Santa Fe Weekly Gazette/La Gaceta,* February 14, 1857, 3.

169. Mora, *Border Dilemmas,* 231–32.

170. E.g., Governor Lionel A. Sheldon's address to the Tertio-Millennial Commemoration, Santa Fe, in "Third of a Century," *Weekly New Mexican Review,* June 30, 1883, 1; Prince, *Historical Sketches of New Mexico,* 13.

171. Mora, *Border Dilemmas,* agrees (234).

172. Iliana Galea, "Cartas de relación de Hernán Cortez: las estrafalarias cartas originales de la conquista de México y su explicación." Grandesporques.com. https://grandesporques.com/cartas-de-relacion-de-hernan-cortes/.

173. Indicated in Villagrá, *Historia de la Nueva Mexico, del capitán Gaspar de Villagrá,* 224; also documents cited by Hackett, *Revolt of the Pueblo Indians of New Mexico* 1: xxix; Dodds, *On Savage Shores,* 23, 37, 183; Frank, *From Settler to Citizen,* 180; Frank, "'They Conceal a Malice Most Refined,'" 82–83; also, "Una Raza Que Se Extingue," *El Independiente,* August 10, 1895, 2; Leopoldo to Editor ("El Eco de la Capital"), *El Nuevo Estado,* August 23, 1915, 1.

174. Chacón, Meléndez, Lomelí, *Writings of Eusebio Chacón,* 139, 140, 144, 149, 153. Hackett (*Revolt of the Pueblo Indians,* 1: xxi) notes the prevalence of *nación* among the early Spanish colonials, e.g., Alonso de Benavides's 1630 *History of New Mexico* (*Memorial,* in Benavides and Morrow), 50, 81.

175. Doob, *Patriotism and Nationalism,* 188; Gans, *Limits of Nationalism,* 5.

176. Pueblo Indian, Hopi, Diné, and the Apache had creation stories of "pure" autochthony, their ancestors said to have emerged "(just as Pericles is said to have held for the Athenians) from the underworld of the soil;" Tuan, *Space and Place,* 154. See also, McPherson, *Viewing the Ancestors,* 33, 52–56, 61; "Creation: A Hopi Tale," *In the Beginning: Native American Creation Stories,* https://www.angelfire.com/ny5/spiritsong/InTheBeginning.html; Diné (Navajo), https://www.angelfire.com/ny5/spiritsong/OrigDine.html.

177. Lozano, *American Language,* 119.

178. Gans, *Limits of Nationalism,* 5.

179. Ting, "Social Construction of Nation," 468.

180. Mark, "Doctrine of Discovery." On the psychological history of "savage," see Jahoda, *Images of Savages.*

181. Scholes, "Civil Government and Society," 71.

182. It is "writing that conquers, treating the "New World as if it were a blank, 'savage' page on which Western desire will be written"; de Certeau, *Writing of History,* xxv; also quoted usefully for the consideration of the linguistic and written implementations of the Spanish conquest of New Mexico in Lane, "On Colonial Forgetting," 54.

183. Frank, "'They Conceal a Malice Most Refined,'" 87. As colonial administration proscribed Pueblo Indian officers such as governor, lieutenant, alguacil, and fiscal agent, the primary allegiance of the Pueblo Indians was to their native priests, including war priests; Kessel, Hendricks, and Dodge, "Introduction," 9, 11.

184. Pino, *Exposición*, 18–19.

185. "Las Aspiraciones e Ideales de Nuevo México," *Revista de Taos*, May 3, 1918.

186. Duchacek, "Antagonistic Cooperation," 6.

187. Kiser, "The Politics of Slavery and Social Hierarchies," 287.

188. Frank, "'They Conceal,'" 86, 81, 85.

189. Rael-Gálvez, "Identifying Captivity," 13–14, 28, 373.

190. Frank, "'They Conceal,'" 79–80.

191. Richmond, "Climax of Conflicts with Native Americans," 57, 60, 62–63, 65, 66; Gómez-Quiñones, *Roots of Chicano Politics*, 128, 149–54.

192. Larson, *Forgotten Frontier*, 39.

193. Mora, *Border Dilemmas*, 68.

194. Ball, "Fort Craig," 158.

195. Owen, *Two Alberts*, 21.

196. Owen, *Two Alberts*, 21–22.

197. "Excellent Conduct of the People of San Miguel," *New Mexican*, January 31, 1864, 2.

198. Instructions to the elected delegate to Congress from the New Mexico convention of 1849, in Prince, *New Mexico's Struggle*, 15–16.

199. Larson, *New Mexico's Quest*, 87.

200. "Our Indian Affairs," *New Mexican*, September 1, 1868, 1.

201. Theisen, "Jose Manuel Gallegos (1815–75)," 172–73.

202. J. J. Jr. to *Gaceta Semanaria de Santa Fe*, February 20, 1869, 3.

203. Jesús María Chávez's address to the New Mexico House of Representatives ("Discurso pronunciado por el Hon. Jesús María Chávez, Representante del Condado del Socrro"), *La Gazeta Semanaria de Santa Fe*, January 16, 1869, 3.

204. "Our Indian Affairs," *Santa Fe New Mexican*, September 1, 1868, 1.

205. Luis A. C. Baca to Editor ("Comunicado"), *Republican Review*, January 8, 1872, 3.

206. "Procedimientos de una junta pública que fue tenida en Abiquiu el dia 1 de Junio de 1872, *El Nuevo-Mejicano*, June 11, 1972, 2.

207. "Proceedings of a Republican Convention Assembled at Santa Fe, N.M., April 29th, 1871," *Santa Fe Weekly Post*, May 6, 1871, 2.

208. DeLay, "Blood Talk," 255.

209. Nelson, *Three-Cornered War*, 214.

210. Greiner quoted in Rael-Gálvez, "Identifying Captivity and Capturing Identity," 147; also 135, 245–46.

211. Brooks, "'Served Well by Plunder,'" 26.

212. Brooks, *Captives & Cousins*, 251–52.

213. Brooks, *Captives*, 254.

214. McNitt, *Navajo Wars*, 410.

215. Ball, "Fort Craig," 157; "responding to," 155.

216. Also phrased in terms of "war turn[ing] people into peoples," 254; and collective violence "facilitat[ing] the constitution of peoplehood on both sides of the borderland," 246; see DeLay, "Blood Talk."

217. "Memorial to the Senate and House of Representatives of the United States of America in Congress Assembled," n.d. (1860?), cited in Mora, *Border Dilemmas*, 63.

218. For the rise of the strongman *patrón* in New Mexico, see Alarid, *Hispano Bastion*, 17–29.

219. As the Abiquiu population was described: "a definite division . . . between those calling themselves *españoles,* and the motley inhabitants of Abiquiu itself who were variously designated as indios, mestizos, coyote, and genízaros"; Chávez, *Très Macho*, 2.

220. Rael-Gálvez, "Identifying Captivity," 18. The name "Genízaro" is said to have derived from the military use of captives, its etymology originating in the Ottoman Turkish Janissaries; see Bolton, *Spanish Borderlands*, 184.

221. An anonymously authored obituary for don Félix García of Santa Fe mourned "*los descendientes de la raza de caballeros españoles quienes primero poblaron este país*" (the descendants of the race of Spanish gentlemen who settled this land); "En Memoria," *Santa Fe Weekly Post*, April 20, 1872, 4.

222. Lamar, *Far Southwest*, 87.

223. Theisen, "Jose Manuel Gallegos," 167–68.

224. "Address of the Legislative Assembly of New Mexico," Santa Fe, January 29, 1862, RG 46, tray 1, folder 7, Territorial Archives of New Mexico, National Archives.

225. Vigil, *Los Patrones*, 77.

226. Tranquilino Luna to Fellow Citizens and Gentlemen of the Convention, *Campaign Bulletin* (Las Vegas, NM), August 25, 1880, 1.

227. Doob, *Patriotism and Nationalism*, 188.

228. Smith, *Myths and Memories of the Nation*, 7. Smith devotes chap. 5 to historical memory in nation construction.

229. O'Sullivan, *Indigeneity*, 35.

230. See, e.g., José Francisco Chaves testimony before Congress, extract from the *Congressional Record*, *Santa New Mexican*, March 17, 1870, 1; Henry Mercure, "The Indian Question in Tierra Amarilla," *Santa New Mexican*, July 13, 1871, 1; William F. Arny to Editors, *Santa Fe New Mexican*, March 16, 1870, 1.

Chapter 2

1. Lind, *Next American Nation*, 66.

2. The AT&SF Railroad spanned the territory north to south by 1881, the east-west axis well under way; see Bradley, *Story of the Santa Fe*, 207; Myrick, *New Mexico's Railroads*, xv–xvi.

3. Bradley, *Story*, 147, 148; Callon, *Las Vegas, New Mexico*, 187; cf. Lamar, *Far Southwest*, 143.

4. "New Mexico Speaks for Progress," *Santa Fe Post*, February 10, 1872, 1.

5. Anonymous to the *Republican Review*, July 15, 1871, 2.

6. Ramírez, "The Hispanic Political Elite," 538, 501, 517.

7. "Santa Fe's Triumph!," *Santa Fe New Mexican*, February 14, 1880, 2; also, Myrick, *New Mexico's Railroads*, 7. For Las Vegas, New Mexico's railroad celebration, see Blackshear, *Honor and Defiance*, 78.

8. "Inauguración del Camino Ferreo," *El Nuevo-Mejicano,* February 14, 1880.

9. Untitled obituary, *Las Vegas Free Press,* July 12, 1892, 1; Poldervaart, "Black Robed Justice in New Mexico," 26.

10. "Santa Fe's Triumph!"; "Inauguración del Camino Ferreo". Sena's remarks would have been translated as interpreters were in common use on public stages; see Lozano, *American Language*, 39.

11. Remarks published in "Santa Fe's Triumph!" For an extract, see Walter, "The Coming of the Railroad," 22–23; cf. Montgomery, *Spanish Redemption*, 55; Mora, *Border Dilemmas*, 188–89.

12. Prince, "New Mexico."

13. Prince, "New Mexico." María Montoya ("L. Bradford Prince," 188–89) suggests that Prince's view of Nuevomexicanos stemmed as a response to what he had read in W. W. H. Davis's *El Gringo*, describing them as "degraded," "naïve," and "pitiful."

14. Prince in "Santa Fe's Triumph!"

15. Prince, "Santa Fe's."

16. Anonymous to *New York Times* ("Greasers as Citizens"), February 6, 1882, 2.

17. Said, *Orientalism,* 31. For a cagy review of works that equate treatments of Nuevomexicanos and Puebloans with orientalism, see Carroll, "Debate over a Crypto-Jewish Presence in New Mexico," 13–14.

18. Davis, *El Gringo*: "cunning," 217; 174–286.

19. Anonymous to Editor.

20. Said, *Orientalism*, 31.

21. "Greasers as Citizens."

22. "Greasers."

23. Prince to Editor, *New York Times*, 2; scrap in Prince Papers, #7, Election 1882, NMSRCA; also, "New Mexico: A Defense of the People and Country: A Reply by Chief Justice Prince to a Slanderous Letter in the New York Times," CSWR.

24. Prince to Editor.

25. Prince to Editor.

26. Prince to Editor.

27. Prince, a graduate of the Columbia University School of Law School, worked for New York's Republican Party. His "good government" views and attempts to down corrupt Republican officials hurt his career. While in private practice, without "any application or request," he recalled, President Rutherford Hayes's administration offered him various federal appointments, including chief justice of the New Mexico Territory, which he turned down three times before accepting "at the urgent request" of Secretary of State William Evarts and the Department of Justice; Montoya, "L. Bradford Price," 182–83; also, "L. Bradford Prince," *Weekly New Mexican Review*, August 28, 1884, 1.

28. In a key difference, Progressives in the South were heavily involved in formal policies for Black uplift, often cast in race essentialist language; see, Hartman, *Wayward Lives*, 19–21, 182, 248, 250.

29. For a thorough critique, see Driver, "Rethinking the Interest-Convergence Thesis."

30. Montgomery, *Spanish Redemption*, 55.

31. "Pointers on Prince," *Daily Optic*, August 23, 1882; Election 1882 folder, Prince Papers #7, 282.

32. Bloom, "Historical Society Minutes," 251.

33. Ritch, *Inaugural Address of Hon. W. G. Ritch*, 2; Meketa, *Louis Felsenthal*, 85–87.

34. Ritch, *Inaugural Address*, 4, 5, 12–14.

35. Ritch, *Inaugural*, 5–6.

36. "New Mexico," *Weekly New Mexican Review*, July 19, 1883, 2.

37. For the claim of Denver inspiring the Tertio-Millennial Exposition, see Snead, "Picturesque, Romantic, Practical," 38–9. On Albuquerque's first territorial fair, see Turo, "Politics, Identity, and Statehood," 392.

38. See letterheads, Tertio-Millennial Collection, box 5, folder 2; Nieto-Phillips, *Language of Blood*, 162; Wilson, *Myth of Santa Fe*, 186. For other press reports and academic work on the Tertio-Millennial Exposition, see Melzer, *Maximiliano Luna*, 11n.50.

39. "Third of a Century," *New Mexican Review*, June 30, 1883, 1. Invitations went to President Arthur, cabinet members, congressmen, senators, and governors; Charles W. Greene to Mr. President (W. W. Griffin), May 17, 1883, Tertio-Millennial Collections, AC 204, folder 1, misc. correspondence.

40. Sheriff Romulo Martínez was on the board of directors and executive committee; County Commissioner Antonio Ortiz y Salazar on the board of directors; letterhead, Santa Fe Tertio-Millennial Anniversary Association and official card, "The Tertio-Millennial Anniversary Celebration, Mining and Industrial Exposition," Tertio-Millennial Collection Card, AC 204, folder 1, misc. correspondence; Tertio-Millennial Anniversary Association Invitation card, folder 2; Ellis, "Santa Fe's Tertio-Millennial, 1883," 123; "Report of Trinidad Alarid Auditor," 9, 102; "The Tertio-Millennial," *New Mexican Review*, July 26, 1883, 1; "Our Exposition," *New Mexican Review*, June 9, 1883, 2.

41. Nuevomexicanos on the board were Trinidad Romero, Rafael Romero, Romulo Martínez, and Antonio Abeytia; "Historical Society of New Mexico," cover page, 1880, Historical Society of New Mexico Collection, box 31; Montgomery, *Spanish Redemption*, 93–94.

42. Olzak, *Dynamics of Ethnic Competition and Conflict*, 162–64.

43. Greene to officers; Tertio-Millennial Collection, AC 204, folder 1, misc. correspondence; Ellis, "Santa Fe's Tertio-millennial, 1883," 123.

44. Stratton, *Territorial Press of New Mexico*, 27.

45. "Program: The Santa Fe Tertio-Millennial Anniversary, Character Celebration and Industrial Exposition" (hereafter Program), Tertio-Millennial Collection, AC 204, folder 1, misc. correspondence, Manuscript Collection, Miscellaneous Correspondence, Fray Angélico History Library, Museum of New

Mexico, Santa Fe (hereafter Tertio-Millennial Collection); "A Day's Doings," *New Mexican Review*, July 7, 1883, 3; "Walks and Talks," *New Mexican Review*, July 26, 1883, 4; "many centuries back," "Exposition Atoms," *New Mexican Review*, July 26, 1883, 3; Chávez, "Santa Fe's Own," 11.

46. "New Mexico Speaks For Progress," *Santa Fe Post*, February 10, 1872, 1.

47. "The Great Anniversary," *New Mexican Review*, June 9, 1883, 2.

48. Haines, *History of New Mexico*, 282. Prince likely gave information for Haines's account, the production of which relied on the "private subscription of more than 100 biographical sketches"; Sive, "Helen E. Haines, 1872–1961," 149.

49. "History of New Mexico," *New Mexican Review*, June 16, 1883, 1.

50. "Ancient City," *New Mexican Review*, June 23, 1883, 2.

51. Governor Lionel A. Sheldon address to the Tertio-Millennial commemoration, Santa Fe, in "Third of a Century," *New Mexican Review*, June 30, 1883, 1. *Denver Tribune* disputed Santa Fe's claim of settlement precedence, its "many years too late," awarding the honor to St. Augustine, Florida. *New Mexican Review* stood its ground; see "Ancient City," *New Mexican Review*, June 23, 1883, 2.

52. "Ancient City," 2.

53. Sheldon's address to the Tertio-Millennial commemoration.

54. Untitled, *New Mexican Review*, June 16, 1883, 4; "Tertio-Millennial," *New Mexican Review*, July 19, 1883, 3. On the Anglo-American search for Quivira and other wondrous sites, see Weber, "Reflections on Coronado," 5.

55. "Ancient City," *New Mexican Review*, June 23, 1883, 2.

56. "Ancient City," June 23. On the importance of "sentimental pastoral for American identity," see Marx, *Machine in the Garden*, 14, 21.

57. "Ancient City," *New Mexican Review*, June 23, 1883, 2.

58. "Ancient City," June 23.

59. "Ancient City," June 23.

60. Hammond, "Search for the Fabulous," 2.

61. Quoted in Curti, *Roots of American Loyalty*, 202; and Kaufmann, "American Exceptionalism Reconsidered," 19.

62. Quoted in "The Nation's Day," *New Mexican Review*, July 7, 1883, 1.

63. See, La Cueva Historic District, New Mexico, *Legends of America*, *https://* www.legendsofamerica.com/la-cueva-new-mexico/.

64. "Muere Quemado Don Rafael Romero en el Hotel de Roy," *Nuevo Estado*, July 29, 1918, 1.

65. Meyer, *Speaking for Themselves*, 169.

66. Bandelier, *Gilded Man*, 214; Knaut, *Pueblo Revolt of* 1680, 22–23; Flint, "Results and Repercussions," 234–35. Recent work argues that Coronado's expedition was foremostly the first of a three-pronged effort sponsored by the Spanish viceroy to find the route to East Asia, the so-called "Columbian project" initiated by Christopher Columbus; Flint and Flint, *Most Splendid Company*, 1, passim.

67. "Nation's Day," *New Mexican Review*, July 7, 1883, 1.

68. Bandelier, *Gilded Man*, 241–45.

69. "Power of precedence" is from Hudson, "'Forked Justice,'" 54.

70. Sarah Lee, "The Politics of Belonging: Autochthony in Modern Societies," n.p.

71. Anderson, *Imagined Communities*, 69.

72. Doob, *Patriotism and Nationalism*, 188.

73. Tertio-Millennial Card; Mauzy, "Tertio Millennial Exposition," 17–18.

74. "Tertio-Millennial," *New Mexican Review*, July 19, 1883, 4.

75. "Coronado's Cohorts," *New Mexico Review*, July 19, 1883, in Wilson, *Myth of Santa Fe*, 187; "Tertio-Millennial," *New Mexican Review*, July 19, 1883a, 3, in Wilson; Twitchell, *Old Santa Fe*, 402. Fifteen trunks of costumes were loaned to the Exposition by a "Madame Purcell" of St. Louis; Snead, "Picturesque, Romantic, Practical," 42–43.

76. Ramírez, "Hispanic Political Elite," 538.

77. Wilson, *Myth of Santa Fe*, 183; Lovato, *Santa Fe Hispanic Culture*, 48; also, "Corpus Cristi," *Daily New Mexican*, June 2, 1870, in Wilson, *Myth of Santa Fe*, 182; "Santa Fé, Sus Fiestas de Septiembre," Twitchell, *Spanish Archives of New Mexico*, vol. 2, no. 179; see also fig. 4.

78. Twitchell, *Old Santa Fe*, 402; "Coronado's Cohorts"; Mauzy, "Tertio millennial Exposition," 20. According to an editorial, "Even the Indian catches the spirit of progress when brought in contact with the railroad and telegraph, and the native Mexican vies with the frontiersman in the ready adoption of eastern fashions and American methods"; "Great Anniversary," *New Mexican Review*, June 9, 1883, 2.

79. "Tertio-Millennial," *New Mexican Review*, July 19, 1883a, 4.

80. On Delgado's career, see Read, *Illustrated History of New Mexico*, 747.

81. "Tertio-Millennial," *New Mexican Review*, July 19, 1883a, 4; "Coronado's Cohorts"; Mauzy, "Tertio Millennial Exposition," 20. Conklin was in 1883 clerk of the probate court; Santa Fe County, New Mexico, Genealogy and History, http://genealogytrails.com/newmex/santafe/bios6.html.

82. "Tertio-Millennial," *New Mexican Review*, July 19, 1883a, 3; Twitchell, *Old Santa Fe*, 406. Baca, from Seboyeta and veteran captain in the Civil War, served several terms in the territorial legislature; "Capt Roman Antonio Baca," *Find a Grave*, https://www.findagrave.com/memorial/17481131/roman_antonio-baca.

83. "Tertio-Millennial," *New Mexican Review*, July 19, 1883a, 4; Twitchell, *Old Santa Fe*, 403; "Coronado's Cohorts"; Mauzy, "Tertio Millennial Exposition," 20.

84. The *New Mexican Review* called it a Coronado portrayal. However, it included details that are not associated with Coronado's encounters with the Pueblos but parallel the events of de Vargas's second entrada and battle with the Santa Fe Pueblos, recognized, it seems, by Thomas Chávez, "Santa Fe's Own: A History of Fiesta," 11. In the following descriptions taken from the *New Mexican Review*, "de Vargas" is substituted for "Coronado."

85. Pacheco, "Nativos, criollos y mestizos en la creación del Camino Real," 28–29; Rabasa, *Writing Violence on the Northern Frontier*, 112. For Rabasa's critique of the overall significance of the *Ordenanzas* for the administration of New Spain, see 5, 112, 114–20, 142–43, passim.

86. Wilcox, *Pueblo Revolt and the Mythology of Conquest*, 6.

87. *Adelantado*: an advance man named as the governor of a frontier region and charged with conquering it "in exchange for funding and organizing the

initial explorations, settlements, and pacification of the target area on behalf of the Crown of Castile"; Fisher, *Viceregal Administration*, 81; also, Carroll, et al., eds., *Exposición de la Provincia*, 165n72.

88. Hernán Cortez recited the requerimiento on his taking of Tenochtitlan; Gunberg, "Poderes y Política de Hernán Cortez," 473–500; Gutiérrez, *When Jesus Came*, 48–49. For an insightful discussion of the codification of the Cortez model of the proclamation in literature and ritual, see Lane, "On Colonial Forgetting," 56–58.

89. See, Williams, *American Indian in Western*, 88–93. For the Spanish language text of Oñate's "Act of Taking Possession of New Mexico," see Villagrá, *Historia de La Nueva México*, 131–138. For the translation, see Read, *Illustrated History of New Mexico*, 203–10; Hammond and Rey, *Don Juan de Oñate*, 329–36; Read and Baca, *Illustrated History of New Mexico*, 203–10; Prince, *Spanish Mission Churches*, 33–37.

90. Martinez, "Spanish Brought the 'Requerimiento.'"

91. Hammond and Rey, *Don Juan de Oñate*, 337–62.

92. Martinez, "Spanish Brought the 'Requerimiento.'"

93. Villagrá, *Historia de La Nueva México*, 1610, 152.

94. Rabasa, *Writing Violence*, 182.

95. The following summary of the events that led up to the 1680 Pueblo Indian Revolt is based on studies citing original sources, including: Scholes, "Civil Government and Society," 80–85; Hammond, *Don Juan de Oñate*, 106–23; Hammond and Rey, *Oñate, Colonizer of New Mexico*, 16–35; Kessell, Hendricks, and Dodge, "Introduction," 12–27; Knaut, *Pueblo Revolt*, 3–10, 34–62, 82, 152–70; Silverberg, *Pueblo Revolt*, 42–130; Gutiérrez, *When Jesus Came*, 120–37; Bancroft, *History of Arizona and New Mexico*, 174–223; Blackhawk, *Rediscovery of America*, 33. For debate on the reasons for the Revolt, see Weber, *What Caused the Pueblo Revolt?*

96. Bailey, *Diego de Vargas and Reconquest of New Mexico*, 1.

97. Formerly spelled Popé.

98. Knaut, *Pueblo Revolt*, 11–15.

99. Leonard, "Introduction:" re. apostasy, 13; re. silver, 33–35.

100. Kessell, Hendricks, Dodge, "Preface," xi.

101. Athearn, "Reconquest of New Mexico," 14–15. On de Vargas's appointment as governor of New Mexico, see Leonard, "Introduction," 31–39.

102. The following outline of the de Vargas's reoccupation of New Mexico in 1692 is taken primarily from Espinosa, *Crusaders of the Rio Grande*, 49, 76–99, 109–37, 142, 158–60, 368, supplemented by Hackett, *Revolt of the Pueblo Indians*, vol.1, xxi–lii; Gutiérrez, *When Jesus Came*, 120–37.

103. Leonard, "Introduction," 185; Bancroft, *History of Arizona and New Mexico*, 185.

104. "Parallel rites such as head washing, or baptism, the aspersal of holy water, singing, and the use of altars encouraged acceptance"; Kessell, Hendricks, Dodge, "Introduction," 6.

105. For de Vargas's own account of these excursions, see Sigüenza y Góngora, *Mercurio Volante* (in Spanish), 111–28; (in English), 69–88.

106. Tertio-Millennial," *New Mexican Review*, July 19, 1883a, 4.

107. Twitchell, *Old Santa Fe*, 404; Spude, "Progressive Santa Fe," 345.

108. Espinosa, *Crusaders of the Rio Grande*, 67–68. With some difference in the wording of the ritual, see Leonard's translation of de Vargas's report, in Sigüenza y Góngora, *Mercurio Volante of Don Carlos de Sigüenza Y Góngora*, 65–66.

109. Xavier's toma is trans. from the original in Hackett, *Revolt of the Pueblo Indians*, vol. 2:210–11.

110. Leonard, "Introduction," 17, 20 , 41, 44.

111. "Apuntes historicos de la Conquista de la Nuevo Mejico," Donaciano Vigil papers.

112. "Tertio-Millennial," *New Mexican Review*, July 19, 1883a, 4.

113. "Tertio-Millennial"; Twitchell, *Old Santa Fe*, 404.

114. The New Mexico governor betrayed forgiveness at Santa Fe, executing seventy rebels, including a chief on the charge of treason "against God and the Royal Crown." Angered by the executions, Pueblos, including medicine-men, fought for their sovereignty until their defeat in the unified revolt of 1696; Espinosa, *Crusaders of the Rio Grande*, 161–62; Bailey, *Diego de Vargas*, 226–45.

115. Wilson, *Myth of Santa Fe*, 208.

116. In "cultural objectification," arrays of cultural events, programs, policies, and regulations are organized, used, projected or proclaimed by ethnonationalists as articles of their people's "authentic" heritage, backed by history, anthropology, and archaeology; see Handler, *Nationalism and the Politics of Culture*, 13.

117. Žižek, *Sublime Object of Ideology*, 102.

118. "Tertio-Millennial," *New Mexican Review*, July 19, 1883a, 4.

119. "Tertio-Millennial," July 19.

120. "Tertio-Millennial," July 19.

121. "Ancient City," *New Mexican Review*, June 23, 1883, 2.

122. "New Mexico," *New Mexican Review*, July 19, 1883, 2.

123. Ellis, "Santa Fe's Tertio-Millennial," 124–25; Tertio-Millennial," *New Mexican Review*, July 19, 1883b. On the Mesilla Scouts, see Lee, "Manliness to Defend Themselves," 321.

124. The following account of Luna's address is based on "Speech of Hon. Tranquilino Luna," *New Mexican Review*, June 23, 1883, 2.

125. "Third of a Century," *New Mexican Review*, June 30, 1883, 1.

126. Simmons, *Spanish Government in New Mexico*, 67–68; Simmons, *Coronado's Land*, 42; Chacón, "Report of Governor Fernando de Chacón, 162–72.

127. Luna public address.

128. "Third of a Century."

129. Hinsley, *Savages and Scientists*, 146–51.

130. "Ancient City," *New Mexican Review*, June 23, 1883, 2.

131. The *New Mexican Review*'s spelling of the chief's name was Pa-Ta-Wah-Ti-Wa. I use Palowahtiwa from Green, *Cushing at Zuni*, 301.

132. For a tribute to Cushing's research, see Bandelier and Rodack, *Adolph F. Bandelier's Discovery of New Mexico*, 93.

133. "Tertio-Millennial," *New Mexican Review*, July 19, 1883a, 4; Twitchell, *Old Santa Fe*, 405. On Cushing's beleaguered fieldwork with the Zuñi, see Pandey, "Anthropologists at Zuni."

134. Palowahtiwa address at the Tertio-Millennial, in "Tertio-Millennial," *New Mexican Review*, July 19, 1883a, 4; also, Green, *Cushing at Zuni*, 301–2; with editorial changes, Twitchell, *Old Santa Fe*, 404–6.

135. Palowahtiwa address.

136. While Cushing explained that Nu-we likely meant Cabeza de Vaca, Twitchell says that the Zuñi "never heard" of him, "except from Spaniards who later explored the country" and had escaped "the fate of a 'long rest in the magic blanket"; Palowahtiwa address, *Old Santa Fe*, 405.

137. Last passage from Twitchell, *Old Santa Fe*, 406. In the *New Mexican Review*, it reads, "But when he opened his sticks that read thunder (so said our grandfathers) the war vanished as a rainstorm does when it lightnings [*sic*], and we found we were brothers."

138. Tertio-Millennial," *New Mexican Review*, July 19, 1883b.

139. Twitchell (*Old Santa Fe*, 407) gives a fuller account of Niit'a-héõde's remarks than the more abbreviated one in "Tertio-Millennial," *New Mexican Review*, July 19, 1883b, 3.

140. Opler and Opler ("Mescalero Apache History in the Southwest") express concern regarding the quoting of Niit'a-héõde's remarks (31–32).

141. San Juan address, "Tertio-Millennial," *New Mexican Review*, July 19, 1883a, 4; Twitchell, *Old Santa Fe*, 406.

142. San Juan address, "Tertio-Millennial," July 19. For a description of Victorio's warpath campaign and death, see Debo, *Geronimo*, 119–24.

143. San Juan (Niit'a-héõde) address, Twitchell, *Old Santa Fe*, 408.

144. "Tertio-Millennial," *New Mexican Review*, July 19, 1883a, 1.

145. Gómez, *Manifest Destinies*, 50–56.

146. Montgomery, *Spanish Redemption*, 96.

147. "Tertio-Millennial," *New Mexican Review*, July 19, 1883b, 3; Twitchell, *Old Santa Fe*, 407–08.

148. One correspondent to a Kansas newspaper deplored the "want of attendance" in July, calling it "deplorable, humiliating, grievous, especially when it is the fact that the exhibition is a good one"; Snead, "Picturesque, Romantic, Practical," 43.

149. "The Tertio-Millennial," *New Mexican Review*, July 26, 1883, 1; also, "Tertio-Millennial," *New Mexican Review*, July 19, 1883b, 4; Ellis, "Santa Fe's Tertio-Millennial, 1883," 122.

150. Montgomery, *Spanish Redemption*, 95.

151. "The Eastern Idea," *New Mexican Review*, January 10, 1884, 2.

152. Turo, "Politics, Identity, and Statehood," 404.

Chapter 3

1. For realms of memory in France, see Nora, *Realms of Memory*, xvii–xviii. Important to note, "Since the 1980s the—perhaps obsessive—pursuit of memory has become omnipresent . . . in such diverse fields as historiography, psychoanalysis, visual and performative arts, information technology, and media studies. It also impacts landscapes, architectures, public art, and public space"; Knight and Senie, *A Companion to Public Art*, 51. For useful reviews of Nora's monumental three-volume project, see Bodnar, "Pierre Nora, National Memory, and Democracy"; Tai, "Remembered Realms."

2. Prince Address, 1883 Territorial Fair, verbatim in "Territorial Fair," *New Mexican Weekly Review*, October 4, 1883, 2; Prince, "New Mexico: Its Wonderful Resources and Products, past and Present: An Address Delivered to the Territorial Exposition at Albuquerque, October 1, 1883, CSWR; "The Territorial Fair," *New Mexican Weekly Review*, October 4, 1883, 2.

3. Turo, "Politics, Identity, and Statehood," 411.

4. Spude, "Progressive Santa Fe," 342.

5. "Baldacci's Break," *New Mexican Review*, October 23, 1884, 1.

6. Quoted in *La Voz del Pueblo*, August 22, 1891, 2.

7. T. B. Catron to Joseph McKenna, Attorney General of the United States, April 17, 1897; Catron Papers, Series 402 (1 box only), folder 1.

8. Néstor Montoya, "La Legislatura," *La Voz del Pueblo*, February 11, 1893.

9. Untitled editorial, *La Voz del Pueblo*, May 18, 1901, 2; G. L. Dybwad and Joy V. Bliss, "New Mexico Territory at the World's Columbian Exposition," *Fair News*, March 1993, https://www.bookstopshere.com/publications/NewMexicoTerritory.pdf.

10. "Gacetilla," *La Opinión Pública*, May 14, 1893, 2.

11. "First Settlement of New Mexico," *Santa Fe New Mexican*, June 29, 1898.

12. Chamita Celebration," *Santa Fe New Mexican*, July 8, 1898. For one major study of the matachines dance, see Rodriguez, *Matachines Dance.*

13. "First Settlement of New Mexico."

14. "Chamita Celebration," *Santa Fe New Mexican*, July 15, 1898, 4.

15. Johnson, "Cast in Stone," 51.

16. "La Restauración del Capitolio," *El Independiente*, February 9, 1895, 1.

17. "Reminiscencia del Pasado," *La Voz del Pueblo*, June 15, 1901, 1; "Discurso del Hon D. Pérez," *La Voz del Pueblo*, June 22, 1901, 2; José D. Sena remarks, "Otro Discurso," *La Voz del Pueblo*, June 22, 1901, 2; Sánchez, "It Happened in Old Santa Fe," 267.

18. Petterson, "Monumental Landscape from Below."

19. "Otros Monumentos," *El Independiente*, August 8, 1901, 1.

20. Los Primeros Pobladores de Nuevo México to the people of New Mexico, in "Dad ayuda a Objeto tan Loable," *La Hormiga de Oro*, September 5, 1903, 1; "Héroes da la Conquista Española," *La Bandera Americana*, September 11, 1903, 2.

21. "Oñate y Vargas—La Propiedad de Erigir Monumentos Á Estos Heroes," *El Independiente*, January 21, 1904, 1, 2.

22. L. B. Prince to Dear Sir, solicitation, November 25, 1904, Secundino Romero Papers, box 2, folder 24.

23. "Historical Society," *New Mexican Review*, January 24, 1884, 2.

24. Meléndez, *So All Is Not Lost*, 126, 127, 130.

25. Lomelí, "A Native of the Southwest," 12; Meyer, *Speaking for Themselves*, 188.

26. Lamadrid, *Hermanitos Comanchitos*, 181–82.

27. Roeder, "Los Comanches," 213, 217; Espinosa, *Los Comanches*. On the plot, see Frank, *From Settler to Citizen*, 62–64.

28. Lomelí, "An Illustrious Pioneer of Early Hispanic Letters," 15.

29. Lamadrid, *Hermanitos Comanchitos*, 182.

30. Chaves, *Defeat of the Comanches*.

31. Lamadrid, *Hermanitos*, 182.

32. Benjamin M. Read, "Apreciones de Don Benjamín M. Read Sobre el Profesor Espinosa y Sus Estudios Nuevo Mejicanos," *La Revista de Taos*, July 28, 1911.

33. "Hon. Pedro Perea, Republican Candidate," *New Mexican*, October 22, 1898, 2.

34. "Hon. Manuel C. de Baca," *El Independiente*, May 12, 1898, 2.

35. "Roman L. Baca," *El Nuevo Mexicano*, October 27, 1906, 1.

36. "ISIDORO ARMIJO, Candidato Republicano, para Escribano de Pruebas, Condado de Doña Ana," *Nuevo Mexicano*, October 27, 1906, 1.

37. "El Hon. Frank A. Hubbell," *El Independiente*, August 1, 1901, 2.

38. "Noticias Locales," *La Voz del Pueblo*, August 25, 1894, 4, 1.

39. "*Crear un bajo y cobarde aborrecimiento en el pecho de los Anglo-americanos contra sus condiudadanos y vecinos de origen español*"; "Un Agitador Pernicioso," *La Voz del Pueblo*, August 25, 1900, 1.

40. "La Restauración del Capitolio."

41. Smith, "Introduction," 6.

42. Smith, "Towards a Theory of Ethnic Separatism," 30–31, 26–27.

43. Smith, *Myths and Memories of the Nation*, 7. Smith devotes chap. 5 to the theme of historical memory and ethnic nationalism.

44. Prince, *Historical Sketches of New Mexico*, front; cf. Mora, *Border Dilemmas*, 188–89.

45. Smith, "Introduction," 6.

46. See Gans, *Limits of Nationalism*, 66.

47. Meléndez, *So All Is Not Lost*, 7.

48. "Los Historiadores," *El Independiente*, March 6, 1895, 1; trans. in Meléndez, *Citizens by Treaty*, 80–84.

49. Saxton, "Ethnocentrism in the Historical Literature of Territorial New Mexico," 373.

50. Smith, *Nations and Nationalism in a Global Era*, 63.

51. "Los Historiadores," *El Independiente*, March 6, 1895, 1.

52. On the literary uses of primal nature, see Marx, *Machine in the Garden*, 27, 35, 36, 43.

53. "Los Historiadores," *El Independiente*, March 6, 1895, 1.

54. "Los Historiadores," March 6.

55. Read, *Historia Ilustrada de Nuevo México*, 460.

56. Lomelí, "Native of the Southwest, 10. Chacón in his youth was constantly reminded of his family's "illustrious lineage" to the Marquis de la Peñuela, Admiral Don José Chacón Medina y Salazar," which could not have been true as the Marquis was childless; Nieto-Phillips, *Language of Blood*, 15.

57. Lomelí, "Native of the Southwest," 10, 11.

58. Lomelí, "An Illustrious Pioneer of Early Hispanic Letters," 16, 17; also, Meléndez, "Introduction," 5.

59. Meléndez, "Introduction," 8.

60. Meléndez, *So All Is Not Lost*, 118.

61. Lomelí, "Servant of the Southwest," 10.

62. Eusebio Chacón, "Descubrimiento y conquista de Nuevo México en 1540 por los Españoles," *Las Dos Repúblicas*, March 14, 1896; Lomelí, *Writings of Eusebio Chacón*, 126–28.

63. Lomelí, "A Native of the Southwest," 10.

64. Bandelier, *Gilded Man*, 1. According to Bandelier, Coronado's travels were worthy of distinction save the abductions of the chiefs at Pecos and the cruelties against the Tiguas at Bernalillo, which Bandelier blamed on García López de Cárdenas. As he claimed, "The conception which has often been formed of Coronado as a wicked adventurer is therefore not just" (249).

65. Chacón, "Descubrimiento y conquista de Nuevo México en 1540 por los Españoles," *Las Dos Repúblicas*, March 28, 1896, 131–33.

66. *Las Dos Repúblicas*, April 18, 1896, 145–48, 150–52, 60–62, 155–57.

67. *Las Dos Repúblicas*, May 23, 1896, 64–65.

68. Lomelí, "Illustrious Pioneer," 18–19.

69. The earliest attempts at having a distinctly Nuevomexicano history came in 1894 in a biweekly series of short biographies, called "textual snapshots"; "New Mexico and its distinguished men," by Pablo Escobar in *La Opinión Publica*"; Meléndez, *So All Is Not Lost*, 115–16. The biographies were bundled separately, sold by subscription, and advertised in territorial newspapers; Meyer, *Speaking for Themselves*, 187.

70. Meyer, "Contesting History," 51.

71. Thoma, *Historia Popular*, 5; Nieto-Phillips, *Language of Blood*, 188. On Thoma's work, see Meyer, *Speaking for Themselves*, 188–90.

72. Saxton ("Ethnocentrism in the Historical Literature") somewhat misleadingly calls the work "essentially a drastically reduced version" of Bancroft (372).

73. Pino, *Exposición Sucinta*, 245–46.

74. Thoma, *Historia Popular De Nuevo México*, 139.

75. Thoma, *Historia*, 141.

76. Thoma, *Historia*, 143.

77. Report of the Governor of New Mexico to the Secretary of the Interior, 1901, 62.

78. Mount, "Nuevo Mexicanos and the War of 1898," 382.

79. Adelfa, "Correspondencia de Trinidad," *El Boletín Popular*, August 19, 1897, 1.

80. "La Asamblea Legislativa," *El Independiente*, January 30, 1897.

81. "El Espíritu Guerrero," *El Independiente*, March 3, 1898, 1.

82. John Bonner, "As We Live Now," *Leslie's Weekly*, July 29, 1897, 74; Spanish trans. in "Los Así Llamados Críticos," *La Voz del Pueblo*, August 7, 1897, 2.

83. "Lealtad Neo-Mexicana," *Hormiga de Oro*, repr. in *El Independiente*, August 4, 1898, 3.

84. Jones, *Birthright Citizens*, 11.

85. Booth, "Communities of Memory," 251.

86. "El Espíritu Guerrero," *El Independiente*, March 3, 1898, 1.

87. For discussion of Nuevomexicano birthrights, see Lozano, *American Language*, 120.

88. Addressed in "Los Voluntarios de Nuevo México," *El Independiente*, May 12, 1898, 1.

89. For analysis, see Mount, "Nuevo Mexicanos and the War of 1898," 388–90.

90. "Nuevo México y los 'Chiflados,'" *El Independiente*, August 4, 1898, 1.

91. Melzer and Mingus, "Wild to Fight," 111.

92. "Los Voluntarios de Nuevo México," *El Independiente*, May 12, 1898, 1.

93. Miguel Antonio Otero, interview extract, in "El Gobernador Otero en Washington," *El Independiente*, August 25, 1898, 2.

94. Melzer and Mingus, "Wild to Fight," 111.

95. Melzer, *Captain Maximiliano Luna*: "American to the core" 103, 104–5; "of pure Spanish blood," 143, 155, 345; "of pure Spanish descent," 313.

96. Mount, "Nuevo Mexicanos and the War of 1898," 385.

97. "¡Viva la Union! Nuevo México al Frente," *El Independiente*, May 5, 1898, 1.

98. "¡Viva la Union!"

99. "Nuevo México y los 'Chiflados,'" *El Independiente*, August 4, 1898, 1.

100. "Nuevo México y los 'Chiflados.'"

101. "Nuestros Primos de Ultramar," *El Independiente*, February 15, 1900, 1.

Chapter 4

1. Un Mexicano, untitled verse, *La Voz del Pueblo*, November 3, 1894, 4.

2. Anonymous to *El Nuevo Mejicano*, "Acrimonia Política Entre Los Nativos de Nuevo Méjico," repr. *El Monitor*, June 11, 1891, 1.

3. "¡Nuestros Conciudadanos Mexicanos!," *El Tiempo*, August 25, 1892, 2.

4. "Para que sepan que los Mexicanos saben resentir los insultos que se les han arrojado los cabecillas de aquel partido en esos condados"; "Larrazola [*sic*] es el Candidato," *El Farol* (Capitán), September 25, 1906, 1.

5. Ebright, *Land Grants and Lawsuits*, 37.

6. The US General Accounting Office identified 295 land grants coming under US adjudication in the nineteenth century, most of them communal; General Accounting Office, *Treaty of Guadalupe Hidalgo*, 22–2; Ebright, *Testimony*, 6–7.

7. Caffey, *Chasing the Santa Fe Ring*, 10; Sánchez, *Forgotten People*, 18–19.

8. For early members of the Ring, see Lamar, *Far Southwest*, 128–29. As Lamar notes, "every five years the personnel changed somewhat" (130). For the Ring and Catron's role in it, see Caffey, *Chasing the Santa Fe Ring*.

9. Stratton, *Territorial Press of New Mexico*, 131.

10. Correia, "Making Destiny Manifest," 92.

11. Deutsch, *No Separate Refuge*, 23.

12. See, "La Mala Política y sus Resultados," *La Voz del Pueblo*, May 9, 1896, 2.

13. Antonio Lucero address before the Archaeological Institute, Santa Fe, August 24, 1914, in "Eloquent Brief for Spanish-American by State Secretary," *Santa Fe New Mexican*, August 25, 1914, 3; trans. in "Habla el Secretario de Estado," *El Nuevo Mexicano*, September 3, 1914, 1.

14. Rosenbaum, *Mexicano Resistance in the Southwest*, 35.

15. Montoya, *Translating Property*, 38–39, 71–75, 96–113, 121–38, 143–56, 192–206.

16. Correia, *Properties of Violence*; Torrez, "La Mano Negra," passim.

17. Rosenbaum, *Mexicano Resistance in the Southwest*, 277, 279, 281; "Mass Meeting," *Daily Optic*, March 8, 1884, 1.

18. "Al Pueblo Mejicano!," *El Boletín Popular*, September 2, 1886, 1; "Ecos Políticos," *La Voz del Pueblo*, September 24, 1892, 1; "Joseph es el Escojido de la Gran Convención," *La Voz del Pueblo*, September 17, 1892, 2.

19. "Plataforma del Condado de Rio Arriba," *La Voz del Pueblo*, June 20, 1908, 2.

20. First quote, Gellner, *Nationalism*, 48; second quote, Gellner, *Nations and Nationalism*, 74; also, Smith, *Nationalism in the Twentieth Century*, 3.

21. R. M. López to Secundino Romero, April 26, 1902, Secundino Romero Papers, box 1, folder 13.

22. "Gran Excursión," *La Voz del Pueblo*, September 3, 1892, 1; also, "Comentos Generales," *La Voz del Pueblo*, March 11, 1893, 1.

23. "Otro Agente," *La Voz del Pueblo*, September 7, 1895, 2.

24. "Soplando el Fuelle," *La Voz del Pueblo*, May 16, 1908, 2.

25. Westphall, *Mercedes Reales*, 43, 45–6, 105–6. Westphall calls the constant attacks on Catron unfair (70–71).

26. "Al Pueblo Mejicano!," *El Boletín Popular*, September 2, 1886, 1; "Ecos Políticos," *La Voz del Pueblo*, September 24, 1892, 1; "Joseph es el Escojido."

27. Anonymous, untitled, *El Hispano Americano*, October 15, 1892, 2.

28. "Pancho y Chepe," *La Gazeta Semanaria de Santa Fe*, January 9, 1869, 3; Cerrando la Sangrieta y Profunda Herida," *La Unión*, repr. *Borderer/ El Fronterizo*, October 26, 1872, 3.

29. According to former Territorial Governor Miguel A. Otero, the "notorious fact [is] that territories had suffered much in the past at the hands of disgraceful carpetbaggers sent out from back east who knew little law and still less about the problems of the West"; *My Nine Years as the Governor*," 24; see also, Gill and Goff, "Edmund Francis Dunne and the Public School Controversy," 372; Limbaugh, *Rocky Mountain Carpet-baggers*; untitled editorial, *New Mexico Union*, June 5, 1873, 1.

30. Anonymous, "Don Tomás Borrego Catron," *La Voz del Pueblo*, October 13, 1894, 4.

31. E.g., untitled editorial, *La Voz del Pueblo*, December 22, 1894, 2; "H. B. Fergusson," *El Labrador*, October 6, 1896, 1; Uno to Editor, *Daily Optic*, repr. *El Labrador*, September 22, 1896, 2.

32. Untitled editorial, *La Voz del Pueblo*, December 22, 1894, 2.

33. "Nuevo México y Sus Honorables Principios," *La Voz del Pueblo*, September 24, 1892, 2; also, "El Partido del Pueblo en Guadalupe," *La Voz del Pueblo*, September 24, 1892, 1; "Ecos Políticos," *La Voz del Pueblo*, September 24, 1892, 1.

34. Anonymous, "Los Americanos," in Espinosa, *Romancero De Nuevo Méjico*, 7.

35. "Concerning Wool," *New Mexican Review*, June 9, 1883, 2.

36. George W. Gregg to R. E. Twitchell, October 22, 1892, Catron papers, box 401, folder 3.

37. Francis H. Atkins, "The Health of Las Vegas, New Mexico," paper read before the American Climatological Association, Denver, September 1890, Huntington Library, Rare Books Collection, 1.

38. Fiske is identified in Otero, *My Nine Years as Governor*, 147.

39. "Cogent Reasons for Statehood: The Evils of Territorial Government. An Appeal to the Senate," June 1902; circular, Thomas Catron papers, Series 402, folder 2, Charges against Governor Otero.

40. Quoted in Dargan, "New Mexico's Fight for Statehood, VII," 169.

41. "La Boleta Legislativa," *El Farol*, October 16, 1906, 4, https://digitalrepository.unm.edu/cgi/viewcontent.cgi?article=1040&context=el_farol_news.

42. Mora, *Border Dilemmas*," 234.

43. "¡Que Descaro!" *El Guía de Santa Fe*, September 2, 1886, 2.

44. In *El Nuevo Mexicano*, repr. in *El Monitor*, June 11, 1891, 1.

45. "Lazos Fraternales," *El Independiente*, December 7, 1895, 1.

46. Untitled editorial, *El Guía de Santa Fe*, October 16, 1886, 4. *El Guía* is catalogued as a campaign sheet with editor and publisher unknown; Stratton, *Territorial Press of New Mexico*, 286.

47. Samuel [C. Clark?] to R. E. Twitchell, October 19, 1892, Catron papers, box 401, folder 3.

48. "Dato Histórico," *El Independiente*, December 22, 1894, 1.

49. Quoted in Holtby, *Forty-Seventh Star*, 111–12.

50. Bonafé, "De la Capital," *El Independiente*, May 8, 1897, 1.

51. On the Las Vegas Land Grant, see Blackshear, *Honor and Defiance*, passim.

52. "El Pleito de la Merced Seguirá Adelante," *La Voz del Pueblo*, April 18, 1908, 1.

53. "Recuerdo al Legislador Nativo," *El Independiente*, March 3, 1901, 1.

54. "Los Métodos Democráticos," *El Independiente*, October 27, 1898, 1.

55. "Editorial," *La Opinión Pública*, February 9, 1895, 1.

56. "La Convención de Silver City," *La Voz del Pueblo*, March 28, 1908, 1.

57. El Ranchero, "La Situación Lastimosa de Nuevo México," *La Voz del Pueblo*, September 17, 1904, 3.

58. "Malo Está el Cuento, Manitos," *La Voz del Pueblo*, February 18, 1911, 1.

59. "Noticia Locales," *La Voz del Pueblo*, March 3, 1894, 3.

60. Untitled commentary, *La Voz del Pueblo*, October 13, 1894, 2; also, "Chimisturre Plantanilla y Chile Verde," *La Voz del Pueblo*, October 27, 1894, 2; "El Manifiesto y el Eclipso del Sol," *La Voz del Pueblo*, February 24, 1894, 2; "Noticias Locales," *La Voz del Pueblo*, October 13; 1894, 4.

61. "Hoja Negra a la Bandera Americana," *La Opinión Pública*, August 4, 1906, 2; untitled editorial, *La Opinión Pública*, August 8, 1906, 2.

62. Edmunson, *Los Manitos*; Romero, "Manitos and the Struggle for Self-Identity"; "Following the Manito Trail," a cultural heritage exhibition at the Millicent Rogers Museum, Taos, New Mexico, March 26–July 31, 2022.

63. For use of this term among Spanish language journalists, see Meléndez, *So All Is Not Lost*, 59–62. According to Bustamante ("Los Hispanos"), the term did not catch on for self-identification among the mass of Hispanos (124).

64. "Through the use of this [Neo-Mexicano] neologism, Nuevomexicanos began to foster an image of themselves as a new and emerging group, heir, on the one hand, to the *Mexicano* culture of their forebears and, on the other, to the technological and societal changes of the industrial age"; Meléndez, *So All Is Not Lost*, 60.

65. "¡¡Viva Antonio Joseph!!," *La Aurora*, August 30, 1884, 2.

66. "Despierten, Mejicanos!," *El Guía de Santa Fe*, October 16, 1886, 4.

67. Untitled editorial, *La Voz del Pueblo*, November 3, 1900, 2.

68. "El Sol de Mayo, "*El Sol de Mayo*, May 1, 1891, 1.

69. "Resoluciones de Condolencia," *La Opinión Pública*, August 4, 1906, 1.

70. "La Sociedad Neo-Mexicana," *El Combate*, April 2, 1903, 2.

71. Meyer, *Speaking for Themselves*, 199; Grove, et al., New Mexico Newspapers, 156; Stratton, *Territorial Press of New Mexico*, 271, 290; Cervantes, *Raíces del Periodismo Hispano*, 104.

72. Author's name smudged, in the printing it appears, "En Marcha," *La Voz del Pueblo*, October 1, 1892, 1.

73. Gutiérrez, "What's in a Name?," 34.

74. J. L. Ronquillo Jacques and Santiago Alvarado, resolutions of a mass meeting of indignation in El Paso, Texas, June 2, 1896, in "Enérgica Protesta," *La Voz del Pueblo*, June 13, 1896, 3.

75. "En Hora Buena," *La Voz del Pueblo*, February 3, 1894, 1.

76. Camilo Padilla to Pedro Sánchez in "Memorias del Padre Martínez," *La Voz del Pueblo*, May 2, 1903, 2.

77. Anonymous, "Al Hon. O. A. Larrazolo," *La Voz del Pueblo*, July 18, 1908, 2.

78. E. to Editor ("Carta Abierta: A Los Representates y Senadores de la Trigésima Segunda Asamblea de Nuevo México!"), *El Labrador*, February 27,1897, 1.

79. La Redacción, "Defectos de Raza: Nuestro Personalismo," *La Estrella*, March 4, 1911, 1.

80. Aguilar and Rojas, *El republicanismo en Hispanoamérica*; "La Exposisión [*sic*] International de los Estados Algodoneros," *El Financiero Mexicano*, repr. *El Estandarte*, May 12, 1895, 2–3; *El progreso; periódico ateo en más circulación en los paises hispano-americanos*, https://fkukso.com/post/149932501375/fuimos-modernos-alguna-vez-entre-1887-y-1916-el.

81. Jesús Islas, "Disposición de 13 de Febrero de 1856: Promoviendo la emigración de la raza hispano-americana existente en la Alta California, para aprovecharla en la colonización del estado de Sonora," cited in Hernández, *Mexican American Colonization*, 103n.14; cf. Islas, *Situación de los habitantes Ispano-Americans* [*sic*] *en el Estado de Alta California.*

82. Hernañdez, *Mutual Aid for Survival*, passim.

83. Gutiérrez, "What's in a Name," 34.

84. Donaciano Vigil papers, correspondence, letters received, 1873.

85. Their spiritual competitor *La Revista Católica* in Las Vegas charged that the project was "designed to pervert the Catholics of New Mexico"; "La Obra de los Misioneros en Embarazos," *La Revista Católica*, repr. in *Albuquerque Review*, May 27, 1876, 4.

86. "La Vigésima-tercera Legislatura," *Revista Católica*, repr. in *Revista de Albuquerque*, February 2, 1878, 3.

87. Bustamante, "Los Hispanos," 125–26.

88. Stratton, *Territorial Press of New Mexico*, 279; Grove, et al., 294, suggest it originated as the *New Mexico American* in Folsom, NM.

89. Meléndez, *So All Is Not Lost*, 87. Meyer (*Speaking for Themselves*) implies that Ochoa restarted *El Hispano-Americano* in Socorro. That he moved a paper called *El Hispano-Americano* is deducible because it existed in El Paso in 1891, disappears after that, and reappears under his ownership and editorship that year in Socorro (215–16); no author, *American Newspaper Directory*, 1628.

90. Meléndez, *So All Is Not Lost*, 81; Cervantes, *Raíces del Periodismo Hispano*, 93; Kanellos, *Hispanic Periodicals in the United States*, 316; Meyer, *Speaking for Themselves*, 215–16; Grove, et al., *New Mexico Newspapers*, 402.

91. "El Nuevo Mexicano," *La Voz del Pueblo*, March 31, 1894, 3.

92. Grove, et al., *New Mexico Newspapers*, 568.

93. "Brillo Marcial," *El Independiente*, July 28, 1894, 3.

94. Untitled editorial, *La Voz del Pueblo*, April 9, 1892, 2.

95. El Casino operated at least to 1899; "Noticias Locales," *La Voz del Pueblo*, January 23, 1892, 1; Dr. F. B. Romero, Martin Delgado, Carlos Tramblez to Apreciable Señor [Secundino Romero], Las Vegas, New Mexico, April 3, 1899, Secundino Romero Papers, box 1, folder 5.

96. "Moctezuma" in the title associates "Hispano" to a Mexican icon. It gave its first dance in February 1893; "Noticias Locales," *La Voz del Pueblo*, February 4, 1893, 2.

97. This drama club, consisting of young members of the town's literary society, posted a substantial repertoire of plays, comedies, and musical acts; "Teatro," *La Voz del Pueblo*, January 16, 1892, 3.

98. "El Sol de Mayo," *El Sol de Mayo*, May 1, 1891, 1.

99. "Nuestro Condado y Nuestra Orden," *El Sol de Mayo*, May 7, 1891, 1.

100. "La Posición de Gobernador," *La Voz del Pueblo*, repr. in *El Tiempo*, December 17, 1896, 1.

101. Ley, "La Legislatura," *La Voz del Pueblo*, February 16, 1895, 1.

102. Beck, *New Mexico*, 210–11; Stratton, *Territorial Press of New Mexico*, 36. For a list of prominent alumnae, see Ogden, *Historical Sketch of St. Michael's College*, 109–10; also, Read, *Illustrated History of New Mexico*, 552–53; "El Colegio de San Miguel," *El Independiente*, September 6, 1900, 2.

103. "A la Prensa Hispano-Americana," and "Sin irnos ni venirnos," *El Hispano Americano*, January 9, 1892, 1.

104. "La Asociación de la Prensa Asociada Hispano-Americana," *La Voz del Pueblo*, February 27, 1892, 1; trans. in Meléndez, *So All Is Not Lost*, 63. Néstor Montoya and Hilario A. Ortiz assisted Salazar in establishing *La Voz del Pueblo* in 1888; untitled, *Sol de Mayo*, July 9, 1891, 3. Salazar may have been persuaded to make the move to Las Vegas from Santa Fe by Félix Martínez, the successful businessman who began publishing the weekly, who served as its president and who apparently became a partner-owner with Salazar. Martínez penned few editorials, but with Salazar as general administrator and editor in chief, he hired Ezequiel C. de Baca for weekly editing and Antonio Lucero as associate editor; Meléndez, *So All Is Not Lost*, 73–74; Meyer, *Speaking for Themselves*, 216–17.

105. "El Primer Paso," *La Voz del Pueblo*, March 26, 1892, 1; cf. Meléndez, *So All Is Not Lost*, 64; Meyer, *Speaking for Themselves*, 14, 216.

106. "El Primer Paso."

107. "El Primer Paso."

108. "El Primer Paso."

109. "La Prensa Asociada: Resoluciones pasadas por la Primera Reunión de Editores Hispano-Americanos," *El Sol de Mayo*, March 31, 1892, 2; "El Primer Paso."

110. "A la Prensa Hispano-Americana," *El Hispano Americano*, January 9, 1892, 1.

111. Gellner, *Nations and Nationalism*, 10–11.

112. For other member weeklies by 1893, see Meléndez, *So All Is Not Lost*, 64.

113. Mesa Directiva, "De Albuquerque," *La Voz del Pueblo*, May 14, 1892, 2. A public-relations report stated that the "greatest harmony" prevailed in the organization; "La Prensa Asociada Hispano-Americana," *El Hispano Americano*, May 14, 1892; "La Prensa Asociada Hispano-Americana," *El Defensor del Pueblo*, May 21, 1892, 2.

114. "La Prensa Asociada Hispano-Americana," *El Hispano Americano*, May 14, 1892; "La Prensa Asociada Hispano-Americana," *El Defensor del Pueblo*, May 21, 1892; Meléndez, *So All Is Not Lost*, 87–88.

115. Jon Grinspan, "2024, I'd Like You to Meet 1892," *New York Times*, April 14, 2024, Opinion, 8.

116. "A la Prensa Hispano-Americana" and n.673; "Sin irnos ni venirnos."

117. *Las Vegas Optic*, cited in *La Voz del Pueblo*, August 22, 1891, 1.

118. Quoted in "Predican una Cosa y Hacen Otra," *La Voz del Pueblo*, April 16, 1892, 1.

119. "Predican una Cosa."

120. Untitled editorial, *La Voz del Pueblo*, May 28, 1892, 4.

121. "La Política y la Personalidad de Nuestro Colega, El Hispano-Americano de fecha 25 se expresa in los sigiente terminos," *La Voz del Pueblo*, June 4, 1892, 2.

122. "Precavemos a nuestros compatriotas en el territorio y fuera de el que es un hombre que no merece ni sus favores ni su confianza"; "Gracias," *El Mosquito*, June 30, 1892, 1.

123. Montoya, "L. Bradford Price," 192.

124. "Gracias"; also, "Sóplate Esta, Prince," *El Mosquito*, June 30, 1892, 2; cf. Meyer, *Speaking for Themselves*, 93–94.

125. "Ecos de la Casa," *El Mosquito*, June 30, 1892, 1.

126. "A Nuestro Amado Cacique y su Parna el Sargento," *La Opinión Pública*, repr. *La Voz del Pueblo*, July 30, 1892, 2; "scourge," untitled editorial, *La Voz del Pueblo*, August 27, 1892, 3.

127. "Los Tres Sastres," *El Nuevo Mexicano*, n.d., Prince Papers, Hispano-Anglo Relations, Contemporary Issues, folder 3.

128. See, "Republicanos en Sesión," *El Nuevo Mexicano*, April 9, 1892, 2.

129. "Al Nuevo Mexicano," *La Voz del Pueblo*, August 27, 1892, 1.

130. "Al Nuevo."

131. Quoted in Meléndez, *So All Is Not Lost*, 72.

132. "Salutatoria," *El Independiente*, March 14, 1894, 2; "La Política," *El Independiente*, June 9, 1894, 1; cf. Meléndez, *So All Is Not Lost*, 75–76.

133. Meyer, *Speaking for Themselves*, 214; Meléndez, *So All Is Not Lost*, 207.

134. A problem that had existed for some time. Anonymous, "Acrimonia Política Entre los Nativos de Nuevo México," sent to Editor, *El Nuevo Mexicano*, repr. in *El Monitor*, June 11, 1891.

135. "Cuestión entre periodistas," *El Boletín Popular*, March 15, 1894, 2.

136. Teresa Palomo Acosta, "Ochoa, Victor L.," *Handbook of Texas Online*, http://www.tshaonline.org/handbook/online/articles/foc05.

137. On Ochoa's revolutionary activities and his life after serving time, see Romo, *Ringside Seat to a Revolution*, 33–37, 45–51, 108–11; untitled, *La Voz del Pueblo*, January 13, 1894, 2; Acosta, "Ochoa, Victor L."

138. "PEDIMENTO—Al Presidente de la Asociación de la Prensa Hispano-Americana de Nuevo México" and "La Impresión de las Leyes en Castellano," *El Independiente*, January 28, 1904, 4, 6.

139. "Los Derechos de la Prensa Hispano Americana," *El Independiente*, June 11, 1904, Prince Papers, Political Issues and Elections.

140. Stratton, *Territorial Press of New Mexico*, 59.

141. "Salutación," *El Farol*, December 12, 1905, 2.

142. "Pueblo Más un Burro Negando," *La Voz del Pueblo*, April 4, 1908, 2.

143. "La Asociación de la Prensa Hispano-Americana," *El Eco del Norte*, November 15, 1909.

144. "El Gobernador ha Renunciado," *El Eco del Norte*, November 15, 1909, 1.

145. "La Propuesta Asociación de la Prensa," *El Eco del Norte*, April 25, 1910, 2.

146. José Montaner editorial, *La Revista de Taos*, repr. "Lo que Dice Montaner," *El Eco del Norte*, May 6, 1910.

147. "Llamada Para la Asociación de la Prensa," *El Eco del Norte*, August 15, 1910, 2.

148. "Llamada a la Prensa Asociada Hispano-Americano Republicana del Estado de Nuevo México," *La Bandera Americana*, February 23, 1912, 2, and *El Nuevo Mexicano*, March 2, 1912, 2.

Chapter 5

1. House Reports, Fiftieth Congress, First Session, vol. 4, Report no. 1025, 1–18; Larson, *New Mexico's Quest*, 147–48; Dargan, "New Mexico's Quest, III," 138–39.

2. "Views of the Minority" [to HR 8466], House Reports, Fiftieth Congress, First Session, vol. 4, Report no. 1025:27–54, 42–45, 35, 39. For the greater controversy, see Larson, *New Mexico's Quest*, 149–55; Dargan, "New Mexico's Fight for Statehood, VI," 69–70; Prince, *New Mexico's Struggle for Statehood*, 37–41.

3. "Views of the Minority," 39; quote from Stratton, *Territorial Press of New Mexico*, 103.

4. *El Tiempo*, April 5, 1888, 2.

5. Gonzales, "La Junta de Indignación."

6. As they did in India, for instance, when it came to a right of independence; Williams, "Liberalism, Colonialism and Liberal Imperialism," 106.

7. "La Junta de Indignación de los Ciudadanos de Las Vegas," *El Boletín Popular*, April 19, 1888, repr. in a clipping from an unknown Spanish language newspaper, in L. Bradford Prince Governor's Papers, Election of 1920, Political Events, 1920–21, folder 30.

8. "La Junta de Indignación."

9. Stratton, *Territorial Press of New Mexico*, 104; Dargan, "New Mexico's Fight for Statehood, III," 139.

10. For the letter, see Dargan, "New Mexico's Fight for Statehood, III," 150–53; quote 151; also Larson, *New Mexico's Quest*, 151–52.

11. Quoted in Dargan, "New Mexico's Fight for Statehood, VI," 68–69.

12. Mora, *Border Dilemmas*, 227–28.

13. Quoted in Dargan, "New Mexico's Fight for Statehood, VI," 68; Larson, *New Mexico's Quest*, 148.

14. "Joseph y El Estado," *El Tiempo*, March 21, 1889, 1; Larson, New Mexico's Quest, 153–55; Dargan, "The Opposition Within the Territory," 172.

Stratton, *Territorial Press*, 104; Montoya, "L. Bradford Prince," 187.

15. "Junta Pública en Gallup," *La Voz del Pueblo*, February 13, 1892; "La Gran Convención," *La Voz del Pueblo*, March 10, 1892, 1; Dargan, "New Mexico's Fight for Statehood, VI," 85–87; "De Albuquerque.," *La Voz del Pueblo*, May 14, 1892, 1; "native sons," Stratton, *Territorial Press of New Mexico*, 131.

16. Quote, "Ojo al Cristo, Neo-Mexicanos!" *La Voz del Pueblo*, January 23, 1892, 1; untitled, *La Voz del Pueblo*, January 16, 1892, 2; "¿No somos Americanos?," *El Hispano Americano*, January 9, 1892, 1.

17. "¿No somos Americanos?"

18. Mora, *Border Dilemmas*, 227–28.

19. "¿No somos Americanos?"

20. Prince to Platt, June 25, 1892, in Prince, *New Mexico's Struggle for Statehood*, 81-90; cf. Larson, *New Mexico's Quest*, 174.

21. "Otra Calumnia en Contra del Pueblo de Nuevo México.," *La Voz del Pueblo*, August 26, 1893, 1.

22. "Estado de Nuevo México," *La Voz del Pueblo*, October 7, 1893, 1.

23. "Otra Calumnia en Contra del Pueblo de Nuevo México."

24. Roberts, "H. B. Fergusson," 238; "Movimiento de los Trabajadores," *El Boletín Popular*, September 3, 1896, 2; untitled, *El Labrador*, October 31, 1896, 2; "Club Democrático de Bryan," *El Boletín Popular*, August 6, 1896, 2; "La Convención Republicana de Las Vegas," *El Boletín Popular*, 8 October 1896, 2; "A Los Pagadores de Tasacion," *El Boletín Popular*, October 29, 1896, 2.

25. "Carta del Honorable H. Fergusson," *El Independiente*, January 27, 1898, 1.

26. "Carta del Honorable H. Fergusson."

27. "Proyecto Núm. 8226," *El Boletín Popular*, March 10, 1898, 2.

28. Analysis based on "Speech of Hon. Harvey B. Fergusson, of New Mexico, in the House of Representatives," Wednesday, February 2, 1898, Fortifications Appropriation Bill, GPO, 1898; copy in A. A. Jones Papers, box 1.

29. "Speech of Hon. Harvey B. Fergusson," 13.

30. Larson, *New Mexico's Quest*, 193, 194; also, Roberts, "H. B. Fergusson, 1848–1915," 245–46; Holtby, *Forty-Seventh Star*, 26.

31. Stratton, *Territorial Press of New Mexico*, 104, 105; Larson, *New Mexico's Quest*, 156; Prince, *New Mexico's Struggle*, 48; Owen, *Two Alberts*, 177.

32. Larson, *New Mexico's Quest*, 158–9, 161; Lamar, *Far Southwest*, 163; Stratton, *Territorial Press of New Mexico*, 141.

33. "Una Carta," *La Cachiporra*, October 19, 1888, 1; Montoya, "L. Bradford Price," 187–88.

34. Untitled editorial, *La Voz del Pueblo*, April 27, 1889, 2.

35. The analysis in this section is based on José D. Sena, "Veinte y Cuatro Razones Porque los Nativos de Nuevo Mexico—o sea los Mexicanos como los llaman—Deben Votar por la Constitución y Erigirse en Estado," *El Nuevo Mexicano*, September 27, 1890, repr. in *La Cachiporra*, October 8, 1890, 2 and Meléndez, *Citizens by Treaty*, 111–17.

36. Stratton, *Territorial Press of New Mexico*, 31.

37. All references to the diálogo taken from Argus, "La Polémica se Vuelve a Entablar y su Tema es el Estado," *El Nuevo Mexicano*, September 27, 1890, 1.

38. "Convención Demócrata del Condado de Taos," *El Monitor*, August 30, 1890, 1.

39. Tobias, *History of the Jews*, 158; see also 70, 74, 118–19.

40. Sandweiss, "Opposing Views," 58.

41. Meléndez, *So All Is Not Lost*, 68.

42. Suzman, *Ethnic Nationalism and State Power*, 12; also, Carr, *Nationalism and After*, 190–92.

43. Argus, "La Polémica."

44. For biographical items, see Enciso and North, "Nestor Montoya."

45. Dargan, "New Mexico's Fight for Statehood, III," 168–69.

46. Dargan, "New Mexico's Fight."

47. Catron to S. B. Elkins, August 15, 1892, Catron papers, box 401, folder 3.

48. Dargan, "New Mexico's Fight for Statehood, III," 187.

49. Larson, *New Mexico's Quest*, 168; Blackshear, *Honor and Defiance*, 147; Montoya, "L. Bradford Price," 188.

50. For the statistical table, see Dargan, 'New Mexico's Fight for Statehood, III: Opposition within the Territory (1888–1890)," 185.

51. Dargan, "New Mexico's Fight for Statehood, IV," 76.

52. Blackshear, *Honor and Defiance*, 140.

53. Bonafé, "Día de Gala en la Capital," *El Independiente*, October 19, 1895, 2; Bonafé, "Festividad Solemne.," *El Independiente*, October 26, 1895, 2; "Unkindest cut of all," *El Boletín Popular*, October 24, 1895.

54. Thomas Malone, from the *Colorado Catholic*, quot. in "Malone Called Down," *Daily New Mexican*, October 28, 1895; "The Colorado Catholic Explains," *Daily New Mexican*, November 8, 1895; Spanish trans. in "Reverendo Calumniador," *El Boletín Popular*, October 31, 1895, and "Malone Llamado a Cuentas," *El Nuevo Mexicano*, November 2, 1895.

55. "Al Fraile Malone," *La Bandera Americana*, November 2, 1895, and *El Boletín Popular*, October 31, 1895; "Reverendo Calumniador," *El Boletín Popular*, October 31, 1895.

56. "*De un pueblo cuyas nueve décimas partes se compone de católicos fieles*"; "Tributo Merecido, *El Nuevo Mexicano*, November 2, 1895, 2.

57. "Un Hipócrita Usurpador del Sagrado Nombre de 'Católico," *La Voz del Pueblo*, November 2, 1895, 1.

58. "Un Hipócrita."

59. Untitled, *La Voz del Pueblo*, November 23, 1895, 2.

60. M. A. D. Rivera to Editor ("Otra Carta Patriótica"), *La Voz del Pueblo*, November 16, 1895, 1.

61. "Al Fraile Malone," *La Bandera Americana*, November 2, 1895 (special edition).

62. "Al Fraile."

63. "Susceptibilidad Excesiva," *El Independiente*, November 2, 1895, 1.

64. "Susceptibilidad."

65. Anderson, *Imagined Communities*, 24.

66. "Nuestro Porvenir," *El Independiente*, November 9, 1895, 1.

67. "Nuestro Porvenir."

68. *Forgotten People.*

69. "Nuestro Porvenir."

70. "Nuestro Porvenir."

71. "Nuestro Porvenir."

72. "Nuestro Porvenir."

73. "Nuestro Porvenir."

74. Prince, *Student's History of New Mexico*, 162.

75. "Tributo Merecido."

76. Thomas Malone, "To the Spanish-Americans of New Mexico," *Colorado Catholic*, repr. in "Colorado Catholic Explains," *Daily New Mexican*, November 8, 1895.

77. Malone, "To the Spanish-Americans."

78. Malone, "To the Spanish-Americans."

79. "A Los Hispano Americanos de Nuevo México," *Colorado Catholic*, repr. in "Apología del P. Malone," *El Boletín Popular*, November 14, 1895, 1; "Se Retracta Malone," *La Voz del Pueblo*, November 9, 1895, 1.

80. Author's trans. of Malone, "A Los Hispano Americanos."

81. Benjamín M. Read, Aniceto Abeytia, and H. L. Ortiz, Proceedings of a meeting of Catholics of Santa Fe's two parishes held on August 8, 1894, in "Comunicado," *El Boletín Popular*, August 16, 1894, 1.

82. "El Rev. Malone," *La Revista de Taos*, November 9, 1895, 1.

Chapter 6

1. "New Mexico's Fight for Statehood, II: The Attitude of the Territorial Press," 121.

2. "El Deber Primordial," *El Independiente*, November 8, 1900, 2.

3. "La Junta de Indignación," *La Voz del Pueblo*, November 2, 1901, 1; extracts of a *Sunday Morning Review* editorial trans. in "La Difamación Refutada," *La Voz del Pueblo*, October 26, 1901, 1.

4. "Insultos Gratuitos," *La Voz del Pueblo*, October 26, 1901, 1.

5. "La Difamación Refutada."

6. "Fanatismo e Hipocrecía," *El Independiente*, October 31, 1901, 1.

7. "Insultos Gratuitos."

8. Durkheim, *Elementary Forms of the Religious Life*, 104–5.

9. "Insultos Gratuitos."

10. "Insultos Gratuitos."

11. "La Junta de Indignación."

12. Nieto-Phillips, *Language of Blood*, 13–14.

13. For Chacón's speech, which forms the basis of the analysis below, see "Elocuente discurso," *La Voz Del Pueblo*, November 2, 1901, 2; "El Hispano Americano," *El Independiente*, November 7, 1901, 2; also, "La Junta de Indignación," *El Independiente*; Arellano, *De Colores*, 38–46; Meléndez and Lomelí, *Writings of Eusebio Chacón*, including a transl., 186–200; Kanellos, et al., *Anthology of Hispanic Literature of the United States*, 130–35.

14. On Nuevomexicanos denigrating Mexicans from Mexico, see Gonzales, "Introduction: Recovering *Impresiones*," 1–14; Lozano, *American Language*, 146.

15. Vignaud, *Toscanelli and Columbus.*

16. "Los Denigradores de Colón," *El Independiente*, October 10, 1901, 2; also on the critical campaign, see "¿Fué un Bien ó un Mal el Descubrimiento de América Para la Humanidad?," *El Independiente*, September 14, 1895, 2.

17. Tempering this ideological view is the conclusion, "New Mexico was poor, not destitute"; Kessel, *Spain in the Southwest*, 111.

18. Morfí, "Account of Disorders in New Mexico," 131.

19. Lomelí, "Illustrious Pioneer of Early Hispanic Letters Background and Social Context," 18.

20. "Resoluciones de Indignación," *El Independiente*, October 31, 1901, 1; untitled resolutions in *La Voz del Pueblo*, November 2, 1901, 1; "Resoluciones de Indignación," *La Bandera Americana*, photocopy with date clipped in Prince Papers, Hispano-Anglo Relations, Contemporary Issues, folder 3; "An Indignation Meeting Held at Las Vegas," *White Oaks Eagle*, November 10, 1901, 1. That Snider left New Mexico is sufficiently clear, though diligent searches have failed to uncover her whereabouts after the controversy.

21. Magnet, "Language Rights as Collective Rights," 294, 295.

22. Lozano, *American Language*, 5.

23. Marshall, "Question of Official Language," 40–41; Hernández-Chávez, 147–48; Magnet, "Canadian Perspectives on Official English," 53; Lozano, *American Language*, 54.

24. Hernández-Chávez, "Language Policy in the United States," 142–43.

25. Lozano, *American Language*, 8.

26. Anderson, *Imagined Communities*, 78.

27. Dargan, "New Mexico's Fight for Statehood, VI," 65–66.

28. "Encargos," *El Independiente*, November 30, 1895, 2.

29. Lozano, *American Language*, 100.

30. Larson, *New Mexico's Quest*, 213–14.

31. For an incisive examination of the Beveridge field hearings, see Lozano, *American Language*, 113–34; cf. Cottrell, "Senate Action on the Omnibus Statehood Bill of 1902," 9–11; Larson, *New Mexico's Quest*, 212, 213, 216.

32. Larson sees Beveridge's most serious concerns concentrated on the low population count and the prospect of such a sparse population's having as equal representation in the Senate as larger ones and that corporate interests would take advantage of New Mexico and Arizona.

33. Report, New Statehood Bill, 1902, Senate Reports, Report no. 2206, Part 1, vol. 1, 57th Congress, Second Session, 1902–03, GPO, 2, 5–7.

34. Report, New Statehood Bill, 29–30, quote, 9. The Report's comments on the Mexican element also applied to Arizona, which had 30,000 of them; Larson, *New Mexico's Quest*, 215–16.

35. Larson, *New Mexico's Quest*, 216.

36. Some went to support the bill; *Albuquerque Journal-Democrat*, December 8, 1902.

37. Resolutions, Mesilla Valley Chamber of Commerce, *Santa Fe New Mexican*, December 30, 1902, 1.

38. Resolutions, Central Labor Union; *Albuquerque Journal-Democrat*, December 15, 1902, 4.

39. Resolutions, Albuquerque Mass Meeting; *Albuquerque Journal-Democrat*, December 9, 1902, 1.

40. "Resolutions, Mass Meeting of the Citizens of Old Albuquerque," *Albuquerque Journal-Democrat*, December 12, 1902, 1.

41. "EL PUEBLO DEBE OBRAR," *El Independiente*, January 8, 1903, 1. The editorial claimed that San Miguel County should "imitate" those communities

that had organized against the Beveridge Report, but no Las Vegas junta on this issue is in evidence.

42. "La Cuestión de Estado," *El Combate*, December 6, 1902, 1.

43. "En lo que Basan su Oposición a Nuevo México y Arizona," *Voz del Pueblo*, December 13, 1902, 1.

44. "El Trabajo del Coronel Chávez," *Voz del Pueblo*, July 25, 1903, 2; "Sin Maestros Buenos Es Imposible Tener Buenos Discípulos," *Voz del Pueblo*, August 15, 1903, 1.

45. "El Trabajo," "Sin Maestros."

46. "El Trabajo," "Sin Maestros."

47. Untitled, *Voz del Pueblo*, August 15, 1903, 2.

48. Hubbard, "Arizona's Struggle against Joint Statehood," 417–19.

49. "El Pueblo Lo Quiere," *El Independiente*, June 23, 1904, 1.

50. "Los Pros y Contras del Estado Consolidado Compuesto de Nuevo México y Arizona," *El Independiente*, February 18, 1904, 2.

51. "Peor Sera el ____ Que La Enfermedad?," *El Independiente*, June 9, 1904, 1.

52. "Los Pros y Contras."

53. "En Referencia Al Nombre de Nuevo México," *El Independiente*, March 3, 1904, 1.

54. "Nombres y Más Nombres," *El Independiente*, May 26, 1904, 1.

55. Noel, *Debating American Identity*: "specifically,"41; Braeman, "Albert J. Beveridge and Statehood for the Southwest": "greasers," 327; also, Meléndez, "Nuevo México by Any Other Name," 153.

56. "Una Alianza Que No Es Solicitada," *El Independiente*, March 17, 1904, 1.

57. A. (Alarid) to Editor ("Sobre el Estado"), *El Independiente*, February 1, 1904.

58. Alarí, "La Cuestión de Estado," *El Independiente*, March 24, 1904, 4.

59. Jesús María Alarid, "El Idioma Español," *El Independiente*, 1905, trans. in Otero, Meléndez, and Lamadrid, *Santa Fe Nativa*, 107–9.

60. J. M. H. Alarid to Editors ("Manifiesto"), *El Independiente*, April 14, 1904, 1.

61. J. M. H. Alarid to Editors.

62. Hubbard, "Arizona's Struggle against Joint Statehood," 419.

63. "Proyecto de Estado Consolidado—En lo que se Refiere Á Nuevo Mexico y Arizona," *El Independiente*, April 21, 1904, 1.

64. "La Infausta Estrella de Nuevo México y Los Neo-Mexicanos," *El Independiente*, April 28, 1904, 1; rpt. in "Los Republicanos y Los Caciques—En Su Porfía Respecto al Estado Consolidado," *El Independiente*, May 12, 1904, 1; "El Pueblo Lo Quiere," *El Independiente*, June 23, 1904, 1.

65. Holtby, *Forty-Seventh Star*, 157; "En Referencia Al Nombre de Nuevo México," *El Independiente*, March 3, 1904,1; Stratton, *Territorial Press of New Mexico*, 111; E. V. Safford to Holm Bursum, August 14, 1906, Holm Bursum Papers, box 4, folder 1.

66. Max Frost to Holm Bursum, August 14, 1906, Holm Bursum Papers, box 4, folder 1.

67. "En Referencia Al Nombre de Nuevo Mexico," *El Independiente*, March 3, 1904, 1.

68. B. S. Rodey to Secundino Romero, February 24, 1904; Secundino Romero Papers, box 2, "Theft Items Returned to Collection."

69. "El Proyecto De Estado Consolidado," *El Independiente*, November 9, 1904, 2; "Comment," *El Independiente*, December 8, 1904, 3.

70. "Joint Statehood Bill, St. Louis Globe, repr. in *Santa Fe New Mexican*, December 9, 1904, 1; "El Proyecto de Estado—Presentado al Senado con Varias Enmendaciones, Apropiación de Cinco Millones para Las Escuelas Públicas del Estado de Arizona," *El Independiente*, December 22, 1904, 1.

71. Leopard, "Joint Statehood," 243; Lamar, *Far Southwest*, 429–30.

72. "Territorial Republican Platform," L. Bradford Prince Papers, Political Issues and Elections—Election of 1906, folder 17.

73. Prince, *New Mexico's Struggle*, 110.

74. "Los Republicanos y Los Caciques—En Su Porfía Respecto al Estado Consolidado," *El Independiente*, May 12, 1904, 1.

75. Untitled, *El Independiente*, May 12, 1904, 2.

76. E. V. Safford to Holm Bursum, August 14, 1906; Holm Bursum to Alfredo Chávez, October 12, 1906, Holm Bursum Papers, box 4, folder 1.

77. Holm Bursum to Max Frost, August 21, 1906, Holm Bursum Papers, box 4, folder 1.

78. Stratton, *Territorial Press of New Mexico*, 110–11.

79. Braeman, "Albert J. Beveridge," 334; also, Stratton, *Territorial Press of New Mexico*, 111.

80. For the list of delegates, see Prince, *New Mexico's Struggle*, 117; *The Eagle*, December 7, 1907, and *El Nuevo Mexicano*, January 12, 1907, Prince Papers, Statehood Movement, 1906–1907, Contemporary Issues, folder 4. Among the Nuevomexicanos were José D. Sena, Romulo Baca, Elfego Baca, O. A. Larrazolo, Miguel Otero, George Armijo. Prominent among the county delegates were Margarito Romero, Gabino Sánchez, Crescencio Hernández, and José García.

81. For the Prince interview, see "Splendid Chance for Statehood," *Santa Fe New Mexican*, September 16, 1907, 1; see also Prince, *New Mexico's Struggle for Statehood*, 113–17; Coan, *History of New Mexico*, 413.

82. "Splendid Chance"; Prince, *New Mexico's Struggle for Statehood*, 113–17; untitled column, *Albuquerque Citizen*, September 17, 1907, 2.

83. Pero Grullo: a nickname used by various Nuevomexicanos; "No Somos Profetas," *La Revista de Taos*, November 14, 1918, 1. In Latin America, Pero was shorthand for Pedro but is also translated as "But." Grullo signifies hayseed. Some writers referred to Pero Grullo as one who spills platitudes while others alluded to his wise observations; "Pero Grullo," https://es.wikipedia.org/wiki/Pedro_Grullo.

84. On the cuando as a corrido form, see Espinosa, *Folklore of Spain in the American Southwest*, 20, 27,128, 131.

85. Pero Grullo, "¿Cuando Será Estado Nuevo México?," *Voz del Pueblo*, February 29, 1907, 2.

86. For bravery at the Battle of Mactan in the Philippines, Curry earned the admiration of Theodore Roosevelt to the degree that Roosevelt appointed him governor.

87. Twitchell would soon author *History of the American Occupation* and *Leading Facts*. Taking interest in New Mexico's Spanish antiquities, he compiled a

catalogue of Spanish archival holdings in New Mexico; Twitchell, *Ralph Emerson Twitchell*, 127–28.

88. "City Asks for Appropriation," *Daily Optic*, February 21, 1907, 1; "New Laws by Legislature," *Santa Fe New Mexican*, March 23, 1907, 1; "great explorer," "Council Passes Monument Bill," *Daily Optic*, March 1, 1907, 1. Twitchell was called the "prime mover of the Coronado enterprise" in "The Coronado Memorial Association Formed at Enthusiastic Convention," *Albuquerque Morning Journal*, October 10, 1907, 1.

89. Governor George Curry, "Proclamation for the Coronado Commemorative Convention," in "To Pay Homage to Early Pioneers," *Santa Fe New Mexican*, August 28, 1907, 1; also, "Call Issued for the Coronado Convention," *Albuquerque Morning Journal*, August 30, 1907, 5.

90. Curry, "Proclamation"; "Call Issued."

91. "Governor Curry Fires First Gun for Single Statehood," *Albuquerque Citizen*, October 8, 1907, 1.

92. "Coronado Memorial Association."

93. "Coronado Memorial Association."

94. See, e.g., Sariñana and Gonzales, *Impresiones de un Surumato.*

95. "Coronado Memorial Association." Part of the speech is in Larrazolo, *Octaviano A. Larrazolo*, 65–67. For brief attention to the speech, see Noel, *Debating American Identity*, 50; Mora, *Border Dilemmas*, 246–47.

96. Lummis, *Spanish Pioneers*, 165–69; "gentle zeal," 159.

97. Wilcox, *Pueblo Revolt of 1680 and the Mythology*, 55–58.

98. "Coronado Memorial Association."

99. "Delegate Andrews' Congratulations," *Santa Fe New Mexican*, December 3, 1907, 1; "Hope for State of New Mexico," *Santa Fe New Mexican*, December 3, 1907, 1; Prince, *New Mexico's Struggle for Statehood*, 121.

100. One on a partial list of ten; "Additional Names Statehood Boosters," *Santa Fe New Mexican*, January 17, 1908, 1.

101. W. S. Hopewell to Secundino Romero, January 13, 1908, Secundino Romero papers, box 3, folder 34.

102. "Personnel of Big Delegation," *Santa Fe New Mexican*, January 15, 1908, 1; W. S. Hopewell to Secundino Romero.

Chapter 7

1. Donnelly, "Making of the New Mexico Constitution," 458; Lamar, *Far Southwest*, 431; Larson, *New Mexico's Quest*, 261–63. "New Mexico," *Journal of the New Mexico Territorial Council*, February 23, 1909, 168–70.

2. Larson, *New Mexico's Quest*, 264–67; Braeman, "Albert J. Beveridge," 339–40.

3. "Los Republicanos en Apuros," *La Voz el Pueblo*, February 10, 1910, 1.

4. The New Mexico representatives were Prince, Charles Spiess, Bird S. Coler, N. B. Laughlin; United States Congress, Senate Committee on Territories. *Statehood. Hearing Before the Committee on Territories, United States Senate* 1910, 8–35.

5. See Palsson, "Arizona Constitutional Convention of 1910: The Election of Delegates," 116–17.

6. United States Congress, Senate Committee on Territories. *Statehood*, 55.

7. Senate Committee on Territories.

8. Senate Committee on Territories, 71.

9. Senate Committee on Territories, 102.

10. Senate Committee on Territories, 55.

11. Senate Committee on Territories, 53–56.

12. Senate Committee on Territories, 71.

13. Senate Committee on Territories, 77–78.

14. Senate Committee on Territories.

15. US Congress, Senate Committee on Territories. *An Act To enable the people of New Mexico to form a constitution and state government*, 559; cf. Larson, *New Mexico's Quest*, 269, 268.

16. US Congress, Senate, Cong. Rec., 61st Cong., 2nd Sess. (1910), 8227; cf. Crawford, *Language Loyalties*, 60; Russell, "State Regionalism in New Mexico," 83.

17. ¿Habrá Estado?," *La Voz del Pueblo*, June 18, 1910, 2; Untitled, *La Voz del Pueblo*, June 25, 1910, 2.

18. Spanish version in J. M. H. Alarid to Editor ("Correspondencias. Remitido"), *La Voz del Pueblo*, 26 March 1910, 2.

19. "Proclama del Gobernador," *El Eco del Norte*, July 18, 1910, 2; William J. Mills, "Proclama," *El Labrador*, July 8, 1910, 2; Larson, *New Mexico's Quest*, 269–70.

20. Gonzales, "Whose Sovereign People?," 162–63, 173–76.

21. "Nuevo México Progresa," *El Eco del Norte*, August 1, 1910, 2.

22. Untitled editorial, *El Eco del Norte*, July 18, 1910, 2.

23. Mount, "Nuevo Mexicanos and the War of 1898," 383; Durand, *Thirteenth Census of the United States Taken in the Year* 1910: Statistics for New Mexico, 568.

24. Holmes, *Politics in New Mexico*, 49; Stumph, "The History of the Referendum in New Mexico," 29; Russell, "State Regionalism in New Mexico," 72–73.

25. Holmes, *Politics*; Stumph, "The History of the Referendum"; Russell, "State Regionalism."

26. Larson, *New Mexico's Quest*, 276.

27. "*Los descendientes de los originales pobladores de este Territorio se hayan quedado sin sus legitimas herencias no deberían de recibir, para nada, el voto de ningún hombre en cuyo pecho se sientan todavía los latidos de un corazón Independiente.*" In untitled editorial, *La Voz del Pueblo*, October 29, 1910, 2.

28. Mabry, "New Mexico's Constitution in the Making," 170; cf. Holmes, *Politics in New Mexico*, 49; Cline, *New Mexico's 1910 Constitution*, 31.

29. Quote, Russell, "State Regionalism in New Mexico," 74; also Holmes, 1967, 49; Westphall *Thomas Benton Catron*, 340; New Mexico, *Proceedings of the Constitutional Convention*, 29; Callary, "Political Biography of Frank A. Hubbell," 99.

30. New Mexico, Constitutional Convention (1910), *Rules of the Constitutional Convention*, 11–15; Larson, *New Mexico's Quest*, 275; Ihde, "Washington Ellsworth Lindsey," 193.

31. Larson, *New Mexico's Quest*, 276.

32. Heflin, "New Mexico Constitutional Convention," 61.

33. See Tarr, "American State Constitutions," 100.

34. Holmes, *Politics in New Mexico*, 49–50.

35. "Nuestro Boleto," *La Voz del Pueblo*, August 27, 1910, 1; "Boleta de Ciudadanos a la Convención Constitucional," *La Voz del Pueblo*, September 3, 1910, 2.

36. Ihde, "Washington Ellsworth Lindsey," 95–96; Holmes, *Politics in New Mexico*, 49; Larrazolo, *Octaviano A. Larrazolo*, 69; Cordova and Judah, *Octaviano Larrazolo*, 7.

37. Reeve, *History of New Mexico*, 333; Larrazolo, *Octaviano A. Larrazolo*, 111; Vigil, *Los Patrones*, 71; cf. Stumph, "History of the Referendum," 43–44.

38. As one historian who interviewed delegates twenty-five years later found, "many Anglo leaders, as well as native . . . insistent that the Spanish-Americans be safeguarded"; Russell, "State Regionalism in New Mexico," 81–82.

39. Stumph, "History of the Referendum," 30–31; cf. Ihde, "Washington Ellsworth Lindsey," 193–94.

40. United States Congress, H. R. 18166, 558; "Constitutional Proposition," *New Mexican*, October 20, 1910, 7; New Mexico, *Proceedings*, 255.

41. New Mexico, *Constitution of the State of New Mexico*, 2.

42. "Criticism of Enabling Act Sharp and Severe," *Albuquerque Morning Journal*, November 1, 1910, 1–2; "Tareas de la Convención," *El Labrador*, November 11, 1910, 1; New Mexico, *Proceedings*, 36.

43. Gonzales-Berry, "Which Language Will Our Children Speak," 175.

44. "Criticism of Enabling Act Sharp and Severe," *Albuquerque Morning Journal*, November 1, 1910, 1–2; New Mexico, *Proceedings*, 194; Cf. Holmes, *Politics in New Mexico*, 49.

45. "Criticism of Enabling Act Sharp and Severe."

46. United States Congress, H. R. 18166, 559.

47. "Criticism of Enabling Act Sharp and Severe"; New Mexico, *Proceedings*, 194.

48. "Criticism of Enabling Act"; also Gonzales-Berry, "Which Language Will Our Children Speak?," 174; New Mexico, *Proceedings*, 194.

49. "Criticism of Enabling Act"; "Which Language Will Our Children Speak?"; *Proceedings*.

50. "Criticism of Enabling Act"; "Which Language Will Our Children Speak?"; *Proceedings*.

51. "Language Provision," *Albuquerque Morning Journal*, November 2, 1910, 2.

52. "Language Provision."

53. "Language Provision."

54. "La Convención Constitucional," *La Voz del Pueblo*, November 5, 1910, 2.

55. *Constitution of the State of New Mexico*, 18.

56. *Proceedings*, 14.

57. Holmes, *Politics in New Mexico*, 51.

58. New Mexico, *Constitution of the State of New Mexico*, 37; Enabling Act, 559.

59. Getz, *Schools of their Own*, 25.

60. "File No. 71," *New Mexican*, October 21, 1910, 5.

61. *Constitution of the State of New Mexico*, 29; "Constitutional Proposition," *New Mexican*, October 20, 1910, 7.

62. Getz, *Schools of their Own*, 27.

63. Gonzales-Berry, "Which Language Will Our Children Speak?," 174–75.

64. Moyers, "History of Education in New Mexico," 497.

65. *Constitution of the State of New Mexico*, 34.

66. Gonzales-Berry, "Which Language Will Our Children Speak?," 173.

67. *Constitution of the State of New Mexico*, 29; *Proceedings*, 116.

68. *Constitution of the State of New Mexico*, 141–42; Gonzales, "Promise and Frustration."

69. "Spiess Elected President of Santa Fe Convention by Solid Vote of Majority," *New Mexican*, October 4, 1910, 1.

70. "File No. 34," *New Mexican*, October 14, 1910, 5.

71. *Constitution of the State of New Mexico*, 29; *Proceedings*, 133; Larson, *New Mexico's Quest*, 279.

72. Holmes, *Politics in New Mexico*, 50–51. However, as Jenson ("Disfranchisement is a Disgrace") observes, "the constitutional compromise protecting the elective franchise of Hispanic males . . . that was achieved, made it virtually impossible to amend the constitution to give women the vote. . . . Women in other western states who achieved state suffrage by 1914 had no such provisions to overcome" (9).

73. "Another Long Step Toward Statehood Accomplished; Organic Act Will Get Support of People," *Albuquerque Morning Journal*, November 22, 1910, 1.

74. Territory of New Mexico, *Proceedings of the Constitutional Convention of the Proposed State of New Mexico*, 289.

75. If rejected, the governor had twenty days to reconvene delegates for another go at it. *Proceedings of the Constitutional Convention*, 252.

76. "Special Dispatch to the Morning Journal," *Albuquerque Morning Journal*, November 22, 1910, 1; "Alabanza á la Constitución," *El Labrador*, December 16, 1910, 1.

77. "42,000 Copies in Spanish are Distributed," *Albuquerque Morning Journal*, December 28, 1910, 4.

78. Paul Larrazolo, *Octaviano A. Larrazolo*, 69–72; Cordova and Judah, *Octaviano Larrazolo*, 7.

79. "Albuquerque Takes Lead in Campaign for Ratification of the Constitution," *Albuquerque Morning Journal*, December 30, 1910, 1–2.

80. "Resultado de la Votación—Cómputo Oficial," *Nuevo Mexicano*, February 11, 1911, also Read, *Historia Ilustrada de Nuevo México*, 607–08; Holtby, *Forty-Seventh Star*, 244; Stratton, *Territorial Press*, 113; Larson, *New Mexico's Quest*, 286; Cordova and Judah, *Octaviano Larrazolo*, 6–7.

81. Cf. Noel, *Debating Identity*, 51.

82. El Corresponsal, "La Voz de la Capital," *La Revista de Taos*, January 27, 1911, 1.

83. "*Y entonces con toda garganta la letrilla cuyo estribillo refrán es, / No hay que abatirse, / Noble cuadrilla, / Valemos mucho / Por más que digan.*" "La Voz de la Capital," *La Revista de Taos*, February 3, 1911, 1.

84. "Triunfo de la Libertad y del Progreso," *La Revista de Taos*, January 27, 1911, 1.

85. Other governments worldwide have formally decreed a particular nomenclature or ethnic heritage as that of its official people; Nagel, *American Indian*

Ethnic Renewal, 27–28. On the state's imposition of authorizing group categories and classificatory schemes, see Brubaker, *Ethnicity Without Groups*, 42–44; Marx, *Faith in Nation*, 20.

86. "Tocante a la Constitución," *La Voz del Pueblo*, December 24, 1910, 2.

87. Quoted in Holtby, *Forty-Seventh Star*, 243.

88. Benjamin M. Read, "Triunfo de la Justicia—Legítimo Regocijo—Sobre Razón," *La Revista de Taos*, January 27, 1911, in Read, *Historia Ilustrada de Nuevo México*, 605–6.

89. Read, "Triunfo de la Justicia."

90. Read, "Triunfo de la Justicia."

91. Read, "Triunfo de la Justicia."

92. Read, "Triunfo de la Justicia."

93. Octaviano Larrazolo, Address on Fiftieth Anniversary of St. Michael's College, Santa Fe, June 22, 1911, in Larrazolo, *Octaviano A. Larrazolo*, 192–94.

94. Benjamín M. Read, "El Estado y Los Hijos e Nuevo Mexico," *La Revista de Taos*, August 25, 1911, 1.

95. Read, "El Estado y Los Hijos."

96. Read, "El Estado y Los Hijos."

97. Read, "El Estado y Los Hijos."

98. Read, "El Estado y Los Hijos."

99. Read, "El Estado y Los Hijos."

100. See Meléndez, *Citizens by Treaty*, 168–70.

101. Aurora Lucero, "Notable Discurso," *Voz del Pueblo*, December 2, 1911, 2; *Nuevo Mexicano*, November 25, 1911, 2; *Bandera Americana*, December 9, 1911, 3; trans. into English in "New Occasions Teach New Duties," *New Mexican*, November 25, 1911, 3. See also, Lozano, *American Language*, 137–38.

102. Lucero, "Notable Discurso."

103. Lucero, "Notable Discurso."

104. Lucero, "Notable Discurso."

105. See Malešević, *Identity as Ideology*, 127.

106. Lucero, "Notable Discurso."

107. "Honor al Mérito," *Estrella*, February 11, 1911, 1.

Chapter 8

1. Before the president signed, Congress had New Mexico adjust its overly conservative procedure for amending the state constitution. Passage of the so-called Blue Ballot amendment required voter confirmation. Owen, *The Two Alberts*, 369; Holtby, *Forty-Seventh Star*, 253; Larson, *New Mexico's Quest*, 293–95.

2. Schermerhorn, *Comparative Ethnic Relations*, 67.

3. Tarr, "American State Constitutions," 100.

4. On the transition from individual rights to collective rights, see Habermas, "Struggles for Recognition in the Democratic Constitutional State."

5. Töpperwien, "Participation in the Decision-Making Process," 48.

6. New Mexico Center on Law and Poverty, "Judge Rules New Mexico Violates Public School Students' Constitutional Right to Sufficient Educational Opportunities."

7. Getz, *Schools of their Own*, 25.

8. See Gonzales, "Promise and Frustration."

9. Fessha, "Federalism, the Subnational Constitutional Framework and Local Government," 82; also Pildes, "Ethnic Identity and Democratic Institutions," 184.

10. "Republicanos, Demócratas y Progresistas Deben Votar por la Enmienda," *La Bandera Americana*, November 1, 1912, 2; "Fergusson Re-Elected by 3,000 or More," *Albuquerque Morning Journal*, November 6, 1912.

11. *Constitution of the State of New Mexico.*

12. Prince, "Opening Address at the First State Convention in New Mexico," 12–13.

13. Cunningham, "Bronson Cutting," 38; "Aquí Les Hablan, Señores Republicanos De Habla Española," *La Voz del Pueblo*, December 9, 1911, 2.

14. Gonzales, "New Mexico Statehood and Political Inequality," 37–38.

15. From a table in Padilla and Ramírez, "Patterns of Chicano Representation in California, Colorado and Nuevo México," 212.

16. Sergeant, "New Mexico, a Relic of Ancient American," 2; partly extracted in "New Mexico, a Relic of Ancient America," *Santa Fe New Mexican*, November 24, 1923, 2.

17. Montgomery, *Spanish Redemption*, 12.

18. Ma, "Reciprocal Relation Between Political Development," 374–75.

19. This compensative conception compares with Charles Montgomery's "Spanish redemption," though "redemption" signifies a psychological compensation among Nuevomexicano elites for their families' loss of lands and political power while compensative leans toward the structural basis of participation rights.

20. "'La Voz del Pueblo,'" *La Revista de Taos*, February 1, 1918, 1.

21. "Two Old Spanish Families United When Miss Sandoval Marries Damian C. de Baca," *Albuquerque Morning Journal*, February 8, 1920, 2.

22. "The Late Pedro Perea," *Santa Fe New Mexican*, January 12, 1906, 2; "Muere Quemado Don Rafael Romero en el Hotel de Roy," *El Nuevo Estado*, July 29, 1918, 1; "La Muerte del Sr. E. C. De Baca," *La Voz del Pueblo*, March 3, 1917, 2; "Biografía Del Gobernador Ezequiel Cabeza de Baca," *Taos Valley News*, March 6, 1917, 4; "One More Formal Tribute to Honorable Alejandro Sandoval is a Monument Located at his Resting Place on the family Lot, at Calvary Cemetery, February 11, 1921," *Albuquerque Journal*, February 13, 1921; "Ambrosio Ortiz, a Resident of State Many Years, Dies," *Albuquerque Morning Journal*, January 7, 1918, 4; "Late Nestor C. De Baca Was Lineal Descendant of the Great Spanish Explorer," *Santa Fe New Mexican*, December 8, 1922, 8.

23. "Obituary: José F. Montoya," *Santa Fe New Mexican*, November 7, 1932, 6; "Obituary: Francisco F. Romero," *Santa Fe New Mexican*, November 18, 1932, 2.

24. Montgomery, *Spanish Redemption*, 151

25. "Nuevo México está Cumpliendo con su Deber," *La Voz del Pueblo*, July 31, 1917, 2.

26. "O. A. Larrazolo and Malaquías Martínez Favor S.A. Regiment," *Santa Fe New Mexican*, August 6, 1917, 2.

27. Montgomery, *Spanish Redemption*, 135–36; untitled, *Santa Fe New Mexican*, June 2, 1911, 4.

28. "Seventeenth Century Glory Recalled in Brilliant Pageant," *Santa Fe New Mexican*, July 5, 1911, partially extracted in Wilson, *Santa Fe Myth*, 198–99.

29. Untitled endorsement of Celso López for mayor, *Santa Fe New Mexican*, March 29, 1912, 7; also untitled, *Santa Fe New Mexican*, June 2, 1911, 4.

30. "Seventeenth Century Glory Recalled in Brilliant Pageant."

31. "De Vargas Pageant Sight of Wonderful Days of Chivalry," *Santa Fe New Mexican*, July 6, 1912, 3.

32. "De Vargas Pageant Sight."

33. George W. Armijo, "La Villa de Santa Fe Tomada en Posesión por de Vargas," in "Proclama de Don Diego de Vargas," *El Nuevo Mexicano*, July 6, 1912, 4.

34. Uncaptioned photograph of George Washington Armijo as Diego de Vargas in conquistador attire, *Nuevo Mexicano*, June 1, 1912, 3. The other of Armijo on his "black charger" was taken by Jesse Nusbaum, published later and reproduced in Wilson, *Santa Fe Myth*, 199.

35. "Fiesta to be Annual Affair," *Santa Fe New Mexican*, September 21, 1919, 1.

36. "Great Events in Santa Fe's History Celebrated in Grand Fiesta," *Santa Fe New Mexican*, September 12, 1919, 1; "The Fiesta," *Santa Fe New Mexican*, September 1, 1919, 5.

37. "La Fiesta de Santa Fe," *La Bandera Americana*, August 13, 1920, 2.

38. "La Fiesta de Santa Fe," *La Bandera Americana*, August 13, 1920, 2.

39. Santa Fe Fiesta Council, "History of Santa Fe Fiesta," Fiesta de Santa Fe site, https://www.santafefiesta.org/history-of-fiesta-de-santa-fe/.

40. As noted in "Fiestas Coming Back," *Santa Fe New Mexican*, August 4, 1932, 4.

41. "Española will Celebrate Oñate's First Settlement in American Southwest," *Santa Fe New Mexican*, March 7, 1933, 2.

42. "Española will Celebrate Oñate's First Settlement"; "Española Celebrates Oñate Day with Parades, Sports, Dances," *Santa Fe New Mexican*, July 5, 1933, 2.

43. Rael-Gálvez, "Reimagining the Española Fiesta."

44. Roxana M. Martínez, "Birthday Bash: Fiestas de Albuquerque Celebrates 313 years Since City's Founding," *Albuquerque Journal*, April 15, 2019.

45. Parallel to regional anthropologists, historians, sociologists, demographers, linguists, folklorists, archaeologists, and lay authors in Quebec who objectified their French identity in publications; Handler, *Nationalism and the Politics of Culture in Quebec*, 3–14.

46. Mora, *Border Dilemmas*, 247–48. For Mora's treatment of Read's biography, writings, and Nuevomexicano identity purposes and contradictions, see 247–53.

47. Isidoro Armijo to Benjamin M. Read, July 14, 1911, published in "Historia Ilustrada de Nuevo Mexico," *La Revista de Taos*, July 28, 1911, 1.

48. Aurelio M. Espinosa to Benjamin M. Read, July 5, 1911, in "Del Profesor Aurelio M. Espinosa Respecto de la 'Historia Ilustrada de Nuevo Mexico,' de

Don B. M. Read," *La Revista de Taos*, July 21, 1911, 1. For other such laudations from friends and peers, see Mora, *Border Dilemmas*, 248.

49. Benjamin M. Read, "Apreciones de Don Benjamín M. Read Sobre el Profesor Espinosa y Sus Estudios Nuevo Mejicanos," *La Revista de Taos*, July 28, 1911.

50. "Asuntos Educacionales," *La Bandera Americana*, February 12, 1904.

51. "Neo-Mexicano que se Distingue," *La Voz del Pueblo*, February 12, 1910, 2.

52. El Corresponsal, "La Voz de la Capital: Un Literato Novo-Mexicano," *La Revista de Taos*, 7 July 1911, 1.

53. Wilson, *Myth of Santa Fe*, 150.

54. Espinosa, "Spanish Folklore in the Southwest," 222; Wilson, *Myth of Santa Fe*, 150.

55. Gellner, *Encounters with Nationalism*, 42–43.

56. For a bibliography of Espinosa's folklore and New Mexico Spanish studies, see Manuel Espinosa, "Spanish Folklore in the Southwest."

57. Wilson, *Myth of Santa Fe*, 150–51.

58. Aurelio M. Espinosa to Benjamin M. Read, July 5, 1911, in "Del Profesor Aurelio." 1.

59. Harroun, "The Plumed Knight," 11; Nieto-Phillips, *Language of Blood*, 180.

60. Espinosa, *Spanish Language in New Mexico*," 1–2.

61. Espinosa, *Spanish Language in New Mexico*.

62. Espinosa, *España En Nuevo Méjico*.

63. Schermerhorn, *Comparative Ethnic Relations*, 67.

64. E.g., Walter V. Woehlke's article in *Sunset Magazine* that says Nuevomexicanos lay outside the US national culture for being "more Spanish than American." "New Mexico Corrupt and Un American, Alleges," *Santa Fe New Mexican*, May 13, 1921; "Insultos Gratuitos a Nuestro Pueblo," *La Voz del Pueblo*, May 28, 1921, 2.

65. Jesús María Alarid to Nestór Montoya, March 28, 1913, *El Independiente*, repr. in *El Nuevo Mexicano*, April 17, 1913, 3. For a similar review of the leading Nuevomexicano figures of Santa Fe, see El Corresponsal, "La Voz de la Capital: Algunas Notabilidades," *La Revista de Taos*, December 9, 1911, 1–2.

66. Antonio Lucero address at the Archaeological Institute, Santa Fe, August 24, 1914 ("Eloquent Brief for Spanish-American by State Secretary"), *Santa Fe New Mexican*, August 25, 1914, 3; trans. in "Habla el Secretario de Estado," *El Nuevo Mexicano*, September 3, 1914, 1.

67. Lucero address delivered at the Archaeological Institute.

68. Lucero address delivered.

69. "No Hay Agravio Donde Hay Derecho," *La Revista de Taos*, October 13, 1915, 5.

70. Enloe, "Internal Colonialism, Federalism and Alternative State Development," 88.

71. Quoted in Montgomery, *Spanish Redemption*, 81.

72. For partial descriptions of the Native Son Movement, see Montgomery, *Spanish Redemption*, 54–88; Gonzales, "New Mexico Statehood and Political Inequality," 39–45.

73. Montgomery, *Spanish Redemption*, 294.

74. See, Gonzales, *Forced Sacrifice as Ethnic Protest.*

75. Juan E. Valdespino, et al., Petition: To His Excellency the Governor of the State of New Mexico and Petition: To the Honorable Nestor Montoya, n.d., Governor Merritt C. Mechem Papers, Special Reports and Investigations, Discrimination Against Spanish-Americans at Deming Road Camp.

76. Clara Olsen [Secretary of Governor] to Hon. Nestor Montoya, May 26, 1921; L.A. Gillett to Hon. Merritt C. Mechem, May 23, 1921, Mechem Papers.

77. Walter, "New Mexico in the Great War," 238.

78. Isaac Montoya to Editor, *La Voz del Pueblo*, October 21, 1916, 2.

79. First quote, "Conferencia de Jefes Indios Relacionada con la Registración, *El Nuevo Estado*, September 2, 1918, 4; second quote, "La Voz del Pueblo," *La Revista de Taos*, October 7, 1921, 1.

80. Isidoro Armijo, "Hon. Elfego Baca," *La Estrella*, June 13, 1914, 1.

81. Armijo, "Hon. Elfego Baca."

82. "Mexico-New Mexico-and Wilson," *Western Liberal*, November 3, 1916, 4.

83. Wilson, *Myth of Santa Fe*, 149.

84. "Hernández in Speech Makes Strong Plea for Quick Action in Avenging Outrages Committed by Villa and his Cutthroats," *New State* (El Nuevo Estado), March 20, 1916, 1.

85. "Una Absurdidad," *El Nuevo Estado*, August 30, 1916, 2.

86. El Corresponsal, "La Voz de la Capital," *La Revista de Taos*, August 15, 1913, 3.

87. "Los Hispano-Americanos," *La Revista de Taos*, May 1, 1914, 1.

88. Jno. J. Boniface, "Separate Report on Second Lieutenant Jesus M. Baca, Troop D, 1st Sep. Sqdn, N.M. Cav., N. G.," in "Mrs. T. H. Baca's Resignation Is Made Public by General Brown," *Santa Fe New Mexican*, July 9, 1921, 1.

89. "Mrs. Baca Out; Reasons Are Sensational, Rumor Today," *Santa Fe New Mexican*, July 8, 1921.

90. "Mrs. T. H. Baca's Resignation is Made Public by General Brown," *Santa Fe New Mexican*, July 9, 1921, 1.

91. "Baca's Resignation is Made Public."

92. "Baca's Resignation is Made Public."

93. "Baca's Resignation is Made Public."

94. "Renuncia su Cargo Porque no Puede Tolerar Insultos a Nuestra Gente," *La Voz del Pueblo*, July 23, 1921, 1.

95. "Renuncia su Cargo."

96. Coronado to Editor ("Del Cercado Ajeno: ¿Es un Ciudadano Americano?"), *La Bandera Americana*, April 8, 1932, 2.

97. Leopoldo to Editor ("El Eco de la Capital"), *El Nuevo Estado*, August 23, 1915, 1.

98. Leopoldo, "El Eco de la Capital: Convención Demócrata de Bernalillo," El *Nuevo Estado*, September 28, 1914, 1.

99. T.A. Bernal to Editor, *La Voz del Pueblo*, April 5, 1919, 2.

100. "El Obrero Mexicano, Escucha," *La Voz del Pueblo*, May 24, 1919, 2.

101. José Sotero Durán to Editor, *La Bandera Americana*, August 8, 1931, 2.

102. José Sotero Durán to Editor.

103. José Sotero Durán to Editor.

104. Refugio B. y García to Editor (Más Tribuna Popular: El Mismo Quejido), *El Nuevomexicano*, November 7, 1929, 3.

105. McWilliams, *North From Mexico*, 43.

106. William G. Brown to H. B. Hening in Callary, "A Political Biography of Frank A. Hubbell," 131.

107. A. A. Hine to Arthur Seligman, September 5, 1918, NM Democratic State Central Committee Records, 1916-1936, box 2.

108. Earl J. Wilson to Arthur Seligman, October 1, 1920, NM Democratic State Central Committee Records, 1916-1936, box 3.

109. "Pro-Raza," *La Voz del Pueblo*, January 13, 1917, 2.

110. "Debemos Identificarnos en el Censo," *El Nuevo Mexicano*, repr. in *La Bandera Americana*, March 21, 1930, 2.

111. L. E. Bernal, "Hispano-Americanos, o simplemente Americanos," *El Nuevo Mexicano*, May 6, 1920, 2.

112. L. E. Bernal, "Hispano-Americanos," 2.

113. L. E. Bernal, "Hispano-Americanos," 2.

114. ROUX, "¿Que Somos, Americanos o Mejicanos?," *La Estrella*, repr. in *La Bandera Americana*, April 18, 1930, 2.

Chapter 9

1. Campa, "Religious Spanish Folk-Drama," 3.

2. Campa, "La Nueva Generación," *El Nuevo Mexicano*, June 1, 1939, trans. by Luzita Girón in Arellano and Vigil, *Arthur L. Campa*, 24–26. On Campa's critical essays in El Nuevomexicano, see Montgomery, *Spanish Redemption*, 222–23.

3. Krauze, *Mexico*, 394.

4. Sue, *Land of the Cosmic Race*, 15.

5. Campa, "Juan de Oñate Era Mexicano: El Cuarto Centenario de Coronado y Los 'Españoles," *El Nuevo Mexicano*, October 12, 1939, transl. in Arellano and Vigil, *Arthur L Campa*, 33–35.

6. Campa, "Juan de Oñate Era Mexicano."

7. Campa, "Nuestro 'Españolismo," *El Nuevo Mexicano*, December 21, 1939, transl. by Christine V. LaCelle in Arellano and Vigil, *Arthur L Campa*, 41, 43–44.

8. Campa, "Nuestro 'Españolismo"; Horton, "Where is the 'Mexican' in 'New Mexican'?"

9. Campa, "La Nueva Generación."

10. Montgomery, *Spanish Redemption*, 219, 220.

11. Orozco, "Regionalism, Politics, and Gender," 467–69.

12. From the guide to the New Mexico Coronado Cuarto Centennial Commission Records, 1935–1940.

13. Montgomery, *Spanish Redemption*, 223.

14. Out of California came the Mexican American Political Association and the Asociación Nacional México Americana; from Texas, the Political Association of Spanish-Speaking Organizations, the League of United Latin American Citizens, and the G.I. Forum; García, *United We Win*, 9; Marquez, *LULAC*.

15. Álvarez, "Psycho-Historical and Socioeconomic Development of the Chicano Community"; García, *Mexican Americans*, 28.

16. Orozco, "Regionalism, Politics, and Gender," 461–63, 465, 481; Padilla and Ramírez, "Patterns of Chicano Representation," 222–23.

17. Orozco, "Regionalism," 480–81.

18. Luján, "Dennis Chavez and the Roosevelt Era," 512–15. See also Gonzales, "Political Construction of Latino Nomenclatures."

19. *Albuquerque Tribune*, November 6, 1958; see also November 15; Gonzales, "Political Construction of Latino Nomenclatures," 170.

20. See the chapters in Anaya and Lomelí, *Essays on the Chicano Homeland*.

21. Interestingly, a Chicano communique invoked a nineteenth-century Spanish heritage script, noting the important fact that "the first colony in the United States was not at Plymouth Rock and that the first settlers of this country were not the pilgrims but, in fact, the first colony was in 1609 in Santa Fe, Nuevo Méjico, 11 years before the pilgrims arrived at Plymouth Rock. This colony was the first in the United States as known today and the first in Aztlán." "Raza, Nos Están Matando. They Are our able to Kill Us, Did You Know?," *La Voz del Pueblo*, May 19, 1970, in Vasquez, *Enriqueta Vasquez*, 182.

22. Américo Paredes, e.g., criticized "Hispanophiles" for overemphasizing New Mexico's isolation from Mexico; *Folklore and Culture Along*, 130. See also, Sánchez, *Forgotten People*, 3; Valdez, "Insurrection in New Mexico," 18; García, "New Mexican Early Ballad Tradition," 151; Chávez, *Lost Land*, 96; Wilson, *Myth of Santa Fe*, 152.

23. Padilla, "Imprisoned Narrative?," 52; Wilson, *Myth of Santa Fe*, 153–54.

24. Mares, "Resolana on Networks," 148–49.

25. Gonzales, "Political Construction of Latino Nomenclatures," 173.

26. Chávez, *My Penitente Land*, xii-xiii, 28–30, 68; see also Simmons, *People of the Sun*, 52, 55; Nostrand, *Hispano Homeland*, passim.

27. Chávez, "A Look at the Background."

28. Suggested in a 1972 survey of 229 "Spanish New Mexicans" in Albuquerque in which 48 percent of the male respondents 20 years of age or younger and 36 percent of those 21–30 years of age chose "Chicano" as their preferred identifier; for similar ratios, see Metzgar "Ethnic Sensitivity of Spanish New Mexicans," 58. As Hunley, et al. note ("Social Identity in New Mexicans"), these results in their own study "are consistent with the notion that the Chicano Movement in New Mexico had roots in politically marginalized communities in rural areas of the state, largely among individuals with deep family ties to the region" (225).

29. Griego, "Presentación a una Junta en la Serie," unpubl. ms, n.d.

30. Gonzales, "The Political Construction of Latino Nomenclatures," 177.

31. Joseph Baca, "Mexican Asks a New Mexican," *Alibi*, March 11–17, 2010.

32. A. Michael Martínez, "Hispanos in New Mexico," *Alibi*, March 25, 2010.

33. Martínez, "Hispanos in New Mexico."

34. Mora, *Making Hispanics*, 10, 13; quote, 159.

35. Lovato, *Santa Fe Hispanic Culture*, 40–41; Salgado, "Mexican American Identity," 185. For analysis, see Gonzales, "Political Construction of Latino Nomenclatures," 175–78.

36. The major attempt to confirm Sephardic Jewish identity in New Mexico is Hordes, *To the End of the Earth.* The claim of a Sephardic tradition in New Mexico is disputed. For a critical inquiry, see Ferry and Nathan, "Mistaken Identity?"

37. Tlapoyawa, *Totacho*, 6; also, Tlapoyawa, *We Will Rise.*

38. See, Gonzales and Lamadrid, eds., *Nación Genízara.*

39. Spicer, "Plural Society in the Southwest," 24–25.

40. Wilcox, *Pueblo Revolt and the Mythology of Conquest*, 8–9.

41. Rhea, *Race Pride and the American Identity*, 25 ; also Nagel, *American Indian Ethnic Renewal*, 162–75; Wilcox, *Pueblo Revolt and the Mythology of Conquest*, 11; Stromberg, "Rhetoric and American Indians," 4–5.

42. Wilcox, *Pueblo Revolt and the Mythology of Conquest*, 8.

43. Andrew Oxford, "Obelisk Redux," *Santa Fe Reporter*, February 03, 2023, 1.

44. On the Soldiers Monument, see Rael-Gálvez, "Centering Truths, Not So Evident." https://medium.com/@estevanraelgalvez/centering-truths-not-so-evident-9573b344d1e6.

45. John Scott, "Hispanic Fraternal Order Sues Santa Fe Mayor," *Daily Lobo*, June 20, 2021.

46. Doss, "Process Frame: Vandalism," 412.

47. Kritzman, "Forward," x.

48. Habermas, "Struggles for Recognition in the Democratic Constitutional State," 109. For a pioneering essay on recognition movements, see Taylor, *The Politics of Recognition.* For a theoretical treatment of recognition struggles and movements for the protection of identity among "subaltern counter-publics," see Young, *Inclusion and Democracy*, 104–8.

49. Appiah discusses African American demands for respect and resistance to the racism of "white culture," "white norms," and "mainstream American conventions" in "Identity, Authenticity, Survival," 152–53.

50. Brooks, "Served Well by Plunder," 27.

51. See Gonzales, "'History Hits the Heart.'"

52. In 1977, the All Pueblo Council of Governors, a confederation consisting of representatives of nineteen New Mexico Pueblos and one in Texas, boycotted Santa Fe Fiesta because organizers banned the selling of native art, jewelry, and wares on the Plaza as it would interfere with the staging of la toma, a decision that was called a "slap in the face to the Indians." In 1980, Pueblo Indians commemorated the 1680 Revolt against Spanish rule; Lovato, *Santa Fe Hispanic Culture*, 53.

53. Lovato, *Santa Fe Hispanic Culture*, 53.

54. Horton, *Santa Fe Fiesta Re-Invented.*

55. Hispanic Culture Preservation League, https://nmhcpl.org/.

56. Doss, "Process Frame: Vandalism," 411.

57. Thompson, *Smashing Statues*, xviii.

58. Larry Barker, "State's $2M visitor center Oñate's final folly," KRQE online, May 17, 2018, https://www.krqe.com/news/states-2m-visitor-center-onates-final-folly/.

59. Pueblo Indian settlement precedences have been legally validated in court decisions over river water usage; see Stevens, "Pueblo Water Rights in New Mexico." Southwest Natives continue invoking precedence as in the disputed waters of the Colorado River; see, Elise Schmelzer, "Tribes Have Rights to a Quarter of Colorado River's Water But Have Been Excluded from Decision-Making. Will That Change?," *Denver Post*, June 8, 2024, https://www.msn.com/en-us/news/us/tribes-have-rights-to-a-quarter-of-colorado-river-s-water-but-have-been-excluded-from-decision-making-will-that-change/ar-BB1popXP.

60. Gonzales, "'History Hits the Heart,'" 227.

61. Gonzales, "'History Hits the Heart,'" 225.

62. Gonzales, "'History Hits the Heart,'" 220–21.

63. Russell Contreras, "Annual New Mexico Hispanic fiesta draws Native American Ire," Associated Press, September 2, 2016, www.dailydemocrat.com/2016/09/02/annual-new-mexico-hispanic-fiesta-draws-native-american-ire/.

64. Gonzales, "'History Hits the Heart,'" 221, 227.

65. Gonzales, "'History Hits the Heart,'" 219.

66. Levin Rojo, *Return to Aztlan*, 84.

67. New Mexican Hispanic Culture Preservation League, https://nmhcpl.org/.

68. Natasha Balwit, "In Santa Fe, Tradition and Identity Clash." *Bloomberg News*, September 15, 2016, https://www.bloomberg.com/news/articles/2016-09-15/fiestas-de-santa-fe-grapples-with-history-and-identity; Elizabeth Miller, "Natives to Entrada: Stop It," *Santa Fe Reporter*, September 9, 2016, https://sfreporter.com/archives/natives-entrada-stop/.

69. Balwit, "In Santa Fe, Tradition and Identity Clash"; Miller, "Natives to Entrada."

70. Miller, "Natives to Entrada."

71. Miller, "Natives to Entrada."

72. Miller, "Natives to Entrada."

73. Aaron Cantú, "Under Protest," *Santa Fe Reporter*, September 14, 2017. Daniel J. Chacón and Andrew Oxford, "At Least Eight Arrested During Entrada Clash at Fiesta de Santa Fe," *New Mexican*, September 8, 2017, https://www.santafenewmexican.com/news/local_news/at-least-eight-arrested-during-entrada-clash-at-fiesta-de-santa-fe/article_bbb99d35-bde1-5195-bc54-7912d6fed3e5.html.

74. Chacón and Oxford, "At Least Eight Arrested."

75. Aaron Cantú, "Entrada Pageant Sparks Fierce Protests, Leads to Eight Arrests," *Santa Fe Reporter*, September 8, 2017.

76. Chacón and Oxford, "At Least Eight Arrested."

77. Cantú, "Under Protest."

78. Cantú, "Under Protest."

79. Cantú, "Under Protest"; "Entrada Pageant Sparks Fierce Protests"; Chacón and Oxford, "At Least Eight Arrested."

80. Chacón and Oxford, "At Least Eight Arrested."

81. Simón Romero, "New Mexico Grapples With Its Version of Confederate Tributes: A Celebration of Spanish Conquest," *New York Times*, September 8, 2018.

82. Estevan Rael-Gálvez, *Creative Strategies 360*, https://www.creativestrategies360.com/.

83. https://decolonizingnewmexico.com.

84. *Culture Connects Santa Fe—A Cultural Cartography*, Creative Strategies 360°, 2016, https://santafenm.gov/media/files/City_SF_Culture_Connects_book.pdf, and, https://santafenm.gov/media/files/125201_City_of_SF_Cultural_Cartography_final_Section_1_reduced_file_size.pdf.

85. Rael-Gálvez, "Raising Consciousness and Imagining Reconciliation: Santa Fe Fiestas," March 19, 2018, https://www.creativestrategies360.com/post/raising-consciousness-and-imagining-reconciliation-santa-fe-fiestas.

86. Rael-Gálvez, "Identifying Captivity": "coercive relations," 8; "internal crisis," 371; "indigenous captivity," 377; on mestizaje, see 126, 187, 301, 373.

87. Rael-Gálvez, "OÑATE ~ REMOVE & REIMAGINE," June 19, 2020, https://www.creativestrategies360.com/post/o%C3%B1ate-~-remove-reimagine; Lane, "On Colonial Forgetting."

88. See, Rael-Gálvez, "Raising Consciousness."

89. Kritzman, "Foreword," xiii.

90. See Rael-Gálvez, "Raising Consciousness." For the 1712 proclamation signed by Juan Páez Hurtado y Rubio and other Spanish colonizers, see Spanish Archives of New Mexico, vol. 2, no. 179.

91. Rael-Gálvez, "Raising Consciousness"; Spanish Archives of New Mexico.

92. All Pueblo Council of Governors, Resolution No. APCG 2017-20, "Reconciliation Negotiations," December 14, 2017.

93. All Pueblo Council of Governors, Resolution No. APCG 2017-20, "Reconciliation Negotiations," December 14, 2017.

94. All Pueblo Council of Governors.

95. Aaron Cantú, "The Entrada is Really Over," *Santa Fe Reporter*, July 31, 2018, https://www.sfreporter.com/news/2018/07/31/the-entrada-is-really-over/.

96. 2018 Entrada/Fiesta Proclamation, https://santafenm.gov/media/files/2018EntradaFiestaProclamation.pdf.

97. 2018 Entrada/Fiesta Proclamation.

98. Chacón, "Fiesta Drops Divisive Entrada Pageant."

99. Romero, "New Mexico Grapples With Its Version."

100. Romero, "New Mexico Grapples With Its Version."

101. Romero, "New Mexico Grapples With Its Version."

102. Carol A. Clark, "Javier Sanchez Elected Mayor Of Española," *Daily Post*, March 7, 2018.

103. Austin Fisher, "Oñate to be Removed from Española Fiesta," *Rio Grande Sun*, April 19, 2018.

104. Morgan Lee, "Española Reconsiders Tribute to Conquistador Juan de Oñate," *Santa Fe New Mexican*, April 18, 2018.

105. Austin Fisher, "Oñate to be Removed."

106. Quoted in Aaron Cantú, "Political Descent," *Santa Fe Reporter*, May 30, 2018.

107. Rael-Gálvez. "Reimagining the Española Fiesta."

108. Quoted in Aaron Cantú, "Political Descent."

109. Rael-Gálvez, "Reimagining the Española Fiesta."

110. Morgan Lee, "Española Reconsiders Tribute to Conquistador Juan de Oñate," *Santa Fe New Mexican*, April 18, 2018.

111. Lee, "Española Reconsiders."

112. Rebecca Atkins, "City of Española Will No Longer Organize Fiestas," KRQE online, Nexstar Media, May 31, 2018, https://www.krqe.com/news/city-of-espanola-will-no-longer-organize-fiestas/.

113. Megan Bennett, "Española Bows Out of Fiesta, Oñate Commemoration," *Albuquerque Journal*, June 1, 2018, A9.

114. Thompson, *Smashing Statues*, xvii.

115. Sarah Mervosh, Simon Romero, and Lucy Tompkins, "Reconsidering the Past, One Statue at a Time," *New York Times*, June 17, 2020, A1, A 13.

116. Thompson, *Smashing Statues*, xviii.

117. Matthew Riesen, "'A Force to be Reckoned With,'" *Albuquerque Journal*, January 3, 2021, A9.

118. John Burnett, "Who Was Juan De Oñate? A Look at The Conquistador's Violent Legacy In New Mexico," National Public Radio, Weekend Edition, July 11, 2020, https://www.npr.org/2020/07/11/890000884/who-was-juan-de-o-ate-a-look-at-the-conquistadors-violent-legacy-in-new-mexico. Betty Sabo, the cocreator of *La Jornada*, passed away in 2016.

119. The statue was created by the late sculptor Donna Quasthoff.

120. KRQE Staff, "Santa Fe Mayor Orders Removal of Three Controversial Monuments," *Santa Fe New Mexican*, June 18, 2020.

121. Unión Protectiva de Santa Fe, Nuevo Méjico, https://unionprotectiva.com/mission/.

122. Virgil Vigil, "Webber's Accounting of Plaza Incident is Fantasy," *Santa Fe New Mexican*, July 4, 2021, updated August 9, 2022.

123. Virgil Vigil, "Mayor Webber's Dark Side," in John Block, "Santa Fe Mayor Alan Webber Triggered after Hispanic Group Blasts Him in Newspaper Ad," *Piñon Post*, April 6, 2021.

124. Union Protectiva de Santa Fe, https://www.facebook.com/unionprotectivadesantafe/.

125. Karla Moya-Crites open letter to Alan Webber, under "Destroying a City that Once was United," *Albuquerque Journal*, June 28, 2020.

126. In Comments, Molly Montgomery, "Hundreds Petition County to Remove Oñate Monument," *Rio Grande Sun*, June 11, 2020, http://www.riograndesun.com/news/hundreds-petition-county-to-remove-o-ate-monument/article_2863c708-ab80-11ea-933f-f7569a3463df.html.

127. Wilcox, *Pueblo Revolt*, 8–9.

128. In Comments, Montgomery.

129. In Comments, Montgomery.

130. Amanda Martínez, "Rio Arriba Work Crews Remove Oñate Statue Ahead of Protest," *Santa Fe New Mexican,* July 15, 21, 2021, https://www.santafenewmexican.com/news/local_news/rio-arriba-work-crews-remove-o-ate-statue-ahead-of-protest/article_41428204-af3c-11ea-b12b-c33ed0b5b099.html.

131. Randall Balmer, "A Spanish Conquistador Gets Pushed Off His Pedestal," *Rio Grande Sun,* June 21, 2020, https://enewspaper.latimes.com/infinity/article_share.aspx?guid=7dd0b0d5-a6c1–416d-acce-15d6986c84ab.

132. Claudia L. Silva, "Celebration of Hispanic Culture Back in Full Swing," *Santa Fe New Mexican,* September 4, 2022.

133. Austin Fisher, "Return of Oñate Pageantry Inflames Debate over Colonial Memory in NM," *Source NM,* July 12, 2022. https://sourcenm.com/2022/07/12/return-of-onate-pageantry-inflames-debate-over-colonial-memory-in-nm/.

134. Daniel J. Chacón, "Fiesta Changes in Santa Fe Leave Some Locals Feeling Cast Aside," *New Mexican,* August 27, 2018.

135. Mo Charnot, "Fiesta Court Stays in School," *Santa Fe Reporter,* August 28, 2023.

136. Julia Goldberg, "SFPS Board: Fiestas Visits Will Continue," *Santa Fe Reporter,* August 29, 2023.

137. See, e.g., Morgan Lee, "Man Shot and Wounded at New Mexico Protest Over Installation of Spanish Conquistador Statue," *Associated Press,* September 28, 2023, https://apnews.com/article/controversial-statue-new-mexico-shooting-dd3b5c671544044dc83eb8bedb480320.

138. KOB, "Santa Fe Officials Approve New Homes for 2 Historical Statues," June 12, 2024, https://www.kob.com/new-mexico/santa-fe-northern-new-mexico/santa-fe-officials-could-approve-new-homes-for-2-historical-statues/.

139. KOB, "Santa Fe Officials Approve." For the Spanish American argument that the Pueblo Indian Revolt had no other meaning than that it was a "massacre," see Sálaz, *Pueblo Revolt Massacre.*

140. KOB, "Santa Fe Officials Approve."

141. Daniel J. Chacón, "No Happy Outcome," *Santa Fe New Mexican,* May 24, 2024, A1, https://www.pressreader.com/usa/santa-fe-new-mexican/20240524/281513641273052

142. Chacón, "No Happy Outcome."

143. *Statue of Diego de Vargas,* Wikipedia; Sean P. Thomas, "Don Diego de Vargas Statue Found in Backyard of Home/Business," *Santa Fe New Mexican,* February 15, 2021, https://research-ebsco-com.libproxy.unm.edu/c/kov46v/viewer/html/dd27td3dlb.

Coda

1. Padilla, *Daring Flight of My Pen*, 9.

2. Millie Santillanes, "Choice for Mayor Comes Down to Mindset," *Albuquerque Journal*, October 25, 1993, A9.

3. Reeve, *History of New Mexico*, 99.

4. Rio Arriba County, "Oñate Center," n.d, https://www.rio-arriba.org/departments_and_divisions/onate_center.html.

5. Kay Matthews, "Oñate's Statue and Monument: Removal at a Troubled Site," *La Jicarita* online magazine, June 14, 2020, https://lajicarita.wordpress.com/2020/06/14/onates-statue-and-monument-removal-at-a-troubled-site/.

6. The facility is currently under the auspice of the federal Northern Rio Grande National Heritage Area. Kay Matthews, "Oñate's Statue."

7. Dictionaries give "homing instinct" and "the heart's true home."

8. Anaya, "Querencia, Mi Patria Chica," xv; Anselmo Arellano quoted in Valenzuela, 182.

9. Gonzales, "La Querencia"; Arellano, *Enduring Acequias.*

10. Arrellano, "La Querencia"; Valenzuela, "Mestiza Consciousness"; Gonzales, "La Querencia."

11. Mary Beth King, "UNM Professor Strives to Keep Traditional Dialect Alive." UNM Newsroom, June 22, 2023, https://news.unm.edu/news/unm-professor-strives-to-keep-traditional-dialect-alive.

12. Raúl Montaño Ayala, "Now is the Time to Raise Monuments to New Mexico's Mexican Era," *Albuquerque Journal*, January 12, 2026, A7.

Conclusion

1. Chanda, et al., "The Role of Ethnic Identity," 165.

References

Collections

Holm Bursum Papers. Center for Southwest Research (CSWR, University of New Mexico).

Official Correspondence of James S. Calhoun, while Native agent at Santa Fé and superintendent of Indian Affairs in New Mexico. Collected mainly from the files of the Indian Office and edited, under its direction, by Annie Heloise Abel.

Thomas Catron Papers, CSWR.

Papers in the Case of J. Francisco Chaves vs. Charles P. Clever, Delegate from the Territory of New Mexico, 40th Congress, House of Representatives, 2d Session.

Additional Papers in the Case of J. Francisco Chaves Against Charles P. Clever, of New Mexico, Mis. Doc. No. 14, 40th Congress, 3d Session.

Rare Books Collection, Huntington Library.

A. A. Jones Papers. New Mexico State Records Center and Archives, Santa Fe (NMSRCA).

William A. Keleher Collection, CSWR.

New Mexico Coronado Cuarto Centennial Commission Records, 1935–1940, CSWR.

New Mexico Democratic State Central Committee Records, Guide to, 1916–1936, CSWR.

Miguel A. Otero, Governor of New Mexico. Interior Department Territorial Papers New Mexico, 1851–1914.

L. Bradford Prince Papers, NMSRCA.

Secundino Romero Papers, CSWR.

Paul S. Taylor Papers, Bancroft Library, BANC MSS 84/38 c.

Tertio-Millennial Collection, Manuscript Collection, History Library, Museum of New Mexico, Santa Fe.

United States. Congress. House. Committee on Elections. February 14, 1856. New Mexico contested election. Papers and testimony in the case of Miguel A. Otero, contesting the seat of Jose M. Gallegos, delegate from the Territory of New Mexico. Washington, DC: 1856.

Donaciano Vigil Papers. Southwest Collection, New Mexico State Archives.
Donaciano Vigil Papers, State Archives of New Mexico.

Government Records

Congressional Record, House of Representatives, June 6, 1896, 54th Congress, 1st session. https://www.loc.gov/classroom-materials/united-states-history-primary-source-timeline/new-nation-1783-1815/policies-and-problems-of-the-confederation-government/.
Papers in the case of Chaves vs. Clever, House of Representatives, 40th Congress, 3d session, Misc. Doc. No. 14.
Laws of the Territory of New Mexico: passed by the Legislative Assembly, 1857–58. *Santa Fe Weekly Gazette*, 1858, HathiTrust. https://babel.hathitrust.org/cgi/pt?id=mdp.35112203967585&seq=86#view=1up&seq=2.
Governor Merritt C. Mechem Papers, Special Reports and Investigations, Discrimination Against Spanish-Americans at Deming Road Camp.
New Mexico. Journals of the Legislative Assembly, December 4, 1865-February 1, 1866, Territorial Archives of New Mexico, microfilm reel 3, CSWR.
New Mexico. Journal of the New Mexico Territorial Council, February 23, 1909.
New Mexico. *The Constitution of the State of New Mexico: Adopted by the Constitutional Convention Held at Santa Fe, New Mexico, from October 3 to November 21, 1910, and Amended November 6, 1911*, November 5, 1912, and November 3, 1914, Santa Fe, 1917.
New Mexico. Constitutional Convention (1910), *Rules of the Constitutional Convention.*
New Mexico. Legislative Assembly. Address of the Legislative Assembly of New Mexico. Manifesto of the Council and House of Representatives to the Inhabitants of the Territory of New Mexico. Signed: Facundo Pino, President of the Council, J.M. Gallegos, Speaker of the House, Santa Fe, N.M. Jan. 29, 1862. (Santa Fe, N.M.): [Publisher not identified], https://archive.org/details/esrp437939782/page/n1/mode/2up.
Records of the Historical Society of New Mexico, 1859–1959 by Historical Society of New Mexico, NMSRCA.

Report of the Governor of New Mexico to the Secretary of the Interior, GPO, 1901.

Santa Fe County, New Mexico, Genealogy and History. http://genealogytrails.com/newmex/santafe/bios6.html.

Territorial Archives of New Mexico, National Archives.

Thirteenth Census of the United States Taken in the Year 1910. Statistics for New Mexico. Department of Commerce and Labor.

US Congress, Senate Committee on Territories. S. 5916. Statehood. Hearing Before the Committee on Territories, United States Senate, 1910.

US Congress, Senate Committee on Territories. H. R. 181166. An Act To Enable the People of New Mexico to Form a Constitution and State Government, 1910.

US Congress, Senate, Congressional Record, 61st Cong., 2d Sess., 1910.

US Congress. HR 8466. "Views of the Minority," House Reports, Fiftieth Congress,

First Session, vol. 4, Report no. 1025, GPO, 1888: 27–54.

Newspapers, Journals

El Abogado Cristiano Neo-Mexicano. Albuquerque, NM

Albuquerque Citizen

Albuquerque Journal

Albuquerque Journal-Democrat

Albuquerque Republican Review/Revista de Albuquerque

Albuquerque Review

Albuquerque Tribune

Alibi. Albuquerque, NM

La Aurora. Santa Fe, NM

La Beliota. Las Vegas, NM

Bloomberg

El Boletín Popular. Santa Fe, NM

The Borderer/El Fronterizo. Las Cruces, NM

La Cachiporra. Las Vegas, NM

The Chicago Tribune

El Combate. Wagon Mound, NM

La Crónica de Valencia. Los Lunas, NM

Daily Lobo. Albuquerque, NM

Daily Optic. Las Vegas, NM

Daily Post. Los Alamos, NM
Daily New Mexican. Santa Fe, NM
The Denver Post
The Eagle. Santa Fe, NM
El Estandarte. Durango, Mexico.
La Estrella. Las Cruces, NM
El Farol. Capitán, NM
El Fronterizo/The Borderer. Las Cruces, NM
La Gaceta Semanaria de Santa Fe
El Guía de Santa Fe
El Hispano Americano. Mora, NM
La Hormiga de Oro. Albuquerque, NM
El Independiente. Las Vegas, NM
El Labrador. Las Cruces, NM
Las Vegas Free Press. Las Vegas, NM
El Metodista Neo-Mexicano. Las Cruces
El Monitor. Taos, NM
El Mosquito. Mora, NM
New Mexico Herald. Santa Fe, NM
The New York Times
El Nuevo Estado. Tierra Amarilla, NM
La Opinión Pública. Albuquerque, NM
El Palacio. Santa Fe, NM
Piñon Post. Santa Fe, NM
Republican Review. Santa Fe, NM
La Revista Católica. Las Cruces, NM
La Revista de Alburquerque
Rio Grande Sun. Española, NM
Santa Fe Gazette/La Gaceta
Santa Fe Post
Santa Fe Reporter
Santa Fe Weekly Post
El Sol de Mayo. Las Vegas, NM
The Source NM. Santa Fe, NM
Sunday Morning Review. Las Vegas, NM
El Tiempo. Las Cruces, NM
La Voz del Pueblo. Las Vegas, NM
La Voz del Pueblo. Santa Fe, NM

Weekly New Mexican. Santa Fe, NM

Weekly New Mexican Review. Santa Fe, NM

White Oaks Eagle. Farmington, NM

Published Sources

Acuña, Rodolfo. *Occupied America: A History of Chicanos*. Harper & Row, 1988.

Aguilar, José Antonio and Rafael Rojas. *El republicanismo en Hispanoamérica: Ensayos de historia intelectual y política*. Fondo de Cultura Económica, 2002.

Alarid, Michael J. *Hispano Bastion: New Mexican Power in the Age of Manifest Destiny, 1837-1863*. University of New Mexico Press, 2022.

Alarid, Trinidad. "Report of Trinidad Alarid Auditor." In *Report of the Governor of New Mexico to the Secretary of the Interior, 1884*. Government Printing Office, 1884.

Álvarez, Rodolfo. "The Psycho-Historical and Socioeconomic Development of the Chicano Community in the United States." *Social Science Quarterly* 53 (March 1973): 920–42.

Ambrosio, Thomas. *Irredentism: Ethnic Conflict and International Politics*. Praeger, 2001.

Anaya, Rudolfo. "Querencia, Mi Patria Chica." In *Querencia: Reflections on the New Mexico Homeland*, edited by Vanessa Fonseca-Chávez, et al.

Anaya, Rudolfo, and Francisco Lomelí, eds. *Aztlan: Essays on the Chicano Homeland*. University of New Mexico Press, 1989.

Anderson, Benedict. *Imagined Communities: Reflections on the Origin and Spread of Nationalism*. Verso, 1983.

Anderson, George B. *History of New Mexico: Its Resources and People*. Pacific States Publishing, 1907.

Appiah, Anthony K. "Identity, Authenticity, Survival: Multicultural Societies and Social Reproduction." In *Multiculturalism: Examining the Politics of Recognition* by Charles Taylor, edited by Amy Gutmann. 2nd edition. Princeton University Press, 1994.

Aragón, Janie Louise. "The People of Santa Fe in the 1790s." *Aztlan* 7, no. 3 (1976): 391–417.

Aragón, Ray John de. *Padre Martínez and Bishop Lamy*. Pan-American Publishing Company, 1978.

Arellano, Anselmo, ed. *De Colores: Journal of Emerging Raza Philosophies* 21 (1975): 38–46.

Arellano, Anselmo. "Through Thick and Thin: Evolutionary Transitions of Las Vegas Grandes and Its Pobladores." PhD diss., University of New Mexico, 1990.

Arellano, Anselmo, and Josué Vigil. *Arthur L Campa and the Coronado Cuarto Centennial.* Editorial Telaraña, 1980.

Arellano, Juan Estevan. "La Querencia: La Raza Bioregionalism." *New Mexico Historical Review* 72 (1997): 31–37.

Arellano, Juan Estevan. *Enduring Acequias: Wisdom of the Land, Knowledge of the Water.* University of New Mexico Press, 2014.

Athearn, Frederic J. "The Reconquest of New Mexico, 1693–1704." In *A Forgotten Kingdom: The Spanish Frontier in Colorado and New Mexico, 1540–1821.* Bureau of Land Management, Cultural Resources Series (Colorado: No. 29), 1989. https://www.nps.gov/parkhistory/online_books/blm/ut/29/chap2.htm.

August 29th Movement. *Fan the Flames: A Revolutionary Position on the Chicano National Question.* 1975. https://marxistleninist.wordpress.com/2010/11/14/fan-the-flames-a-revolutionary-position-on-the-chicano-national-question-a-pamphlet-by-the-august-twenty-ninth-movement-m-1 /.

Austin, Mary. "Mexicans and New Mexico." *Survey Graphic* 19, no. 2 (1931): 141–44.

Bailey, Jessie Bromilow. *Diego de Vargas and Reconquest of New Mexico.* University of New Mexico Press, 1940.

Ball, Durwood. "Fort Craig, New Mexico, and the Southwest Indian Wars, 1854–1884." *New Mexico Historical Review* 73, no. 2 (1998): 153–73.

Bancroft, Hubert Howe. *History of Arizona and New Mexico, 1530–1888.* History Company, 1889.

Bandelier, Adolph Francis Alphonse. *The Gilded Man: (El Dorado) and Other Pictures of the Spanish Occupancy of America.* Appleton, 1893.

Bandelier, Adolph Francis Alphonse, and Madeleine Turrell Rodack. *Adolph F. Bandelier's The Discovery of New Mexico by the Franciscan Monk Friar Marcos De Niza in 1539.* University of Arizona Press, 1981.

Barth, Fredrik. "Introduction." In *Ethnic Groups and Boundaries: The Social Organization of Culture Difference,* edited by Fredrik Barth. 1969; Waveland Press, 1998.

Beck, Warren A. *New Mexico: A History of Four Centuries.* 1962; University of Oklahoma Press, 1977.

Bélanger, Claude. "Quebec Nationalism." *Quebec History*. Last revised August 23, 2000. http://www2.marianopolis.edu/quebechistory/events/natpart4.htm.

Benavides, Alonso de, and Baker H. Morrow. *A Harvest of Reluctant Souls: Fray Alonso de Benavides's History of New Mexico, 1630*. University of New Mexico Press, 2012.

Benedict, Kirby. *Anniversary address delivered before the historical society of New Mexico at Santa Fé, December 31, 1860*. Manderfield & Tucker, 1860.

Blackhawk, Ned. *The Rediscovery of America: Native Peoples and the Unmaking of U. S. History*, Yale University Press, 2023.

Blackshear, James Bailey. *Honor and Defiance: A History of the Las Vegas Land Grant*. Sunstone Press, 2013.

Bloom, Lansing Bartlett. "New Mexico Under Mexican Administration 1821–1846: Part III New Mexico as a Department 1837–1846." *Old Santa Fe* 2, no. 1 (1914): 37–46.

Bloom, Lansing Bartlett, ed. "Historical Society Minutes." *New Mexico Historical Review* 18, no. 3 (1943): 252–311.

Bodnar, John. "Pierre Nora, National Memory, and Democracy: A Review." *Journal of American History*, 87, no. 3 (2000): 951–63.

Bolton, Herbert E. *The Spanish Borderlands*. Yale University Press, 1921.

Booth, W. James. "Communities of Memory: On Identity, Memory, and Debt." *American Political Science Review*, 93, no. 2 (1999): 249–63.

Brading, D. A. *The Origins of Mexican Nationalism*. Cambridge University Press, 1985.

Bradley, Glenn Danford. *The Story of the Santa Fe*. Gorham Press, 1920.

Braeman, John. "Albert J. Beveridge and Statehood for the Southwest 1902–1912." *Arizona and the West* 10, no. 4 (1968): 313–42.

Breton, Raymond. *The Governance of Ethnic Communities: Political Structures and Processes in Canada*. Greenwood Press, 1991.

Breuilly, John. *Nationalism and the State*. Manchester University Press, 1993.

Bridgers, Lynn. *Death's Deceiver: The Life of Joseph P. Machebeuf*. University of New Mexico Press, 1997.

Brooks, James F. "'Served Well by Plunder': La Gran Ladronería and Producers of History Astride the Río Grande." *American Quarterly* 52, no. 1 (2000): 23–58.

Brooks, James F. *Captives & Cousins: Slavery, Kinship, and Community in the Southwest Borderlands*. University of North Carolina Press, 2002.

Brubaker, Rogers. *Ethnicity Without Groups*. Harvard University Press, 2004.

Bruner, Michael Lane. *Strategies of Remembrance: The Rhetorical Dimensions of National Identity Construction*. University of South Carolina Press, 2002.

Bullis, Don. "A Brief History of Education in New Mexico." Triple A Livestock Report. Sponsored by *New Mexico Stockman & Livestock Market Digest*, 2012. https://aaalivestock.wordpress.com/2012/07/27/a-brief-history-of-education-in-new-mexico-by-don-bullis/.

Bushman, Claudia L. *America Discovers Columbus: How an Italian Explorer Became an American Hero*. University Press of New England, 1992.

Bustamante, Adrian Herminio. "Los Hispanos: Ethnicity and Social Change in New Mexico." PhD diss., University of New Mexico, 1982.

Caffey, David L. *Chasing the Santa Fe Ring: Power and Privilege in Territorial New Mexico*. University of New Mexico Press, 2014.

Calhoun, Craig. *Nationalism*. University of Minnesota Press, 1997.

Callary, Carol N. "A Political Biography of Frank A. Hubbell, 1862–1929." MA thesis, University of New Mexico, 1967.

Callon, Milton W. *Las Vegas, New Mexico . . . The Town that Wouldn't Gamble*. Las Vegas Publishing, 1962.

Campa, Arthur L. "Religious Spanish folk-drama in New Mexico." *New Mexico Quarterly 2* (1932): 3–13.

Campa, Arthur L. *Spanish Folk-Poetry in New Mexico*. University of New Mexico Press, 1946.

Carr, Edward Hallett. *Nationalism and After*. Macmillan, 1945.

Carroll, Michael P. "The Debate over a Crypto-Jewish Presence in New Mexico: The Role of Ethnographic Allegory and Orientalism." *Sociology of Religion* 63, no. 1 (2002): 1–19. https://doi.org/10.2307/3712537.

Cervantes, Leo. *Raíces del Periodismo Hispano en el Suroeste de Estados Unidos: El Caso de Nuevo México*. Editorial Orbis Press, 2005.

Chacón, Eusebio, Meléndez A. Gabriel, and Lomelí Francisco A. *The Writings of Eusebio Chacón*. University of New Mexico Press, 2012.

Chaves, Amado. *The Defeat of the Comanches in 1717*. Historical Society of New Mexico, Publications in History, no. 8.

Chávez, Angélico. "A look at the Background of New Mexico Cultures." *Albuquerque Journal*, December 18, 1970.

Chávez, Angélico. *My Penitente Land: Reflections on the Spanish New Mexico.* William Gannon, 1979.

Chávez, Angélico. *But Time and Chance: The Story of Padre Martínez of Taos, 1793–1867.* Sunstone Press, 1981.

Chávez, Angélico. *Très Macho—He Said: Padre Gallegos of Albuquerque, New Mexico's First Congressman.* William Gannon, 1985.

Chávez, Angélico, and Thomas E. Chavez. *Wake for a Fat Vicar: Father Juan Felipe Ortiz, Archbishop Lamy, and the New Mexican Catholic Church in the Middle of the Nineteenth Century.* LPD Press, 2004.

Chávez, John R. *The Lost Land: The Chicano Image of the Southwest.* University of New Mexico, 1984.

Chávez, Thomas E. "Santa Fe's Own: A History of Fiesta." *El Palacio* 91 (Spring 1985): 7–17.

Chovanec, Johanna and Olof Heilo, eds. *Narrated Empires.* Perceptions of Late Habsburg and Ottoman Multinationalism. Cham, Switzerland. Palgrave Macmillan, 2021. https://download.e-bookshelf.de/download/0014/1645/60/L-G-0014164560-0051700787.pdf.

Cline, Dorothy I. "Constitutional Politics in New Mexico: 1910–1976." In *New Mexico Government,* edited by F. Chris Garcia and Paul L. Hain.

Cline, Dorothy I. *New Mexico's 1910 Constitution, A Nineteenth Century Product.* Lightning Tree, 1985.

Coakley, John. "Introduction: The Challenge." In *The Territorial Management of Ethnic Conflict,* edited by John Coakley.

Coakley, John. *The Territorial Management of Ethnic Conflict.* 2nd rev. and expanded ed. London: F. Cass, 2003.

Cocker, Mark. *Rivers of Blood, Rivers of Gold: Europe's Conquest of Indigenous Peoples.* Grove Press, 1998.

Connor, Walker. *Ethnonationalism: The Quest for Understanding.* Princeton University Press, 1994.

Cooper, Frederick. "Modernizing Colonialism and the Limits of Empire." *Items and Issues* 4, no. 4 (2003–2004): 1–9.

Cordova, Alfred C., and Charles B. Judah. *Octaviano Larrazolo: A Political Portrait.* Publication 32. University of New Mexico Press, 1952.

Coronado, Raul. *A World Not to Come: A History of Latino Writing and Print Culture.* Harvard University Press. 2013.

Correia, David. "Making Destiny Manifest: United States Territorial Expansion and the Dispossession of Two Mexican Property

Claims in New Mexico, 1824–1899." *Journal of Historical Geography* 35 (2009): 87–103.

Correia, David. *Properties of Violence: Law and Land Grant Struggle in Northern New Mexico*. University of Georgia Press, 2013.

Crawford, James. *Language Loyalties: A Source Book on the Official English Controversy*. University of Chicago Press, 1992.

Cronin, Sean. "The Ideology of the IRA and the Roots of Conflict in Northern Ireland." PhD diss., New School for Social Research, 1979.

Crutchfield, James A. *Tragedy at Taos: The Revolt of* 1847. Wordware Press, 1995.

Cunningham, Jonathan Ray. "Bronson Cutting: A Political Biography." PhD diss., University of New Mexico, 1940.

Curti, Merle Eugene. *The Roots of American Loyalty*. Columbia University Press, 1946.

Dargan, Marion. "New Mexico's Fight for Statehood 1895–1912, I: The Political Leaders of the Latter Half of the 1890s and Statehood." *New Mexico Historical Review* 14, no. 1 (1939): 1–33.

Dargan, Marion. "New Mexico's Fight for Statehood 1895–1912," II: The Attitude of the Territorial Press, 1895–1901," *New Mexico Historical Review* 14, no. 3 (1939): 121–42.

Dargan, Marion. "New Mexico's Fight for Statehood, 1895–1912, III: Opposition within the Territory (1888–1890)." *New Mexico Historical Review*, 15, no. 3 (1940): 133–87.

Dargan, Marion. "New Mexico's Fight for Statehood, 1895–1912, IV: Opposition within the Territory During the Nineties." *New Mexico Historical Review*, 16, no. 1 (1940): 70–103.

Dargan, Marion. "New Mexico's Fight for Statehood 1895–1912, V. The Silencing of the Opposition at Home." *New Mexico Historical Review* 16, no. 4 (1941): 379–400.

Dargan, Marion. "New Mexico's Fight for Statehood 1895–1912, VI: Advertising 'The Backyard of the United States.'" *New Mexico Historical Review* 18, no. 1 (1943): 60–96.

Dargan, Marion. "New Mexico's Fight for Statehood 1895–1912, VII. The Part Played by the Press of the Southwest." *New Mexico Historical Review* 18, no. 3 (1943): 148–75.

Davis, W. W. H. *El Gringo; or, New Mexico and Her People*. Harper & Brothers, 1857.

Debo, Angie. *Geronimo: The Man, His Time, His Place.* University of Oklahoma Press, 1976.

de Certeau, Michel. *The Writing of History.* Translated by Tom Conley. Columbia University Press, 1988.

de la Peña, Guillermo. "A New Mexican Nationalism? Indigenous Rights, Constitutional Reform and the Conflicting Meanings of Multiculturalism." *Nations and Nationalism* 12, no. 2 (2006): 279–302.

DeLay, Brian. *War of a Thousand Deserts: Indian Raids and the U.S.-Mexican War.* Yale University Press, 2008.

DeLay, Brian. "Blood Talk: Violence and Belonging in the Navajo-New Mexican Borderland." In *Contested Spaces of Early America,* edited by Juliana Barr and Edward Countryman. University of Pennsylvania Press, 2014.

Deutsch, Karl W. *Nationalism and Its Alternatives.* Alfred A. Knopf, 1969.

Deutsch, Sarah. *No Separate Refuge: Culture, Class, and Gender on an Anglo-Hispanic Frontier in the American Southwest, 1880–1940.* Oxford University Press, 1987.

Diffie, Bailey W. "The Ideology of *Hispanidad.*" *Hispanic American Historical Review* 22 (August 1943): 457–82.

Dodds Pennock, Caroline. *On Savage Shores: How Indigenous Americans Discovered Europe.* Alfred A. Knopf, 2023.

Donnelly, Thomas C. "The Making of the New Mexico Constitution, Part I." *New Mexico Quarterly* 11, no. 4 (1941): 452–62.

Doob, Leonard W. *Patriotism and Nationalism: Their Psychological Foundations.* Yale University Press, 1964.

Doss, Erika "The Process Frame: Vandalism, Removal, ReSiting, Destruction." In *A Companion to Public Art,* edited by Cher Krause Knigh, and Harriet Senie. Wiley, 2016.

Driver, Justin. "Rethinking the Interest-Convergence Thesis." *Northwestern University Law Review* 105, no. 1 (2011): 149–97.

Duchacek, Ivo. D. "Antagonistic Cooperation: Territorial and Ethnic Communities." *Publius* 7, no. 4 (1977): 3–29.

Durkheim, Émile. *The Elementary Forms of the Religious Life, a Study in Religious Sociology.* Free Press, 1947.

Ebright, Malcolm. *Testimony in Status of Community Land Grants in Northern New Mexico.* Oversight Hearing Before the Subcommittee on General Oversight and Investigations of the House Committee on Interior and Insular Affairs. Washington, .C. Governing Printing Office, 1989.

Ebright, Malcolm. *Land Grants and Lawsuits in Northern New Mexico.* University of New Mexico Press, 1994.

Ebright, Malcolm, and Rick Hendricks. *Pueblo Sovereignty: Indian Land and Water in New Mexico and Texas.* University of Oklahoma Press, 2019.

Edmunson, Munro S. *Los Manitos: A Study of Institutional Values.* Tulane University. 1957.

Ellis, Bruce T. "Santa Fe's Tertio-millennial, 1883." *El Palacio* 65, no. 4 (1958): 121–35.

Enciso, Carmen E. *Hispanic Americans in Congress, 1822-1995.* United States Congress Joint Committee on Printing. 1994,

Enloe, Cynthia H. *Ethnic Conflict and Political Development.* Little, Brown, 1972.

Enloe, Cynthia H. "Internal Colonialism, Federalism and Alternative State Development Strategies." *Publius* 7 (Fall 1997): 145–60.

Espinosa, Aurelio Macedonio. "*Los Comanches,* A New-Mexican Spanish Heroic Play," *University of New Mexico Bulletin* 45, no. 1 (1907).

Espinosa, Aurelio Macedonio. *The Spanish Language in New Mexico and Southern Colorado.* Historical Society of New Mexico, Publication No. 16, 1911.

Espinosa, Aurelio Macedonio. "New Mexico." *The Catholic Encyclopedia.* Vol. 11. Knights of Columbus Truth Committee, 1913.

Espinosa, Aurelio Macedonio. *España En Nuevo Méjico: Lecturas Elementales Sobre La Historia De Nuevo Méjico y Su Tradición Española.* Allyn and Bacon, 1937.

Espinosa, Aurelio Macedonio. *The Folklore of Spain in the American Southwest.* University of Oklahoma Press, 1990.

Espinosa, Aurelio Macedonio, ed. *Romancero De Nuevo Méjico.* Revista De Filología Española. Añejo, 58. Consejo Superior de Investigaciones Científicas, 1953.

Espinosa, J. Manuel. *Crusaders of the Río Grande: The Story of Don Diego de Vargas and the Reconquest and Refounding of New Mexico.* Institute of Jesuit History, 1942.

Espinosa, J. Manuel, ed. *The Folklore of Spain in the American Southwest: Traditional Spanish Folk Literature in Northern New Mexico and Southern Colorado.* University of New Mexico Press, 1985.

Espinosa, J. Manuel. "Spanish Folklore in the Southwest: The Pioneer Studies of Aurelio M. Espinosa." *Americas* 35 (1978): 219–37.

Everett, Dianna. "The Public School Debate in New Mexico, 1850–1891." *Arizona and the West* 26, no. 2 (1984): 107–34.

Ferry, Barbara, and Debbie Nathan. "Mistaken Identity? The Case of New Mexico's 'Hidden Jews.'" *Atlantic Monthly* 286, no. 6 (December 2000): 85–96.

Fessha, Yonatan Tesfaye. "Federalism, the Subnational Constitutional Framework and Local Government: Accommodating Minorities Within Minorities." *Perspectives on Federalism* 4, no. 2 (2012): 77–100.

Fisher-Onar, N. "Remembering Empires: Between Civilisational Nationalism and Post-National Pluralism." In *Narrated Empires: Perceptions of Late Habsburg and Ottoman Multinationalism*, edited by J. Chovanec and O. Heilo. Palgrave Macmillan, 2021.

Flint, Richard. "Results and Repercussions of the Coronado Expedition to Tierra Nueva from Documentary and Archaeological Sources." *New Mexico Historical Review* 77, no. 3 (2002): 233–59.

Flint, Richard, and Shirley Cushing Flint. *A Most Splendid Company: The Coronado Expedition in Global Perspective.* University of New Mexico Press, 2019.

Florescano, Enrique. *Étnia, Estado y Nación: Los Indigenas y la Sociedád Colonial.* Nuevo Siglo, 1997.

Fonseca-Chávez, Vanessa, Levi Romero, and Spencer R. Herrera, eds. *Querencia: Reflections on the New Mexico Homeland.* University of New Mexico Press, 2020.

Fowler, Will. "Valentín Gómez Farías: Perceptions of Radicalism in Independent Mexico, 1821–1847." *Bulletin of Latin American Research* 15, no. 1 (1996): 39–62. http://www.jstor.org/stable/3339403.

Francis, E. K. "Padre Martinez: A New Mexican Myth." *New Mexico Historical Review* 31, no. 4 (1956): 265–89. https://digitalrepository.unm.edu/nmhr/v0131/iss4/2.

Frank, Ross. *From Settler to Citizen: New Mexican Economic Development and the Creation of Vecino Society, 1750–1820.* University of California Press, 2000.

Frank, Ross. "'They Conceal a Malice Most Refined': Controlling Social and Ethnic Mobility in Late Colonial New Mexico." In *Choice, Persuasion, and Coercion: Social Control on Spain's North American Frontiers,* edited by Jesús F. de la Teja and Ross Frank. University of New Mexico Press, 2005.

Freise, Kathy. "Contesting Oñate: Sculpting the Shape of Memory." In *Expressing New Mexico*, edited by Phillip B. Gonzales.

Fukuyama, Francis. *The End of History and the Last Man.* Free Press, 1992.

Gamio, Manuel. *Mexican Immigration to the United States: A Study of Human Migration and Adjustment."* 1930; Dover, 1971.

Gans, Chaim. *The Limits of Nationalism.* Cambridge University Press, 2003.

García, F. Chris, and Paul L. Hain, eds. *New Mexico Government.* University of New Mexico Press, 1976.

García, Ignacio M. *United We Win: The Rise and Fall of La Raza Unida Party.* University of Arizona Press, 1989.

García, Mario. *Mexican Americans: Leadership, Ideology, and Identity, 1930–1960.* Yale University Press, 1989.

García, Peter J. "The New Mexican Early Ballad Tradition: Reconsidering the New Mexican Folklorists' Contribution to Songs of Intercultural Conflict." *Latin American Music Review / Revista de Música Latinoamericana* 17, no. 2 (1996): 150–71.

Gellner, Ernest. *Nations and Nationalism.* Basil Blackwell, 1983.

Gellner, Ernest. *Encounters with Nationalism.* Blackwell, 1994.

Gellner, Ernest. *Nationalism.* New York University Press, 1997.

General Accounting Office. *Treaty of Guadalupe Hidalgo: Definition and List of Community Land Grants in New Mexico.* Exposure Draft. GAO, January 2001.

Getz, Lynne Marie. *Schools of Their Own: The Education of Hispanos in New Mexico, 1850–1940.* University of New Mexico Press, 1997.

Gill, Mary E., and John S. Goff. "Edmund Francis Dunne and the Public School Controversy, 1875." *Journal of Arizona History*, 25, no. 4 (1984): 369–84.

Glazer, Nathan. "Federalism and Ethnicity: The Experience of the United States." *Publius* 7, no. 4 (1977): 71–87.

Glenn, Evelyn Nakano. *Unequal Freedom: How Race and Gender Shaped American Citizenship and Labor.* Harvard University Press, 2002.

Gómez Laura E. *Manifest Destinies: The Making of the Mexican American Race.* New York University Press, 2018.

Gómez-Quiñones, Juan. *Roots of Chicano Politics, 1600–1940.* University of New Mexico, Press, 1994.

Gómez-Quiñones, Juan, and Irene Vásquez, *Making Áztlan: Ideology and Culture of the Chicana And Chicano Movement, 1966–1977.* University of New Mexico Press, 2014.

Gonzales, Moises. "La Querencia: The Genízaro Cultural Landscape Model of Community Land Grants in Northern New Mexico." In *Querencia: Reflections on the New Mexico Homeland*, edited by Vanessa Fonseca-Chávez, Levi Romero and Herrera R. Spencer. University of New Mexico Press, 2020.

Gonzales, Moises, and Enrique R. Lamadrid. "Introduction." In *Nación Genízara*, edited by Moises Gonzales and Enrique R. Lamadrid.

Gonzales, Phillip B. "'A Perfect Furor of Indignation:' The Racial Attitude Confrontation of 1933. PhD diss., University of California, Berkeley, 1985.

Gonzales, Phillip B. "Spanish Heritage and Ethnic Protest in New Mexico: The Anti-Fraternity Bill of 1933." *New Mexico Historical Review* 61, no. 4 (1986): 281–99.

Gonzales, Phillip B. "The Political Construction of Latino Nomenclatures in Twentieth Century New Mexico." *Journal of the Southwest* 35, no. 2 (1993): 158–85.

Gonzales, Phillip B. *Forced Sacrifice as Ethnic Protest: The Hispano Cause in New Mexico and the Racial Attitude Confrontation of 1933.* Peter Lang, 2001.

Gonzales, Phillip B. "La Junta de Indignación: Hispano Repertoire of Collective Protest in New Mexico, 1884–1933." *Western Historical Quarterly* 31, no. 2 (2000): 161–86.

Gonzales, Phillip B. "History Hits the Heart": Albuquerque's Great Cuartocentenario Controversy, 1997–2005." In *Expressing New Mexico: Nuevomexicana/o Creativity, Everyday Ritual, and Collective Remembrance.* University of Arizona Press, 2007.

Gonzales, Phillip B. Review of *The Spanish Redemption: Heritage, Power and Loss on New Mexico's Upper Rio Grande, by Charles Montgomery. New Mexico Historical Review* 78, no. 1 (2003): 329–37.

Gonzales, Phillip B., ed. *Expressing New Mexico: Nuevomexicana/o Creativity, Everyday Ritual, and Collective Remembrance.* University of Arizona Press, 2007.

Gonzales, Phillip B. "Mexican Party, American Party, Democratic Party: Establishing the American Political Party in New Mexico, 1848–1853." *New Mexico Historical Review* 88, no. 3 (2013): 253–85.

Gonzales, Phillip B. "New Mexico Statehood and Political Inequality: The Case of Nuevomexicanos," *New Mexico Historical Review* 90, no. 1 (2015): 31–52.

Gonzales, Phillip B. *Política: Nuevomexicanos and American Political Incorporation, 1821–1910.* University of Nebraska Press, 2016.

Gonzales, Phillip B. "Promise and Frustration: On the History of Spanish-language Bilingual Education in New Mexico, 1846–1975." In *Standing on their Shoulders: A History of Bilingual Education in New Mexico,* edited by Rebecca Blum-Martínez and Mary Jean Habermann López. University of New Mexico Press, 2020.

Gonzales, Phillip B. "Whose Sovereign People? The Campaign of Nuevomexicanos for Delegates to the 1910 Constitutional Convention." *New Mexico Historical Review* 98, no. 2 (2023): 157–89.

Gonzales, Phillip B. "Introduction: Recovering *Impresiones.*" In *Impresiones de un Surumato en Nuevo México,* edited by Manuel Sariñana.

Gonzales, Phillip B. "Reading *Impresiones,* Explicating Manuel Sariñana." In *Impresiones de un Surumato en Nuevo México,* edited by Manuel Sariñana.

Gonzales-Berry, Erlinda. "Which Language Will Our Children Speak? The Spanish Language and Public Education Policy in New Mexico, 1890–1930." In *The Contested Homeland,* edited by Erlinda Gonzales-Berry and David R. Maciel.

González Casanova, Pablo. "Internal Colonialism and National Development." *Studies in Comparative International Development,* 1, no. 4 (1965): 27–37. doi:10.1007/bf02800542, S2CID 153821137.

Green, Jesse, ed. *Cushing at Zuni: The Correspondence and Journals of Frank Hamilton Cushing, 1879–1884.* University of New Mexico Press, 1990.

Gregg, Josiah. *Commerce of the Prairies.* 1844; Henry G. Langley, 1926.

Grove, Pearce S., Becky J. Barnett, and Sandra J. Hansen, eds. *New Mexico Newspapers: A Comprehensive Guide to Bibliographical Entries and Locations.* University of New Mexico Press, 1975.

Guardino. Peter. *The Dead March: A History of the Mexican–American War.* Harvard University Press, 2017.

Gunberg, Bernard. "Poderes y Política de Hernán Cortés (1518–1528)." *La Biblioteca Jurídica de Investigaciones Jurídicas de la UNAM*: 473–500. https://archivos.juridicas.unam.mx/www/bjv/libros/15/7025/24.pdf

Gutiérrez, Ramón A. *When Jesus Came, the Corn Mothers Went Away : Marriage, Sexuality, and Power in New Mexico, 1500–1846.* Stanford University Press, 1991.

Gutiérrez, Ramón A. "What's in a Name: The History and Politics of Hispanic and Latino Panethnicities." In *The New Latino Studies Reader*, edited by Ramon A. Gutiérrez, and Tomás Almaguer.

Gutiérrez, Ramón A., and Tomás Almaguer, eds. *The New Latino Studies Reader: A Twenty-First-Century Perspective*. University of California Press, 2016.

Habermas, Jürgen. "Struggles for Recognition in the Democratic Constitutional State." In *Multiculturalism: Examining the Politics of Recognition* by Charles Taylor, edited by Amy Gutmann. 2nd edition. Princeton University Press, 1994.

Hackett, Charles W. *Revolt of the Pueblo Indians of New Mexico and Otermín's Attempted Reconquest, 1680-1682.* 2 vols. Translated of original documents by Charmion Shelby. University of New Mexico Press, 1942.

Haines, Helen E. *History of New Mexico: From the Spanish Conquest to the Present Time, 1530-1890 : With Portraits and Biographical Sketches of Its Prominent People*. New Mexico Historical Publishing, 1891.

Hammond, George P. *Don Juan de Oñate and the Founding of New Mexico.* El Palacio Press, 1927.

Hammond, George P. "The Search for the Fabulous in the Settlement of the Southwest." *Utah Historical Quarterly* 24 (1956): 1–19.

Hammond, George P., and Agapito Rey, eds. *Don Juan de Oñate Colonizer of New Mexico 1595-1628.* University of New Mexico Press, 1953.

Handler, Richard. *Nationalism and the Politics of Culture in Quebec.* University of Wisconsin Press, 1988.

Hannon, Michael. "Public discourse and its problems." *Politics, Philosophy & Economics* 22, no. 3 (2023): 336–56. https://journals.sagepub.com/doi/pdf/10.1177/1470594X221100578.

Harper, Wayne A. "Juan Bautista Vigil y Alarid, a New Mexico Bureaucrat, 1792–1866." MA thesis, Brigham Young University, 1985.

Harroun, W. S. "The Plumed Knight." *El Palacio* 4 (1917): 11–17.

Hartman, Saidiya V. *Wayward Lives, Beautiful Experiments: Intimate Histories of Social Upheaval.* W. W. Norton, 2019.

Hechter, Michael. "The Dynamics of Secession," *Acta Sociologica* 35 (1992): 267–74.

Hechter, Michael. *Internal Colonialism: The Celtic Fringe in British National Development* Transaction, 1999.

Heflin, Reuben W. "The New Mexico Constitutional Convention." *New Mexico Historical Review* 21, no. 1 (1946): 60–68.

Hernández-Chávez, Eduardo. "Language Policy in the United States: A History of Cultural Genocide." In *Linguistic Human Rights,* edited by Tove Skutnabb-Kangass and Robert Phillipson.

Hernańdez, José Amaro. *Mutual Aid for Survival: The Case of the Mexican American.* Krieger, 1983.

Hernández, José Angel. *Mexican American Colonization during the Nineteenth Century: A History of the U.S.-Mexico Borderlands.* Cambridge University Press, 2012.

Hills, E. C. "New-Mexican Spanish." *PMLA* 21, no. 3 (1906): 706–53. https://doi.org/10.2307/456770.

Hinsley, Curtis M. *Savages and Scientists: The Smithsonian Institution and the Development of American Anthropology, 1846-1910.* Washington, DC: Smithsonian Institution Press, 1981.

Holmes, Jack E. *Politics in New Mexico.* University of New Mexico Press, 1967.

Holtby, David V. *Forty-Seventh Star: New Mexico's Struggle for Statehood.* University of Oklahoma Press, 2012.

Hordes, Stanley M. *To the End of the Earth : A History of the Crypto-Jews of New Mexico.* Columbia University Press, 2005.

Horgan, Paul. *Lamy of Santa Fe, His Life and Times.* Farrar, Straus and Giroux, 1975.

Horton, Sarah B. "Maintaining Hispano Identity Through the Santa Fe Fiesta: Re-Appropriating Key Symbols and Resisting Anglo Dominance." *Kiva* 66, no. 2 (2000): 250–65.

Horton, Sarah B. "Where is the 'Mexican' in 'New Mexican'?" Enacting History, Enacting Dominance in the Santa Fe Fiesta." *Public Historian* 23, no. 4 (2001): 41–54.

Horton, Sarah B. *The Santa Fe Fiesta Re-Invented: Staking Ethno-Nationalist Claims to a Disappearing Homeland.* School for Advanced Research Press, 2010.

Horton, Sarah B. "Ritual and Return: Diasporic Hispanos and the Santa Fe Fiesta." In *Expressing New Mexico*, edited by Phillip B. Gonzales. University of Arizona Press, 2007.

Hubbard, H. A. "Arizona's Struggle against Joint Statehood." *Pacific Historical Review* 11, no. 4 (1942): 415–23. https://www.jstor.org/stable/3633254.

Hudson, Angela Pulley. "'Forked Justice:' Elias Boudinot, the US Constitution, and Cherokee Removal." In American *Indian Rhetorics of Survivance*, edited by Ernest Stromberg.

Hunley, Keith, Heather Edgar, Meghan Healy, Carmen Mosley, Graciela S. Cabana, and Frankie West. "Social Identity in New Mexicans of Spanish-Speaking Descent Highlights Limitations of Using Standardized Ethnic Terminology in Research." *Human Biology* 89, no. 3 (2017): 217-28. Available at: https://digitalcommons.wayne.edu/humbiol/vol89/iss3/4.

Hunt, Aurora. *Kirby Benedict: Frontier Federal Judge*. Beard Books, 2000.

Huntington, Samuel. *Who Are We? The Challenges to America's National Identity*. Simon & Schuster, 2004.

Ihde, Ira C. "Washington Ellsworth Lindsey." *New Mexico Historical Review* 26 (3, 1951): 177–96.

Irving, Washington. *The Life and Voyages of Christopher Columbus*. J. Murray, 1830.

Islas, Jesús. *Situación de los habitantes Ispano-Americanos en el Estado de Alta California, 26 Junio 1855*. Imprenta de Rafael Carreon, 1855.

Jahoda, Gustav. *Images of Savages: Ancient Roots of Modern Prejudice in Western Culture*. Routledge, 1999.

Jarrett, Henry. *Peace and Ethnic Identity in Northern Ireland: Consociational Power Sharing and Conflict Management*. Routledge, 2017.

Johannsen, Robert W. *To the Halls of the Montezumas: The Mexican War in the American Imagination*. Oxford University Press, 1985.

Johnson, Nuala. "Cast in Stone: Monuments, Geography, and Nationalism." *Environmental Planning D: Society and Space* 13, no. 1 (1995): 51–65.

Jones, Martha S. *Birthright Citizens: A History of Race and Rights in Antebellum America*. Cambridge University Press, 2018.

Kanellos, Nicolás. *Hispanic Periodicals in the United States, Origins to 1960: A Brief History and Comprehensive Bibliography*. Arte Publico Press, 2000.

Kanellos, Nicolás, Kenya Dworkin y Méndez, and Alejandra Balestra Herencias. *The Anthology of Hispanic Literature of the United States*. Oxford University Press, 2002.

Karst, Kenneth L. *Belonging to America: Equal Citizenship and the Constitution*. Yale University Press, 1989.

Kaufman, Eric P. "American Exceptionalism Reconsidered: Anglo-Saxon Ethnogenesis in the 'Universal' Nation, 1776–1850." *Journal of American Studies* 33, no. 3 (1999): 437–57.

Kaufman, Eric P. "Introduction: Dominant Ethnicity: From Background to Foreground." In *Rethinking Ethnicity*, edited by Eric P. Kaufman. https://doi.org/10.4324/9780203563397.

Keating, Michael. *State and Regional Nationalism: Territorial Politic and the European State*. Harvester-Wheatsheaf, 1988.

Keating, Michael. "Regionalism and Regionalization." *Encyclopedia Princetoniensis*. Princeton University, n.d. https://pesd.princeton.edu/node/626.

Kellas, James G. *The Politics of Nationalism and Ethnicity*. St. Martin's, 1998.

Kelly, Michael J. "Political Downsizing: The Re-Emergence of Self-Determination, and the Movement Toward Smaller, Ethnically Homogeneous States." *Drake Law Review* 47 (1999): 209–78.

Kessell, John L. "Preface." *To the Royal Crown Restored: The Journals of Don Diego de Vargas, New Mexico, 1692–94*. University of New Mexico Press, 1995.

Kessell, John L. *Spain in the Southwest: A Narrative History of Colonial New Mexico, Arizona, Texas, and California*. University of Oklahoma Press, 2002.

Kessell, John L., Rick Hendricks, and Meredith D. Dodge. "Introduction." In *By Force of Arms: The Journals of Don Diego de Vargas, 1691–1693*, edited by John L. Kessell, Rick Hendricks, and Meredith D. Dodge. University of New Mexico Press, 1992.

Kiser, William S. "The Politics of Slavery and Social Hierarchies in Colonial, Mexican, and Territorial New Mexico." *New Mexico Historical Review* 92, 3 (2017): 285–309. https://digitalrepository.unm.edu/nmhr/vol92/iss3/4.

Knaut, Andrew L. *The Pueblo Revolt of 1680: Conquest and Resistance in Seventeenth-Century New Mexico*. University of Oklahoma Press, 1995.

Knight, Cher Krause, and Harriet Senie, eds. *A Companion to Public Art*. Wiley, 2016.

Krauze, Enrique. *Mexico: Biography of Power: A History of Modern Mexico, 1810–1996*. Translated by Hank Heifetz. HarperCollins, 1997.

Krieger, Alex D., and Gonzalo Fernandez de Oviedo y Valdes. *We Came Naked and Barefoot: The Journey of Cabeza de Vaca Across North America*, edited by Margery H. Krieger. University of Texas Press, 2002.

Lamadrid, Enrique R. "Santiago and San Acacio: Slaughter and Deliverance in the Foundational Legends of Colonial and Postcolonial New Mexico." *Journal of American Folklore* 115, no. 457–58 (2002): 457–74.

Lamadrid, Enrique R. *Hermanitos Comanchitos: Indo-Hispano Rituals of Captivity and Redemption*. University of New Mexico Press, 2003.

Lamar, Howard W. *The Far Southwest 1846–1912: A Territorial History*. Rev. ed. University of New Mexico Press, 2000.

Lane, Jill. "On Colonial Forgetting: The Conquest of New Mexico and Its Historia." In *The Ends of Performance*, edited by Peggy Phelan and Jill Lane. NYU Press, 1998.

Larrazolo, Paul F. *Octaviano A. Larrazolo: A Moment in New Mexico History*. Carlton Press, 1986.

Larson, Carole. *Forgotten Frontier: The Story of Southeastern New Mexico*. University of New Mexico Press, 1993.

Larson, Robert W. *New Mexico's Quest for Statehood, 1846–1912*. University of New Mexico Press, 1968.

Lee, Ian Anson. "'The Manliness to Defend Themselves': Race and Civilian/Indigenous Warfare in New Mexico, 1598-1898." PhD diss., University of Texas at El Paso, 2020.

Lee, Sarah. "The Politics of Belonging: Autochthony in Modern Societies." NumberAnalytics, May 24, 2025. https://www.numberanalytics.com/blog/politics-belonging-autochthony-modern-societies.

LeFebre, Derek J., "Pedagogies of Resistance and Self-Preservation: Hispano Education and the Struggle for Land in Northern New Mexico, 1846–1919." PhD diss., University of Colorado Boulder, 2024.

Leonard, Irving A. "Introduction." In Sigüenza y Góngora, *The Mercurio Volante of Don Carlos de Sigüenza Y Góngora: An Account of the First Expedition of Don Diego de Vargas into New Mexico in 1692*, translated by Irving A. Leonard. Quivira Society, 1932.

Leopard, Donald P. "Joint Statehood: 1906." *New Mexico Historical Review* 34, 4 (1959): 241–47. https://digitalrepository.unm.edu/nmhr/v0134/iss4/2.

Levin Rojo, Danna. *Return to Aztlan: Indians, Spaniards, and the Invention of Nuevo Mexico*. University of Oklahoma Press, 2014.

Lijphart, Arend. *Democracy in Plural Societies: A Comparative Exploration*. Yale University Press, 1977.

Limbaugh, Ronald H. *Rocky Mountain Carpet-baggers. Idaho's Territorial Governors 1863–1890*. University Press of Idaho, 1982.

Lind, Michael. *The Next American Nation: The New Nationalism and the Fourth American Revolution*. Free Press, 1995.

Lomelí, Francisco A. "A Native of the Southwest." In *The Writings of Eusebio Chacón*, edited by Eusebio Chacón, A. Gabriel Meléndez, and Francisco A. Lomeli. University of New Mexico Press, 2012.

Lomelí, Francisco A. "An Illustrious Pioneer of Early Hispanic Letters Background and Social Context." In *The Writings of Eusebio Chacón*, edited by Eusebio Chacón, A. Gabriel Meléndez, and Francisco A. Lomeli. University of New Mexico Press, 2012.

Lomnitz, Claudio. "Nationalism as a Practical System: Benedict Anderson's Theory of Nationalism from the Vantage Point of Spanish America." In *The Other Mirror: Grand Theory Through the Lens of Latin America*, edited by Miguel Angel Centeno and Fernando Lopez-Alves. Princeton University Press, 2000.

Lovato, Andrew Leo. *Santa Fe Hispanic Culture: Preserving Identity in a Tourist Town*. University of New Mexico Press, 2004.

Lozano, Rosina. *An American Language: The History of Spanish in the United States*. University of California Press, 2018.

Lucero, Aurora. "Shall the Spanish Language be Taught in the Schools of New Mexico." *New Mexico Normal University Bulletin*, no. 23 (1911): 1–7.

Luján, Roy. "Dennis Chavez and the Roosevelt Era, 1933–1945." PhD diss., University of New Mexico, 1987.

Lummis, Charles F. *A New Mexico David, and Other Stories and Sketches of the Southwest*. C. Scribner's Sons, 1891.

Lummis, Charles F. *The Land of Poco Tiempo*. Charles Scribner's Sons, 1893.

Lummis, Charles F. *The Spanish Pioneers*. 1893. Rio Grande Press, 1963.

Ma, Shu-Yan. "Reciprocal Relation Between Political Development and Ethnic Nationalism." *Social Science Journal* 36, no. 2 (1999): 369–79.

Mabry, Thomas J. "New Mexico's Constitution in the Making: Reminiscences of 1910." *New Mexico Historical Review* 19 (April 1944): 168–84.

Magnet, Joseph E. "Canadian Perspectives on Official English," In *Perspectives on Official English: The Campaign for English as the Official*

Language of the USA, edited by Karen L. Adams and Daniel T. Brink.

Magnet, Joseph E. "Language Rights as Collective Rights." In *Perspectives on Official English: The Campaign for English as the Official Language of the USA*, edited by Karen L. Adams and Daniel T. Brink.

Malešeić, Siniša. *Identity as Ideology: Understanding Ethnicity and Nationalism.* Palgrave MacMillan, 2006.

Mantena, Karuna. "The Crisis of Liberal Imperialism." In *Victorian Visions of Global Order*, edited by Duncan Bell.

Mares, E. A. "The Many Faces of Padre Antonio José Martínez: A Historiographic Essay." In *Padre Martínez: New Perspectives from Taos*, edited by E. A. Mares, Bette S. Weidman, Thomas J. Steele, Patricia Clark Smith, and Ray John De Aragon.

Mares, E. A. "Padre Martínez and Mexican New Mexico." In *New Mexican Lives*, edited by Richard W. Etulain. University of New Mexico Press, 2002.

Mares, E. A. "A Resolana on Networks: Chicanos, Connections, and Culture." In *Resolana: Emerging Chicano Dialogues on Community and Globalization*, edited by Miguel Montiel, Tomás Atencio, and E. A. Mares. University of Arizona Press, 2009.

Mark, Joshua J. "Doctrine of Discovery," *World History Encyclopedia.* https://www.worldhistory.org/Doctrine_of_Discovery/.

Marquez, Benjamin. *LULAC: The Evolution of a Mexican American Political Organization.* University of Texas Press, 1993.

Marshall, David F. "The Question of an Official Language: Language Rights and the English Language Amendment." *International Journal of the Sociology of Language* 60 (1986): 7–75.

Martin, Ben L. "From Negro to Black to African American: The Power of Names and Naming." *Political Science Quarterly*, 106, no. 1 (1991): 83–107. https://doi.org/10.2307/2152175 https://www.jstor.org/stable/2152175.

Martínez, Antonio José. *Esposición que el presbítero Antonio José Martínez, cura de Taos de Nuevo México, drije al Gobierno del Exmo. Sor. General Antonio López de Santa Anna.* Taos: J.M.B., 1843). Imprint No. 5, n.p. In *Northern Mexico on the Eve of the United States Invasion*, edited by David J. Weber. Arno Press, 1976.

Martínez, Rob. "Spanish Brought the 'Requerimiento' Claiming Rule." *Santa Fe New Mexican.* August 5, 2022, updated Sep 10,

2023. https://www.santafenewmexican.com/news/local_news/spanish-brought-the-requerimiento-claiming-rule/article_a0a3639a-119a-11ed-a904-0f8f0b6ae146.html.

Marx, Anthony W. *Faith in Nation: Exclusionary Origins of Nationalism.* Oxford University Press, 2003.

Marx, Leo. *The Machine in the Garden: Technology and the Pastoral Ideal in America.* Online ed. Oxford University Press, 2000.

Mauzy, Wayne. "The Tertio Millennial Exposition: A Santa Fe Celebration Fifty Years Ago." *Santa Fe Magazine* 29, no. 5 (1935): 17–23.

McCrone, David. *The Sociology of Nationalism: Tomorrow's Ancestors.* Routledge, 1998.

McNierney, Michael. *Taos 1847: The Revolt in Contemporary Accounts.* Johnson Publishing, 1980.

McNitt, Frank. *Navajo Wars: Military Campaigns, Slave Raids, and Reprisals.* University of New Mexico Press, 1972.

McPherson, Robert S. *Viewing the Ancestors: Perceptions of the Anaasází, Mokwič, and Hisatsinom.* University of Oklahoma Press, 2019.

McWilliams, Carey. *North from Mexico: The Spanish-Speaking People of the United States.* Greenwood Press, 1948.

Meketa, Jacqueline. *Louis Felsenthal, Citizen-Soldier of Territorial New Mexico.* University of New Mexico Press, 1982.

Meléndez, A. Gabriel. *So All Is Not Lost: The Poetics of Print in Nuevomexicano Communities, 1834–1958.* University of New Mexico Press, 1997.

Meléndez, A. Gabriel. "Nuevo México by Any Other Name: Creating a State From an Ancestral Homeland." In *The Contested Homeland: A Chicano History of New Mexico*, edited by Erlinda Gonzales-Berry and David Maciel. University of New Mexico Press, 2000.

Meléndez, A. Gabriel. "Introduction." In *The Writings of Eusebio Chacón*, edited by Eusebio Chacón, A. Gabriel Meléndez, and Francisco A. Lomelí. University of New Mexico Press, 2012.

Meléndez, A. Gabriel. *Citizens by Treaty: Texts by Hispanic New Mexicans, 1846-1925.* The Modern Language Association, 2025.

Melzer, Richard. *Captain Maximiliano Luna: A New Mexico Rough Rider.* Rio Grande Books, 2017.

Melzer, Richard, and Phyllis Ann Mingus. "Wild to Fight: The New Mexico Rough Riders in the Spanish-American War." *New Mexico Historical Review* 59, no. 2 (1984): 109–36.

Metzgar, Joseph V. "The Ethnic Sensitivity of Spanish New Mexicans: A Survey and Analysis." *New Mexico Historical Review* 49, no. 1 (2021): 49–73. https://digitalrepository.unm.edu/nmhr/vol49/iss1/4.

Meyer, Doris. "Contesting History: The Unpublished Manuscripts of Benjamin Read," *New Mexico Historical Review* 76, no. 1 (2001): 47–64.

Meyer, Doris. *Speaking for Themselves: Neomexicano Cultural Identity and the Spanish Language Press, 1880–1920*. University of New Mexico Press, 2006.

Mignolo, Walter D. *The Idea of Latin America*. Blackwell, 2005.

Montejano, David. *Anglos and Mexicans in the Making of Texas, 1836-1986*. University of Texas Press, 1987.

Montgomery, Charles. *The Spanish Redemption: Heritage, Power, and Loss on New Mexico's Upper Rio Grande*. University of California Press, 2002.

Montoya, Maria E. "L. Bradford Price: The Education of a Gilded Age Politician." *New Mexico Historical Review* 66, no. 2 (1991): 179–201. https://digitalrepository.unm.edu/nmhr/v0166/iss2/4.

Montoya, Maria E. *Translating Property: The Maxwell Land Grant and the Conflict over Land in the American West, 1840–1900*. University of California Press, 2002.

Mora, G. Cristina. *Making Hispanics: How Activists, Bureaucrats, and Media Constructed a New American*. University of Chicago Press, 2014.

Mora, Anthony P. *Border Dilemmas: Racial and National Uncertainties in New Mexico, 1848–1912*. Duke University Press, 2011.

Morfí, Juan Agustín de. "Account of Disorders in New Mexico, 1778." In Marc Simmons, *Coronado's Land: Essays on Daily Life in Colonial New Mexico*. University of New Mexico Press, 1991.

Mount, Graeme S. "Nuevo Mexicanos and the War of 1898." *New Mexico Historical Review* 58, no. 4 (1983): 381–96.

Moyers, Robert A. "A History of Education in New Mexico." PhD diss., University of Tennessee, 1941.

Myrick, David F. *New Mexico's Railroads: An Historical Survey*. University of New Mexico Press, 1990.

Nagel, Joane. *American Indian Ethnic Renewal: Red Power and the Resurgence of Identity and Culture*. Oxford University Press, 1997.

Nelson, Megan Kate. *The Three-Cornered War: The Union, the Confederacy, and Native Peoples in the Fight for the West*. Scribner, 2020.

Netanyahu, Benzion. *The Origins of the Inquisition in Fifteenth Century Spain.* Random House, 1995.

New Mexico Center on Law and Poverty. "Judge Rules New Mexico Violates Public School Students' Constitutional Right to Sufficient Educational Opportunities." *NM Center on Law and Poverty Newsletter*, July 21, 2018. https://www.nmpovertylaw.org/2018/07/21/judge-rules-new-mexico-violated-public-school-students-constitutional-right-to-sufficient-educational-opportunities/.

New Mexico. *Laws of the Territory of New Mexico: Passed by the Legislative Assembly, Session of 1869–70.* Manderfield & Tucker, 1870.

New Mexico. *Laws of the Territory of New Mexico Enacted by the Legislative Assembly of 1871-1872.* A. P. Sullivan, 1872.

New Mexico. *Constitutional Convention.* Proceedings of the constitutional convention of the proposed state of New Mexico held at Santa Fe, New Mexico, October 3rd, 1910, to November 21st, 1910. Press of the Morning Journal, 1910.

New Mexico. *Rules of the Constitutional Convention.* The New Mexican Printing Company, 1910: 11–15.

New Mexico. *The Constitution of the State of New Mexico: adopted by the Constitutional Convention held at Santa Fe, N. Mex. from Oct. 3 to November 21, 1910.* GPO, 1911.

Nielson, François. "The Flemish Movement in Belgium after World War II: A Dynamic Analysis." *American Sociological Review* 45 (1980): 76–94.

Nieto-Phillips, John. *The Language of Blood: The Making of Spanish-American Identity in New Mexico, 1880s–1930s.* University of New Mexico Press, 2004.

Noel, Linda. *Debating American Identity: Southwestern Statehood and Mexican Immigration.* University of Arizona Press, 2014.

Nora, Pierre. *Realms of Memory: Rethinking the French Past.* Vol. 1. Edited by Lawrence D. Kritzman; translated by Arthur Goldhammer. Columbia University Press, 1996.

Norval, Aletta J. "Thinking Identities: Against a Theory of Ethnicity." In *The Politics of Difference: Ethnic Premises in a World of Power*, edited by Edwin N. Wilmsen and Patrick McAllister. University of Chicago Press, 1996.

Nostrand, Richard L. *The Hispano Homeland.* University of Oklahoma Press, 1992.

Ogden, Raymond. *Historical Sketch of St. Michael's College.* College of Santa Fe, 1974.

Olzak, Susan. "Ethnic Mobilization in Quebec." *Ethnic and Racial Studies* 5 (1982): 254–75.

Olzak, Susan. "Ethnic Protest in Core and Periphery States," *Ethnic and Racial Studies* 21, no. 2 (1998): 187–217.

Olzak, Susan. *The Global Dynamics of Racial and Ethnic Mobilization.* Stanford University Press, 2006.

Opler, Morris Edward, and Catherine H. Opler. "Mescalero Apache History in the Southwest. *New Mexico Historical Review* 25, no. 1 (1950): 1–36. https://digitalrepository.unm.edu/nmhr/v0125/iss1/2.

Orozco, Cynthia E. "Regionalism, Politics, and Gender in Southwest History: The League of United Latin American Citizens' Expansion into New Mexico from Texas, 1929–1945." *Western Historical Quarterly* 29, no. 4 (1998): 459–83. https://doi.org/10.2307/970404.

O'Sullivan, Dominic. *Indigeneity: A Politics of Potential: Australia, Fiji and New Zealand.* Policy Press, 2017. https://search.ebscohost.com/login.aspx?direct=true&scope=site&db=nlebk&db=nlabk&AN=1571966.

Otero, Miguel Antonio, II. *My Nine Years as Governor of the Territory of New Mexico, 1897-1906.* University of New Mexico Press, 1940.

Otero, Rosalie C., A. Gabriel Meléndez, and Enrique R. Lamadrid. *Santa Fe Nativa: A Collection of Nuevomexicano Writing.* University of New Mexico Press, 2009.

Owen, Gordon R. *The Two Alberts: Fountain and Fall.* Yucca Tree Press, 1996.

Pacheco Rojas, José de la Cruz. "Nativos, criollos y mestizos en la creación del Camino Real a Santa Fe, Nuevo México." In *Patrimonio e Identidad en el Camino Real de Terra Adentro y el Camino Nacional*, edited by Luis Carlos Quiñones Hernández.

Padilla, Fernando V. and Carlos B. Ramírez, "Patterns of Chicano Representation in California, Colorado and Nuevo México." *Aztlan* 5, nos. 1 & 2 (1974): 189–234.

Padilla, Genaro. "Imprisoned Narrative? Or Lies, Secrets, and Silence in New Mexico Women's Autobiography." In *Criticism in the Borderlands: Studies in Chicano Literature, Culture, and Ideology*, edited by Héctor Calderón and José David Saldívar. Duke University Press, 1991.

Padilla, Genaro. *The Daring Flight of My Pen: Cultural Politics and Gaspar Pérez de Villagra's Historia de La Nueva Mexico, 1610.* University of New Mexico Press, 2010.

Palsson, Mary Dale. "The Arizona Constitutional Convention of 1910: The Election of Delegates in Pima County." *Arizona and the West* 16, no. 2 (Summer, 1974): 111–24.

Pandey, Trikoli Nath, "Anthropologists at Zuni." *Proceedings of the American Philosophical Society* 116, no. 4 (1972): 321–37.

Paredes, Américo. *Folklore and Culture Along the Texas-Mexico Borderland.* University of Texas Press, 1993.

Patterson, Henry. *Ireland Since 1939.* Oxford University Press, 2002.

Peckham, Robert. "Internal Colonialism: Nation and Region in Nineteenth-Century Greece." In *Balkan Identities: Nation and Memory*, edited by Maria Todorova. NYU Press, 2004.

Perrigo, Lynn I. "New Mexico in the Mexican Period, as Revealed in the Torres Documents." *New Mexico Historical Review* 29, no.1 (1954): 28-40. https://digitalrepository.unm.edu/nmhr/vol29/iss1/4.

Petterson, Anne. "The Monumental Landscape from Below: Public Statues, Popular Interaction and Nationalism in Late Nineteenth-Century Amsterdam." *Urban History* 46 (2019): 722–46. https://www.cambridge.org/core/journals/urban-history/article/monumental-landscape-from-below-public-statues-popular-interaction-and-nationalism-in-late-nineteenthcentury-amsterdam/B036D19BE3D4C1119BAAC6F60E7E5F0C.

Pildes, Richard E., "Ethnic Identity and Democratic Institutions: A Dynamic Perspective," In *Constitutional Design for Divided Societies: Integration or Accommodation?*, edited by Choudhry Sujit. Oxford University Press, 2008.

Pino, Don Pedro Baptista. "Exposición Sucinta y Sencilla de la Provincia del Nuevo México: Hecha Por Su Diputado en Cortés. Cádiz: Estado Mayor General, 1812." In *Three New Mexico Chronicles: The Exposición of Don Pedro Bautista Pino, 1812; The Ojeada of Lic. Antonio Barreiro, 1832; and the Additions by Don José Agustín de Escudero, 1849*, edited and annotated by H. Bailey Carroll, Juan Villasana Haggard, James H. Sutton Jr., and Sylvia Leal.

Poldervaart, Arie. "Black Robed Justice in New Mexico, 1846–1912." *New Mexico Historical Review* 23, no. 2 (1948): 18–50.

Preucel, Robert, and Matero, Frank G., "Placemaking on the Northern Rio Grande: A View from Kuaua Pueblo." In *Archaeologies of Placemaking: Monuments, Memories, and Engagement in Native North America*, edited by Patricia E. Rubertone. Routledge, 2009.

Prince, L. Bradford. *Historical Sketches of New Mexico From the Earliest Records to the American Occupation.* Leggat Brothers, 1883.

Prince, L. Bradford. *New Mexico's Struggle for Statehood.* Santa Fe: New Mexican Printing Company, 1910.

Prince, L. Bradford. "Opening Address at the First State Convention in New Mexico." September 28, 1911. Political Issues and Elections, folder 22. New Mexican Printing Company, 1912.

Prince, L. Bradford. *Spanish Mission Churches of New Mexico.* Torch Press, 1915.

Prince, L. Bradford. *The Student's History of New Mexico.* 1921; Sunstone Press, 2008.

Pulido, Alberto L. *The Sacred World of the Penitentes.* Smithsonian Institution Press, 2000.

Rael-Gálvez, Estevan. "Identifying Captivity and Capturing Identity: Narratives of American Indian Slavery, Colorado and New Mexico, 1776–1934." PhD diss., University of Michigan, 2002.

Rael-Gálvez, Estevan. "Raising Consciousness and Imagining Reconciliation: Santa Fe Fiestas." March 19, 2018. https://www.creativestrategies360.com/post/raising-consciousness-and-imagining-reconciliation-santa-fe-fiestas.

Rael-Gálvez, Estevan. "Reimagining the Española Fiesta." *Creative Strategies 360°*. April 13, 2018. https://www.creativestrategies360.com/post/reimagining-the-espa%C3%B10la-fiesta.

Rael-Gálvez, Estevan. "Centering Truths, Not So Evident," *Creative Strategies 360°*. August 13, 2020. https://www.creativestrategies360.com/post/centering-truths-not-so-evident.

Ramírez, Carlos Brazil. "The Hispanic Political Elite in Territorial New Mexico." PhD diss., University of California, Santa Barbara, 1979.

Read, Benjamin M. *Historia Ilustrada de Nuevo Mexico.* Compañía Publicista del Nuevo Mexicano, 1911.

Read, Benjamin M. *Illustrated History of New Mexico.* Translated by Eleuterio Baca. New Mexican Printing Company, 1912.

Reeve, Frank D. *History of New Mexico.* Vol. 2. Lewis Historical Publishing, 1961.

Reeves, René. *Ladinos with Ladinos, Indians with Indians: Land, Labor, and Regional Ethnic Conflict in the Making of Guatemala.* Stanford University Press, 2006.

Resendez, Andrés. *Changing National Identities at the Frontier: Texas and New Mexico, 1800–1850.* Cambridge University Press, 2005.

Resendez, Andrés. *A Land so Strange: The Epic Journey of Cabeza De Vaca.* Basic Books, 2007.

Rhea, Joseph Tilden. *Race Pride and the American Identity.* Harvard University Press, 1997.

Richmond, Douglas W. "The Climax of Conflicts with Native Americans in New Mexico." *New Mexico Historical Review,* 80, no. 1 (Winter 2005): 55–86.

Ritch, William G. "Inaugural Address of Hon. W. G. Ritch, President: Delivered Before the Society, Feb. 21, 1881." Historical Society of New Mexico, no. 1. New Mexican Book Job and Printing, 1881.

Ritch, William G. *Illustrated New Mexico: Historical and Industrial.* Bureau of Immigration (Santa Fe), 1885.

Roberts, Calvin A. "H. B. Fergusson, 1848–1915: New Mexico's Spokesman for Political Reform." *New Mexico Historical Review* 57, no 3 (1982): 237–55.

Rodríguez, Sylvia. *The Matachines Dance: A Ritual Dance of the Indian Pueblos and Mexicano/Hispano Communities.* Sunstone Press, 2009.

Roeder, Beatrice A. "*Los Comanches:* A Bicentennial Folk Play," *Bilingual Review/La Revista Bilingüe,* 3, no. 3 (1976): 213–20.

Romero, Cecil V. "Apologia of Presbyter Antonio J. Martinez." *New Mexico Historical Review,* 3, no. 4 (1928): 325–46.

Romero, Juan, and Moises Sandoval. *Reluctant Dawn: Historia del Padre A. J. Martínez, Cura de Taos.* Mexican American Cultural Center, 1976.

Romero, Levi. "Following the Manito Trail: A Tale of Two Querencias." In *Querencia: Reflections on the New Mexico Homeland,* edited by Vanessa Fonseca-Chávez, Levi Romero and Herrera R. Spencer. University of New Mexico Press, 2020.

Romero, Orlando. "Manitos and the Struggle for Self-Identity in the Hispano Homeland." In *Cultural Convergence in New Mexico: Interactions in Art, History & Archaeology,* edited by Robin Farwell Gavin and Donna Pierce. Museum of New Mexico Press, 2021.

Romo, David Dorado. *Ringside Seat to a Revolution: An Underground Cultural History of El Paso and Juarez: 1893–1923.* Cinco Puntos Press, 2005.

Rosenbaum, Robert J. *Mexicano Resistance in the Southwest: "The Sacred Right of Self-Preservation."* University of Texas Press, 1981.

Royce, Anya Peterson. *Ethnic Identity: Strategies of Diversity.* Indiana University Press, 1982.

Russell, John C. "State Regionalism in New Mexico." PhD diss., Stanford University, 1938.

Said, Edward W. *Orientalism.* Vintage Books, 1979.

Sálaz, Rubén Dario. *The Pueblo Revolt Massacre.* Cosmic House, 2008.

Salgado, Casandra. "Mexican American Identity: Regional Differentiation in New Mexico." *Sociology of Race & Ethnicity* 6, no. 2 (2020): 179–94.

Salpointe, John Baptist. *John Baptist Salpointe: Solider of the Cross.* Diocese of Tuscon, 1966.

Sánchez, George I. *Forgotten People: A Study of New Mexicans.* University of New Mexico Press, 1940.

Sánchez, Joseph P. *Between Two Rivers: The Atrisco Land Grant in Albuquerque History, 1692–1968.* University of Oklahoma Press, 2008.

Sánchez, Joseph P. "It Happened in Old Santa Fe, The Death of Governor Albino Pérez, 1835–1837." In *All Trails Lead to Santa Fe*, edited by Vicki Ahl, Marc Simmons, Orlando Romero, and Joseph P. Sánchez. Sunstone Press, 2010.

Sandweiss, Naomi. "Opposing Views: New Mexico Territory's Jews and the Statehood Debate." In *The Jewish Legacy in New Mexico History*, edited by Richard Melzer. Rio Grande Books, 2015

Sariñana, Manuel. *Impresiones de un Surumato en Nuevo México: A Bilingual Edition of the Original 1908 Picaresque Novella.* Edited and translated by Phillip B. Gonzales. University of New Mexico Press, 2023.

Saxton, Russell S. "Ethnocentrism in the Historical Literature of Territorial New Mexico." PhD diss., University of New Mexico, 1980.

Schermerhorn, R. A. *Comparative Ethnic Relations: A Framework for Theory and Research.* University of Chicago Press, 1978.

Scholes, France V. "Civil Government and Society in New Mexico in the Seventeenth Century." *New Mexico Historical Review* 10, no. 2 (1935): 71–111.

Schwaller, Robert C. *Géneros de Gente in Early Colonial Mexico: Defining Racial Difference*. University of Oklahoma Press, 2016.

Sergeant, Elizabeth Shepley. "New Mexico, a Relic of Ancient America." First published in *Nation*, vol. 117, issue 3046 (1923): 577–579; reproduced in the *Santa Fe New Mexican*, November 24, 1923.

Seton-Watson, Hugh. *Nations and States: An Enquiry into the Origins of Nations and the Politics of Nationalism*. Methuen, 1977.

Shils, Edward. "Primordial, Personal, Sacred and Civil Ties." *British Journal of Sociology* 8, no. 2 (1957): 13–45.

Shoup, Paul. "Foreward." In *Irrendentism: Ethnic Conflict and International Politics*, edited by Thomas Ambrosio. Praeger, 2001.

Sigüenza y Góngora, Carlos de. *The Mercurio Volante of Don Carlos de Sigüenza Y Góngora: An Account of the First Expedition of Don Diego de Vargas into New Mexico in 1692*, translated by Irving A. Leonard. Quivira Society, 1932.

Silverberg, Robert. *The Pueblo Revolt*. Weybright and Talley, 1970.

Simmons, Marc. *Spanish Government in New Mexico*. University of New Mexico Press, 1968.

Simmons, Marc. *The Little Lion of the Southwest: A Life of Manuel Antonio Chaves*. Sage, 1973.

Simmons, Marc. *People of the Sun: Some Out of Style Southwesterners*. University of New Mexico Press, 1979.

Simmons, Marc. "The Chacón Economic Report." *New Mexico Historical Review* 60 (January 1985): 81–88.

Sive, Mary Robinson. "Helen E. Haines, 1872–1961: An Annotated Bibliography." *Journal of Library History (1966–1972)* 5, no. 2 (1970): 146–64.

Smith, Anthony D. "Theories and Types of Nationalism," *European Journal of Sociology* 10, no. 1 (1969): 119–32.

Smith, Anthony D. "'Ideas' and 'Structure' in the Formation of Independence Ideals." *Philosophy of the Social Sciences* 3 (1973): 19–39.

Smith, Anthony D. "Introduction: The Formation of Nationalist Movements." In *Nationalist Movements*, edited by Anthony D. Smith. Macmillan, 1976.

Smith, Anthony D. *Theories of Nationalism*. Duckworth, 1971.

Smith, Anthony D. *Nationalism in the Twentieth Century*. Martin Robertson, 1979.

Smith, Anthony D. "Towards a Theory of Ethnic Separatism." *Ethnic and Racial Studies* 2, no. 1 (1979): 21–37.

Smith, Anthony D. *Nations and Nationalism in a Global Era*. Polity, 1995.
Smith, Anthony D. *Myths and Memories of the Nation*. Oxford University Press, 1999.
Smith, Anthony D. *The Ethnic Revival*. Cambridge University Press, 1987.
Smith, Anthony D. "Ethnic Cores and Dominant Ethnies." In *Rethinking Ethnicity*, edited by Eric P. Kaufmann.
Smith, Timothy L. "Protestant Schooling and American Nationality, 1800–1850." *Journal of American History* 53, no. 4 (1967): 679–95.
Snead, James E. "Picturesque, Romantic, Practical: Selling Santa Fe at the 1883 Tertio-Millennial Exposition." *El Palacio: The Magazine of the Museum of New Mexico* (Summer 2021). https://elpalacio.org/2021/05/picturesque-romantic-practical/.
Spencer, Philip, and Howard Wollman. *Nationalism: A Critical Introduction*. Sage, 2002.
Spicer, Edward H. "Plural Society in the Southwest." In *Plural Society in the Southwest*, edited by Edward H. Spicer and Raymond H. Thompson.
Spude, Robert. "Progressive Santa Fe, 1880–1912." In *All Trails Lead to Santa Fe*, edited by Vicki Ahl, Marc Simmons, Orlando Romero, Joseph P. Sánchez. Sunstone Press, 2010.
Stegmaier, Mark J. "New Mexico's Delegate in the Secession Winter Congress, Part 2: Miguel A. Otero Responds to Horace Greeley, and Greeley Takes Revenge." *New Mexico Historical Review* 86, 4 (2011): 513–23. https://digitalrepository.unm.edu/nmhr/vol86/iss4/5.
Stevens, Anastasia S. "Pueblo Water Rights in New Mexico." *Natural Resources Journal* 28, no. 3 (1988): 535–83.
Stratton, Porter A. *The Territorial Press of New Mexico 1834–1912*. University of New Mexico Press, 1969.
Stromberg, Ernest. "Rhetoric and American Indians: An Introduction." In *American Indian Rhetorics of Survivance: Word Medicine, Word Magic*, edited by Ernest Stromberg. University of Pittsburgh Press, 2006.
Stumph, Roy C. "The History of the Referendum in New Mexico." MA thesis, University of New Mexico, 1941.
Sue, Christina A. *Land of the Cosmic Race: Race Mixture, Racism, and Blackness in Mexico*. Oxford University Press, 2013.
Sunseri, Jun U. *Situational Identities along the Raiding Frontier of Colonial New Mexico*. University of Nebraska Press, 2017.

Suzman, Mark. *Ethnic Nationalism and State Power: The Rise of Irish Nationalism, Afrikaner Nationalism and Zionism.* St. Martin's, 1999.

Tai, Hue-Tam Ho. "Remembered Realms: Pierre Nora and French National Memory." *American Historical Review* 106, no. 3 (2001): 906–22.

Tarr, G. Alan. "American State Constitutions." In *Federalism, Subnational Constitutions, and Minority Rights,* edited by G. Alan Tarr, Robert F. Williams, and Josef Marko.

Taylor, Charles. *Multiculturalism: Examining the Politics of Recognition.* Edited by Amy Gutmann. 2nd edition. Princeton University Press, 1994.

Taylor, Charles. "The Politics of Recognition." In *Multiculturalism: Examining the Politics of Recognition,"* edited by Amy Gutmann. 2nd edition. Princeton University Press, 1994.

Teja, Jesús F. de la, and Ross Frank, eds. *Choice, Persuasion, and Coercion: Social Control on Spain's North American Frontiers.* University of New Mexico Press, 2005.

Territory of New Mexico, *Proceedings of the Constitutional Convention of the Proposed State of New Mexico Held at Santa Fe, New Mexico.* Press of the Morning Journal, 1910.

Theisen, Gerald Arthur. "Jose Manuel Gallegos (1815–75): The First Mexican-American in the United States Congress." PhD diss., University of New Mexico, 1985.

Thoma, Francisco de. *Historia Popular De Nuevo México, Desde Su Descubrimiento Hasta La Actualidad.* American Book, 1896.

Thompson, Erin L. *Smashing Statues: The Rise and Fall of America's Public Monuments.* W. W. Norton, 2022.

Thompson, Jerry. "Brave Christian Soldiers: The New Mexico Territorial Militia in the Civil War." *New Mexico Historical Review* 89, no. 3 (2014): 263–320.

Ting, Helen. "Social Construction of Nation—A Theoretical Exploration." *Nationalism and Ethnic Politics* 14, no. 3 (2008): 453–82.

Tlapoyawa, Kurly. *We Will Rise: Rebuilding the Mexikah Nation.* Trafford, 2000.

Tlapoyawa, Kurly. *Totacho: Our Way of Talking: The Nawatl Presence in New Mexico and Southern Colorado.* Mesonewmexico.org, 2016.

Tobias, Henry J. *A History of the Jews in New Mexico.* University of New Mexico Press, 1990.

Töpperwien, Nicole. "Participation in the Decision-Making Process as a Means of Group Accommodation." In *Federalism, Subnational*

Constitutions, and Minority Rights, edited by G. Alan Tarr, Robert F. Williams, and Josef Marko.

Torrez, Robert J.. ""El primer y principal ramo": An Examination of the Status of Education in Mexican Era New Mexico." *New Mexico Historical Review* 99, 2 (2024). https://digitalrepository.unm.edu/nmhr/v0199/iss2/1.

Tuan, Yi-Fu. *Space and Place: The Perspective of Experience.* University of Minnesota Press, 1977.

Turo, Bryan. "Politics, Identity, and Statehood at the New Mexico Territorial Fair, 1881–1912." *New Mexico Historical Review* 87, no. 4 (2012): 392–421.

Twitchell, Daniel Jason. *Ralph Emerson Twitchell: The Historian Who Found New Mexico's Future in the Present.* Sunstone Press, 2018.

Twitchell, Ralph Emerson. *The History of the Military Occupation of New Mexico.* Arno Press, 1976 [1909].

Twitchell, Ralph Emerson. *The Leading Facts of New Mexican History* Vols. 1 and 2. Torch Press, 1911, 1912.

Twitchell, Ralph Emerson. *The Leading Facts of New Mexican History.* 1914; Horn & Wallace, 1963.

Twitchell, Ralph Emerson. *Old Santa Fe: The Story of New Mexico's Ancient Capital.* Rio Grande Press, 1963.

Twitchell, Ralph Emerson. *Spanish Colonial Lives: Documents from the Spanish Colonial Archives of New Mexico, 1705–1774: A Companion in Part to the Spanish Archives of New Mexico by Ralph Emerson Twitchell.* Edited by Linda Tigges and translated by J. Richard Salazar. Sunstone Press, 2013.

United Mexican American Students. "The Chicano and UNM: A Proposal for a Chicano Studies Program at the University of New Mexico." Unpublished, 1969.

Valdez, Armando. "Insurrection in New Mexico—the Land of Enchantment." *El Grito* 1 (1967): 15–24.

Valenzuela, Norma A. "Mestiza Consciousness a la MeXicana in Última and Agueda Martínez: Bridging and Legitimizing Querencia in the Borderlands." In *Querencia: Reflections on the New Mexico Homeland*, edited by Vanessa Fonseca-Chávez, Levi Romero and Herrera R. Spencer. University of New Mexico Press, 2020.

Vallen, Nino. "The Conqueror and the Archive: Social Struggles and Practices of Memorialization in Viceregal New Spain." In *What's*

Left Behind. The Lieux de Mémoire of Europe beyond Europe, edited by Marjet Derks, Martijn Eickhoff, Remco Ensel en Floris Meens. Vantilt Publishers, 2015.

Vasquez, Enriqueta. *Enriqueta Vasquez and the Chicano Movement: Writings from el Grito del Norte*, edited by Lorena Oropeza and Dionne Espinoza. Arte Publico Press, 2007.

Vaughn, John H. *History and Government of New Mexico*. L. H. Jenkins, 1931.

Vigil, Donaciano. *Address to the New Mexico Assembly*, 18 June 1846 (trans. as "Vigil on Arms, Munitions, Trade, North Americans, and Barbaric Indians," 1–8, and "Vigil opina sobre armas, municiones, comercio, norteamericanos, y indios Bárbaras," 9–17). In *Arms, Indians, and the Mismanagement of New Mexico*, 7, 15, edited by David Weber. Texas Western Press, 1986.

Vigil, Donaciano, and David J. Weber. *Arms, Indians, and the Mismanagement of New Mexico*. Texas Western Press, 1986.

Vigil, Maurilio E. *Los Patrones: Profiles of Hispanic Political Leaders in New Mexico History*. University Press of America, 1980.

Vigil, Maurilio E., and Helene Boudreau. *Donaciano Vigil: The Life of a Nuevomexicano Soldier, Statesman, and Territorial Governor*. University of New Mexico Press, 2022.

Vigil, Ralph H., Frances W. Kaye, and John R. Wunder, eds. *Spain and the Plains: Myths and Realities of Spanish Exploration and Settlement on the Great Plains*. University Press of Colorado, 1994.

Vignaud, Henry. *Toscanelli and Columbus: The Letter and Chart of Toscanelli on the Route to the Indies by Way of the West, Sent in 1474 to the Portuguese Fernam Martins, and Later on to Christopher Columbus; a Critical Study on the Authenticity and Value of These Documents and the Sources of the Cosmographical Ideas of Columbus, Followed by the Various Texts of the Letter*. Sands, 1902.

Villagrá, Gaspar Pérez de. *Historia de la Nueva Mexico, del capitán Gaspar de Villagrá*. 1610.

Villoro, Luis. *Los grandes momentos del indigenismo en México*. Ediciones de la Casa Chata, 1979 [1950].

Waldstreicher, David. *In the Midst of Perpetual Fetes: The Making of American Nationalism, 1776-1820*. University of North Carolina Press, 1997.

Wallerstein, Immanuel. "The Construction of Peoplehood." In *Race, Nation, Class: Ambiguous Identities*, edited by Étienne Balibar and Immanuel Wallerstein. Verso, 1991.

Walter, Paul A. F. "New Mexico in the Great War." *New Mexico Historical Review* 1, no. 3 (1926): 229–64.

Walter, Paul A. F. "The Coming of the Railroad." *El Palacio* 39 (July 1935): 23–33.

Warner, Louis H. *Archbishop Lamy: An Epoch Maker.* Santa Fe New Mexican Publishing, 1936.

Weber, David J. "'Scarce More Than Apes.' Historical Roots of Anglo American Stereotypes of Mexicans in the Border Region." In *New Spain's Far Northern Frontier*, edited by David J. Weber. University of New Mexico Press, 1979.

Weber, David J. "Reflections on Coronado and the Myth of Quivira." In *Myth and the History of the Hispanic Southwest: Essays*, 1–17, edited by David J. Weber. University of New Mexico Press, 1990.

Weber, David J. *The Mexican Frontier 1821-1846.* University of New Mexico, 1982.

Weber, David J., ed. *What Caused the Pueblo Revolt of 1680?* Bedford/St. Martin's, 1999.

Weigle, Marta. *The Penitentes of the Southwest.* Ancient City Press, 1970.

Weigle, Marta. *Brothers of Light, Brothers of Blood: The Penitentes of the Southwest.* University of New Mexico Press, 1976.

Westphall, Victor. *The Public Domain in New Mexico, 1854–1891.* University of New Mexico Press, 1965.

Westphall, Victor. *Thomas Benton Catron and His Era.* University of Arizona Press, 1973.

Westphall, Victor. *Mercedes Reales: Hispanic Land Grants of the Upper Rio Grande Region.* University of New Mexico Press, 1983.

Whiting, David V. "Minutes of the Historical Society of New Mexico." In "Historical Society Minutes, 1859-1863." *New Mexico Historical Review* 18, no. 3 (1943): 247–311, edited by Lansing B. Bloom.

Wilcox, Michael V. *The Pueblo Revolt and the Mythology of Conquest: An Indigenous Archaeology of Contact.* University of California Press, 2009.

Williams, David. "Liberalism, Colonialism and Liberal Imperialism." *East Central Europe* 45, no. 1 (2018): 94–118.

Williams, Robert A. *The American Indian in Western Legal Thought: The Discourses of Conquest.* Oxford University Press, 1992.

Williams, Robert F., and G. Alan Tarr. "Subnational Constitutional Space: A View from the States, Provinces, Regions, Länder, and Cantons." In *Federalism, Subnational Constitutions, and Minority Rights*, edited by G. Alan Tarr, Robert F. Williams, and Josef Marko. Prager, 2004.

Wilson, Chris. *The Myth of Santa Fe: Creating a Modern Regional Tradition.* University of New Mexico Press, 1997.

Wimmer, Andreas. "Dominant Ethnicity and Dominant Nationhood." In *Rethinking Ethnicity*, edited by Eric P. Kaufmann. Routledge, 2004.

Wirth, Louis. "Types of Nationalism." *American Journal of Sociology* 41 (May 1936): 723–37.

Wolf, Eric R. *Peasant Wars of the Twentieth Century.* Harper and Row, 1968.

Yack, Bernard. *Nationalism and the Moral Psychology of Community.* University of Chicago Press, 2012.

Young, C. M. *Politics in the Congo.* Princeton University Press, 1965.

Young, Iris Marion. *Inclusion and Democracy.* Oxford University Press, 2000.

Zeleny, Carolyn. "Relations between the Spanish-Americans and Anglo-Americans in New Mexico: A Study of Conflict and Accommodation in a Dual-Ethnic Situation." PhD diss., Yale University, 1944.

Žižek, Slavoj. *The Sublime Object of Ideology.* Verso, 1989.

Index

www.ingramcontent.com/pod-product-compliance
Ingram Content Group UK Ltd.
Pitfield, Milton Keynes, MK11 3LW, UK
UKHW012230200926
475760UK00001B/21

9 780826 369734